CW01024259

Passenger of Silence

@ Éditions Albin Michel - Paris 2003
For the present edition:
@ 5 Continents Editions 2024 /
Waddington Custot Gallery /
Fabienne Verdier
ISBN 979-12-5460-063-4

Fabienne Verdier

Passenger of Silence

My Quest for the Ancient Arts
in Post–Cultural Revolution China

Translated from the French by Young Kim
With an afterword by Corinna Thierolf

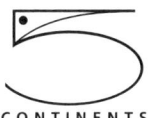

CONTINENTS

CONTENTS

* All quotes at the beginning of the chapters are inspired by Chinese poet Li Po, who lived in the eighth century.

In my white socks and blue skirt

*While the impetuousness of youth has yet to be tamed . . . **

Childhood is endured, but youth has choices. My choice was to paint, but first I had to master a technique, and this would take me to China.

Life can have the beauty of a bonsai or an old wind-buffeted pine tree by the seaside. We find its craggy form appealing, but how much did it suffer to grow this way? If its beauty is unique, it is because it was battered by storms and all manner of harsh weather. Everyone and everything is what they are as a result of the violent forces and torments they have braved. It has always been this way.

I'm not writing to settle scores with family, friends, institutions, or even the age into which I was born. What I hope to relate here is the story of the journey I took to find my own style of painting. Along the way, I will tell some stories from my life, as I also want to describe the realities of living in China during this time. In spite of the Kafkaesque prison-like world it was in the 1980s, after the ravages of the Cultural Revolution, the vestiges of a magnificent civilization still survived.

Some people criticize my approach to Chinese painting and call it inauthentic, but they have no problem when Asians study in the West and become great international artists—artists like the painter Zao Wou-Ki, or the cellist Yo-Yo Ma, or the academician and writer François Cheng, who became the first Asian elected to the Académie Française. Why, then, shouldn't a European woman like me take the reverse path? Why shouldn't I become a student of Chinese painting, learn its poetic and philosophical codes, extract their essence, and, using this ancient tradition, create my own original works?

I was sixteen when I told my mother I wanted to be a painter. I was the eldest of five, and my mother unhappily resigned herself to my early departure. She had done her best to raise us alone. She was a woman deeply wounded by divorce; not only by the painful loss of my father, her first love, but also by his betrayal of the solemn vows made before God, which broke her belief in promises.

Throughout childhood, I picked up on the slightest signs of my mother's suffering and, at her side, silently relived these injustices over many years. This might explain why I was so difficult back then, with a muted internal rebellion. I was so young but already so sad, a child searching for an escape.

Wearing white socks and a blue skirt, I left my mother and my Catholic school to join my father, with whom I had not lived since I was eight. As my father had studied art, an initial training with him seemed a natural place to start my journey of apprentice painter. All I took with me was my mother's good upbringing.

He lived in a large remote hillside farm on sixty hectares facing the Pyrenees Mountains. Not a soul lived for miles around. The house had a 180-degree view of forests, little valleys, and vineyards planted along the Malepère hills between Carcassonne and Limoux. It had a magical beauty, perfumed by wild thyme, but this idyllic life turned out to be ruthless and austere. Our neighbors did not like Parisians. They considered us affluent strangers and we were not welcome. However, the initial jolt was good for me, and, for better or worse, I was forced to train in the tough school of life in the country.

My father was an idealist who had taken part in France's revolutionary May '68 protests. He constantly pursued unreachable ideals and left a lot of destruction in his wake. His motto was: "If you love me, you'll follow." He compared raising children to the harsh realities of nature and believed in pushing his fledglings out of the nest to teach them to fly. If some perished, it was because they were not strong enough, and ultimately for the best. The countryside proved the perfect place for his perpetual questioning. He loved intense, exhausting experiences, often seeking out unknown territory where he had to learn and understand everything to survive. We were forced to follow.

He loved seemingly impossible challenges. We were left to fend for ourselves and to manage on our own. Survival depended on how clever we were out on the battle-field of life. There was no respite. However, he managed to instill in us an awareness of ecology and harmony with nature. He also taught us about intuition and living in the present. My father would constantly ask me, "How does this work?" before answering himself, "It's simple: if you're an idiot, you die!" This principle applied in equal measure to painting, exercises, and chores around the farm.

Living cut off from everything, I was immersed in a sensory world that intro-duced me to the solitude of the painter. Though it was difficult to endure, this solitude and isolation would prove necessary and ultimately essential for deep self-exploration. I didn't know it then, but one day I would return to such austerity.

For days on end, my father locked me away in a room with a still life arrange-ment made from a few iron pots salvaged at the dump. Positioned before these with my hog bristle brushes and a makeshift palette, I tried to understand the catch of the light and the perspective of the composition as well as the right mix of color pigments with the oils and refined solvents. I contemplated the profound presence of life in these simple saucepans.

From time to time, my father would drop in, pitchfork in hand or trailed by his favorite pig, and ask with a sly smile if I was still as committed to painting. At night, he would correct my work. He was an excellent draftsman, and he passed on what knowledge he had. This routine, a kind of test, went on for many months. Every day, on my own, I had to teach myself by figuring things out. Each day brought discoveries as well as anger. Sometimes I was successful, and sometimes I became enraged by my lack of skill and my inability to express what I wanted. This frustration taught me modesty. I learned humility and, above all, unlimited patience when I set out with shears in hand to prune the first row of twenty-four hectares of vines. Looking out, there was no end in sight. I was also in charge of the kitchen garden, so I learned the art of gardening. I turned to the country people, who were a treasure trove of knowledge and taught me many things. A farmer showed me how to stake tomatoes, grow good melons, sow seeds, and hunt mushrooms. My kitchen garden flourished and I discovered an enduring love for creating from nature.

Overcoming these obstacles, I managed to survive in the countryside and grow from a Catholic schoolgirl into an apprentice painter and farmworker. I became more hardened and proud of the calluses on my hands. This initial training in solitude and the open fields helped prepare me for what would be waiting in the People's Republic of China.

Although I learned a lot living out in the country, the situation with my father and his new family was uncomfortable, so I decided to move out. I enrolled in the local art college in Toulouse and found work in a graphic design firm to pay for my studies. In a street behind the college, I rented a shabby room over a garage that looked out over a faded courtyard. The room was too small to even hold my work. The graphic design job was interesting. Creating posters and brochures, we had to work within parameters set by clients while continually coming up with fresh ideas. However, I did not like the lack of artistic integrity—the only goal was to satisfy the client. There was nothing authentic in this practice, nothing solid, and ultimately nothing aesthetically worthy.

The art college proved disappointing. There was no more study of the great masters in the curriculum. There were no more models to learn from, no instruction in technique nor pictorial expression. It was all out of fashion. "Lock yourself in a room and express yourself!" our professors would repeat ad nauseum—no doubt the result of the psychoanalytic theories that were making such a dramatic impact on the national curriculum. But how could I express myself if they didn't give us the necessary tools? It drove me mad. Of what use were teachers then?

A few courses in classical drawing still existed—figure drawing, still lifes, copying from plaster models. But it wasn't very inspiring or engaging. I yearned to capture life in a brushstroke. The painting classes were appalling. It didn't help that the professor was a chauvinist who hated women. But that was nothing compared to his irritating demands that we "express" ourselves when he himself didn't know how to express anything. He painted what he called a "form of lyrical abstraction" while ranting about "beautiful gestures," admiring dynamic zeal over preparation or compositional technique. The art of extemporizing had somehow been raised to the level of beauty and substance.

Braque famously said that art colleges serve only one purpose: making friends. Unfortunately, even in that respect, I was disappointed. I didn't fit into this university structure. I was cut off from others and lonely. There was a nice group of people always up for a good time, but I never joined. They claimed I intimidated them. I don't know why. We were a generation lacking passion—the kind of passionate curiosity that spurs a soul to discover the world and experience the exhilaration, and even poetry, offered by life.

One day we were copying a bust of Beethoven when my drawing teacher, a small man resembling Napoleon, exploded at me in class. He walked up, knocked over my easel, and insulted me in front of the other students, shouting, "Admit it. You're bored!"

"Yes, I am!" I answered. "I'm interested in life, not the shape of a nose or a lifeless head."

"Get out! Leave!"

I left in despair carrying my portfolio. What was I going to draw? I had to bring back something. I wandered about until I stumbled upon a place of marvels: the garden of the Museum of Natural History.

From that day on, I would skip class and my school became the Museum of Natural History. Or perhaps it was a church populated with sacred objects. I went every morning to take part in a sort of ritualized study. I worshiped Egyptian snakes in jars and galleries of exquisite taxidermy, from the tiny lizard of the *Squamata* order to the *Paleosuchus* of South America. Javanese scorpions were placed side by side with African frogs. There were extraordinary collections of butterflies and display cases packed with flying creatures of all kinds—a hoopoe, a little owl who seemed just barely dozing, skeletons of wild geese and cranes. All these helped me to understand the internal structure of insects and birds. This dusty universe reeking with formaldehyde was a place of ceaseless fascination. There were few other visitors at such a bizarre place, and day after day I found myself alone with my sketchbooks. I meandered along the old, creaking parquet floors, thrilled. I discovered nature and, oddly, in this cloister of stuffed reality, my passion for the living was born.

I made peace with the drawing professor. Sometimes I would meet him in a Garonne bistro across from the college. I'd invite him for coffee and a *pain au chocolat* while he looked over my sketches and offered me useful feedback. He became encouraging and obtained permission from the museum curator for me to spend more time among the collections.

I started with pencil drawings but the lead was too dry for me. It scraped at the paper and hampered my perception. One of my friends worked like Giacometti. When drawing a face, she would immediately try to find the skeleton, the structure of the traits, building, erasing, and stumping so that she could then reconstruct it. It was somehow distressing for me to watch her working like a fiend until the soul of the subject would suddenly appear out of the tormented strokes, as she pulled an imaginary face out of the void. I preferred thick black felt-tip markers, which I felt allowed for a better rendering of movement. What fascinated me was to capture the moment in a single stroke. I would get up at five, and before beginning my drawing session at the museum, I would stop at the park. There, with my markers, I would try to suggest the movement of two swan necks in conversation, moorhens bathing, or magpies chattering in the shade of a walnut tree.

When there was a live model at the drawing class, I would return to sketch the curve of a breast, a buttock, or the silhouette of an old woman's profile. I thought for a while about becoming an animal painter and traveling to study nature. To obtain our degree, we had to select a subject and create an exhibition around it. My drawing professor told me, "Since you find animals so fascinating, take them as the theme of your final project." With my night job at the graphic design agency, I had all the necessary equipment to enlarge, reduce, edit, and present my work. I created plates and put together a fairly elaborate presentation that included studies of barnyard hens and various nests from around the world with their eggs rendered in oil paint.

One class that did interest me was calligraphy. Purely by chance, I found myself at the only college in France that still taught it, for by then it had become completely overlooked. My professor, Bernard Arin, was kind and determined, useful qualities in a discipline that required students to relearn how to draw a single letter and then an alphabet. We studied different Western styles: rustic capitals, Roman square capitals, of which I was particularly fond, Latin primitive uncial, Roman cursive of the sixth and seventh centuries, Merovingian and Visigothic. From the chancery hand of the fifteenth century and the bastarda to the didone and sans serif of the twentieth century, we traced the history of written letters and words. We copied pages and pages of capital and lowercase letters using horizontal or inclined surfaces, to explore the different movements needed to render a letter. So much depended on the angle at which the pen nib was applied to the surface. This brought on exhaustion and frequent cramps since the exercises required endless patience and extreme precision.

I interpreted classical texts by the ancient Greeks that we either selected or were assigned. We were given models of the different scripts to copy over and over:

Carolingian primitive for fragments of the Old Testament from the time of Pepin the Short; fifteenth-century humanist for texts by Seneca that we wrote with a quill; bookplates in gothic Flemish bastarda; excerpts from fragments of old manuscripts; or even, for a little fun, old menus. My taste for concise philosophical maxims was born from this. I adored experimenting with different styles to express phrases like "Nature loves to hide" from Heraclitus (excerpt from Fragment No. 123) or "A thing of beauty is a joy forever" by John Keats. From such simple pleasures, I began to harbor a conviction that an art of living could be located within the art of writing.

Professor Arin also taught us about the different nuances that various nibs could produce, leading to my first collection. Some nibs were extraordinary: German and English, a few of which had a special image on the tip, for example a knight of the Middle Ages or the outline of a moon; very narrow little nibs and the Baignol & Farjon *baïonnettes*, whose angles allowed for some very original strokes. I had even uncovered a magnificent eagle feather which rendered lines with striking integrity.

I regretted that my time with Professor Arin was so short. He managed to pass on to his students the ineffable grace of the art of Western calligraphy in an institution that did not hold his work in high esteem. At that time, it was sadly against the trends in art-school teaching. However, with his instruction, the training I had already done with my father, and my work at the graphic design agency, I graduated in three years instead of the five normally required.

My drawing professor had told me one day that I wouldn't find what I was seeking within the Western tradition . . . "Focus on Asian art. You might find what you seek is there." So I supplemented my life studies and calligraphy by exploring libraries and bookshops. The first book I came across was one by François Cheng, *Vide et Plein*; then the enchantments of Hokusai and the great Japanese masters of nature studies. Hokusai's images of plant and animal life were a particular favorite. I would stay up all night poring over interpretations of dragons, carp, flower fields, courtesans, and other fascinating subjects, such as a bat sleeping upside down or a butterfly under its chrysalis. Given my ardor for nature, I wanted to learn how the great animal painters had worked, the English masters but also Pisanello, Leonardo da Vinci, and finally, Dürer, even if I did not really understand his work until many years later, when I returned home from China and fixated upon his watercolor *The Great Piece of Turf*.

I was introduced to the Italian and Flemish primitives in an art history class. I admired them but the teaching was so dull. Lists of dates and names are not inspiring; artistic expression is. Nevertheless, the basic knowledge I acquired was enough for me to build upon later.

It was the Chinese and Japanese nature paintings that would prove my starting point. I admired these artists' sense of humor and venerated their contemplative study of the world and the elaborate perfection in their work. To me, they appeared to be the most accomplished artists, so I resolved to study Chinese. As usual, I tackled it on my own, buying manuals that were available at the time. I took lessons from a Chinese woman who taught me how to write certain characters, grammar basics, and a few essential words in the spoken language. This was the beginning of a great passion.

For the final examination, the other students took on lyrical abstractions or disturbing morbid subjects. These trends repulsed me. They thought themselves the followers of the German Expressionists, whose work expressed the suffering and misery they had experienced during the political upheavals of the early twentieth century, mainly the First World War. However, these students had no such feelings or experiences to draw from. They were self-indulgent petit bourgeois from the provinces. Without the anguish, there was nothing to transcend to feed into the work. It was hollow.

Like a good student, I read the required reference works. Among them I found a quote from Kandinsky that encouraged me: "The artist must be blind to 'recognized' and 'unrecognized' form, deaf to the teachings and desires of his time. His eyes must look to his inner life and his ears must listen to the voice of inner necessity." Although I presented works that deviated from those of my peers, I passed with flying colors and was offered a scholarship to Paris.

I turned it down. China was calling.

To learn more about China, I went up to Paris for a few days to stay with my aunt Yvonne Verdier. Yvonne was an ethnologist and her husband a mathematician. They were both intellectuals, researchers, and serious scholars. They taught me a great deal about thinking and living. "If you are really serious about this," my aunt suggested one day, "I know a unique Chinese teacher, Jacques Pimpaneau. He has put together a sort of museum of Asian folk traditions that you should visit. Tell him I sent you."

I headed to a warehouse in the Marais district clutching my portfolio and went up to the mezzanine where the director had his office. There, I discovered an extraordinary atmosphere similar to the Toulouse Natural History Museum, but here the space was packed with puppets, ancient theater costumes, funeral masks, and deities of all sorts. The collection had a disturbing beauty, and I hardly dared move for fear of upsetting any of the carefully labelled spirits. Pimpaneau, a mad Sinologist, had traveled around the world and returned with a sampling of the ancient folk traditions of Asia. I was impressed and amazed by this explorer of the universe, and our meeting had a decisive impact on me. Despite living on a modest teacher's salary, he had spent his life paying homage to a master of Chinese theater called Kwok On, creating a collection which may have been unique in the world. Hidden from view behind a pile of books, he lived amid indescribable clutter. I developed a deep affection for this man hunched at his desk, lost in reverie in his big black threadbare coat, while a forgotten cigarette scorched down between his fingers. It was as if I had known him forever, as if we shared a common fate.

"Sir," I said by way of introduction, "my aunt sent me to you. I want to make a book with these animal drawings I have done. I want to accompany them with some Chinese poems. Can you help me find a publisher while I am in Paris?"

"Mademoiselle, I doubt any publisher would undertake this type of publication. It would be unmarketable."

"You mean my drawings aren't good enough?"

"I'm not talking about the quality of your work, but publishers are there to sell books. You will never convince them, especially not in three days."

"I can assure you, I will find a publisher," I told him.

"I hope so. If you don't, stop by to see me again before you go."

I returned three days later, disheartened. "You were right, I could not find a publisher," I admitted.

"In that case, I will publish your book!"

"It would require a very good printer, capable of bringing out all the nuances of the brushstrokes . . ."

"The best printer in Paris is Union, they work for the Louvre. Let's get them to print it!"

I had met a fellow enthusiast.

He suggested the poems. We translated them, and two thousand copies of the book *Les singes crient leur chagrins* appeared some months later, published by the Musée Kwok On. Ten years later only fifty copies had been sold. Regardless, I had a new mentor, and he showed me around his museum, explaining the myths and stories told by the woodcuts and the reconstitutions of scenes with opera costumes, puppets, and shadow theater with cutout figures in donkey or cattle hide. He told me, "If you want to learn the energy in motion at the origin of Chinese painting you will have to study calligraphy, but you cannot do it here—you have to go to China."

When I returned to Toulouse, I managed to secure a meeting with the mayor, who offered me a place on the official visit to establish a sister-city relationship with Chongqing, in Sichuan province. I showed him my drawings and told him, "No, I want to go to China and learn from the great masters. I'm teaching myself Chinese and my goal is to go there only for serious study."

"Mademoiselle, you are very difficult to please! First, you refuse a scholarship to study in Paris, and now you turn down a free trip with me! But perhaps you're right after all. I'm going to arrange the sister-city program. I will inquire while I'm at it if you can participate in the first student exchange."

And so my dream of China was on the way to being realized. Unfortunately, I had no money for the plane ticket. Jacques Pimpaneau came to the rescue. "It's marvelous that you have managed to find a way to study in China. I will buy your ticket and we'll say that I owe it to you for the book." Very touched, I accepted his gift. Although I could not find the words to thank him, I felt I had a duty not to disappoint this beautiful soul who instinctively believed and trusted in my ambitions.

I was twenty-two years old when I left my family and friends. After a crisis of conscience, I decided to abandon everything without looking back. I even left my treasured stamp collection, which I passed along to the college caretaker.

It was life or death for me. I was in search of an initiation that would open the doors to another reality. I was driven by a force pushing me to leave without knowing where I was going or what I would do when I arrived. I could never say which way was north, let alone where China was. But, like a migratory bird, I sensed a magnetic force that would not let up. It was time to go out and discover the world. I took along the book that would become my constant companion, *Comments on Painting*, a parting gift from my new friend Jacques who told me, "Shitao's manual on painting will help you in your training; put it in your backpack it will sustain you."

Beijing via Karachi

Distant traveler, why come here to follow such an arduous path?

I was headed for the land of literati and painters, refinement and poetry, wisdom and great cuisine. It felt like a dream. But I still had to get there. I had bought a ticket to Beijing on Air Pakistan. At the airport in Paris, I learned that the flight had been delayed by a day for mechanical reasons so I was put up in a drab hotel overnight. When we arrived in Karachi for a stopover, a flight attendant informed us that we would have to wait another twenty-four hours because of a defective jet engine.

I had my first experience of the developing world at the airport. It was a shock that I will remember for the rest of my life. It was summer, the heat was stifling, and the light terribly harsh. I found myself facing a crowd of destitute people and starving children with flies in their eyes. A European meant wealth, so they pulled at my hair and clothes, grabbing my backpack. I couldn't get away. They kept coming in increasing droves. At the exit more beggars, in even greater numbers, pressed up against me. I fainted.

I came to inside a car with windows veiled by little curtains. I recognized the men in the car from the flight—a team of field hockey players returning home. I wondered what had happened to me. Where was I? Where was I going? "You fainted," someone told me. "We'll take care of you. Don't worry." I peeked through a slit in the curtains. We were driving through slums and it was already pitch dark. I was terrified. When I begged them to stop the car, they burst out laughing. "You'd never find your way. This is a bad part of town. A woman can't just walk around freely here. You'd be torn to pieces." They took me to a deserted old house in an isolated area and locked me up in the bedroom. There were bars across the windows. The whole team was there, with the coach lewdly eyeing me. The entire group was gearing up for the fun. I was frightened, but I decided it was better to be raped by one than many, so I bargained with the coach: "I understand. I'll spend the night together with you, but could you please make sure the others stay in the next room?"

All night long, the others drank and pounded on the door for their share of the prize. They didn't think about anything else, shouting crude jokes to the chosen one. The sole comfort I had was the presence of the moon, my only solace in this place of sordid violence. There was nothing I could do; screaming was no use. Submission was the only way to survive. After the night of debasement, I said to the coach, "They're expecting me at the French Embassy." My greatest fear was that I would not be able to return to the airport. Perhaps moved by my plight and our "memorable" night together, he took me where I asked.

By the time I landed on Chinese soil I was in a terrible state. I had been told by the French Ministry of Foreign Affairs that someone would be sent to meet me. Since I was twenty-four hours late, though, no one was at the airport. Because it was a Saturday, the diplomatic offices were closed. To make it worse, it was raining. It was September 1983, and while it was still very hot in Karachi, in Beijing the weather was dreary. My arrival was a disappointment—I felt like I had landed in a military camp surrounded by loudspeakers. I did not have a yuan to my name and needed to change money. I was miserable and I was bleeding.

I did have a few addresses of Chinese professors at the China Central Academy of Fine Arts in Beijing. I turned up at the home of one, who was baffled by my presence. I explained to him that I had just arrived via Karachi and experienced some problems along the way. I was to leave for the Sichuan Fine Arts College but first I had to fill out papers at the French Embassy, which, unfortunately, was closed for the weekend. Would it be possible to stay at the school? There were dormitories at the academy back then, although they were more like cells with bunk beds, with one thermos per person. The kind professor went to fetch me something to eat in a numbered mess tin. My smattering of Chinese did not get me very far. I had my little dictionaries, but could only say some basic words: eat, thank you, good evening. I stayed the weekend in the school, chaperoned by my young protector, who was distressed to see me in such a state. He offered to take me to the health center, though I did not dare tell them what I had been through. The nurses were very kind and looked after me.

Asia was not at all what I had pictured. I arrived, accompanied by my trusty Shitao, the writings of the great ancient scholars, and beautiful Chinese poetry, only to find myself in a gray, heavily polluted city with infernal traffic jams. The professor introduced me to some colleagues as the new student heading to Sichuan province. This generated much guffawing. "They are not at all set up to host foreigners in Sichuan. It is the most remote fine arts college in China! What on earth are you going to do there? We already have a hard enough time getting by here." They said all of this in Chinese so I could only follow with great difficulty. "That's exactly the point," I answered. "I understand there are some remarkable artists in Sichuan and that is what I want: a school where nothing is organized for foreigners."

On Monday, I called the embassy. An official car was sent for me and I entered a small room full of beaming Chinese. A woman in a Chanel suit greeted me with apologies. What a contrast from the Chinese surroundings that I had just been in! What is interesting in China is that one is often thrown into surreal situations. I was amused to discover Beijing—the Beijing of foreigners that was not the Beijing where I had first landed or even that of the old districts that still existed at that time. The woman from the embassy very kindly allowed me to stay in her apartment for a few days while embassy officials wavered as to whether to allow me to go to Sichuan: they were convinced I was making a huge mistake.

The ambassador was furious: How could a young French woman be sent to study anywhere other than Beijing or Hangzhou, where the only two suitable schools were located? The art college in Chongqing had never been open to foreigners. "I cannot let you go there," he told me. "You are a French citizen and it is my duty to look after your physical and emotional well-being." Fortunately, I still had told no one about what had happened to me in Pakistan. Inexplicably, I continued to insist on going, even though I was in bad shape, barely able to stand on my own. The ambassador was angry at the French administration in general and the mayor of Toulouse in particular for having signed agreements between the two cities without going through the French Ministry of Foreign Affairs. This was turning into a diplomatic incident.

"Let me try," I told him. "No Westerner has lived in that province since 1949. Allow me to study at the school. I promise you that if life there is as unbearable as you say, I will ask you to arrange for my transfer. Won't you please trust me?" "All right," he finally conceded. "In any case, the agreements have already been signed."

I left on the next train, my first such experience in China. Unfortunately, the embassy had reserved a couchette for me in a "hard" compartment. I learned only later that there are "hard" and "soft" couchettes. An entire family, the father, mother, and their three young children, was installed on mine. Seeing them crammed together and not knowing that the trip would last three days, I politely took the bench. I was sandwiched between people who were sleeping with me on the hard couchette with the big compartment windows wide open. It was lively and amusing, a kind of nineteenth-century version of travel. We picnicked all together, sharing dishes. I began to observe the daily life of the Chinese. An employee went up and down the train with hot tea in a garish thermos. I drank nearly a gallon. Even if the toilets, smells, close quarters, and lack of privacy started to get to me, the atmosphere was friendly and the travelers were kind and tried to communicate. I started to practice my Chinese and got out my dictionaries, only to learn that we would arrive in three days—three days and two nights to cover the distance from Beijing to Chongqing, less than twelve hundred miles. The day that we were meant to arrive, I discovered that we were back in Beijing! I thought I would lose my mind. I could not understand what they were saying on the loudspeaker. Someone explained to me, "This is highly unusual. There was an accident on the tracks. During the night, the train started back in the other direction; we have to start the journey over again from Beijing by taking different train tracks."

I thought the trip would never end. After six long days, I finally arrived in Chongqing in a pitiful state. I had not eaten much, as I had fallen ill from the revolting train food. I had bought some rice cakes, sweets, a duck wing, and bones to suck from the little vendors on the platforms, all cooked in pork fat or rancid oil. In the mornings, we were served a spicy rice soup off a trolley. This was to be my first lesson about life in China.

When we pulled into Chongqing station, a horrific vision rose up before me: bodies packed together so tightly they had to be straddled, peasants with lined faces waiting for a week or more to leave for some far off destination, entire families, starving people—it was a heartbreaking human landscape. In the immense hall, posters hung everywhere, loudspeakers squawked in total pandemonium with whistles going off, spit pooled on the floor, meanwhile security staff attempted to control the crowd. Workers in blue or green overalls and white pollution masks swept up. It reminded me of a routed army. All of these people slept in the station; they could not get tickets and ceaselessly pushed in and out of lines, insulting and fighting one another. In the midst of this chaos, a delegation wearing Mao collars was waiting for me in a tinted-window limousine sporting little red flags. The officials yelled, pouring out insults and kicking their way to get to me in the middle of the crowd. I was shocked by their behavior, treating the people like dogs as they elbowed their way through to me.

I was barely able to stand after my endless train journey, but this was to be an official Chinese welcome. They were taking me to the city hall for a banquet. How I would have preferred a room and a shower!

We crossed Chongqing, a gray city, lost in a thick fog. It had the feel of a 1930s film noir. Out the window I saw a teeming population. Along one side of the street there were old wooden houses with laundry hanging among the flower pots, bonsais, and endless staircases—as the city is built along the slopes of the Yangtze—while along the other loomed austere buildings in the socialist-realist style, red flags, and gold stars over the doors.

The city hall reception room was furnished with grimy red velour armchairs with white cotton headrests, loud carpets, and glass-covered coffee tables with doilies bearing saucers of peanuts and old candy and white cups decorated with pandas or horses in the style of the painter Xu Beihong. I suffered through the official speeches, translated by a woman into English, in which the Chinese expressed their joy to host the very first foreign student in the largest city in Sichuan. I looked at them, dressed in the rigid uniform of their social and political function, and on some of the faces I thought I could read their past suffering. Next, I was taken into the banquet room. The officials rose one at a time to toast my arrival while I, on an empty stomach, was expected to swallow a glass of rice alcohol after each.

When the first dish was presented to me, it was grilled grasshoppers. My interpreter, Mrs. Liu, explained that this was an ancient custom, an honor that could not be refused. So, traditions *did* still exist! But that did not make swallowing the grasshoppers any easier. At the end of the banquet, they offered me gifts. One was a little notebook with a pretty red silk cover. I opened it and saw the first page was adorned with a Party star.

The welcome ritual was over. We left for the college. There was no doubt about it: I had finally arrived in China.

Chinese campus

There is no moment when
alone, hidden,
she does not weep,
only to realize the futility of tears.

Accompanied by officials, we left for the art college, which was located in the suburbs, far from the city center. I was introduced to many people during the luncheon, but I could not keep them straight. I couldn't tell you who was Li or Wang. But in the car I figured out who was the head of the college. I thought his open, pleasant face boded well. Next to him sat the Party official at the college, with whom I would come to have many difficulties, and finally there was Mrs. Liu, who spoke perfect English. She would be my interpreter throughout these years. I immediately tried to practice the few words of Mandarin that I could say, but the little I knew turned out to be useless as everyone spoke Sichuanese, leaving me utterly lost.

They very politely explained to me that I would encounter no difficulties, and that I would enjoy a privileged status. Mrs. Liu would translate everything for me. As they showed kindness, I thought they were honest and trusted them at first. I was naive. Later, I learned that below the surface were hidden agendas forged in the harsh reality that they were subjected to. They had organized my life, and I would not be able to take any initiative of my own. I would not escape.

Upon our arrival, I was shown around the college. The Fine Arts Center was a new five-story building with galleries on several floors. It was clearly a source of pride, but it looked out of place in such a neglected district of low, run-down buildings. We then visited the dormitories of the students, who were all boarders. I was informed that it was unthinkable to house me there as a post-graduate researcher. I would need peace and quiet, and as I came from another culture it would be too difficult for me to mix with the others.

Then we came to the administrative building. In the middle of a little garden with brick-bordered shrubs, members were clearing out a room with a barred window just across from the Party office. They brought in a little bed with a straw mattress, an enamel basin, and a desk. A fluorescent tube gave off a pale light. This was my room—a cell. I put my bag down. My hosts closed the window, saying, "You should rest. We'll come and get you later for dinner."

I wanted to wash and asked the "comrades" in blue overalls next door where to find water. "Impossible," they told me. "There is no place to wash in the university; there is no water either; and above all, don't drink the tap water. Rest in your room. You will be looked after." They introduced me to an old peasant, toothless and wrinkled, shuffling along the hallway. "This woman will take care of you. Her job is to bring you water every day, but hot boiled water is provided only in the morning." There was just one boiler at the college where the two thousand students filled their thermoses.

In the evening, the Party official took me to the dining hall. I crossed an area where the students were waiting in line, each with their numbered mess tin; they ate while walking or in their rooms, while the teachers took their meals home with them. The Party official led me through a side door to the "guest dining room." There were crushed mosquitoes on the wall, pools of spit on the unswept floor, a dirty table sticky with grease, plastic chairs in a lurid blue color, and a nauseating burning smell. An elderly cook came in, apparently delighted to have made twelve dishes especially for me. It was a change for him from the huge vats he was used to cooking. I had pork with peanuts, pork with bamboo shoots, and pork with greens, all delicious, though the Sichuanese love of chili peppers would tear my insides out. The Party official left me alone to eat and went to queue for her own dinner. She followed the same procedure as everyone else, carrying her cutlery in a plastic bag, meal tickets in hand. It was a touching and pitiful spectacle of inhumanity in a country that was home to subtle flavors and one of the richest and most convivial culinary traditions in the world. When the dinner was over, she returned to escort me back to my room.

The first meeting to decide what to do with the foreign student was held the following day in the new building. I found myself in a large room, furnished like the town hall with the same glass-covered coffee tables, armchairs, and little doilies. The vulgar style and cold ambience astonished me in a country I had imagined so refined. The head of the college and the heads of the oil painting, Chinese painting, woodcutting, art history, and sculpture departments were all present.

I showed them my book, *Les singes crient leur chagrins*, which they passed around. "We heard you were a very good student in France," began one of the professors. "What can we teach you? What did you come here to do? You already graduated first in your class."

"I have come to study your culture," I answered.

"Yes, but looking at this beautiful book, what more can we teach you?"

"Let's see what she can do," suggested another professor who was more crafty. Someone brought in paper, an ink stone, and a paintbrush and placed them on the floor. "Paint a tree and we'll see your level and what we can teach you."

"I can't. I've never used ink cakes or an ink stone. Though there are some artists in the West, such as Jackson Pollock, who have experimented with painting on the floor, I have never tried to work on the ground, on a horizontal surface. I'm not familiar with your methods. But if you allow me to get my sketchpads and study the trees in the garden, I could come up with a composition. This, I was taught. I'll need a canvas, an easel, some tubes of paint, one or two hog bristle brushes, a palette, and, let's see . . . a palette knife."

I explained how I would rough out a sketch in successive strokes and start building the painting by stretching out the colors, adding layers and going back over the work during different sittings. After that, I would patiently construct a painting between long drying times and, little by little, begin the impasto. It would be weeks before I could show the results.

"I am very sorry," I continued, "but I don't know how to paint you a tree right at this very moment."

This made them laugh. "All right," they decided, "you'll have to start from the beginning."

This was a huge blow to me. But then I realized they were right: I would have to start with their basics; they were working from traditions that I knew absolutely nothing about. They selected the classes that I would take, and I found myself once again, just like in my class in Toulouse, facing a bust of Beethoven. But here the goal was to use hard lines, born of the spirit of socialist realism.

I worked in several studios. The classroom ambience was very different from that of Toulouse. In France, the students didn't care, their life was not on the line. But in China a remarkable silence reigned over the class; students applied themselves in a charged atmosphere. Sichuan province had ninety million inhabitants, and to be admitted to the art college was the dream of thousands of young students. The selection by competitive examination was draconian. Families would arrive with gifts to curry favor so that their child could be among the two thousand chosen. Recommendations from political figures also played an important role. At the end of their studies, the students would be assigned jobs correlated to their classroom performance. During the five years spent at the college, any missed class, any deviation in the interpretation of ideology, any slackening, could mean the student would be sent back to the countryside. This threat elicited a devotion to work that I had never before thought possible.

I wanted to learn the language but my request was denied. I was there to study Chinese art, not poke my nose into Chinese affairs. The less I knew about the reality of life in China, the better. Mrs. Liu, my interpreter, accompanied me to my classes. At night, in my room, I memorized the dictionary that I'd brought with me so that slowly, I nonetheless started to practice speaking.

At the college, everyone had to pick up their supplies, just like in the army: portfolio, little stool, thermos for a day's worth of tea, paintbrushes, and ink stone. Everything was inventoried and due back at the final exam. Nothing belonged to us, which was very strange to me. Painters or musicians normally work with their own instruments. Everything here felt dehumanized. These first months, I learned exactly what I was taught; indeed, I learned a lot. I learned how to hold a paintbrush, paint vertically without an easel, and grind up ink on a wet stone; I learned about the qualities of the different papers.

In the Chinese painting studio, they didn't teach us poetry, aesthetics, or the calligraphy strokes used in traditional painting. It was still considered decadent. The great scholarly painting style had been rejected, and many works were destroyed during the Cultural Revolution. The prevailing ideology required the depiction of people's lives in a popular manner. Inspiration was to be sought in folk art—for example in paper cutouts and auspicious New Year images of protective gods that decorated the homes of peasants. Themes were expected to come from life in the countryside or old legends. Artists were periodically sent into the villages to "study among the people."

This policy proved a double-edged sword since it sent intellectuals and city dwellers to witness what was really happening to the silent majority of peasants usually living in poverty or at least in precarious circumstances. Probably the artists in China were the ones who were the most familiar with the reality of their country and knew that an immense disparity existed between the official Party line and the truth.

The ideology imposed socialist realism, no longer that of the Soviet Union but that of Mao's famous discourse on art and literature: condemning bourgeois Western art. If references were needed, ancient popular art could be consulted, even if it was feudal and highly stylized in its own way.

Obviously, art could raise no challenge, even a veiled one. This very particular aesthetic that young artists had to interpret—imitating peasants, while at the same time achieving a modern look or personal expression within a rigid political context—sometimes resulted in pleasant work and even alluring images; for example, the paintings by Wang Yishi, who studied with me at the college and who has since become a celebrated artist, even beyond China's borders.

I also took classes in woodcut printing, a medium that is very advanced in China. Since the invention of paper by Cai Lun two millennia ago, works have been printed by applying a succession of carved woodblock plates onto rolls of paper. The Chinese invented movable type at around the same time as Gutenberg, but hardly ever used it, since the Chinese language includes too many characters for it to be practical.

When the book first appeared, there was one plate per double page and some of them included illustrations. Even if they were folk art, the book illustrations, either full page or captioned (a sort of precursor to the cartoon) and the New Year images seemed to me to be as much a part of the great Chinese tradition as scholars' ink paintings.

Before the war, Lu Xun, a great writer of the 1920s, and Zheng Zhenduo, a historian who had studied the popular literary genres and restored them to favor, tried to renew interest in woodcut printing. They had plates recut from old prints and organized exhibitions of the work of the Belgian woodcut artist Frans Masereel to show how a traditional technique could be revived by creators of modern art.

The woodcut printmaking professor was married to the head of the college. She was much celebrated and supported by the authorities, as she fit the profile they sought. A high-ranking cadre who had taken part in the Cultural Revolution, she wanted to build a new China and fervently believed in the creation of a world free from the past.

She had created a new style. She used large blocks of pear wood that must have been very costly given their size, but the Party paid. Her theme was the glorification of women and ethnic minorities. These national minorities, as they were called, were people that the Han, or ethnic Chinese, had driven to border regions or into the mountains. Despite government efforts at Sinicization they had managed to preserve their customs and language. Their traditional dress had not yet been replaced by the blue Mao suit, so their exotic appearance attracted painters. Our professor had followed the official instructions. She had gone to visit these peoples and, inspired by reproductions of Gustav Klimt's work, had created a strange style that distorted Klimt into sentimentality by pushing him closer to the Czech poster artist Alphonse Mucha.

The problem was, she wanted to teach me her discovery and she was tyrannical. I explained to her that the themes she proposed did not inspire me, especially in her style. Instead, I showed her reproductions of old Chinese woodcuts and told her, "This is what I'm interested in, what I find fascinating." This upset her. I was rejecting her artistic approach though she was famous all over the province, featured in reviews and journals, and was politically connected.

I offended her in a way that no student would have dared, and I saw on the faces of the other students that they were thrilled that a foreigner was setting the cat among the pigeons. Nonetheless, we reached a compromise: I asked her to teach me the folk legends that inspired her woodcuts. This required the services of Mrs. Liu, my interpreter.

The first tale was about Zhong Kui, the eighth-century ruler of spirits. When he failed his imperial exams, he committed suicide and appeared in the emperor's dream. In the dream, Zhong Kui caught the demons that haunted the imperial palace. He explained to the ruler that as he had not been able to serve him while alive, he was protecting him after death. The emperor had Zhong Kui's portrait painted and hung to scare away the evil spirits. This practice was then emulated by the people, so Zhong Kui became a theme for woodcuts.

A second story concerned Guanyin, a bodhisattva who took the form of a princess. She refused to marry, against her father's wishes, and instead became a nun in a Buddhist monastery; her father, furious, had the monastery burned down, but Guanyin managed to escape. When her father fell ill and could only be saved by someone who would sacrifice an eye and a hand, Guanyin tore an eye out and cut off a hand. Filled with remorse, her father forgave her and she appeared to him in her true form of as compassionate bodhisattva with one thousand eyes and hands. Later on, I saw this representation of Guanyin in temple sculptures.

There is also the myth of the Cowherd and the Weaving Maid. Cowherd, driven from his brother's home, heard his water buffalo speak. It told him to go to a lake where he would see celestial fairies bathing. Cowherd hid the clothes of one of the fairies and ended up marrying her. Eventually, the couple had two children. One day, the Queen of Heaven came to look for Cowherd's wife, for it was this fairy, known as the Weaving Maid, who embroidered the clouds of the setting sun. When the Cowherd returned that evening, he discovered his wife had disappeared, and had left the two children crying. He remembered that the water buffalo had told him before its death to save its hide and if he wore the hide on his shoulders and made a wish, it would be granted. Cowherd put on the hide and placed his two children in baskets at each end of a yoke. He then made a wish to join his wife. His wish was granted and they started their ascension toward the heavens. When the Queen of Heaven realized that he'd catch up with Weaving Maid, she pulled a hairpin out of her hair and drew a line in the sky to block him; this was the beginning of the Milky Way and, ever since, Cowherd and Weaving Maid have been two constellations separated by the Milky Way. Fortunately, on the seventh day of the seventh lunar month, magpies form a bridge, allowing the lovers to meet again.

Another legend tells of the Door Gods. Emperor Xuanzong had fallen ill, victim of a dragon's evil spells. Only the soothsayer knew why the emperor was ill and how to save him, but he had been sentenced to death by the prime minister because his prediction of rain had not come true. The dragon had deliberately delayed the rain. In order to save himself and the emperor, the soothsayer appeared to the emperor in a dream and asked for his help. The emperor agreed, summoned his prime minister and, on the date set for the execution, ordered the prime minister to play chess all night with the soothsayer. When the prime minister dozed off for a brief moment, there was just enough time for the soothsayer to decapitate the dragon. To prevent the dragon's ghost from seeking revenge on the emperor, two generals offered to guard the entrance to the imperial bedroom day and night. Taking pity on his generals, the emperor had their portraits painted on the two door shutters in order to relieve them. This is why, ever since, prints of the two generals have been stuck on people's doors.

I was inspired by these legends and went to the college library to see some old woodcuts. This turned out to be difficult. "There is nothing left," the librarians told me. "Nearly everything was destroyed during the Cultural Revolution, and we are not permitted to show you those that remain." I insisted, explaining that I was studying woodcut printing, and managed to consult a few. I did some sketches that I would put on a block, or I would draw directly on the wood, then carve. I had to remember that what was on the left would then be on the right and vice versa. With a little roller, I spread the ink and applied the sheet of Chinese paper with the back of a spoon or a stone polished by the waters of the Yangtze. I spent many enjoyable evenings doing this work. It helped with the depression that sometimes came over me.

But my relationship with my woodcut printing professor remained strained. When I showed her my work, she would grab my pear woodblock and correct it by gouging a line I was instructed to follow. She defaced my work to fit her ideology.

The students were delighted that I dared to question the teachings of a high-ranking official and mouthpiece for the reigning ideology. Since I made no attempt to hide my opinion that, contrary to the official view, she was no great artist, she soon became hysterical. It made me think of the old Empress Dowager Cixi, who ruled with fear. Like her, my professor had her own court, whose members reported my comments to her. I learned later that upon hearing them, she flew into such a rage that she broke everything in her home. Subsequently, she made sure that the local press published articles glorifying her artistic talents. I was coming dangerously close to serious trouble, especially since her husband was the head of the college. Fortunately, the head—a very attractive man, the most handsome Chinese man I ever saw—was completely different from her. Intelligent and humane, it was thanks to him that my situation at the school would undergo a radical improvement. After a month or two, I attended other classes and left woodcut printing for the paintbrush.

Besides classes, my daily routine began with an alarm at 5:30 a.m. There was no escape since the loudspeaker was fixed directly under me, on my building. After the raising of the national flag, the students made their way to the dining hall to collect their steamed buns, while I reported to the guest dining room to partake of my elaborately concocted dishes. When I inadvertently glanced into the kitchen, I saw monstrous black roaches crawling on the day's mounds of buns and soy bean cakes.

Next, we had to report to the stadium, to the spot assigned to our registration number; mine was at the back, on the right. Any hole indicated an absence, duly noted by the Party official, and meant points would be deducted from the absentee's report at the end of the month. Students who did not have the minimum number of points would be expelled. Then a gym teacher with a whistle had us jump in place for an hour. He brayed like a donkey to set the pace. It felt like a juvenile detention center. These exhausting calisthenics to disco music re-mixed by the Chinese were a far cry from tai chi or daoyin, the Taoist form of stretching and physical movement. Afterward, we had to go around the stadium four or five times, often in the fog since Chongqing is located on the slope of a deep valley carved out by the Yangtze. Since there was so little visibility when we did our laps around the track, the students took the opportunity to speak to me, asking me questions that, for many months, I could not understand. My Sichuanese was limited to a few phrases jotted down in a notebook and learned by heart. "I would like to buy some sugar." "Where are the toilets?" "How much is this pencil?" Unfortunately, on the track I did not have my notebook.

The poor students, with their drawn faces, were very thin. I knew that they sold their meal tickets to buy more tubes of paint. We were provided housing, but their stipend was limited to sixty yuan per month,[1] on which they had to live, buy meal tickets, and art supplies. I was paid one-hundred and twenty yuan, equal to a teacher's salary, and I was fed. I had not realized when I left France that my scholarship would be paid for by the Chinese government and the Chinese students sent to Toulouse would in turn receive a French scholarship. Many of the Chinese students wore thick glasses; if the students wanted to keep working after the electricity was cut at 10:00 every night, they had to continue by candlelight, which damaged their eyesight.

From time to time, a rebellion would break out in the middle of the night at the college. The students' anger was so great that when the lights went out, they banged on their mess tins for at least an hour. It was unbearable. However, the professors, housed near the student buildings, kept silent and the college officials did not react. From my room, I never saw the lights come back on after one of these nocturnal concerts. I felt very uneasy alone in the dark under my duvet, feeling the discontent of the students rising like a tsunami, a powerful sentiment that might one day destroy everything in its path.

---

[1] Roughly $25 USD, approximately $75 in 2024.

Classes went until 11:30 a.m., when we returned to the dining hall for lunch. Then we had a one-hour nap for digestion, a delightful Chinese custom that I would eventually take back with me to France. In the afternoon, classes continued until 6:00 p.m., when dinner was served.

After the meal, we had free time until lights out at 10:00 p.m. We could go back to our rooms and work or go to the cinema, as there were showings every night. The days were long and full, but I rarely missed a film. It was a way to learn Chinese and I found it relaxing. As a result, I saw a lot of Chinese films, but also classic foreign films. The sound was hard to make out, but it was a unique experience hearing Alain Delon and Catherine Deneuve speak Chinese!

My neighbors constantly cracked sunflower and watermelon seeds so that the ground was strewn with shells. This was their big splurge, the only one that they could afford at the little college sweet shop. I copied them and ate seeds as well. They also smoked a lot. The constant fatigue and stress may explain why the Chinese are heavy smokers. Some students took advantage of the cover of night, when there was less surveillance, to approach me and shake my hand. Before heading off to bed, we could return once more to the dining hall for some sweet sticky rice soup, or a stuffed steamed bun. It was the reward at the end of a hard day's work. The schedule was grueling, six days a week, and, with the ceaseless supervision, I often wondered whether this was a college or a correctional facility.

On Sunday, the only rest day, I started to explore the nearby area, but the college was far from the city center. I found some bookstores, very poorly stocked, where, unsurprisingly, it was impossible to find any books in a Western language. After three weeks, I finally managed to buy a bedside lamp to save me from the neon light. For want of something better, a cardboard box served as my nightstand. To wash, I had only the basin and the thermos of hot water that the attendant brought me every morning. She also folded my duvet, swept a little, and took away my dirty clothes to be laundered; that way she could inspect my private life for her daily report!

The toilets were the only place where people could talk freely. They looked like the pigsties where my father kept his livestock. They were divided in two, one side for men, the other for women. On each side, there was a trench to squat over. The stench was nauseating, but this was the one place where the female students dared approach me. "What's your name?" "Let's have a look at you." "Look at that, you have hair there." Embarrassed, I got out of it by joking around. "You want to see my bottom? Well then, take a good look!" The girls would giggle. I started to make my first friends.

Every other Saturday afternoon we had shower privileges. There were no showers at the college, so each person with their towel and enameled basin headed to a Soviet-built power plant pouring out asphyxiating pollution. There was a large room with showerheads and numbered spots. Here, generations mixed, from little girls of three to women in their eighties, because the college professors and plant workers came with their families. A whole range of naked bodies was on display. We had to wear plastic shoes because we were wading in dirty, stagnant water. I felt paralyzed and didn't dare take off my clothes. There was no place to be alone or even to hide a bit. We were a far cry from the hammam scenes dreamt up by Ingres or Chassériau. I took off my top and did the best I could to wash. The others made fun of me. When you are prudish, it is very hard to strip off in front of 150 women who are staring at you because it is the first time they have seen the body of a Westerner. Mrs. Liu would try to encourage me. "Don't pay them any attention. It doesn't matter, just take off your clothes." The women scrubbed themselves with enough intensity to turn lobster red and also scrubbed each other. When they finished, their towels were black with grime. It was a kind of purification ritual for them. They offered to help me and scrub me, but in the end, I decided I preferred the basin and hot water from my thermos in my room.

I washed what needed washing when it was needed. China taught me to manage on my own: you dip your little towel into very hot water, wring it out, then rub it all over your body. There is no need to dry off; in a few seconds it is already done.

The whole situation was difficult to bear, especially the official ideology that was embedded in every stroke of the paintbrush, whether by teachers or students. But in spite of everything, I did not stop learning.

I felt terribly lonely, as I had no one to talk to. What kept me going was reading Shitao's meditations at night. When I felt too sad, I would dive back into the book, sprawled on my straw mattress reading by candlelight after hours. I had nothing else to read except my dictionaries, which I was learning by heart.
I was often racked by massive doubts, the kind that kept me awake at night and filled me with anxiety. I had come to China as a kind of painter-ethnologist to observe what China had become after Mao. But what if I had made a mistake? What if the Chinese officials actually had destroyed their ancestral knowledge? Had I really come all this way for nothing?

I could not quite accept that the art of these ancient aesthetes and poets had completely deserted the Chinese world. I decided that I would not leave this hell without investigating properly.

The teahouse in Jiu Long Po

The southern wind
blows my forsaken spirit,
setting me down
outside a friendly tavern

After six months, I started to sink into serious depression. One day, my Chinese had improved enough to decipher the sign stuck on my door, which was an official notice issued by the local Party office. I discovered it said: "Disturbing the foreigner is forbidden. Any student acting in violation of this rule shall be expelled from the college." I now understood why no one dared speak to me except in secret while running around the stadium or at night during the film screening. And all along, I had thought that I did not know how to fit in.

Furious, I ripped down the sign. I headed straight to the director to express my indignation, as he seemed to be the most open and receptive. I took along Mrs. Liu, who had started to become my friend. I had sensed for some time her increasing discomfort; human feelings, which exist in China like anywhere else, had eventually cracked the official veneer. The campus Party official stopped me, insisting I had to speak to her and not to bother the director. This woman reigned over the college, and her primary task was to write reports about professors and students. I'd get nowhere with her. "Sorry," I told her. "You're not the one I want to speak to, it's the director." She began to shriek and make a scene. The director, whose door was open, came out to see what was the matter. Pushing past his ferocious gatekeeper, I exclaimed, "What is this notice? I'm a model student. For six months, I have done everything you asked of me. Why am I being ostracized? This sign forbids anyone from speaking to me. Now I understand why everyone has been avoiding me like the plague. No one even says hello. Isn't that the first rule of hospitality? So much for Chinese manners!"

Mrs. Liu closed the door and spoke to the director. I saw then that they shared an intimacy that I had not noticed before. She blew up at him in a local dialect, but I caught at least one bit: "This can't go on. We can't impose such a miserable existence on her." Fortunately, they understood. My forced isolation had aroused compassion. The Chinese do not bear solitude well. When they arrive in a strange place, they form a group; they even prefer sharing a hotel room. If you want to punish a Chinese person, shut him up alone; he will very quickly break down.

"What is the problem?" asked the director. I told him about my trouble with his wife, the woodcut professor. "I understand," he said, smiling. He also suffered from her tyranny. She was known for her hardline ideology, and I suspect she was very tiresome. He taught sculpture, and I had visited him at his giant studio. It was like a cathedral full of bamboo scaffolding. Perched fifty feet above, he tackled vast marble blocks. I appreciated his masterly, energetic sculpting, and watching him work was a real pleasure. However, when I saw, several months later, a monument to the glory of Mao emerge from the block of marble—a female farmer and her crying child—I had my doubts. I acknowledged that his realism was artistic but wouldn't it be better to let the rough stone speak through its natural irregularities?

"What do you want?" asked the director. "What are we supposed to do for you? You have to understand that no one can do as they like here. Mrs. Liu and I, in fact *all* of us, have someone to answer to. We all have duties to the Party. Both of us have dual roles: I am the director of this college and a sculptor; Mrs. Liu is an English teacher, and at the same time, responsible for you. That is no small task. You're starting to become a real burden. We aren't totally ignorant of how you live in the West. In fact, we didn't think you'd last six months, but look, you're still here!"

"I want to live like the others," I answered. "Trust me. I'm not irresponsible, let alone an agitator. I know that I haven't made things easy for you but I have learned a lot in these six months. I want to meet professors and speak with the other students. I'm here to study, nothing more. I want to understand Chinese culture. You have to let me have contact with Chinese people. I want to try to master Chinese techniques because they are an important contribution to the rest of the world." I stressed the latter to better strengthen my cause.

"I'm not looking for special treatment. The cook always serves me delicious food, but dining alone every day is unbearable. The door to the guest dining room stays open, so when I eat, seated before my twelve different dishes, I see two thousand students laughing at me. This is torture. You're punishing me in front of everyone. You say that we should live like the common people and yet you force me to live like a capitalist. Do you want to humiliate me?" I demanded, using their own politics to argue mine.

"You're right," he admitted, "our system is flawed. But can't you see, we're trying to give you what we cannot give ourselves? Don't think that we have been trying to hide the reality from you, we know that's not possible. We wanted to spare our Western visitor the harsher aspects of life here. Our intention was not to treat you like a capitalist. We know that you are not one. We've been treating you as a foreign guest because that is what you are. Perhaps we've gone about it in the wrong way. I understand that you find certain classes disappointing, but you are not alone in your dissatisfaction."

I was touched in spite of myself, even though I knew that he was employing the usual double talk. "I have to learn Chinese," I told him, "even just to study painting. Mrs. Liu's dedication is admirable. But don't you see, she cannot stay with me all the time; she also has classes herself, plus English is not my native language—I have to retranslate what she tells me into French. You have to admit it's not easy."

"You came here to study art. You want to be a painter, not a Sinologist."

"Of course, but it is impossible to live in a country for several years without speaking the language. Films are not enough to learn from."

"Fine, then. We will give you meal tickets, like the other students. But if you fall ill, don't come complaining. You'll be allowed a certain amount of rice and meat per day. This is how the system functions here. As to classes, especially my wife's, that is a more delicate matter. Could you please continue attending them? If not, war will break out in the college. You would be setting a bad example for the others, who would love to use you as an excuse to make demands. In exchange, you may consult the last of the old masters who still live here. They are retired; they have not been reinstated and do not have the right to teach. However, you could learn brushwork from them, since that is what you're interested in. I will issue instructions to that effect. I'll get into a lot of trouble for this, but I understand you."

I later learned that he had faced great difficulties getting me admitted into his institution in the first place because the local Party administration deemed it unthinkable to invite a foreign student there. After my departure, he was arrested for supporting the students in the demonstrations held in Tiananmen Square in June 1989, which eventually spread across China.

Overnight, a new life began. I queued with the others in the dining hall, clutching my numbered mess tin for my bowl of rice with meagre toppings—"to make the rice go down easier," as the Chinese say. Once a week, I attended a meeting where college officials delivered their reports with the requisite moralizing speeches. But I was excused from Marxism classes. Instead, I was invited to visit the various studios. Students began to speak to me in the dining hall. "Finally! It's about time!" they exclaimed. I could not understand them well, but we did our best to communicate. Sitting on the ground outside, we ate from our mess tins and played games, throwing peanuts in the air and catching them in our mouths.

Some classmates asked me out, hoping to win my hand to escape abroad. Others were curious and wanted to learn about my country. Having started out so alone, now I barely had a moment to myself.

One day at a painting session I met a student called Houmei, who soon became a friend. She was a tomboy, tiny as could be with a strong personality. Dressed in green army surplus right down to her trainers, she always carried a regulation canvas backpack in the same color. Her hair was like a mane, as if she wanted to hide behind it. She walked up and nonchalantly offered me a cigarette.

"Do you want to come with me to the teahouse?" she asked.

"Teahouses still exist?"

"Sure, we didn't tell you before because they wouldn't have allowed you to come with us. We go there between classes to get away from campus and sketch the river. It's very beautiful, you'll see. Come on, I'll show you."

I readily accepted her invitation. I could not imagine a teahouse in this gloomy, polluted, industrial suburb.

On Sundays, I had tried to go out and take the bus to the city center, but the streets were jammed and the buses overflowing. You had to fight your way on board, otherwise you'd be left behind. I hadn't realized that all I had to do was cross a congested boulevard, turn into a short series of alleyways and go down a few steps to see a different China. There were black wooden houses built on top of one another and a maze of stairs going down to the river. Old women sat on little worn-out bamboo chairs in doorways chatting away while sifting rice; corn cobs and chili peppers lay drying; children wearing trousers with the backs cut out, exposing their bottoms, played in the courtyards. In the windows, miniature potted trees sat like talismans among the drying clothes. Fat bricks of coal shaped like disks with holes pierced in the middle to improve chimney draught were stacked up around the houses as fuel for cooking on little round stoves. In the winter I took the same route when it was already dark. During power outages, I'd see children being bathed by candlelight in wooden tubs. It was like a Georges de La Tour painting, where life suddenly surges out of the darkness. I enjoyed experiencing this slice of history and felt that in spite of the totalitarian system, life rose above it. In Singapore, when the old Chinese district was razed to build breathtakingly high towers and "offer" people modern, sanitary residences, the suicide rate shot up as fast as the new buildings. I learned later the same thing happened in all the big cities in China, including Chongqing.

The teahouse was a wooden shack clinging to a rock that overlooked the valley. Everything about it was filthy, with spit puddled on the floor, but it was a unique place. Cement blocks served as tables and stools. Old men in faded gray suits sat around playing mah-jongg and chess. Sometimes, a storyteller would sing ballads, beating time with sticks on a kind of drum made from a long wooden tube closed at one end by a pig's bladder squeezed under his arm. For a few maos, the proprietor would bring a white porcelain cup and saucer with a cover containing tea leaves for the afternoon. An elderly woman came around regularly to fill the cups with hot water from a long-spouted copper teapot. The inside of the cups had turned brown from the tannins that no one bothered to wash away. The layer was so thick that simply pouring hot water into the cup was enough to give it the taste of tea. A few maos more would buy you a plate of sunflower seeds or roasted peanuts. From this high vantage point, you had a clear view of the boat traffic on the river and the ever-changing sky. Holes in the mist made for a kind of hide-and-seek, where the scenery would come and go. Sitting there, you could travel somewhere else. These were times of respite, happiness, and escape from the college campus and its barrack-like atmosphere.

In former times, there was a teahouse culture in China—of which this one was but a vestige—similar to that of pubs in England or cafes in France. Teahouses were meeting places where customers could sip different kinds of tea, savoring flavors in the same way that the French enjoy wine. They were also a place to play games, especially chess, like in the eighteenth-century cafes of Paris's Palais Royal. Moreover, teahouses were where folk culture lived on. Storytellers and singers would narrate long ballads in the afternoons and evenings, in which the history of China was performed as a fantasy full of heroism and magic.

It has always been difficult in China to criticize authority. But thanks to these mythical characters, it was possible to remind those in power of their responsibilities. They never fundamentally challenged the State, but only protested against those who did not observe the same rules that they imposed on others. How could this purely moral presentation of history fail to attack the government itself, whether imperial or Communist? This is probably because the Chinese authorities didn't solely use force or censorship to check dissent, but somehow imposed self-censorship. The romantic history of China was not written by the people but for the people by disgruntled scholars blocked from civil service after failing their imperial exams. In their frustration, they denounced the authorities who did not obey their own laws. These learned men dreamed up an ideal state from the past, made more marvelous because it was set as far back in ancient times as possible. A spectacular tool for propaganda was created, whether intentionally or not. Storytellers and ballad singers spread that propaganda without realizing that they were instruments in a quest for justice by those incapable of attacking the real source of their grievances. I witnessed the guardians of ideology recycle these old methods at the college, where they managed to impose a kind of self-censorship more stifling than any other form of oppression. The students might dare to criticize one form of excess or another, but no one would have admitted, even to himself, that it was Mao's socialism that had to be brought down.

It was hard for me to gain acceptance at the teahouse. When I entered, a dreadful hush fell over the place, bringing all conversation to a halt: a foreigner would attract the attention of the authorities to their little haven! They were troubled and I did not know how to win over my hosts or prove that I had no desire to disturb their sanctuary. One day, I opened my sketchbook and started to draw some of the faces around me. A gray-haired man, curious, drew closer and chuckled as he recognized himself. I had found a way in! It broke the psychological barrier that had prevented them from seeing me as a human being capable of understanding them. I gave the drawing to my model and was soon surrounded by the others. I knew the local dialect well enough at that point to speak a bit with them, but what no words could express I managed to get across with a few strokes of my pencil.

To fully grasp how just a few sketches sufficed to gain their trust, the importance of the brushstroke in China must be appreciated. In the West, a person's word carries no weight. Only when something is in writing is it deemed official or lasting. In China, a verbal agreement is difficult to obtain during negotiations because, traditionally, the Chinese do not go back on their word. Like farmers in France, the Chinese believe a yes is as good as a signature. But they have learned the hard way that words can also be deceptive. A painting, on the other hand, or a drawing or calligraphy, anything related to the stroke of a pen or brush, cannot deceive. The moral virtue of its author reveals itself. It is bared for all to see and is impossible to fake. It is the character of the artist as much as his work that is judged in a painting or calligraphy. He who masters *hua* (the brushstroke) possesses this particular language that can only be true.

This is one of the singularities of Chinese thought, and it reminds me of a Chinese friend who was inspired by a Western painting style to execute a series of works. They were shown at a gallery in a European capital, where all of them sold. The painter was left with only one. He could only show me the images. He wondered to himself: "With this style of painting, I can create illusions. I can seduce. But if I am honest, it's not part of my culture or my education. It's a disguise." From then on, this painter worked only in Chinese calligraphy because, as he put it, it was unforgiving. It could not be used to deceive people. An artist in China enjoys a unique status because the Chinese believe art communicates one's true spirit. I could have tried to win the teahouse patrons over with fine words but my drawings revealed my genuine intentions.

There is a classic Chinese tale about a fisherman who managed to train some seagulls to come and land around him on his boat. One day, his father asked him to catch one of the birds and bring it to him. The next day, the seagulls remained in the air, circling over the little boat but never landing. Their instinct told them not to. Man no longer possesses this animal instinct; culture and speech have distorted it. But the Chinese have created an original art form that forces the artist to speak the truth. During the Cultural Revolution, temples were destroyed. Afterward, the sculptures of the deities sitting atop the altars were recreated. They are exact reproductions yet they ring false. It is hard to pinpoint why, but it's because they are the work of artists for whom religion no longer has any meaning beyond a set of outdated beliefs.

Once they had adopted me, the old-timers who visited the teahouse every day introduced me to their games, as this peaceful oasis doubled as a gambling joint. I learned how to play and was happy to discover I was good, even if we were only playing for beans. This was also the place where I could spend time with classmates who were discouraged from associating with me. We "ran into" each other there. I often had to juggle things around so it didn't look like I was closer to one friend than another. The teahouse was full of secrets.

My friend Houmei, who had first introduced me to the teahouse, was antisocial and withdrawn but she opened up to me. Her life at home was unbearable. Her father had gone mad and suffered violent episodes. He drank and beat her mother. Her sister had a disability. When Houmei came home at night and showed her father her paintings, he insulted her and threatened to hit her because she was not following the Party line. In truth, he was afraid she would suffer like he had during the Cultural Revolution. He had been a lacquer craftsman, one of the most highly regarded in the province. Since we spent a lot of time together, I asked her to introduce me to her parents.

When I met her father, I tried to win him over. On his bed and table I saw remnants of his creations.

"Did you make these?" I asked him.

"You're interested?" he replied, with a frantic look in his eye.

"Of course," I answered. "What is your technique?" That broke the ice. On a section of wood, he explained, a piece of fine silk was laid as a base and then coated with successive layers of lacquer, a kind of resinous veneer. Each layer was left to dry before it was sanded and polished. Up to fifteen or twenty coats were necessary, taking months. The result was solid but appeared fragile, sublime to touch and deep and translucent in its contemplative beauty. Decorative motifs were then engraved into the thick lacquer. He added with a smile that the glazing technique used in Flemish painting was most likely inspired by Chinese lacquer.

"Where does that theory come from?" I asked, surprised.

"In Europe, painters in the twelfth and thirteenth centuries didn't have the drying oil necessary for their technique. The surface of their paintings remained viscous because they never dried properly. But in China, the use of resinous oil–based lacquers dates back to medieval times.

We Chinese were the first to create an effect of infinite transparency in the use of varnish. They say that great Flemish and Venetian explorers who were invited to China in the age of the Mongolian dynasties became fascinated with lacquer techniques. Once back in Europe, inspired by what they had seen, they purportedly created the process of drying oil varnishes used in oil painting, which was a real revolution at that time."

I was astonished by this information. No one taught this in our art schools! He went on to tell me about his training, first in the countryside, then in a workshop. Through the telling of his story, he seemed to come alive again. He had been barred from teaching his art after the Cultural Revolution. Accused of perpetuating a backward culture and branded a lackey of feudalism, he had been humiliated, beaten, tortured, and ostracized. Now, forced into retirement, he was free to come and go but he stayed inside his home as though imprisoned, for as soon as he set foot outside, he would inevitably cross paths with his former torturers.

No family had been spared during the Cultural Revolution. Even if a person informed against someone, the informer could find himself among the accused the next day. There were no guarantees of impunity. Any weakness, any attempt to promote your traditional art could rank you among the enemies of the people and then nothing could save you. You would be eliminated. One professor, hoisted upon a window ledge high up in a building and about to be dropped, was saved at the last moment when his torturer was called away. Another had his fingernails torn out. Merciless beatings were an ordinary occurrence. Being dragged through the streets in the middle of a roaring crowd, wearing a tall paper hat and a sign around your neck with a list of your alleged crimes, was the least of all humiliations you might suffer. Many committed suicide, and suicides were greeted with cries of joy: the bastard had confessed to his crimes! A respected intellectual's daughter was forced to work as a cashier in a supermarket where men, feeling she deserved nothing but contempt, insulted, pinched, and mocked her. She ended her life by swallowing a bottle of detergent. Wives informed against their husbands and children denounced their parents out of panic or overcome by a frenzy of fanaticism.

Now these same people had to live together: children with the guilt of their crimes, colleagues with the terror and shame they had caused others to suffer, or with hatred for their sadistic torturers. When two individuals ran into one another on the street, a simple glance or a face turned away spoke volumes. You could sense this hatred between members of the college, who seemed ready to blow up at any moment. It is perhaps not the least of the government's accomplishments that it managed to prevent an explosion of retaliation until time had passed and memories had faded.

I was profoundly moved by a film titled *Night Rain in the Bashan Mountains*. It starts with a group of people who board a boat in Chongqing to go down the Yangtze to Wuhan, crossing the river gorges that separate Sichuan from the neighboring province. A young girl tearfully parts from a boy. A man passes, handcuffed, flanked by a man and a woman, who despite their plain clothes, are clearly security agents. The story takes place on the boat over the course of a day and night. The passengers settle into their quarters, and through their words and actions, are introduced to the viewer. An opera actor who had played clowns chooses to be deaf to all speech and buries his head under a blanket because he was so mistreated for having participated in such backward traditional theater. An old woman brings along a basket of jujube fruit to throw into the river as an offering when the boat passes the place where her son was killed in a battle between Red Guard groups. The girl eventually reveals that she has been forced to leave her beloved because her father is sending her to marry another in the neighboring province in order to repay a debt.

A poet, arrested in a restaurant while having lunch, is alone at a table. A young man finds a moment when the two guards are distracted and approaches the poet to inform him that he was among the Red Guards who burst into the poet's home at a university, dragged him outside to beat him, ransacked his house, and burned his books. Instead of destroying the handwritten poems found in a drawer, the Red Guard took them home to read. He then realized that this man, the poet, was not the enemy he had imagined. Since then, he regrets his cruelty and has come to respect the poet.

During the night, stretched out on his bunk, the poet cannot sleep. When he sees the woman go outside with her jujube basket, he joins her on deck to keep her company. Later, the girl appears. She quietly climbs over the railings of the boat and throws herself into the river. The poet dives in to save her. At dawn, at the first stop, the passengers plot to help the poet escape. The final scene is the boat setting off again. The wife of the security agent approaches his colleague and says that she is the one who should be in handcuffs because she knew about the poet's escape plan and chose to ignore it. The colleague answers that he himself organized the poet's escape with the passengers.

Immediately after the film, I found the happy ending rang terribly false and overly sentimental, like so many modern works of literature. Later, though, I came to understand what the filmmaker was trying to say. In the mind of each person, the Cultural Revolution simply had to become an aberration, a moment of madness, where the participants, possessed by fanaticism or fear, had committed horrible crimes. But the torturers and sufferers were still human, all of them victims of the situation. Otherwise, there would be too many reprisals and society would be stuck in an endless cycle of revenge.

When I returned to France, I was often asked how I could have borne the living conditions in the school for six years, and why I never left. But every day I learned of more adversity, and people told me their stories about those ten dark years. I saw that many were still traumatized by their pain. Students my age disobeyed the program rules to try and express themselves through their art. I explained that, in this context, problems involving showers and toilets seemed fairly trivial. In this college, at least, I felt alive and enjoyed a privileged status; the lack of comfort or my problems with the educational system did not have the same meaning as they would have had in France. I became so attached to students and professors alike that I felt compelled to be a part of their life, a life to which history had given heart-breaking dimensions. I felt as though my own life prior to living there was limited to trifling matters. It took coming to China to truly grasp what tragedy meant. In the end, the only thing that separated me from the Chinese was the fact that they had lived through such experiences while I had not.

Avatars from Courbet to Millet

Although half of the university students were enrolled in the oil painting department, few studied traditional Chinese painting because it was considered an art form doomed to extinction. There were two woodcut printmaking workshops. There was the one given by the college head's wife, which, in line with the prevailing ideology, focused on images of national minorities. The other was with an instructor inspired by Munch and Expressionism, in which morbid fear was conveyed through the use of violent contrasts. The latter allowed her students complete artistic freedom, but she suffered from the presence of her colleague, who sought to crush any form of creativity other than her own.

Houmei was fascinated by Daumier and was constantly drawing Don Quixote and Sancho Panza in her sketchbook. Her work was so dark and tortured, I found it painful to look at. Haunted by a violence that she struggled to control, she was aggressive, unhappy, and misunderstood. I listened and tried to cheer Houmei by teasing her and sharing sunflower seeds. I made her smile with my impressions about the official classes.

I took classes with another professor who followed the Party line but practiced an unusual technique: he reconstructed scenes on a stage using male nudes that we had to sketch with a brush and India ink. Traditionally, the scholar's brush was used to render scenery and scenes in an abstract way. But since the present ideology advocated a return to nature, studies of nudes or still lifes were done using the ancient Chinese technique on a sheet of paper placed atop our portfolio. This mix of two cultures, which attempted to create new art forms, was interesting.

Sometimes the professor took us deep into the countryside to sketch using his method, which gave me the opportunity to study village life. It was very difficult, with just a little brush made of three rat hairs, to depict a farmer or an old man in his overalls, much less include the wrinkles that would bring the character to life.

Unfortunately, the instructor was disagreeable and extremely misogynistic. He constantly poked fun at me, and the atmosphere was dreadful. I was the only woman and foreigner in the group. Out of two thousand graduates, only eight researchers were chosen each year to continue post-graduate studies for another two or three years on a State scholarship. That meant the others were technically excellent and far beyond me.

I also took an art history class that required Mrs. Liu's help. Every instructor had suffered greatly during the Cultural Revolution, but each had felt the horror differently and had taken their own path. I found the art history professor particularly touching. He had been very young during the Cultural Revolution, and believing in it, had wanted to see everything destroyed. Now that it was over and China was opening up, he was discovering his own culture. He had started to read the classics, and Chinese philosophy was a revelation for him.

Even if the curriculum on ancient China in schools had been fairly limited, the other students had learned enough to understand their art history, whereas I knew nothing. The slides shown during class provided an introduction to certain works, but it was not enough. How could one understand Western painting, from the Roman frescoes to Delacroix, without an initial understanding of Christianity, Greek and Roman mythology, the humanism of the Renaissance, etc.? Then there was the field of aesthetics for which my entire frame of reference was my solitary book on Shitao. I therefore requested that this professor give me an introduction. Gradually, he took me through the whole of Chinese civilization. He got caught up in it and went looking for sources, often admitting to me, "This is so frustrating. I've been searching the archives desperately, but there is nothing left." He introduced me to the *I Ching*, the Taoist philosophies, Laozi and Zhuangzi, Confucianism and Buddhism. The further we ventured, the more passionate I became, and I often asked him, "But why was everything destroyed? You sawed off the very branch you were sitting on." I knew I was placing him in an awkward position, because he could no longer understand himself why he had participated in such insanity. You can't play with madness or stupidity with impunity: when you treat people like idiots they become idiots. Fanatical behavior turns out bona fide fanatics.

This teacher took real pleasure in teaching me what he himself was learning. I became concerned about him because he was turning into an insomniac and developed a kind of monomania. He would rush to my room with the interpreter, often exhausted and overexcited, proclaiming, "Miss, I've just discovered new aspects of our culture!" The audacity of what he dared to teach me put him in a cold sweat. At the end of class, he always said, in a trembling voice, "This must remain just between us. Above all, don't tell anyone about the content of our classes."

I owe a huge debt to this young professor because he helped me surmount two major handicaps. Although I finally managed to speak Chinese by picking it up as I went along, and learned certain characters to reproduce in calligraphy through dictionaries, I did not know enough to read classical Chinese works. And while I believed I was capable of not only learning the Chinese technique but mastering it, I lacked the cultural base that the others had acquired naturally from school and their family. I was like a student beginning a graduate course in mathematics without the slightest notion of binary arithmetic or trigonometry. I was confined within frustrating limits, more a prisoner of my own ignorance than of the exasperating college rules. This teacher helped me to overcome these obstacles blocking my progress.

In this college, oil painting alone held distinction when I arrived in 1983, and it represented the fast track to fame. This generation, working with hog bristle brushes on easels, did not learn how to use a Chinese brush loaded with ink and held vertically.

Unfortunately, their oil painting was painting without finesse, with paint squeezed straight from the tube applied thickly with a palette knife, without even any glaze to give off light. Some artists had learned glazing in the West, but apparently the technique had been lost. The available materials were of poor quality, the oils crude and the pigments unrefined; moreover, no one seemed to know how to use any of them properly.

The current Chinese painters had been trained by the Soviets in a previous era when the USSR—the "Big Brother Country" as it was known before the split with Khrushchev—had dispatched experts in all fields to its socialist ally. If an artist wanted to avoid trouble and continue to paint, then Communist ideology had to be served one way or another. At that time, giant formats like huge frescoes exalting rural life were encouraged. Starting in the 1950s, the favored aesthetic was referred to as "romantic realism." It was both surprising and impressive, with a Delacroix-like intensity to it. However, just as in Europe, when most works were commissioned by the nobility and bourgeoisie, the Chinese artists, working for the State, slipped in some kind of personal mark alluding to the source of his inspiration. Whereas Europeans artists used hidden meanings and symbols, the Chinese embedded theirs in steles or inserted brief phrases and poems.

Certain village scenes recalled Géricault in their power or could be seen as an homage to Millet and his earnestness. There was a recurrent theme celebrating women working in fields that recalled *The Gleaners* by Millet. Other artists received official encouragement by following a harder ideological line in which they would depict people's misery and the injustices suffered by the poor social classes. These paintings of people's suffering—before their liberation, of course—were distressing in realism and horror, but very well executed. They brought to mind scenes of the retreat from Russia by Joseph-Ferdinand Boissard de Boisdenier. I saw large scenes of workers set in dramatic chiaroscuro with terrifying machines looming in the background. Certain works recalled our campus kitchens with bloody chunks of pork hanging from hooks in the red glow of cooking fires like the gates of hell. These suggested Goya and even Soutine. Others were closer to Courbet's *Stone Breakers*. I was a great admirer of Courbet, particularly of works such as *L'Atélier du peintre*, which ignited my imagination.

The successful manipulation of minds and techniques by the Chinese to serve political ends, and the cruel reality of their approach, both amazed and distressed me. It was astonishing to witness the transformation of Courbet's *The Trellis (Young Woman Arranging Flowers)* to the young pioneer girl in a red scarf offering a bouquet to the glory of the Great Helmsman. I had to admit it was ingenious.

To understand this new form of Chinese painting, the role of the prominent artist Xu Beihong must be taken into consideration as well as that of the Soviets. Xu was already famous when the Communists came to power and in the best position to play the role he would be assigned. He had studied in Paris and Berlin and was an expert in both traditional Chinese and Western painting. Appointed head of the China Central Academy of Fine Arts in Beijing, which was to serve as a model for all future institutions, Xu decided which subjects were to be studied, decreeing that modernists like Matisse and Picasso were decadent and that Rembrandt should be emulated. He facilitated a path toward Soviet-style painting and blocked any experimentation in other styles of art.

No one, in the beginning, forced him to make such choices. He illustrates a phenomenon I observed many times in China. Xu Beihong was not a Communist but a celebrity who sought to rally around the regime. Perhaps because he was uneasy with his choice, he felt compelled to be even more orthodox than the survivors of the Long March. His famous horses, with their undertone of Chinese Army propaganda, began to invade porcelain. Posters and reproductions of them were presented to important foreign visitors.

He was capable of executing Chinese painting with great refinement and an extraordinarily vivid brushstroke, but he made it a point to stamp art with socialist realism to please the new masters. There were many Chinese like him, practitioners of self-censorship even more exacting than any official version, who, regardless of their true feelings, chose to bow to the new ideology.

However, it was also Xu Beihong, well acquainted with survivors of the traditional arts like Qi Baishi and Wu Zuoren, who protected those artists. Furthermore, he arranged for Huang Yong Ping, the greatest Chinese traditional landscape painter, to teach in Beijing. Thanks to him, Li Keran, another great painter, joined the academy. So Xu Beihong's role is controversial. He was without doubt an artistic genius, and the authority that he wielded was admittedly less strict than that of the Soviet professors who reigned after him. Later, I met his wife and son, who solicited me to organize an exhibition of his work in Paris. However, I could never bring myself to do it, for I had seen too many artists suffer from the many artistic avenues he had denied them, including abstract painting.

Since artists were forced to leave their studios to go out and study real life, many creative possibilities opened up for them. They immediately favored depicting ethnic minorities in colorful costumes living on the high Tibetan plateau, in the hills of the southwest, or in the semi-arid regions near the edge of the Gobi Desert. Numerous paintings of Tibetan women milking yaks resulted, as well as of horse racing in Mongolia, portraits of women from minorities such as the Miao, Naxi, and Yao, and troglodyte houses in the loess cliffs of the northwest.

This interest in ethnic minorities corresponded perfectly with the government's policy of Sinicizing them while preserving their folklore for tourism. These paintings of minorities, by the very nature of their subject, differed from other works that were more strictly "socialist realist." The colors were more vivid and sparkling because these populations had to be portrayed as happy under Chinese domination.

Chinese painters became great travelers, setting off with their backpacks and portfolios, undeterred by harsh living conditions. Artists aimed to return with the most extraordinary stories or venture into the farthest reaches of the country. It was wonderful at night to hear about their journeys, meeting people with different customs and cultures. What these new kinds of explorers reported was far from the official Party line, which was that the Chinese government respected the habits and beliefs of minorities and provided them with decent living conditions. In reality, most of these people lived in poverty unless they were lucky enough to be turned into zoo animals for tourists.

These painter-travelers very quickly realized the material opportunities they could exploit through their expeditions. They acquired costumes, masks, statues, and religious paintings for a few pennies from the destitute, and resold them when they returned home. How many times did I hear, "Miss Fa" (their nickname for me), "don't you know any foreigner who would like to buy this?" I was very sorry to not be able to buy some of the marvelous old objects myself.

A new school of painting began to appear, thanks to an intrepid few and the head of our college who allowed their "decadent" innovations. These students formed a separate group that I naturally gravitated to. They chose Cézanne and Picasso for their models and wanted to deconstruct form to achieve another kind of expression. *Les Demoiselles d'Avignon* inspired a style that might have amused Picasso. Meanwhile, Van Gogh—a mad and accursed artist who fit their ideal—was all the rage. They practically cut off their own ears! It was their way of rebelling by imitating an artist who, like them, painted by taking his easel out into nature or setting it before a figure outdoors. Some of them painted nudes *en plein air*, reminiscent of Gauguin, Derain, or Matisse, with Fauvist touches and great force expressed in the lines. Then there were my friends, the romantics, who painted, like Chagall, young newlyweds floating through the sky over a murky urban background. A sincere and authentic approach brought these paintings to life from their birth in the industrial suburbs of Chongqing.

It was extraordinary to witness these young people drawing their entire inspiration from a foreign culture. But what of their own had they been allowed to keep? They had been denied their heritage under the pretext that it was just a lot of counterrevolutionary nonsense. Appropriating a culture that they knew only from reproductions remained a completely artificial process for some, but for others it became astonishingly integrated. I wondered about this process because it directly concerned me. At heart, I wanted to take the exact opposite course to theirs. Watching the best of them find their own language, little by little, encouraged me. Together with my young professor and painter friends from that period, Zhang Xiaogang, Ye Yongqing, He Duoling, and Zhou Chunya, we spent many years engaging in lively and heated discussions about art. I have fond memories of entire evenings in front of our paintings with bottles of local alcohol in hand, getting carried away by passion and inspiration, engaged in unwinnable debates. Some of them are very successful today and show their work in prominent international galleries. If a foreigner could practice the traditional Chinese art of the brush as well as they mastered oil painting, she might succeed in creating a new kind of painting.

I very quickly realized that two prerequisites were necessary to reach my goal. The first was to master the Chinese technique, initially that of calligraphy, since it contained all the brush strokes I needed to use later in landscapes and other subjects. This meant a huge amount of work and patience, and called for the same determination and conscientiousness that the Chinese students showed in applying themselves to our oil painting. Learning to write just a few characters, in a crash course as some foreigners do, leads at best to mere amateur work, and at worst impresses only the uninitiated.

The second requirement was to not limit myself to technique. I had to acquire the inner culture that accompanies it—not just book learning. I had to absorb

Chinese thought, become a bit Chinese in spirit, in my way of being, and even in my way of living.

It is no coincidence that the Chinese students were drawn to Courbet and Millet. The art of these French painters is inseparable from the socialist thinking of the nineteenth century, which could be compared, to a certain extent, to the socialist painting they envisioned. For the Chinese, though, political ideas were too omnipresent to break free from. Even when their paintings contained real power, the propaganda element of their work prevailed over the aesthetic impression. In contrast, those who had studied Modigliani or Braque eventually created a signature style in painting that is recognized today. I observed their approach: they started by copying, endlessly copying, and it was only much later, after dedicated practice, that some of them found their own style. And in doing so, they honored a Chinese method.

In the West, students strive to produce an original work of art as soon as possible. The Chinese, on the other hand, continue to paint as before by copying the old masters. There is no disdain for copies as in the West—quite the contrary. Only after the copying stage did they begin to travel and to allow the Chinese landscapes, their traditional culture, and in particular their current one, to enrich their work.

As time passed, a Chinese aesthetic emerged, a new art form different from that of the West. At the time, the Chinese were not familiar with Jackson Pollock, the abstract gesture, Antoni Tàpies, Barnett Newman, Mark Rothko, or even early modernists like Piet Mondrian. They were familiar with Picasso though, and could paint a sunset over the rice patties of Sichuan with large trees, in the style of Charles-François Daubigny painting the banks of the River Oise. This was a bit of a crazy experiment, and a bit disconcerting.

At the beginning of the 1980s, Pop art had not yet arrived in China, but soon after, Martial Raysse, Roy Lichtenstein, and Andy Warhol hit upon the idea of Maoist images reworked in a Pop art style. It was an enormous success, as there was a market for this work. Westerners were excited to discover Chinese art interpreted in a familiar way. For the Chinese, this ease with copying everything while adapting national subjects presents an obvious danger: catering to the public, creating what people like, what sells. Chinese artists have no qualms about following the crowd or fashion. I have heard Chinese artists declare outright, "I can do anything; just tell me what to paint to appeal to the Western market."

This dangerously easy road, which many of them would eventually take, served as a warning to me. It reminded me of the theater in France. Certain directors, familiar with Asian theater, dressed the characters of the Greek tragedies or Shakespeare in Kathakali or Kabuki costumes or hung a Tibetan cloth over the stage. This interpretation might impress an uninitiated public, but it is superficial. In contrast, director Peter Brook's explorations were a model for me. Significant work went into drawing out the very essence of Asian or African theater. Before directing *The Mahabharata*, he took several research trips to India with his actors.

I knew that my approach was risky, that certain people would criticize me: I was not Chinese, I would never be, and I wanted to create a foreign pictorial language. But if a Korean conductor could be hired by the Paris Opera to direct Western music, and the Chinese could stage productions of *Swan Lake*, *Carmen*, and Shakespeare, and Chinese artists could go beyond the limits of the Chinese aesthetic to create a new modern art form, why couldn't a Westerner forge her path in Chinese pictorial language? No one thinks to criticize a writer who writes in a foreign language if he has sufficiently mastered it. Disparaging my pictorial language is like condemning Joseph Conrad, a Pole, for having written in English and French.

I learned the traditional Chinese technique of *marouflage* from Professor Li. *Marouflage* is a paper-backing method for mounting paintings. Professor Li, whose studio was on campus, used *marouflage* on the work of students and professors. To obtain my degree, I had to present works of calligraphy, landscape painting, and sketches from my travels, so I asked to attend his classes to learn how to back paper and make the glue which resembled boar sperm. I enjoyed spending whole days at a time with him, and we shared unexpectedly delightful moments.

Li was small, stuffed into his apron; his hands, eaten away by moisture and glue, were covered with a microscopic fungus. Little bandages were wrapped all over his fingers.

The professor taught me to mount paintings onto scrolls, explaining the traditional rules of color and border composition. I helped him mount works for several months. After being granted permission, I became his apprentice for a time.

He was extremely attentive to the time needed to stretch the canvas while drying, never going too fast. Chongqing is, as the saying goes, one of China's four ovens. His studio was unbearably hot in the summer. Even with a fan running, it was intolerable at night. The tap water was warm. We were all constantly bathed in sweat. With such high humidity, drying paintings on paper is a delicate operation. It was very hard for me to stay in the *marouflage* studio, but it was a good vantage point to see what the students and professors were doing and what they were planning to submit.

Chinese *maroufleurs* are so skilled that some of them, working with a precious old painting, are even capable of separating different layers of paper by cutting with such infinite care that they reveal another original painting underneath.

After a month, I proposed to him, "Why don't we have a bit of fun with all these techniques?"

"What do you mean, fun?"

"At night, we could try some new compositions for presenting the works by varying the materials that we use."

He was intrigued by the idea. "Let's do it. What do you want to try?"

I invented a new range of scroll mounts and experimented in every way possible. I mounted sketches made in the Chinese countryside onto sheets of newspaper. I mixed special dyes to obtain colors and blends like yellow, black, and the red of the Yi peasants. After a few weeks of experiments, a revolution had taken place on the drying racks of the *marouflage* studio.

Only Western painting and Chinese traditional folk art were taught at the college. There were no classes at all on the literary arts. I asked around to see if any students practiced calligraphy and someone told me about a doctoral student who practiced in secret. "Haven't you met him? He lives in a box room over the classroom." When I went to his door, at the end of a dark corridor, I don't know why, but I felt intimidated.

He had taken over an office reserved for use by the supervisors. Dozens of calligraphies were hung from the ceiling covering his bed. A slight breeze jostled them, and the rustle of drying papers created a wave of sound like so many brushstrokes. His dark and squalid box room had been transformed into a kind of sacred temple, and this impressed me at once. I felt an intense joy looming out of the shadowy light. It was astounding. At last, a rebel! Despite the absolute ban on studying calligraphy by the school officials, he had created his own calligraphic world. Not only was he a lover of calligraphy, he was also a wonderful young man—very handsome, tall, sincere, and likeable. Like all the young intellectuals, he lived in a tiny space with nothing. The only items on the ground were his thermos, mess tin, and a threadbare towel.

"I've seen you around the college for a while now," he said. "I'm so happy to know that there are still calligraphers. I've been searching for months!" I exclaimed. I began to talk to him in my broken Chinese, and we became friends. I started paying him regular visits. He showed me books and his favorite works of calligraphy, and he explained his work to me. He was like a Paul Klee of calligraphy, exploring a naive, childlike style. I appreciated his sense of humor, and his company did me good. Thanks to him, I started to find meaning in my experience there. And, through him, I discovered the existence of a clandestine cultural life and met courageous people who ignored the bans and kept the aesthetic traditions alive. He spent his evenings copying and recopying rubbings of old texts while developing his own personal style. One day I asked him if he knew anyone who might teach me his art. "There are still two professors at the college. One is Feng Jianwu, the other Huang Yuan. Go and see them. But be warned, they are not easy. They don't want to see anyone. They haven't taught since the Cultural Revolution."

Excited, I found out where they lived on campus. First, I went to see Feng Jianwu, who was very well known. The old gentleman was not at all pleased to be disturbed without warning. The Cultural Revolution had left him very bitter, and I felt no interest or desire to pursue it any further. I apologized and left.

A few days later, I tried my luck with Huang Yuan. He lived in poverty in a filthy tower block. The stairwells were filled with bicycles blocking the way. Clothes, chili peppers, and other condiments hung from the hall ceiling, and toys sat abandoned in the dirt. The place was in a sorry state. I knocked on his door. He opened it. He was feeding his bird. I liked him immediately in his old worn-out jacket, beautifully shiny from years of wear, a long lock of hair falling across his face and a cigarette dangling from his lips that he didn't bother to remove when speaking. His whole being evoked ancient China. I was entranced. There was extraordinary nobility in his face, supreme detachment, subtle intelligence, and a wisdom that I can't describe but which I felt instinctively, deep inside. I had never felt that before for any of my professors.

"What are you doing here? Are you lost?" he asked mischievously.

"No, I'm looking for professor Huang Yuan."

This he found amusing, but he politely answered, "Professor Huang Yuan, as you say, miss, has not existed for many years! Come in!"

He poured me a cup of tea. "I was told about you," I told him, "and the head of the college has given me permission me to come and study your work."

A crude obscenity followed in Sichuanese.

"Even my own children can't understand my work! My son is a student here, but he would rather sell jeans at the market so that he can go to America than understand my work. My wife spends every evening playing mah-jongg to forget our lowly existence and win a few pennies. Me, I talk to my bird. What you are proposing is impossible. Anyway, calligraphers are rarely women, and on top of that you're a foreigner."

Then, after a long silence that seemed to carry the weight of history, he told me with a touch of irony that he no longer shared his knowledge and preferred to avoid the whole sad subject. "Besides," he added, "at this point, I'm incapable of teaching."

However, I had finally found the world that I had been searching for. Among his household objects, his birdcages, books, paintbrushes, water pipe, the honey pot under the bed, his Yixing teapot, and the stone he used to grind his ink, I had found an art of living that enchanted me. I saw a culture, a living source, the very teacher who might be able to provide me with what I sought. I left him with a song in my heart, thanking him for making me feel welcome. He was utterly bewildered to see my pleasure when he had just issued a flat refusal.

I had read that before a master accepts a student, he first needs to be sure of your motivation, earnestness, and determination. He would test you. You had to prove your tenacity and perseverance. I thought of the story of the man who wanted to learn Taoist magic. He found a master and carried out the menial household chores he was ordered to do. After several months, impatient at having learned nothing, he complained to the master and asked to be taught at least one magic trick. The master agreed and taught him the secret for passing through walls, adding that he had to throw himself against the wall with complete abandon. The disciple followed these instructions, and to his surprise, found himself on the other side of the wall. Tired of the hard, monastic life and thrilled to have turned into a wall-passer, he went home and boasted to his wife. He recited the formula and threw himself against the wall only to fall to the ground earning his wife's derision and a large bump on his forehead. To avoid ending up like that man was going to require relentless determination.

I went out and bought paper and books containing woodblock reproductions of works by the most famous calligraphers. I started to copy those that seemed to me the most beautiful and interesting. Every night, after class, I tied up a roll of calligraphic exercises with string and went to leave it on Huang Yuan's doorstep. This solitary experience went on for months, with no response.

I persevered for six months, as I knew from his son, who was in the graduate program with me, that his father pored over my exercises with great attention and found them surprising. The son was a bit envious. "My father doesn't care about what I do. When I put something in front of him, he pushes it away. He's not interested in my work. But you're lucky, he looks at your pages every night." The son didn't understand that his attraction to the West and modernity, and his abandonment of Chinese tradition, made his father sad.

I still had no feedback and was working in the dark, but what he said gave me the strength to continue. However, I did not go as far as the disciple of Bodhidharma, who cut off his left arm so that his meditating master would notice his presence and agree to teach him. In class, everyone made fun of me because, each day, I took my scrolls to a silent master. I was teased and told that I was deluding myself and that he must find me annoying and ridiculous, even disrespectful, to disturb his retirement like that.

During this long waiting period, while facing the jibes of my classmates, I sought out a little company. I took my savings and went to the market to buy a bird to liven up my tiny room. I eventually found a man selling birds and cages. I was starting to manage fairly well in the local dialect and had my university card with me. "I am a student at the art college. I'm feeling lonely. Could you help me?" I asked the seller straight out.

"Of course. You need a talking bird."

"A talking bird? You mean we could have conversations?"

"Yes. I even have birds that can teach you the local dialect. This is a mynah bird. He belonged to an old professor who died. He's fantastic. He'll probably not speak at first, but once you have tamed him, he will. He already knows 'please,' 'come in,' and 'what are you doing, you blockhead?' Unfortunately, he has a penchant for insults."

"It's a good idea, but do you think he'll like living in a tiny student room?"

"Is there a garden?"

"Yes, just across from my building, where the statue of the great writer Lu Xun stands."

"Then hang his cage from the arm of Lu Xun, and you'll see how he talks to him!"

When he announced the price, I told him that was too much. It was the equivalent of one month's scholarship stipend. In the end, he gave me a deal and I left with my mynah bird. When I got on the bus with him, everyone started laughing; I had become the laughingstock of the college. The Party official declared me a bit mad, like all artists. "There's nothing we can do for her. We have to understand her, she's lonely. Maybe having a bird for company will calm her down."

I didn't want to leave my bird shut up in his cage all the time, so at night, when I did my exercises, I let him out. I had replaced the desk with a long board on two trestles; one end was reserved for calligraphy, the other for woodcarving. I had hung a network of string on the ceiling to dry my laundry and exercises on paper. Amid all this chaos, my bird had free rein. When it was time to go to bed, I had trouble getting him back into his cage. In the beginning, he said nothing and I thought I had been cheated. But one day, three weeks after I bought him, someone knocked on my door and he cried out, "Come in!"

I was overjoyed. I started to talk to him, spoiling him. One night, when I was copying a rubbing, he started walking on my ink stone, taking ink onto his beak and splashing it across my worktable, calling me stupid! I almost fell over backward. It was the best day of my life. Once, he walked on the table with his wings slightly spread, crossed behind his back as if in deep contemplation. Suddenly he looked at me and screeched, "You blockhead!" He was very good with insults. I retorted tit for tat with *bendan* (idiot), which amused everyone. I took him for walks in the garden. On Sundays, I sometimes ran into the old cook, who also took out his bird. We hung up our birdcages in the shade and chatted. Sometimes I got very angry at my bird. His favorite trick was to fly into my calligraphy pieces hanging from the ceiling, piercing them in a straight line. Or he would soak his feet in ink and then sign my works with his footprints. Still, he was extraordinary and he was good for me. We had happy times together.

One morning I was working with my bird when someone knocked on my door. My bird cried, "Come in!" He must have thought that I was not moving toward the door fast enough or that the visitor was deaf to his invitation, so he called out again, "Come in, you idiot, come in!" I opened the door: there was Huang Yuan with my rolls of calligraphy exercises under his arm.

The master's teachings

Who can tell the end of the endless changes?

My dream had come true: the master was there. Huang Yuan stood on my doorstep looking at me calmly. He came in, sat down, and rolled himself a cigarette.

"Make me some tea," he said. "Frankly, this is crazy. You're a foreigner, but seeing your exercises these past six months, I can discern the moral and spiritual worth in your brushstrokes. This is surprising. Did you select the works you copied yourself?"

"Yes. After I met the graduate student who works alone in his box room, I went and spent a few maos for these books of reproductions of stele rubbings of famous calligraphy. I chose those I liked best and tried to figure things out by looking up the same characters in dictionaries to compare the printed form with that of the calligrapher."

"You've singled out the great masters, which shows that you have a sound cultural base. There is a resonance inside of you that even my own son lacks. It is the source of works to come, and I have hopes that you will create interesting things. I am impressed by what you have accomplished on your own in six months. I like your spirit. For a Westerner, your level of comprehension is surprising. Your intuition is good. You possess an intelligence of the heart that spontaneously points you toward the best. You deserve to be taught properly. I have been living at this university for over fifty years and I have never seen such a gifted student. No one has asked my opinion of a brushstroke since the Cultural Revolution. It will cause me a world of trouble, but I will start the official process to try to obtain permission to teach you. To undertake a proper training, you cannot come to visit me secretly at night. Our status has to be official, even to hold weekly lessons. From there, we will slowly be able to build up to more comprehensive study. However, I should warn you: if you begin with me, it is ten years of apprenticeship, or nothing . . ."

All of twenty-two years old, I was so elated that I answered yes without realizing the importance of this decision to my future. Huang Yuan was there and his presence justified all my efforts. With his guidance, I would learn the fundamental notions that I had somewhat gleaned from books but were absent from my formal education. On impulse, I agreed to be his apprentice for ten years.

Although he was supported by the head of the college and Mrs. Liu, he had a lot of difficulty getting the proper permission. Even the local Party official, who had eventually developed a bit of sympathy for me, had to refer the matter to those higher up since Huang Yuan had never been reinstated after the Cultural Revolution. In the end, an exception was made and he was assigned the task of giving two or three lessons a week to initiate the foreigner in "the use of the Chinese paintbrush." We had succeeded. The practice of the paintbrush could easily be extended to a more comprehensive education, since the art of letters brings together poetry, philosophy, music, and painting. The creative spirit plays all these different instruments. Sadly, blamed as the source of the rot responsible for China's decadence, these arts had been destroyed, eradicated. It was only at the beginning of the 1980s that the art of the literati, with their unique vision of the world, started to return to a place of honor, and classic books as well as ancient and modern studies began to be published again. It is impossible to understand Chinese painting without understanding Chinese culture. But is that so surprising? We easily forget that our own painting is rooted in Greco-Roman civilization, Christianity, the Renaissance, classicism, romanticism, and realism, and the same classicism pervades the work of Le Brun, Vermeer, Mansart, Rubens, and Racine.

Huang Laoshi's[2] first assignment was disconcerting, and it was not until much later that I saw it as judicious. "Before beginning to paint or practice calligraphy," he told me, "I would like you to study with a master seal carver. I will not show you how to use a paintbrush before you have understood the power of the strokes illustrating the steles that you have studied. Works by great calligraphers were carved in stone, then stamped over the years so that they could be circulated. At that time, there was no photographic reproduction. It was by carving the texts in stone that the intrinsic quality was captured. Therefore, you will need to start with sigillary writing, which consists of the most ancient characters. You have to work with the chisel before beginning to produce your first strokes with the brush. I'm going to send you to the greatest master in the province but be warned: he has suffered great misfortune. I hope that you can bear it. In any case, I won't begin to teach you until you have done this training." He gave me the address of the seal carver, Cheng Jun, together with a letter of introduction.

Thus, one morning, I set off to see the master seal carver. I arrived in a dusty, polluted part of town which was covered with soot that often fell like a light rain, apparently spilling out of a Russian power plant. The inhabitants of this godforsaken place developed cancer at a very young age. In the middle of a construction site surrounded by factories, I asked for directions. "It's over there," someone told me, "in the abandoned buildings, fourth floor, third door on the left." When I knocked, a man with only one hand answered. "Are you Miss Fa? I was told to expect you. Come in." The interior was terribly shabby, furnished with a sofa blackened with grime and a little table upon which sat a teapot on a towel. On the wall hung prints of remarkable carved seals. "Don't be afraid," he told me, pouring the tea, and the teaching began. Huang Laoshi had told me that this man had suffered greatly, but who would have imagined that during the Cultural Revolution

---

2   I soon adopted the Chinese habit of calling my professor "Huang Laoshi." *Laoshi* is a traditional title of respect.

they had been so cruel as to cut off a man's hand merely because he was a traditional artist of great talent? Despite his suffering, he still had an extraordinarily bright spirit. "Don't be afraid of my hand," he said. "You see, I am still carving my seals, even if they cut it off." He had made himself a leather pouch to protect his stump, and, holding the stone with his arm, he managed to carve. I worked hard with him, spending months copying seals by the great masters.

The surprising paradox in these totalitarian regimes—a recognized phenomenon that I can confirm—is that among the weakest, the individual is annihilated: his personality and liberty. But for others, like this seal master, who were forced to endure such terrible tribulations, their suffering creates or unleashes a violent inner energy, a renewed power of survival. These individuals go on to reveal a poignant and stirring knowledge of truth because everything was forbidden. In normal circumstances, it is unlikely this would have happened.

When you meet exceptional people who share their art with you regardless of the risks (the least of which is looking bad to the authorities) and who offer you all of their knowledge—the fruits of their internal struggle: the rebirth and the preservation of their art—the least you can do is respond to their generosity. How could I not follow them?

Upon a backdrop straight out of a Zola novel, China was for me an extraordinary accelerator of progress and rare knowledge.

My professor and I went hunting for steatite stones at the market. At night I carved my seals. The next day, he would correct them, explaining every line. He taught this special form of writing to me, deciphering poetry and philosophy. In this way I came to appreciate that seal carving is an art in its own right, like painting. I understood why Wen Yiduo, the greatest Chinese poet of the twentieth century, chose to devote his life to it. The seal that an artist stamps on her painting becomes an integral part of it; it must convey the spirit of the painted work and be in harmony with it. These seals conserve the oldest forms of writing.

Calligraphers must be initiated in it, as this writing only survives in seals; this is the only way to access the origins of this art. It is only through seals that we can study ancient calligraphy. Other mediums used for writing have not survived, except for bronze, but there is no question today of recasting bronzes.

I studied the distinctive style of characters on seals. I copied and recopied the work of the great masters, whose seals I carved and then stamped on paper, from bronze seals of the Shang era to historiated seals from the Spring and Autumn period, which depict marvelous little animals. I interpreted characters in different styles, like "dangling needles" or "birds and insects" from the classical era.

As we had limited means, I carved each face of the same stone. To my great dismay, we would sand down the previous week's exercises to obtain new miniature work surfaces. The art of the "iron brush" is nerve-racking. More than once, out of fatigue, poor skill, or simply being too lazy to place the stone in the little rosewood holder and blocking instead with my left hand, when the knife in my right hand slipped, the beveled tempered steel blade would quickly gash my skin. After a few weeks, the fingers on my left hand were covered in plasters. That's normal, Huang Laoshi would say, you're just learning the hard way!

At night, I translated the seals made by the great scholar-painters. I was overjoyed to discover their poetry and subtle humor. Shitao, the memorable author of my precious *Comments on Painting by Monk Bitter Pumpkin*, was also known as *Disciple of Great Purity* and *Venerable Blind Man*. Mountain-man monk Bada Shanren had pseudonyms like *Singular Snow*, *The Donkey*, and *Woodcutter of Broken Clouds*. Finally, the day came when I was given permission to carve my own: *Paintbrush Tempest* and *The Universe As My Master*. I was better behaved back then. Later I carved names for myself like *Cooked Vegetable*, *Enraged Tigress*, or *Imbecile Before the Eternal*. You see, I learned something in twenty years of practice.

After several months, I took my work to Huang Laoshi and told him I thought I had a good grounding. He looked at my left hand and my work before answering, "Not bad."

When I started to show him what I had learned in the traditional painting studio, he stopped me right away. "I don't want to see any of that, it's demoralizing. Starting today, forget what you've learned, what you think you've understood, aesthetic categories of beauty or ugliness. Throw all of that out! You're going to begin by drawing lines, just lines, for several months. In Chinese painting, everything is based on strokes of the brush; they are your building blocks. Don't imagine for a moment that we are going to copy rubbings of old calligraphy right away. You'll need a solid base first. This base is the horizontal line. Until you can bring the horizontal line to life, we will not move on to other strokes or write characters. The unity of the brushstroke is the foundation. Remember in the middle of the *Tao Te Ching* by Laozi: one gives birth to two, two gives birth to three, three gives birth to all things."

"It seems to me," I told him, "that Heraclitus, one of our Greek philosophers, expressed the same thought: 'All things are one and from one, all things.'"

"That's right," he answered. "The horizontal stroke is the one, the others are the two; they give birth to thousands of characters. The brushstroke is a living entity of its own—it has structure, flesh, and vital energy; it's a creature of nature, like everything else. You have to capture the thousands of variations that can be expressed in a single stroke."

I practiced for months, and every time he stopped by, he corrected me. First, he taught me to grind my ink sticks on the ink stone and to make the most of this ritual of repeated movements to prepare myself mentally for the act of painting. It is a kind of meditation to leave the human world and empty one's mind. He also taught me to load the brush with ink, since deep within its cloak of horsehair there is an internal reserve that one must learn to master vertically. For that, an awareness of mass and universal gravity has to be developed so that the brush becomes a veritable pendulum, a link between the universe and the center of the earth. Huang Laoshi taught me how to hold my body: both feet firmly anchored to the ground, drawing the earth's energies upward. I had to practice staying upright so that the energy currents between heaven and earth could pass through me. This is not a joke! I had to turn myself into a kind of lightning rod to harness telluric forces. The idea may seem simple but it is not easy to apply. I had never dreamed that to handle a paintbrush and draw a stroke on a blank sheet of paper I would need to intuitively master the fundamental laws of physics.

Huang Laoshi rarely came to visit. He left me to paint my lines, my *hua*, alone all day long. "I want your brushstroke to represent a cloud formation, with the indistinct, ever-changing nature of clouds, this breath that stirs the vaporous matter," he would tell me. "Try," he would urge, and leave. I continued my strokes while trying to keep in mind what he had said.

Later, he would return. "Your brushstroke, here, is wrong. Think of a horse, of its femur bone. Try and show this bone with your stroke, including its marrow, because even inside a bone, there is movement. Draw your line while imagining a bone." So for a week I drew my lines with a bone in mind. When he looked at this work he observed, "Your horse bone isn't bad, but there is still something missing. Your stroke is not alive. Do you know the vital principle of plant life?" He went out into the garden to break off a branch. "Look, there is an outer structure and the sap inside, the fluid that nourishes the stem. There is an internal movement and a stable, external covering. I would like you to reproduce that with your heart." Then he disappeared again for a week. When he returned, he said, "Not bad. You have more or less grasped how plant life is ordered. But you are too dry. Your stroke needs more water. Water is in every form of life found on earth. For man, without water there is no flesh. You understand the structure. You are beginning to understand the underlying movement, but there is no flesh. Think of rivers, waterways, the movement of a wave, humidity, and mountain torrents, then try to render that." And then he left me again for many days to try to apply this latest teaching.

During this period, my classmates, who saw me perpetually drawing the same line for several months, made fun of me. "You must be thrilled to have endured so much to come to China to draw lines like in nursery school for months at a time!" They failed to understand the principle of my professor's teaching. But this teaching interested me, even if Huang Laoshi only uttered a single sentence per class. He smoked cigarettes, drank a cup of tea, and spoke to my bird, which he adored. He did not say much, but no one before had ever asked me to think about what a brush can convey in its most basic expression: a stroke. I found his demands very difficult to meet and yet they made sense. His teachings touched upon a certain essential knowledge about the art of painting. As a result, I buckled down, working relentlessly.

One day, he asked if I knew how to ride a horse. "Yes," I answered. "I love to ride."

"How do you stop your horse?"

"I pull on the reins."

"That movement of tension, when you pull the reins: can you show it with your brushstroke?"

Nothing escaped him; he saw that I had not yet reached what could be contained in the matrix that we call the brushstroke. His short sentences, very simple, boiled down to one principle: how to bring life to matter, and calligraphy was part of this principle. "Everything found in nature, all human movement, is an ideal metaphor to teach your mind to give life to a brushstroke," he would say. "Until you have learned to endow your brushstroke with a physical and spiritual tension, there is no reason to go any further."

Over and over, I practiced for months until one day—a miracle!—my brushstroke was perfect. We celebrated my success: he invited me out to dinner, then to the opera. "Tonight, I'm having a drink!" he exclaimed. "You've understood the fundamental basis. We can now go on to other brushstrokes, and we'll go much faster. The first step is the hardest; afterward, there are no limits."

He introduced me to the dot, which could convey a boulder hurtling down a mountain, ready to explode; the diagonal stroke, which resembled a rhinoceros's horn; the vertical stroke, like a rusty nail; the curved stroke, like a wave crashing on the sand and finishing with a roll of thunder. He used poetic images to teach me each stroke. But it was not just images: he forbade me to paint without first picturing the roll of thunder, the breaking of the waves, or the hurtling boulder. "They have to be present in your mind before you even set the paintbrush on the paper; without that, you will not succeed in expressing them. This is not a question of technique."

After two seasons of infernal exercises, I finally understood and applied the crucial mental focus. For an apprentice painter, it was a brilliant lesson.

His critiques were along the lines of: "Your brushstroke lacks muscle. There is not enough tension." "This one should be more lively, more nimble." "There is no harmony in its unctuousness, it lacks music." "Your structure is too weak, too limp. What's the matter? Are you ill?" He could read my inner life in my writing. When I was feeling down, he could see it right away. "This is no good at all; you've lost your mastery. You need a break." "Here, there is too much flesh." "There is not enough fullness in the consistency of your ink." He had an anthropomorphic vision of the brushstroke. To him, calligraphy was a living organism. You had to start with inner preparation, the mental and physical attitude necessary to bring the line to life. This took me several years of practice.

I spent long days at his home, consulting reproductions and rubbings of old works of calligraphy. It was another part of his teachings. He wanted to train my eye, to teach me to discuss brushstrokes. "What mood does it express? What impression or perception do you have?" He borrowed books from friends to show me the largest possible variety. We spent hours leafing through them. He explained to me what he read in this or that mind and why. Then he asked me, "What do you think of this brushstroke, what flavor does it have?" I would tell him what I thought and he would approve or disapprove. I spent many hours this way, trying to understand the secret inspiration of various works. It was long and tiring, but it taught me an enormous amount and helped me in my later training. I developed an acute instinct about the substance and essence of a brushstroke. Fortunately, our sessions also included the tea ritual, a great luxury, when he took out his pot of honey to sweeten our hot water. It was a break with time to chat with the birds.

We started our copying exercises. Together we chose rubbings from the *Forest of Steles* of the Beilin Museum in Xi'an. The seal writing stage went rather quickly, as I had already learned it with the master seal carver and I had acquired the strength that is required for this script. Afterward, we began to tackle regular writing, where each character had to fit within a box, but I got bored aligning the characters like little soldiers in a parade. This was where Huang Laoshi proved his genius. Another teacher would have assigned me many months of regular characters before proceeding any further; but he understood right away that I did not like this. We moved on very quickly to the cursive style, which interested me.

At nights, I tried to find the characters I had copied in my dictionary, but it was very difficult. "I don't understand the meaning of the characters I'm writing in calligraphy," I told him. "I feel frustrated, like this work is beyond me. Is this important?"

"It is not important at all," he reassured me. "Don't worry about the meaning for now. Don't spend your life with your nose in a dictionary. Follow my principle: reveal the energy, the movement, the master strokes. I'm not looking for technical prowess. You must achieve complete mastery over the ink and brush so as to breathe life into your brushstroke."

He often visited my room to calligraph sentences that he would then explain and assign. My walls were covered with them so I fell asleep reading them. My brain would absorb the path the brush took in space. The texts were philosophical because he wanted to lead me imperceptibly from the technique to its underlying thought. He distilled his teaching down for me into small doses.

Having spent so much time perusing dictionaries and trying to understand characters, I wanted to calligraph a poetic thought of my own. I arrived one day, very proud of having managed to write a little poem in Chinese. My professor flew into a terrible rage and cast my work aside, saying, "I don't care what your calligraphy means. It could be the luminous ray on your bird's beak, the evening breeze whispering its stories, or the thunder knocking at your door. It is a spiritual spark that must generate the work; thought must not outweigh the naturalness of the whole. The meaning of the character is beside the point for now. The important thing is the unity. You wanted to express your thought at the cost of the harmony of the composition. One can sense how you toiled; your work was dead before it was even born. Always start from poetic intuition and aim to convey the substance of things; that is the guiding principle. Where is the manifestation of the marvelous mystery? You let the naturalness escape. It is too forced."

He told me two stories that appeared in *Zhuangzi*, which I later found in a translation by Liou Ka-hway.

When Prince Wen-Hui's butcher was cutting up an ox, he gripped the animal, pushed it with his shoulder, and held it with his knees. With feet riveted to the ground, he plunged his knife into the animal with a musical rhythm that kept perfect time with the famous tunes played during the *Mulberry Woods Dance* and the *Meeting of the Feathered Heads*.

"Ah!" exclaimed the Prince. "How can your art have attained such a level?"

The butcher put down his knife and said, "I love the Tao and this is how I progress in my art. When I first started as a butcher, I only saw the ox. After three years,

I no longer saw the ox. Now, it's my spirit acting instead of my eyes—my senses are no longer involved. I know the anatomy of the ox and I only cut through the empty spaces. I don't damage the veins, arteries, muscles, or nerves, and certainly not the large bones! A good butcher wears out one knife per year because he only cuts flesh with it. An ordinary butcher wears through one knife per month because he dulls it on the bones. I have had the same knife for nineteen years. It has butchered several thousand oxen but the blade is as sharp as new. There are gaps between the bones so if you can weave the thin blade through these openings, you can cut through with great ease. Because I use it this way, my knife remains perfectly sharp, even after nineteen years. Each time I have to carve through bone joints, I first note the tricky parts, then hold my breath, focus, and move slowly. I work my knife very carefully and the joints separate as easily as dirt falls to the ground. Then I withdraw my knife and stand up; I look all around and feel satisfaction in the work. Finally I clean my knife and place it back in its sheath."

In the second story he taught me, Duke Houan was reading upstairs in his hall, while below, the wheelwright Pien was making a wheel. Setting down his hammer and awl, Pien climbed the stairs to ask the Duke, "What are you reading there?"

"The words of the saints," answered the Duke.

"Do saints still exist?" asked the wheelwright.

"They're dead," the Duke responded.

"So, what you're reading is only the refuse of long departed men."

"When I read," answered the Duke, "a wheelwright is in no position to offer me his opinion. However, I will allow you to explain yourself. If you cannot, you'll be put to death."

"This is what I have observed in my own craft. When I make a wheel, if I chisel slowly, the work is pleasant, but not sturdy. If I am fast, the work is difficult and botched. I need to go neither slow nor fast but find just the right pace to suit my hand and heart. This is something that cannot be expressed in words, so I was not able to teach it to my son and he could not learn from me. This is why, at seventy years old, I am still making wheels. What the men of old are unable to pass on dies with them, and books are just their refuse."

I was fortunate that Huang Laoshi could render Zhuangzi's philosophy and teachings so accessible. He asked me, "You want to become a painter, right? The sole aim of my teaching you calligraphy is to help you understand the creative process. The hard work it took to interpret your thoughts purged all life from your composition." Ever since that day, I haven't been concerned about not knowing the meaning of all the Chinese characters. "Forget it, it doesn't matter," Huang Laoshi reassured me. Thanks to him, calligraphy was no longer writing, it was painting. My professor had liberated me from Chinese book culture. From then on, I could work with a light and carefree heart; I was now a full-fledged painter and no longer felt bound to become some kind of Sinologist.

I got bored working with black ink, so I asked Huang Yuan if I might brighten up my exercises with a bit of color. "Not only are you not going to add any color, but you will continue working in black for years. You have to get to the point where you perceive within the monochrome the infinite variations of India ink and you can interpret the thousand and one varieties of light found in the universe. If you turn to color now, you will never go further in exploring the possibilities of the washes, or the way a wash captures light. It is hard, but you have to trust me. When after a few years you come to color, the depth of your interpretation of the light will be far more precious. Black contains infinite colors; it is the matrix of them all. Even if this sounds absurd to you now, you will understand it later. With the possibilities of black and the emptiness of white paper, you can create anything—like nature, at the origin, created everything with two opposing and complementary elements, yin and yang, which blend into one. All transformations originate there. Black plays the primary role in revealing light in matter."

He showed me old landscape paintings in books. The inner structure of the world and the essence of the mist were revealed through the delicacy and transparency of the wash. Little by little, he was moving me from calligraphy to landscapes. "Chinese painting is not, as in the West, a representation of the reality surrounding us. We are not interested in likeness. That is vulgar."

I interrupted him to tell him that in France, Charles Baudelaire had made a similarly damning observation. In the West, he said, paintings of landscapes have no other rule than the genuineness of the subject, supposedly an exact science. He deplored the lack of spiritual elevation of his time, its meager poetic imagination. "Of course," my professor continued, "we also use our mountains and valleys, just like we use our written characters as sources of inspiration. There is still a relationship with reality, but the latter represents, if you will, an alphabet we use to create our inner vision, the spirit of the life of the mountain or a landscape that we may choose to interpret. Chinese painting is a painting of the spirit; its only aim is to communicate the spirit of things from their forms, but the latter are merely a means to an end."

I understood these words but it was hard for me to know how to apply them. Now and then, when I was feeling low, he would say to me, "Come with me. This evening I've made you an almond soy-milk custard." Or when I was tired, he calligraphed me a poem for pleasure:

Humble flower standing in the hollow of a wall
Your joy in being yourself is enough
To be at the center of the universe.
—Bing Xin, twentieth century

Then he might serve me a ginger infusion to restore my strength. He went to the market to buy the root fresh and cut it up into thin strips, adding a large spoonful of honey. He was particularly attentive to my health.

He would constantly repeat, "To find unity in the brushstroke, you have to understand its opposite and its match. I don't want a stroke that is too supple, too light, or too rough; it needs to be nimble and restrained, marked by neither strength nor weakness. It needs both power and delicacy. The touch should not be too light or too heavy. Press into the brushstroke, but lightly, like a feather. The brush should not be too wet or too dry; your touch should not be too unctuous. To bring forth life, you have to find the correct middle ground. Everything in life is the right balance of opposing forces. In the West, you like extremes; for you, the happy medium is synonymous with insipidness. We Chinese find the happy medium by embracing life and peace. The harmony of nature is based on this middle ground. Aim toward this and a natural energy will appear in your works, which will then find their own unity and an organic physical quality."

Leafing through art books, if he came across a beautiful painting, he fell silent, practically communing with the work of a great old master. I respected his silence and tried to meditate on the spirit of the painting, even if I only had poor reproductions before me. I liked his saying: "Memory, this furtive, ephemeral trace, teaches us slowly but surely the taste of immortality."

Contemplating these images that would become living entities helped me to grow internally. I trained myself in this advanced art form like one might train to listen to Mozart. A connection appeared spontaneously between what I was trying to understand, with the hand led by the heart, and what I was slowly learning with my eye. There is a moment when all of it comes together. I learned to live a brushstroke by contemplating it, as one communes with music.

When I told him that my classmates were making fun of my exercises in repetition, he told me the story of the mad old man who moved a mountain because it blocked his view. When the man doggedly began to dig at it, the whole village laughed at him. "It doesn't matter," he retorted. "My son, my grandsons, and my great-grandsons will continue my task until eventually they will move the mountain."

After many years of training, one winter morning I blew up in front of Huang Laoshi. "This isn't working; I don't know what I'm doing. I don't understand anything anymore."

"All right, good."

"I don't know where I'm going."

"All right, good."

"I don't even know who I am."

"Even better!"

"I don't know the difference between 'me' and 'nothing.'"

"Bravo!"

The more I thundered, the more delighted he became, expressions of joy and amazement crossing his face. He even stamped his feet, tears in his eyes. I went on, overwhelmed by a pain deep inside me, convinced that he did not understand what I was saying. "After all these years of practice, I realize that I remain ignorant. I will never be able to accomplish what you're asking."

"Yes, that's it exactly," he answered, clapping his hands with joy. He did a little dance. His glee was incomprehensible. I thought he was out of his mind.

"You have no idea how happy you've made me. There are people who after a lifetime still fail to grasp their ignorance." He thought for a moment, then held out his grimy handkerchief so that I could dry my eyes. "I am quite old now and I have not managed to do it. But you, little fool that you are, maybe with your solitary and tenacious heart, you will get there. My intuition at this very moment tells me so. The fact that you recognize that you are ignorant in the face of eternity is the very attitude I want you to have toward painting. It is the only valid attitude to have in becoming a painter. Without it, there is no use even trying. At last, you have had a sudden and accurate understanding of reality! This is the first time you have shown a spontaneous reaction, a clear and distinct intelligence. You are finally on the path of wisdom that I have been trying to help you find for years, the path of true painting, the one that is in harmony with the natural flow of things. You are exhausted; come over for dinner tonight. I will make you wonton soup and we'll drink to celebrate this happy event."

Before leaving him, feeling dazed, I thought of a quote by Fernando Pessoa whose depth I had never fully appreciated before. I tried to translate it. "He who achieves nonbeing, is."

"Ah!" exclaimed Huang Laoshi. "How did a Westerner come to understand such life wisdom?" After a long pause, he mischievously asked, "Who is this Mr. Pei-Zuo-A?"

My professor also taught me to be attentive to the smallest acts of daily life, for it is in them the painter finds inspiration. Total receptivity makes us aware of the vibrations of things, of the nuance of the dawn. He taught me, when I get up, to feel the morning mist, to observe how it differs every day. It illuminates an aspect of the self yet to be explored, a feeling one is unaware of. "Your painting is enriched by fully living in harmony with the mood of the day," he would say. "The painter does not copy nature, yet nature is her primary revelation; she restores its lines, states, and inner structure. A blade of grass is a source of knowledge. It teaches the painter the heavy, sharp, dense line. A bird's dance in flight shows you how to spread your wings, gather momentum, and dive toward the earth. You need to draw sustenance from the lives around you. They will arouse emotions and perceptions that will become increasingly rich and varied. Painters, in the course of their lifetime, build themselves a psychological database from their complicity with the world. That's what they express in their brushstrokes. One day from this store, a spontaneous movement, a creative act, will spring forth naturally."

In the mornings, instead of attending the compulsory calisthenics, Huang Laoshi assigned me to sit cross-legged for up to an hour to empty my mind. This may sound simple but it is remarkably difficult. As soon as a thought arises, thousands of feelings are triggered. "It does no good to fight it. You have a fiery nature, accept its disorder.

If a thought comes along, let it go by, don't try and capture it. You will see that, little by little, everything will quieten down. Practice every day. This conditioning will be very good for you. It is an important practice in order to see things clearly, heighten inspiration, and awaken your sudden perception. You should also study plant life." He brought me a little potted plant. "You should speak to your plants, give them a little water, and talk to your bird. After that, prepare your tea. This ritual will put you in the proper frame of mind." He also taught me to purify my space with incense. "Pay tribute to your elders, to spirits and gods. Think of your ancestors in burning incense. Sweep your doorstep as well, reconnect with natural acts."

Even today I live this way. I cannot settle down to work without a spotless, dusted table. I scrub and clean. This approach, which may seem rather banal, helps to create peace of mind. In the past, I often sat in the garden, but now I prefer walking. To chase away negative thoughts and return to a place of serenity, each person must find their own approach; walking works better for me than stillness.

After an initiation to calligraphy that lasted about three years, Huang Laoshi suggested four-handed landscape painting sessions. When I arrived, my task was to prepare the tea, speak to his bird, then remain silent while he ground the ink. Then he rolled out some blank paper, diluted the ink, and chose a paintbrush for me and another for himself. The first time, paralyzed by the emptiness of the white paper, I could not follow him. He said to me, "We are going to do a piece for four hands. I've invented this system for you. I don't see any other way to introduce you to the infinity of landscapes contained within the void."

He made a mark and asked me, "What do you see there?"

"A form coming to life."

"What else?"

"It could be a rock."

"Yes, it could be a rock."

"It could be the beginning of a rock face."

"Behind the rock face, what do you see?"

"I don't see anything!"

"Of course you do! Look behind the rock face." The work of the imagination had begun.

"Try to imagine a landscape," he instructed me. I had studied, along with calligraphy exercises, manuals like *The Garden as Big as a Mustard Seed*. It was a different kind of nomenclature, that of the representation of the world: one stone, two stones, three stones, a way to place them in space, bringing them together to form mountains, young and aggressive or those worn by time and erosion, a bridge, a row boat, the secret of the thirty-six flaws in painting cherry blossom trees, how to paint bark and tree trunks, faraway dunes and basic teaching on painting irises by the master of the House of Qing. In this *Garden*, I also discovered the writing in the heart of flowers, of stamens and calyxes, those of the apricot tree, which are so different from those of the wild apple. Manuals like these are of unequalled poetic value. The apprentice painter puts them to constant use, like a musical score, following the strokes of the paintbrush like notes he plays in order to capture the life of each and every thing. When, at night, I had the energy to open my dictionary and try to translate a quotation accompanying a plate, I came across a marvelous thought. "Flowers come in numerous shapes: some are like peppercorns, the eyes of a crab, or even a smile . . ."

I had studied the *Garden* textbook on my own, but this exercise was a big leap and I had nothing to refer to anymore. It was no longer about copying; I had to invent, improvise, dream, and spontaneously create. My professor had hidden all the manuals. I had hesitations and doubts but he pushed me through. "Each of us is going to take our turn and paint a brushstroke," he said. "It's like a game of chess: we'll see which one of us wins. If the brushstroke is not suffused with life, your composition dies. But I can also lose the game. Who will win? Who will add the master stroke? Who will finish the work with the right spirit? It's difficult." Naturally, for many long months, I lost what he called "The Four-Handed Games." Often during the first painting sessions, I was the one who messed up the painting. Each time, he explained to me why. "Here, behind this rock face, you wanted to add a tree, but the tree is not clinging the way it should, it doesn't fit there, it's not spontaneous." There was always something wrong; I was not trained for his quickness of mind. As the sessions progressed, he taught me the theories of composition and learning and how to first empty my mind before approaching the paper, an attitude I had to cultivate in order to bring life to the landscape from my inner self.

If I arrived for a session nervous, worried or irritated by everyday problems, my brushstroke would be trembling, blurred, hesitant, uncontrolled, unintelligible. At the end of the class, he might write "relaxation" on a piece of paper. "At our next session, you have to work on this idea." Back home, I worked on the idea of idleness and detachment to awaken my natural power of expression. One day, I arrived at the session sure of myself, in top form, ready to take on any challenge—I felt audacious. As a result, my brushstroke was incisive, violent, loaded with ink, dense, too black, easily veering toward the vulgar: it was pride. He wrote down: "humility." "You've already forgotten what I taught you about being self-effacing, about forgetting yourself. If you want to work on infinite perceptions through the wash of the ink, you need a humble and transparent attitude; this is the only way that a subtle presence will appear in your paintings. If you arrive proud of yourself, sure to win, your work will be crude. You'll have lost your chess match."

At one painting session, I launched a scheme to impress my old professor, but my brushstroke gave me away. Jerky, it betrayed my cunning. I lost my way all by myself. He wrote on the slip of paper, "Quiet, calm, silence." "I explained to you," he added, "that before coming to paint you have to empty your mind. It is this emptiness that will nurture your future painting. It is out of this virgin territory that your inspiration will arise and your thought will spring, like a spark the moment I pass you the brush. If you think about it beforehand, you are no longer in the moment; inevitably, you will be unsettled."Sometimes, I arrived with a fragmented mind—I was too close, obsessed by the subject. My brushstrokes were scattered, one could sense me toiling, forgetting the overall composition. I went over different parts of the painting, but I could not locate the unity of the subject. Huang Laoshi then wrote down, "Study the far-off distance." "This distance is what will allow you to embrace the whole without getting too attached to details. You have only seen the moss on the stone; this can feed your inspiration while still keeping in mind the fundamental unity. With simplicity, the composition will reveal itself, leaving just the sublime solitude of your painting."

We saw transformations on the blank paper: the metamorphosis of the sky into water, of the earth into sky, a rock becoming a cloud, a boat becoming a reef. Suddenly, everything was possible, offering us the freedom to invent a universe.

"Thought ricochets with the void, it teaches us to probe the depths of nothingness, and, from the darkness, light may spring. From movement serenity may be born." I thought of the film where Picasso transforms one subject into another. Following one's intuition, this game with the mind becomes exciting, fascinating, surprising. And, with time, evolves into an acquired taste. The taste of discovery, like musical improvisation, here transforms into impromptus of the imagination. It is intoxicating; you forget everything, living in a trance-like state with the fruitful joy of creative thought. My brushstroke would echo his, his would echo mine—we were inventing in space. He called these exercises to reveal spontaneous intelligence.

"It is the attitude of your heart," Huang Laoshi told me, "that brings your landscape to life or not. If it is calm and unimpeded, it will be the mirror image of passing inspiration. Through restraint and humility, it will suggest the elusive, and the elements of the landscape will naturally place themselves in the space of the composition."

"Your teaching brings to mind the great landscape painter Caspar David Friedrich, whom I admire very much," I said to him. I tried to translate some of the artist's theories for him: "The only true source of art is our heart." Or, "Close your eyes, so that your picture will first appear before your mind's eye." My professor was delighted to hear references from my culture that sometimes echoed his own teachings. This never failed to surprise him, and he adored such exchanges.

Once the principles of composition were mastered, my fear of the blank paper was overcome. I understood the unlimited variety of effects and rich moods that I could express with the tip of my paintbrush. We chose a different theme for each session. Each time, he added a challenge of some kind. "Today, we will interpret a snowy landscape: how to represent the cold, the singular, on a lake. Before we begin this subject, I'll read you a poem:

Over the thousand mountains, the birds no longer fly,
Over hundreds of paths, the traces of man have disappeared
In a solitary boat, a fisherman, in his hat and straw cape
Fishes, alone, in the middle of the icy river and snow

Then I had to think of an autumn landscape. I was spirited, too energetic, while he brought audacity, maturity, modesty, and wisdom. He also taught me humor through human presence in the landscapes—comical or funny situations, with figures fishing or urinating in the mountains. Huang Laoshi always smiled at these figures, laughing at how small man's place was in the universe. He showed me that we are of little significance. Each painting represented for him a survival space of dreams that helped him bear his daily reality. He lived only through his imaginary compositions. During our four-handed exercises, I often thought of the beautiful story by Marguerite Yourcenar of master Wang-Fô and his disciple Ling. Master and disciple so succeeded in self-effacement that together they boarded the row boat they had just finished painting. They disappeared in a subtle wash representing the pale twilight over the infinite jade sea created by the master. Wasn't Huang

Laoshi, like Wang-Fô, initiating me into transcendence through the act of painting? "According to the old masters," he said, "beauty in painting is not beauty as it is understood in the West. Beauty, in Chinese painting, is the brushstroke infused with life, when the sublime is attained. Ugliness does not mean the ugliness of a subject, which, on the contrary, may be interesting: if it is authentic, ugliness nurtures the painting. What is ugly is the labored brushstroke, work that is too well executed, too finely honed, or mere craft.

"Expressions of madness, the strange, the bizarre, the naïve, and the childlike are disturbing because they exist in what is around us. They have a particular personality and flavor, an intelligence of their own. These are states of mind that have to be developed. You, as a painter, must grasp these subtleties. But the deftness, skill, and dexterity that in the West are often considered desirable qualities are in fact disastrous, because they miss the essential. Clumsiness and blunders are much more alive."

During our four-handed sessions, when I commented that I had lost a game or botched my brushstroke, he would answer with a laugh, "Botching is not bad at all. Weakness can even be a mad sort of elegance. Clumsiness, if it comes from the heart, is very moving. What you have just done here is very moving. Clumsiness may even constitute the spirit of the painting. If the expression is sincere, it is bound to enter the mind contemplating it. Keep the crudeness, this freshness in the rendering. Raw vegetables that retain their flavor are tastier and more nourishing than those simmered in a sauce for a long time. You have to work with both freedom and rectitude."

He was hard to keep up with; he said one thing and then the contrary the next day. His teaching never involved lecture, demonstration, or theory. He proceeded by taking small steps, both conflicting and complementary, so that, little by little, I could achieve balance by myself. I felt as though he was teaching me to walk on a high wire, like a tightrope walker.

"The idea is to suggest without ever showing things," said my professor. "The ineffable in painting is born of this secret: suggestion. You have to find a way to capture this state, between the said and the unsaid, between being and nonbeing. A nephew remarked to his uncle, a scholar who had written a poem about thought, 'If thought exists, a poem would not be able to express it perfectly; and if there is no thought, why write a poem?' 'That is exactly where my poem lies: between thought and the absence of thought,' replied the scholar."

"There must be discontinuity in the continuity of the brushstroke. The dance of the paintbrush in space leaves open spaces that allow the viewer to live in the imagination at work in the painting, to enter and make their own discovery of the landscape, through suggestion, without saying too much, letting thought flow. If you try to finish a work, to lock in a composition, it dies at that very moment." That made me think of a quote by the philosopher Vladimir Jankélévitch: "It is in the unfinished that we allow life to move in." "If you try to finish the painting," said Huang Laoshi, "it dies. There is always one brushstroke too many. You should ceaselessly strive to find the singular, the uncommon, to break down the barriers or aesthetic categories created by our cultures and not be afraid of appearing mad or eccentric at times because the idea is to find the thousands of expressions of the nature of things. This is of the utmost importance to a painter's explorations. And forget all of the metaphysics of painting!" This last advice was perhaps the hardest of all, as it requires maturity to achieve.

One day, my dear professor asked me if I wanted him to find me a Chinese name. "No, certainly not," I answered. "I am not Chinese, and I don't want to pretend I am."

"You're right. Anyway, your destiny is inscribed in your French first name: fa-bi-enne corresponds in Chinese to *fa,* the rule, but also she who is seeking her spiritual path, the method, the example to follow; *bi* means comparative study; and *enne* kindness and generosity, which you must not bury beneath your desire to be a successful painter. Write your name with these Chinese characters; it looks a little like the name of a Buddhist nun. You have entered painting the way others enter religion."

The capricious march of time

The moon deepens the sorrows of our intimate secrets.

I wanted to work and earn a little money to buy some books from the local shops. I asked my interpreter if she had any ideas. "I'll look for a publication that might need illustrations," she suggested. A children's magazine offered to publish twenty illustrations on the theme of Chinese children's games, so I went for walks along the riverbank to research. In the evenings, with my paintbrush, I tried to draw these games. I worked on this for several months, then sent off my twenty plates. The editors were satisfied and published my drawings. One day, I received a postal order for the payment of the months of work. When I ran to collect my money, I discovered it was only a couple of yuan! (My stipend was one-hundred and twenty yuan a month.) My classmates all had a good laugh. I realized it was no use trying to work in China. I could not hope for more than what I was already receiving from the State, which was double the grant of the Chinese students. I was privileged: I had a room to myself, whereas the others lived eight to an unheated room, four bunk beds on each side with a study area in between.

One day, I'd had enough of the military parade music that woke me up at five in the morning every day for the raising of the flag. I rebelled. When the music came on, I opened my window and blasted a cassette of traditional music at full volume. The other students found it very funny. Unfortunately this didn't really solve the problem, so I cut the loudspeaker's wire which was just outside my room. "I understand the need for the loudspeakers," I complained, "but that they should be just over my window is enough to drive anyone mad." The Party official lectured me, "Do you realize the seriousness of what you did? If we accept it, can you imagine what people will think around the college?" But they were kind and didn't reconnect the loudspeaker.

Over the years, I became well assimilated and professors invited me to dine with their families. It was touching: they were very poor but they always received me warmly. I knew they made sacrifices for these meals. During one of these evenings, someone played the accordion in my honor. We amused ourselves by playing drinking games: two people facing each other call out a number from one to ten. At the same time, both players have to make a smaller number with the fingers of one hand. The person who calls out the sum of the numbers indicated by the hands of the two adversaries wins and the loser has to drain a small saucer of rice alcohol. Another variation was rock, paper, scissors. Since I lost so often, I consumed a lot of alcohol, which must have weakened my liver—probably one of the reasons, besides fatigue and poor diet, why I caught hepatitis later.

In the 1980s, surprise parties arrived at the college and I was often invited. One time the students decorated the classroom with little red lights. The beginnings of decadence! There were interminable slow dances to Frank Sinatra, reminding me of the art schools in France.

One Chinese New Year, I was asked to be on television. When they asked me to perform the latest Chinese hit song, I couldn't refuse. They shoved a cap on my head and I stood trembling under the spotlights, in front of the cameras singing with a slip of paper in my hand. It was dreadful. "Look! Foreigners appreciate Chinese culture!" exclaimed the commentator. Journalists had been brought in to take my picture. The propaganda machine had manipulated me without my realizing it. The Chinese authorities are experts.

I was invited to every festival. One was the Day of the Dead, on April 4, the only festival that falls annually on the same Western date because it is based on the solar calendar and not the lunar. The celebration is referred to as "Sweeping the Tombs." Tribute is paid to one's ancestors and there is a picnic. The first year, some friends offered to take me along to their family burial plot, which was in the garden of the Southern Mountain, not far from the city. This meant a pilgrimage by truck deep into the countryside. We crossed the river by ferry and drove up valleys, past rice paddies and fields. It gave me a chance to admire the landscape beyond the city. When we reached the grandfather's tomb, the family gathered around it and we spent the day cleaning the grave, dusting, sweeping, making offerings, burning fake money and incense and taking each other's photos. We picnicked in the presence of the ancestor's spirit. I found this celebration very moving. When we returned, night was already falling. My friends proudly showed me the view of the city lit up in the distance. Afterward, each year I chose an ancestor, anyone, and I went to sweep his tomb.

On the fifth day of the fifth lunar month, we celebrated Double Five, the ancient water festival, with dragon-headed boat races on the Yangtze. This was the folk reenactment of an old custom that still survived. I attended from the home of my interpreter's mother because she lived at the starting line of these famous races. The old woman prepared cones of sticky rice mixed with candied fruit, sesame seeds, and shelled almonds wrapped in bamboo leaf tied up and steamed. These were the famous *zongzi*. I adored them and could eat five in one sitting, to my professor's amusement. He knew the little shop that sold the best *zongzi* in the whole province.

He told me the story of Qu Yuan, a poet from very ancient times whose work he greatly admired: Qu Yuan had thrown himself into the river out of despair, because his king had banished him and was running the country into the ground instead of following the poet's advice. In tribute to the great man, and also to distract the fish so that they would not feed on the poet's body, people threw *zongzi* into the river.

There was also the Double Nine or Chrysanthemum Festival, when my friends would climb to the top of a mountain to drink, visit the moon, and play games. Another time I attended the cremation of a classmate's father. A public writer, he had calligraphed thoughts and maxims to hang from the walls of houses. We obtained special permission to attend the ritual and rode in an army truck with the body. The truck was decorated with white flowers and a photo of the deceased was stuck to the front, draped with black banners. Everyone wore a black armband. Strangely, everyone seemed rather cheerful. A little group played music but, since the family did not have much money, the pomp was fairly limited. When we arrived at the crematorium, it was buzzing with activity. We joined the queue to cremate our dead, advancing truck by truck.

Once the entrance ticket and necessary permit were obtained, we went down into a giant pit that reminded me of a communal shower: a factory to burn the dead, only automated. There were about ten tracks on which ten families would place their dead at a time, each in front of the number that they had been assigned. A machine would start up, and with a clang the coffins would move off on rollers. The doors of the ovens would open and the families would wail loudly as the coffins made their way toward the furnace. It was like of a kind of diabolical factory: a number, an assigned space, the queue, then on to the next corpse. It was a descent into hell before stunned onlookers. The atmosphere was unbearably violent. Smoke from the burned bodies rose from the crematorium and heavy grief filled the atmosphere. I could not bear to watch and vomited several times behind the factory. Each family would leave with their box full of ashes, crying, joining an atmosphere of collective hysteria.

Overpopulation required these assembly-line cremations. It was nothing like the rituals in the countryside with their ceremonial rhythm since the dawn of time, where the respect of elders and the cult of ancestors were still faithfully observed. Here, there was nothing sacred about death. In a large city dead bodies can pile up quickly. Overpopulation is the cancer of society. It is hard to imagine the inhumanity, hysteria, and indifference engendered by overpopulation. The body is no longer a person, the individual is subsumed by the multitude and becomes a mere number.

After the cremation, the mood changed, and we resumed a festive atmosphere. Back in the truck, we gathered to attend the reception given by the family and snack on peanuts and sweets.

At night, I was not allowed to go out. My friends tried to cheer me up, saying, "That can't last. Don't worry, we'll find a way around this. Have you been to the local opera house?" "No," I answered, "but I would like to go. In France, I often listened to opera." And so I started to climb the wall with a group of friends.

Like in a barracks, a moving searchlight trained its beam along the exterior wall, while at the gate an old man monitored comings and goings, recording them in his little log. We had to start the moment the light moved away from the spot we had to climb over. I had a hard time keeping up with the agile boys, who had a lot more practice than me. Every time, they had to push from behind to help me get over the wall. We took the bus on the way out because we were about half a dozen miles from the center of town, but on the return trip we had to walk because by the end of the performance it was too late for any form of transportation. We drank as we walked and would arrive home very drunk. Once again, we would jump over the wall while dodging the searchlight.

I loved these little excursions but the city was not safe: there were stories of appalling sex crimes. Anything could have happened to us. Of course, I was not alone, but it was truly dangerous. The day the college officials found out about my escapades I was severely reprimanded for such recklessness. Yet I have wonderful memories.

I saw some extraordinary operas with excellent performances. They went on for hours. My friends always had an uncle or another relative working at the theater, so I got to go backstage and see the singers putting on their makeup and preparing their roles. We did not go every night given the long distance, but we still managed to attend fairly regularly. Certain students were real opera lovers, but otherwise, there were hardly any young people. The room wasn't packed the way it would be for a film with Catherine Deneuve. Most of the audience consisted of older people who had been left badly shaken by the Cultural Revolution. The singers were admirable although not in the least respected. They fought to continue the tradition in the midst of discouraging indifference, but these were not grand productions. This was unfortunate, since the stories and legends that constitute folk culture—and, like writing, make China unique—would unfold upon the stage in this theater.

During my long years in exile in Sichuan, I received a number of visits. One day, a foreigner, a famous photographer, asked to meet me. I invited him to my modest lodgings and offered him tea. When I asked what brought him to China, he responded, "I'm looking for a beautiful tree." I was surprised and awed: he was roaming the world, looking for trees! We had a real connection. He left the polluted city and went into the rice paddies to discover a tree inhabited by a spirit worshipped by the locals. He made a magnificent book about trees. Frank Horvat and I became friends.

Another time, at Chongqing airport, I ran into the Dutch filmmaker Joris Ivens, who was in a wheelchair, pushed by his wife, Marceline Loridan. When I asked what he was doing there, the old man answered: "I'm looking for the wind. I'm still searching for the impossible reality of the wind!" I was astounded. He wanted to climb the high plateaus of Sichuan and dreamt of capturing the constant changes of the invisible gust with his heart's vision and movie camera. Wasn't that the same thing that I was looking for, tirelessly, at the tip of my brush? The inner beauty of this great figure made an impression on me. I was very touched by our meeting. I felt profoundly happy and a little less alone. There were other eccentrics in the world who sought great poetic adventures. Later, I learned that in 1988 he finally made his film, *Une histoire de vent (A Tale of the Wind)*, which won the Golden Lion at the 65th Venice Film Festival.

Friends from Toulouse also visited me in China, hoping to bring me back into the fold. Certain fellow students who were suiters came to find me, hoping to put a ring on my finger.

One was a young biologist who crossed the world to see me. We spent a few days together at the college before he left, disappointed. I felt sorry for him, as he was very likeable and kind. He left me with a pile of books whose value was priceless in my remote corner of the world: Giacomo Leopardi, Walt Whitman, William Blake, and philosopher Gaston Bachelard. To read such writers deep in the heart of China was an absolute joy since I had acquired, thanks to old Huang, a new appreciation for reading. I could not have received a more beautiful gift. Shitao was no longer alone on my bedside table.

Later, my engraver boyfriend from Toulouse College arrived to try to convince me to leave. He was very worried. "You're out of your mind! Come home with me. Why do you want to stay in this hell hole?" he demanded. How could I explain myself? I had completely changed, not only because of what I had experienced but also for reasons I could not account for. How could I make him understand the internal shift I felt then? I felt that I had to stay, to take this path, even if it seemed incomprehensible. I had embarked on a true initiation and it was too late to turn back. I felt weak in his presence, but that did not make me particularly kind. "I can't go back with you. Let me live my life the way I want," I told him. "I am like a chrysalis, busy creating the pretty butterfly I might turn into one day."

Perhaps he can understand me better now, having seen my paintings. But at the time, it was hard for him and for me. I would have liked to share this sentence from Dante's *Paradiso* (I, 112–114) with him: "And they are drifting toward different ports, on the vast ocean of being, and each carried by the instinct that he has been given." I was happy for him when I learned later that he had gone to Japan on his own important journey of discovery.

Another friend, the son of a famous writer, who was deeply in love with me, came to visit me at the college. He was very clever but lived in the shadow of his father and was convinced he would never succeed at anything. He could not find a way to exist on his own. For a time, I believed that China could help him develop his personality and give him the strength to become his own person like it had helped me.

He learned Chinese within a few weeks and loved the Chinese game Go. So I found him a Go master and he translated a theoretical manual on this Chinese pastime. He spent the evenings with his head buried in dictionaries and worked through the whole book with a burning and unsettling passion.

Then, he became interested in the seven-stringed Chinese sitar. I introduced him to a well-known musician and he studied the musical theories of this instrument, effortlessly assimilating the principles of traditional Chinese musicology.

He owned an old Soviet camera with a 180-degree panoramic view, so we went into the countryside to do photo reportage together. He developed his own photos at night. I liked learning how to process the prints with him.

He also wrote very well, but was incapable of conquering his inner demons. At times he would fall into serious, violent fits that I was unable to calm. Why does genius often come with madness? I hope one day his translations or his photographs of these forbidden places that we visited together will be published, as he had dreamed of.

The Chinese families at the college found these foreigners' visits highly entertaining. Everyone had a favorite, and I was at the center of much merry gossip.

We were also graced with the first visits from French lecturers, purported specialists in contemporary art. They were sent by the French government or the Association for Artistic Initiative to promote French culture with the unbearable cultural imperialism of the West. They knew nothing about China, yet they preached. "It's ages since we dropped paintbrushes. We're interested in concrete surfaces in Ripolin colors, the repeated columns of Buren, or videos on violence, self-flagellation, decay . . ." They started by showing the students Duchamp's urinal and other breakthroughs of a similar sort, and concocted various theories in obscure language. When I heard these lectures advising us to put down our paintbrushes, I was furious and ashamed to be a Westerner. I tried to make myself invisible in the lecture hall. Already, in France, there was a disconnect between regular people and the discourse of art historians and critics. Unsurprisingly, the Chinese students sometimes reacted violently. They had expected ideas, techniques, and information to use in their own work, instead of pure theory. My fellow students mocked me. "These professors from your country take us for idiots. Is this what you learned in France?" The form of expression being advocated to them was as totalitarian as their own.

Yet for twenty years, many Chinese artists grasped the concepts of our contemporary art very well. They have more to say about emotional, physical, and moral suffering than well-fed Western artists. Some young Chinese artists have dared to question everything. The spirit of Chinese thought, despite the ravages of the Cultural Revolution, is still alive and incredibly rich for some. Thus Chinese artists like Cai Guo-Qiang and Huang Yong Ping figure among the most inventive and audacious artists of our generation.

The head of the college wanted to create a market to sell student artwork. With the help of the tourism bureau of the province, he arranged for busloads of foreign tourists to take a detour to the college. We amused ourselves by betting on what would sell: "They will definitely buy the ugliest works!" We won every time. Each department displayed its works in the gallery the officials were so proud of. My work was completely overlooked. However, the traditional painting department made a lot of money. A small sum was paid to the artist but the rest went to the school to continue building works, in particular the new dining hall. This even allowed one young painter to launch his early career to some success. Today he sells to the United States and has earned millions of dollars. A star of hyperrealism, he depicted the rural world that was truer than life, right down to the last wrinkle of the village elders, to the delight of the authorities.

My presence gave the officials an idea to generate income for the college. Following the lead of other Chinese institutions, they sent out brochures to attract foreign students, and charged very high tuition. Some American students turned up but they did not last two months, except one who did manage to hang on longer. Unfortunately, he caught hepatitis when an epidemic spread through the college—the same that got me. The poor man was unable to walk and had to use a cane. He soon returned home.

Another time, some representatives from the Avignon Festival in France stopped by during a tour of China to scout for shows. "We're looking for boatmen from the world's greatest rivers," they told me, "but it is impossible to make any headway with the Chinese. You live on the banks of the Yangtze—could you find out if these men still exist and if it would be possible to put together a performance with their musical repertoire?" I started by asking my painter friends, their families, and the old ladies I knew who lived along the river, whose homes I had visited during the dragon boat races. I made my inquiries discreetly because if the Party official knew I was looking for boatmen, she would have caused trouble. I learned that there were still a few boat-haulers. I finally located some living in a remote area in small, makeshift huts. I got friends to translate their patois and asked if they remembered the songs. We spent long evenings drinking with them. They told me about their hard and dangerous life working like mules and how they tugged boats along the riverbank. Many died from exhaustion, falls, or illness from their feet constantly being in the water. Those who survived were robust. They were full of joie de vivre and had a great sense of humor. My favorite sang me love songs and songs of encouragement. He knew them all and told me, a mischievous twinkle in his eye, "I'll go see my old friends. I'll get you what you're looking for." He brought his friends together and we traveled down the mountain gorges of the Yangtze. It was terrifying in certain spots but they knew every rapid and bend of the river. They had tamed the spirit of the wild waters.

Alas, this countryside, one of the most beautiful in China, has since disappeared under water as part of the giant Three Gorges Dam project. Entire villages were evacuated. I recorded the songs of my boatmen on tape and wrote the festival organizers that I had found some wonderful performers who were very likeable and had a repertoire of old tunes. At that point, I had to inform my college, and as predicted the Party official had a fit. "How can you be interested in those poor wretches, those tramps who live in makeshift shacks? It is unthinkable to send such a pathetic bunch to represent our culture abroad."

I appealed to my friend, the head of the college, who was always amused by my adventures, but he had never heard the boatmen's songs. The project was off to a bad start and I decided to speak about it with my friends, in order to find out which *danwei* or work unit these men belonged to. My question was met with peals of laughter. "It's been years since we've had work units!"

When I returned for a second visit, the boatmen were all gone. At one of their homes, I found the man's wife in tears. "I can't tell you what happened. I can't let you in anymore. I'm sorry." She gave me a cup of tea but begged me to go. At another home, I was met with a similar welcome. Furious, I went to see the Party official.

"You wrote a report, didn't you?"

"I spoke to the authorities—they were very alarmed by your initiative."

Headstrong and rash, I caught the train to Beijing and took steps myself with the Ministry of Culture. I asked to meet the official in charge of negotiations with foreign diplomats. I explained the assignment I had been given and played him the tapes. "These boatmen are keeping an important part of your heritage alive," I pleaded. "Why would you deny their participation in the Avignon Festival, one of the largest in the world? The province is cowed by the central government. With your help, we may have a chance. If not, the songs of the Yangtze boatmen will be lost, and no recordings of them will exist."

The official was moved; he had never seen a foreigner take such initiative and promised to help. The wait was drawn out and I worried because the deadline was approaching fast. A month later, the Party official came to me with a bitter smile that said, "Fine, you've won!" She had a telegram in her hand. "It's incredible—we received instructions from the Culture Ministry in Beijing to help you with your project. It is indeed an art form recognized by the central government. An official from the music school will help you put together your production. There also will be someone to supervise the organization. I have ordered a car for you."

Overnight, I was treated like a Chinese official, provided with a car fitted with little curtains and a red flag. I met an official from the city hall and the requisite banquet took place. I was introduced to the music specialist, a very nice man and a true enthusiast who had studied the songs of the boatmen and minorities. My boatmen reappeared immediately, but it was decided that, out of the five I had chosen, only two would be selected. I engaged in a telegram battle to keep the other three, but in vain. The specialist therefore turned himself into a boatman, and was given a pop singer from the music school as an assistant. It was farcical: the two old boatmen learned to sing pop music while the musicologist played a boatman. Little by little, we somehow managed to put together a production. Then, in the summer of 1987, we went to France. My boatmen in France! At the Avignon Festival, people still remember them. As they were not accustomed to French food, I had to find them a burner and some pots so they could make rice soup by their beds and in the corridor of the hotel. It nearly drove the proprietor mad. I escorted them around town, where they were a great success.

I was happy to have accomplished this; it was not a great performance, but it did give an accurate idea of what we were trying to represent.

Back in China, I was astounded by the outrageous proportions the boatmen event took on over the next few years. It had immense repercussions across the whole of China, with articles about it appearing in all the papers. They became nationwide celebrities. Films were made about them and their songs were remade and recorded by pop singers. Television channels fought over them. They made movies and commercials. The pop singer became an even greater star. The life of the boatmen changed. They were proud, in their little homes, to show their photos taken in front of the Eiffel Tower, on the *bateaux-mouches* around Paris. I thanked the Festival d'Avignon and the Festival d'Automne. We had to overcome many obstacles, but I was pleased with the result: together we had saved a part of the Chinese heritage and celebrated the value of a cultural treasure that had previously been disparaged.

At the college, political propaganda seemed a greater priority than the spreading of Chinese culture. One day, while I queued with my mess tin at the dining hall, I discovered photos of Nanking and Shanghai during the Sino-Japanese War exhibited on the walls. They showed the Japanese decapitating the Chinese and bowling with the heads. Displaying these monstrous photos in the 1980s was not innocuous. It was deliberately intended to incite hatred to serve political aims. No one can be completely immune to this kind of manipulation.

One day I was invited to dinner at the home of a very nice couple of painters. We sat having peanuts and a drink, surrounded by their work in their home studio. They were disturbed and told me, "We just learned that in the neighborhood not far from here, a man ate his baby."

I had often heard stories in China that were beyond all comprehension. I answered, "That's impossible."

"Unfortunately, it's true," they insisted. "We know that, in the countryside, if a girl is born, she can be abandoned to another family or even killed. We read in the official press that a couple of farmers, in terror over having a baby girl, fed her to the pigs. Such practices still exist. Officially, a couple may only have one child. Out in the countryside, the birth of a girl is a calamity. There is no retirement system for farmers. If they have a son, he will support his parents when they can no longer work. If it's a girl, she will be married into another family and her parents will end up destitute."

Today, the law has been changed. In the countryside, if the first child is a girl, the couple may try a second time, but not a third. There are also other possible arrangements: a fine can be paid for each additional child. If the farmer is rich, he can pay; if not, abortion is the only alternative.

Another day, on my way to the market, I saw a crowd yelling when huge trucks transporting chained prisoners went past. There was no respectful silence accompanying this final journey: people spat on the poor men and threw bits of watermelon at them. "What is their crime?" I asked. "Murder? Rape?"

"They're thieves. That young man stole watermelons. In the old days we would have cut off his hand; today we shoot them, and rightly so because we need to set examples. If we don't, we'll never survive. Serves them right!"

I was shocked. The behavior of the masses can be atrocious. A man in the crowd told me, "In any case, there are too many of us, any means of eliminating some is fair game . . . A man's life has no value for us, miss."

Most of these prisoners were very young. Their families even had to pay for the bullets that killed them. "There is no reason why the public should pay," people said. Suddenly, these people whom I had begun to like became detestable and inhuman. They had no consideration whatsoever for the lives of others. Yet these very same people had suffered so much. Didn't they understand what these poor prisoners were feeling?

There was an island in the river from where shots would regularly ring out.

I learned it was where they executed common criminals. They were first driven around town in trucks, standing, crammed in, chained up, shaved and carrying signs on their backs, like in the Middle Ages. Next to the driver, an official would cry out the list of crimes committed by these men into a loudspeaker, while onlookers insulted them as they passed by. When the Party believed petty crime might be getting out of control, which happened frequently, they carried out campaigns against criminality. At such times, the theft of a bicycle, for example, could be punished by a bullet in the neck. Every month, we heard gunshots coming from the island, then a long silence. Afterward, I became accustomed to the sound of those unmistakable shots intended as fatal punishment for those judged guilty. I could pick it out amid the city din.

The tense atmosphere was a permanent weight on my shoulders, like lead. A diet best described as spartan and the associated fatigue, coupled with an exhausting academic schedule, ended up compromising my health. When I had a cold or a minor complaint, I went to the health center. The doctors gave out little pills of traditional Chinese medicine wrapped in a paper with the dosage written across the top. If we had the flu, they gave us a jab. The needles were boiled, all jumbled up together in rusty containers, and I always wondered if the nurse had not used some other student's. When I arrived, she would order me, "Bare your left buttock. You have a bad case of flu, it's nothing serious. One shot and tomorrow it'll be gone." I have to admit that it worked.

Unfortunately, I grew weaker, I often felt nauseated and had no desire to work. One night, when I suddenly felt terribly ill, I went to the toilet, outside my room, near the Party offices. Early the next morning someone found me, passed out, with rats nibbling at my toes. When I came to, I was on a drip feed in the local hospital near the college. I was told I had been in a coma for twenty-four hours. The first thing I saw when I awoke was little blue holes along the veins of my arm. I asked the nurse about them. "It's because of the cold that the injections leave their marks. You've been on a drip for a week. You caught a *ganyan* and were delirious." I had no idea at the time that this meant a very bad case of hepatitis.

I had heard the morbid story of a young French student in Chengdu who had had an appendectomy in the capital before returning to France. Several months after his return, he was still feeling very poorly so he went to see his doctor. The doctor asked him what operation he had undergone on his lower back. The student answered with confusion that the Chinese had merely taken out his appendix. Alarmed, the doctor told him that a kidney had been removed as well. He was the victim of organ theft. The student lodged a complaint with the Chinese Embassy in France, and eventually received 10,000 francs in damages.

Very worried, I therefore asked what exactly a *ganyan* was.

"It's very serious. Do you want us to notify the French authorities?"

"Oh no, certainly not! Let's wait a bit. I'm sure you'll take good care of me." In fact, I was afraid of jeopardizing my apprenticeship with Huang Laoshi, which had started out so well. Every day, several doctors stopped by to see me. "You're going to pull through," they reassured me. "Trust us. But this is going to take time. You'll need to stay in hospital at least a month." I was still on a drip and the food was a far cry from the college cook's delicious little dishes. I could hear the groaning of elderly patients near death in the rooms nearby. The sick had accidents in the corridors or peed on themselves; they could be dying but no one looked after them. Hooked up to my rolling drip, I gave up on walking. I was completely exhausted and unable to keep anything down. The nurses were kind and kept asking me what I would like to eat, since I would throw up anything I swallowed.

"Do you have any boiled potatoes?" I finally murmured, desperate.

The nurses were worried: potatoes were only for pigs. "So we'll go to the market and buy potatoes to fix her pig food, if that's the only thing that she wants . . ."

I had collected an incredible group of friends during those few years at the college. The doctors could not believe their eyes. I had gone from the cruelest solitude to being inundated with friendship. Alone in a room with two beds, the second was piled to the ceiling with gifts: fruit, bags of oranges, potted plants, sweets, etc. There was enough for all the sick forgotten out in the corridor. The old cook, dressed in his Sunday best, came by once a week with homemade chicken broth—rich, he told me, with all the necessary ingredients to recover my health. I drank it in secret so as not to upset the doctors.

Seeing the steady stream of visitors, the staff intervened. "Stop stuffing her. She needs to regain her strength bit by bit." The old woman who grumbled about me every morning and monitored what was happening in the privacy of my room made me a sticky rice cake with candied fruits. It was, she claimed, the food of the Eight Immortals, and could only do me good. All the students came. One offered me a painting, another a print that I put on my second bed. Another declared me surprisingly beautiful, exhausted as I was, my complexion pallid, my eyes bright with fever. Even the Party official visited, with food she had cooked. They showed me so much kindness.

I dragged along like that for four or five months. But others died in this epidemic, including a few students.

On my return to the college, the old cleaning woman had a new task: to prepare my daily dose of traditional medicine. Every morning, she would show up with her broom and her earthenware pot exhorting me, "Drink this, or else! Do it now, while it's hot!" Unfortunately, I did not keep the recipe for the concoction. Its composition was incredibly poetic, a real witch's brew that stank horribly. I heard later that it consisted of crushed tortoise shells, "nine-sided and fried over low heat"; various powders "ground or sautéed in alcohol"; substances like *radix glycyrrhiza*, which was meant to "dissipate the fire of the fullness of the liver"; and another substance which "curbs acuteness, soothes pain, and controls liver reflux." I also had to swallow more digestive medicines, like "the pill to maintain harmony," taken with tepid boiled water to treat my revulsion to food and the frequent nausea that I suffered from food smells. As I improved, I eventually moved on to hearty and energizing soups and a brew intended to "rebuild the core and improve energy": a bowl of lukewarm potion to be consumed between meals. This clever pharmacopeia, like something straight out of the *Great Formulary of State Pharmacies* of the Taiping era, saved me!

Afterward in France, noted specialists told me that the treatment had completely regenerated my liver. "You would never have achieved the same result with today's Western medicine," one of them acknowledged.

When I got back to the college, the Party official offered to order a special diet for me. I was so afraid of falling ill another time from eating at the dining hall that I declined. Whenever I set foot inside, I felt unwell all over again. "I have a problem," I told the authorities. "I would like to continue my studies here. There is no question of my going back to France, but I would like to be allowed to prepare my meals myself."

I was given special permission to buy a little electric hotplate for my room. This privilege earned me the wrath of some students: not only were such appliances forbidden, but I was also consuming more electricity than forty classmates combined. I bought a woven bamboo backpack and went to do my shopping. Soon, I became very well known by the farmers near the college. I found all the vegetables I could possibly want. While boiling them, I felt like I was coming back to life. Finally, simple, healthy food! I ate only boiled vegetables and cooked fruit, and, little by little, as I began to feel better, I bought a few pieces of meat that had not hosted too many flies. I tried to make do as best I could with what I had at hand, with some families helping me. When some friends found out that I had been seriously ill, they taught me how to prepare certain dishes. Sometimes they bought some vegetables for me. For example, Huang Laoshi's wife would say to me, "Come by and see me, I'll give you some bamboo shoots," and so I would come away from one home or another with fresh produce. The poor cook was sorry to not be able to prepare his special dishes for me any longer. He found my cooking pathetic, but I still preferred to keep to my own diet.

I had not heard from my family for several years. It felt like an exile. But it was my fault, as I had chosen this total retreat. In the beginning, I wrote, but after no response, I gave up. My family told me later that they wrote two or three times but that they never received anything back, apart from a few letters when I first began to study in China. I had also asked a friend to send me some books on modern art that some students had requested. When I ran into him at an opening after my return to France, I chided him for not having sent me the books. He answered that he had spent a fortune on the books and was very surprised when I did not write to say I had received them. Embarrassed, I apologized and decided to drop it. Had I been the victim over the years of a postman, stamp-collecting customs officer, or Chinese censor monitoring my activities in the country a little too closely? It remains a mystery.

During my convalescence, I received a telegram from my father informing me that he planned to be in Hong Kong on business. He asked me to join him there for a few days. I was still exhausted but I managed to obtain permission to leave the country and get the money together for a plane ticket.

How could I possibly explain to him that I wanted to continue studying in China despite the miserable living conditions? Since it was impossible, I decided to say nothing. I couldn't understand myself the reasons for my obstinacy. I only told him that my studies were going well, even if things were difficult. He noticed that I had lost a lot of weight and voiced his concern. "Are you sure you've made the right choice? Don't you want to come home?"

We were in one of those Hong Kong hotels, a modern skyscraper; I felt uneasy in the vertiginous elevators, where you are suddenly catapulted up over a drop. I was like a country bumpkin come to the big city. I was completely disoriented, totally out of synch between two Chinese worlds.

My father was set on going to Macao. At the casino, I won a lot of money, having been introduced to small-time gambling by the old men at the teahouse. My father was stunned and I was delighted: I won several months' stipend. Before he left, he told me, "You left some things with us in boxes; your stepmother says they're in her way and wants to know what we should do with them." Not only did he know nothing about my life, he wanted to get rid of the little that I owned, which was at his house in France! People are often oblivious to the impact of a single sentence. "Burn everything," I snapped. "Then I won't exist there anymore." I returned to Chongqing heavy-hearted, lost, in tears after our botched reunion, where I hadn't known how to share anything of what I was going through.

One day in April, I was informed that a parcel had arrived for me from France. I thought there must be a mistake, but I ran up the street to the post office with my heart pounding. I felt like the Little Prince receiving a gift from the moon. As usual, I queued for forty-five minutes. I fidgeted with impatience in the perennially crowded place before I collected my parcel. In my room, very emotional, I stood looking at the package, not daring to open it. I wanted to savor every second of this happiness, this sweet thought that had come all the way from home. Even the stamps and the wrapping paper smelled like France.

I was cruelly starved of love and small signs of affection from "back home," but did not realize it until this parcel arrived. The return address was rue d'Assas in Paris. It was from my Aunt Yvonne. Suddenly, memories came flooding back: the post office at Port-Royal, tea at La Closerie des Lilas, the books I found browsing at the Tschann bookshop.

Carefully, I opened the package. Much to my surprise, it was a chocolate Easter egg, wrapped in a fat yellow ribbon and smashed to pieces by the journey. I broke out in sobs—tears of happiness, sadness, amusement at my situation and solitude. It was Easter but I had forgotten! I spent more than twenty-four hours staring at my broken egg, alone, in tears, bemoaning my own existence, asking myself how long I could continue inflicting this unbearable situation on myself. It was the most beautiful parcel I ever received in all the years I spent deep in the heart of China.

My illness was not the only reason for my weakened state; another event had profoundly affected me. I had fallen in love with the calligraphy student living up in his box room.

Much later I learned that I was watched twenty-four hours a day. Working late in my room, I noticed that a young man, cigarette dangling, stood behind a tree watching who came and went from my room, and disappeared as soon as I turned out the light. Friends had also warned me, "We have been lectured for visiting you on a certain day at a certain time." Alerted that my visitors were being watched, I resorted to a ruse to visit my friend: at night, I would turn out the lights and pretend to go to bed, then cross the college halls in the dark with a scarf on my head to avoid recognition. In those darkened rooms, my heart beat wildly because I was breaking a major rule. My little ploy was very quickly found out, since even at 1:00 in the morning there were always people about who returned from who knows where, who could recognize me in the shadows. My boyfriend was severely reprimanded. "If you want to get your doctorate, you should probably stop distracting Miss Fa from her studies. You are getting too close to her." This frightened him because his goal was to become a curator. He was from Nanking, and his dream was to work for the museums of that city.

We saw each other without ever being able to meet, exactly like in the film *In the Mood for Love*. Every time we ran into each other, we were in the presence of others, never able to say anything or even to wordlessly express the emotions that moved us so deeply. For me, this relationship took on exaggerated proportions, given my solitude.

He made it clear that I should not come to him as often because it was too dangerous for him. I could not sleep at night. I found it difficult to admit that he could accept this so easily. At the same time, upon reflection, I told myself I was too young to embark on such a love affair and throw away everything for him. He came from a good family. I did not know that, before leaving for college, he had been promised to a young woman from another important family, as is the custom. The Party official contacted his fiancée and arranged to bring her to campus.

One evening when I went to his room, I found laundry drying, the calligraphies tidied up, his little world all in order. A young Chinese woman asked me what I wanted. She was pretty, petite, and slender. I could see that she was madly in love with the calligrapher. I understood then that it was over: his fiancée was back. I was desperately unhappy. He took his exams and obtained his doctorate. But before leaving, he came over and took me in his arms one last time, a moment that I will never forget.

Once again I was alone. However, I didn't lack suiters. I went out with friendly woodcut printmakers whose company I enjoyed, and young professors who painted interesting things, with whom I had traveled. But I was in love with this calligrapher because he was different from the others. He had taught me so much.

One day, a bit tired of the Chinese characters, I was inspired to paint some budding branches, a bit like the style I paint in today. When I showed him my initial attempt, he told me, "This is good. This is the path you should follow." At that time, I was still a young apprentice, but he sensed talent in me and admired what I did. We had passionate exchanges, though we never made love because we had no contraceptives and could not obtain any without possibly being informed against. We had to stick to the party line. I never dared cross it. The risk would have been fatal to us both.

A few days after the calligrapher left, someone found me dead drunk from rice alcohol and heartbreak, wandering aimlessly around the college stadium. I was taken to Huang Laoshi, who looked after me. My love story with the calligrapher had been doomed from the start.

Years later, while browsing in a bookshop in Beijing, I turned around and there he was, the tall fellow with an impish smile who had somehow picked up my trail. He had married his fiancée, had a child, and been appointed curator of the Nanking Museum. I was happy for him, even as I felt the torments from our indescribable relationship reawaken. Once again he courted me: he had let the love of his life go and wanted to have now what we had not had before—it was now or never. For me, though, it was too late: I had already met the man I was going to marry.

My mad calligrapher paid a visit to my home to offer me metaphorical paintings: two little birds sitting on a branch. When he walked into my studio in Beijing, he was shocked. "Did you paint this?"

"Yes."

He fell into a chair, looking contrite. "You're the one who will have success. I loved you, but I had no choice. Please forgive me," he begged, "please, please forgive me."

The head of the college and I were getting on better and better, though his wife continued to make nasty remarks about me and criticized those who had contact with me. I would go and watch him working in his studio. We talked about art and he always inquired about my progress. Sometimes he invited me to taste *huoguo*, the famous spicy specialty of the province.

One day, my interpreter, who had become a friend, turned up at my place very upset. I asked her what had happened. "We are close enough now that I can tell you what a mess I am in. You know my husband, he is a photographer. You know my daughter. Well, she is not my husband's child."

I understood right away. "Is she the head's child?" Although she did not dare answer, her look was affirmative. "You chose well, my friend, because I also find him very attractive," I said, trying to make her laugh.

"The problem," she went on, "is that his wife knows about us. I'm going to be exiled to the countryside. She's scheming to have me transferred far up on the

Tibetan plateaus. But I love him, and there is nowhere we can meet anymore." Others had the same problem as what I experienced with my poor calligrapher.

"How can we possibly be together?" she lamented. "I'm constantly being watched."

"Meet at my place," I suggested. "I'll figure something out. Don't worry."

Since I couldn't make myself happy, I could at least feel the joy of helping others. A very strong friendship was born of these secret rendezvous. I would go out to the cinema and leave them the keys. One of them would arrive, as if just casually dropping by, followed by the other half an hour later. This subterfuge was not easy to pull off because the old woman assigned to my room checked everything. But it made me a bit closer to the private lives of the Chinese.

One day, I had taken my bird out to give the head some time with his mistress, when a student asked if he could get back some old woodblocks he had lent me. "I'll bring them to you right away," I said, holding out the birdcage. "Sorry not to invite you in but my bird needs some fresh air . . ." I made a lot of noise before putting the key in the lock and found the head hiding under the bed!

An English teacher came to me one day with a confession. Without the slightest prior comment or introduction he declared passionately, "I love you. Let's go away together. I'll teach you all about Chinese culture." Some Chinese did border on madness from their desire to escape the hell they lived in. Any means was fair game to escape their country. When I told my friend the interpreter about her colleague, she said, "Do you know that he beats his wife every night? She's covered in bruises. He's mad!"

The Party official's son did manage to get out by making the most of the exchange program with Toulouse. He was a horrible man, arrogant and macho, a pure product of a Chinese youth born into a family of the political elite. He treated his mother like a dog; she had spoiled him too much and gave him every possible privilege. No one liked him and everyone feared him. He ate like a pig, never washed, and stank. He dressed like a cowboy in jeans, a perpetually filthy pale pink American shirt, and fake Ray-Bans. He thought he was Van Gogh and copied his sunsets, believing himself to be a great artist.

When he found out he was going to France, he walked into my room without knocking and tried to charm me. He presented me with his hideous Van Gogh imitations and asked me to introduce him to my family. His mother even invited me to dine. It was impossible to refuse. She went to a lot of trouble preparing the meal. Eventually she even left me alone to do as I pleased, taking risks regardless of the rules. I gave her offspring my father's details. He did invite him over but he never quite recovered from the experience. My father later recounted that the young man did not flush the toilet and left the toilet paper on the floor, and eating in his company proved a real challenge. I ran into the son much later at some Paris openings: he had found a French girlfriend, managed some success as an interior decorator, and still believed he was a genius of a painter. Of course, he never wanted to return to China, to the great shame of his mother. The professors had a field day trading snide remarks about this paragon of socialist education.

The toilets were putrid, horrifying places, but they were also a prime meeting spot. There were no stalls, only a wall separating men and women. Some men jumped over. One evening, a young man came to meet a girl there. Any woman could have walked in. He was risking his life. Some men had been shot for having forced their way into the women's toilets.

I had the terrifying experience of witnessing a young woman abort in the toilets, on her own, with a pair of wooden chopsticks. When I tried to go for help or to dissuade her, she became irate. "Leave me alone!"

"But you might die," I told her. "You're losing too much blood. I want to help you."

"The only thing you can do for me is to let me die. If you want to help me, above all keep quiet. If not, it will be over for me, I'll be sent out to the countryside. Let me finish the job and go away!"

Once outside, I decided to guard the door and protect her. I trembled at hearing her groans of pain. After she left, I cleaned up the blood and got rid of the chopsticks.

I did not see her again in the following days. Others also would disappear: those who were deemed "decadent" either in their behavior or in their art. Certain painters were sent off to work camps or even to insane asylums. One student told me about his visit to one of these so-called nursing homes to see one of his best friends, a painter of very personal and original work. He lived in a cell, forgotten by the world, slowly dying in a place where no one could come to his aid. I had reason to worry about this girl who had performed her own abortion: either she had fallen ill and not recovered, or she had been sent away somewhere. Six months later, she reappeared: she must have arranged to leave the city under the pretense of an illness. She had managed to get through it.

Short and long journeys

The earth for a pillow and a blanket made of heaven.

During my studies, I went on nearby excursions organized by the college. We traveled by bus. Each of us took a numbered folding chair, a portfolio in the colors of the People's Army (yellow and red), and of course a glass jam jar to serve as a cup for the hot water in our thermoses. From time to time, we added a few leaves of green tea to flavor the boiled water. The countryside was magnificent with its rice paddies, working oxen, farmers laboring under wide straw hats, and their low, white houses with little wooden shutters tucked in among clumps of old pines, banana trees, and bamboo. If we stopped by their homes, they often invited us in for a meal. In the half-light of their communal rooms, we discovered the ancestral altar with images of their deities, statuettes, and all kinds of offerings. One day, when I asked a farmer where to find the toilet, he pointed me to a shed in the middle of a field that was dark and foul-smelling. I had just pulled my underwear down when an enormous creature suddenly licked my backside. It was a huge black pig! I flew out screaming, with my trousers still down. The other students died laughing.

Our school holidays consisted of one week for the Chinese New Year, one month in summer, and one day for the national holiday. During these times, professors frequently invited me to their homes when they returned to their villages. I would spend the first week with one, then the second week with another. At the beginning of my time in China, I stayed for some time in what was known as Dinosaur Village with my art history professor's family. It later became the largest dinosaur museum in the world. Unfortunately, before paleontologists claimed a monopoly over the site, a good number of bones from these prehistoric animals were excavated, collected, and ground into powder as ingredients for traditional medicines.

My great pleasure was escaping Chongqing to the city of Chengdu. Chongqing was the largest city in the Sichuan province, built on a hillside at the junction of the Yangtze and Jialing rivers. There were still some alleys that ended in steep steps plunging toward the river. But it was a martyred city: a martyr to the war, and afterward to builders. From 1938 to 1945, the Kuomintang transformed the province into a veritable fortress to resist the Japanese invasion and set up government in Chongqing. It was so heavily bombarded that the Chinese established war production facilities inside the hills, in spaces dug out for that purpose. There were vestiges of these caves all over town. Street vendors opened little restaurants inside them where you could get a quick meal: bowls of cold spicy noodles or rice soup and soy fritters served on tables covered with dubious-looking oilcloths. In the streets above, the latest Chinese pop hit blared. After the war, Chongqing became an industrial city with affordable housing for workers, factories pouring out pollution to blend with the frequent fog, and overpopulation that made each outing a superhuman effort to force one's way through the crowd. A huge round building, a monstrous caricature of the Temple of Heaven in Beijing, further defaced a city that was already far from inviting, despite its park and location overlooking the river.

Chengdu, on the other hand, was still very lovely. An old city, it retained its status as provincial capital, and although it featured two large intersecting avenues lined with hideous new buildings, behind them lived the old China with its wooden houses and handicraft shops. It was the only city where you could still feel—but for how much longer?—a typically Chinese atmosphere. It had always been an important cultural center. In 1927 the province's university was founded in a very beautiful park housing a large collection of carved stones from tombs dating back to the Han Dynasty. Inside Du Fu Park, the thatched cottage of its namesake, the great eighth-century poet, was but a pale imitation, but the little museum and the river flowing through the trees suggested some of the pleasures that life offered in that era. Along the Brocade River, all kinds of bamboo grew, and one could visit the well that had supplied water to the courtesan and poet Xue Tao for making her patterned paper.

I recall one of her quatrains on the moon, recited by Huang Laoshi:

Her soul takes the form of a slender sickle,
To slowly weave a circular fan.
When her slim figure blossoms, becoming full,
Almost everywhere, men lift their gaze to her.

Brocade weaving workshops lined the opposite bank, hence the river's name. The temple dedicated to the strategist and Taoist sage Zhuge Liang was surrounded by tall conifers, endowing the place with a unique majesty. Though the Taoist temple of the Copper Goat no longer communicated a sense of sacredness, it was a pleasant spot for tea. Inside was a statue of the goat, which was said to have accompanied an apparition of Laozi. There was also the Hall of Original Chaos. "When you believe yourself lost in the chaos," Huang Laoshi had told me, "you are returning to the origin from which creation is possible."

In the Workers' Park, a local troupe performed operas and a group of ballad singers entertained some old-timers who were nostalgic for the ancient legends. Objects for worshipping the dead had once again become available near a Buddhist monastery. In a shop run by an old woman, traditional Chinese shoes of fabric were still sold, as well as extremely rare ox hide shoes that were both comfortable and sturdy. A teahouse built around a pond was adjoined by a little opera theater that was so popular that it was sometimes hard to find a seat. Local painters gathered together in a traditional house where each had their own studio. If I had settled in China, this city is where I would have chosen to live.

My professor was born in Chengdu and we often went together. We would stay a few days in a small hotel as a break from the college; we went for bicycle rides and he would proudly show my work to his friends. One morning a young scholar arrived at my door to pay me a visit. My professor said, "Young man, we are right in the middle of a painting session; it will last for several years so do not disturb us anymore." Annoyed, I protested, since I rather liked the attention. "I know," he answered, "you are at that fiery age of youth where love naturally blooms, but beware of passions, feelings, and resentments. Emotions are disruptive. We get bogged down in attachments—sources of worry, excitement, doubt, anger—all those states steer you off your path as a painter." I was still furious, but it was undeniable that the young man's presence hampered my concentration. I had indeed drifted, and at that moment, had only one desire: to flirt with him.

Once, at a teahouse in Chengdu, I witnessed something strange. An old man seemed overwhelmed by the struggles in his life and suffered from profound melancholy. He began rummaging around in a pocket of his quilted jacket and drew out a container that he had been keeping warm against his chest: a kind of dried gourd, covered with little air holes. He spoke to this container. His face lit up when he removed the finely carved bone cover and took out a tiny creature: a cricket. With a deep smile, he chatted to his friend. He forgot his worries and traveled in the world of the infinitely small. He expounded at length as to why his cricket was the ideal life companion and then abruptly broke off to castigate the teahouse patrons: the smoke from their water pipes would damage the health of his little friend! The whole room immediately ceased smoking to allow the cricket to breathe freely.

Occasionally, we took the bus to the Taoist temple of the Mountain of Purity. Along the way, Huang Laoshi admired the yellow expanses of blooming rapeseed.

We would stop in a small town and have lunch with one of his sons, who had been assigned to work in a run-down factory. It was always a great sadness for the father to see his child living such a dreary life. In the little town we would see luxury cars, donkeys, and men in rags pulling heavy loads, passing each other on the street. These sights for a sensitive person were often truly painful. It was also a tourist destination; people came to see the ancient dam built by Li Bing, which divided the river into three diverging streams that irrigated the Chengdu plain.

When we arrived at the foot of the mountain, we went through the first gate, which had an inscription across the pediment I cherish to this day: *Hua tu ran tian*, meaning "painting by heaven" or "painting-cartography by celestial nature." What more exquisite pilgrimage could exist for a painter seeking beautiful landscapes? My professor would say that we were going to attend an "audience on the mountain." The first gate reminded us that we were leaving the human world behind for that of the spirits. We climbed up winding paths through a forest clinging to the slopes. We were not the only ones; along the way, we shared the trail with young Chinese on excursions and old women on their pilgrimages, winded from the fairly steep slope. Once we arrived, my professor would be overcome by a radical change. Despite his seventy-three years, he would regain the vitality of youth. He would insist we stop for a drink at a little inn he knew well.

When we arrived at the temple, we would have dinner and spend the night there; like many temples, this one served as an inn both for the true pilgrims and for the modern version known as tourists. Old Taoist monks and nuns lived at the temple site. I remember one of the latter, a tall and very beautiful girl, who on the morning of our departure filled our bags with little oat and barley rolls. In the courtyard, the tops of the stone balustrades featured sculptures of grotesque characters making love in a variety of positions and even with animals. I had a secret theory that the old Taoists reached their advanced age by maintaining their sexual prowess by following instructions found in *Classic of the Dark Girl*, among other publications. This was the sort of observation that I dared not share with Huang Laoshi. He, on the other hand, inspired by the setting, explained Taoism to me: the difference between the Taoist religion, founded two thousand years ago, which had imbued popular religion; and the Taoist philosophy of very ancient times, as handed down by Laozi and Zhuangzi. The same Tao was at the root of both, represented as concrete beings and divinities by farmers and as abstract notions by the men of letters. When you knew how to read and interpret religious and philosophical thought, you understood that, ultimately, they were simply two aspects of a single notion: some preferred to personify it, the better to grasp its many facets; others would juggle the concepts to understand the ultimate unity.

Another time, I went to Tibet with a group of young professors. We traveled by bus over dangerous roads; once we crossed the border between Sichuan and Tibet, we pushed inland. It is best not to set off too late in the season since bad weather, ice, and snow block the roads. At the foot of the mountains, we caught sight of waterfalls, steep cliffs, walls of ice, peaks as high as twenty thousand feet, but also car wrecks lying at the bottom of ravines. The driver would regularly point out accidents that had left twenty or thirty dead. The bus was sometimes stopped for several days due to floods blocking the road. Once, we ran out of petrol and had to walk twelve miles before finding a place to sleep, and we waited there for two weeks until we could leave again. We experienced forced and unexpected isolation, often under austere conditions. But on these high plains, the soul could soar toward the heavens like the prayer flags. With this kind of journey you never know when you will arrive or even if you will ever return.

"We will not go to Lhasa since we will be noticed there," my travel companions had warned me. "The army presence is too strong. We have to stick to the countryside." We stopped over in small towns and from there set off with nomadic Tibetan yak herders; along the way, we visited remote and isolated religious sanctuaries.

I was ecstatic in these magical places—these stretches of infinite space; I could better understand how the heavens governed the world order, as my old professor had taught me. The air was bracing, pure and exhilarating, inspiring forgotten thoughts to spontaneously arise in my heart, especially those of Giacomo Leopardi: " Seated here, I contemplate the supreme silence of the beyond. In this profound peace, I drown all thought."

I was so happy up there. The beauty of the mountains, the clouds so close to the earth and their shadows dancing across fields of yak herds filled my heart with joy.

I visited Shigatse, a remarkable site with a monastery of simple and understated architecture perched on the side of the mountain. The frescos inside depicted Sakyamuni, the arhats and bodhisattvas. There was a stupa decorated entirely in silver leaf and precious gems. My young professors dreamed of lost monasteries containing unknown frescoes. The pleasure they took in discovering a remote culture was heartening, since up to that point the Chinese had not shown any interest in the Tibetan civilization.

We traveled from countryside to desert, then across a kind of savannah. We traveled by horseback and on yaks, with children, crossing rivers and following mountain paths through wild scenery. In this world of extremes, we encountered places where deep religious practices were in evidence. We lived among the Tibetans and stayed in monasteries. We came across Tibetan women on the road who made the journey on foot, prostrating themselves. I tried to do the same but could not manage even half a mile. When by chance our eyes met, they would offer a beatific smile of indescribable grace. This kind of pilgrimage demands a great deal of physical and mental strength plus limitless faith. These women were engaging in a practice that went beyond bodily suffering, and by their active prayers, gave of themselves. Some of them did not hesitate to travel long distances to reach a monastery. I was profoundly impressed to see such devotion.

Life was not easy for the Tibetan women; there were no pharmacies and they had to make do on their own. But I had some wonderful times with them. They were lively, intelligent, and funny. The youngest ones were always joking and loved to tease me. They would take me to the riverbank to show me how to wash myself. When I was completely submerged in the water, they would run off with my clothes. This annoyed me very much but we always laughed about it afterward.

Everything there was hard. The climate was arid and the nights freezing. The Tibetans gave me clothing made from animal skins. Yet life up there bestowed wholesome, genuine happiness. I cannot explain why. After long days of walking at high altitude, we felt inebriated by our very existence. At such altitudes, the body is subjected to abnormal demands. It was difficult for me to keep up with the Tibetans, who were accustomed to the hard life up on the high steppes since birth.

When we were hungry, they cut up pieces of fresh meat that we ate voraciously. Morning, noon, and night we ate *tsarnpa*, a thick barley porridge garnished with sesame or sunflower seeds. They carried tea in the form of bricks, breaking away a piece and preparing a drink with rancid yak butter; we drank it without hesitation because we were cold and we knew our bodies needed it. Fortunately, I took this trip before I caught hepatitis.

My hosts made me a contraption to use if I left the tent at night. Called a *dagu*, it was a weight of forged iron at the end of a leather strap. When I left the tent, scared to death, to go to the toilet, I was supposed to spin it around over my head until it whirred. This device was supposed to prevent dogs from approaching and biting my bottom. Though their tents were fairly comfortable with little rugs to sit and sleep on, I picked up a lot of parasites living with them. If we had not lived like nomads we would not have survived.

The Tibetans were exceptional men, very cheerful, yet solitary with a rich inner life. I enjoyed their company. On the deserted plateaus, we were free—as free as the eagles soaring over the plains. It was a delicious sensation to feel it so intensely.

Near Shigatse, we visited a monastery reportedly restored in the fourteenth century. It was a mix of Chinese, Tibetan, and Nepalese styles, with the oldest and most beautiful frescoes in all Tibet. They covered the walls of every room and depicted, along with the deities, scenes from everyday life. These monasteries, places of such utter emptiness, contained an astonishing richness of life.

As soon as we arrived in a city, we immediately sensed the Chinese presence; as soon as we left, we would return to Tibetan territory. The Tibetans' hatred toward the Chinese was palpable, even if on the surface they were more restrained than other minorities.

What struck me the most were the Tibetan houses. They were built entirely of stone, like castles, with corn drying on the roof alongside long poles with sacred texts attached. The inscriptions on colored fabrics were like the ephemeral temples floating in the wind that we would discover in forgotten places. Their bases were surrounded by little wooden plaques of excerpts from the sutras. I have never seen more fragile and moving structures. There reigned an unbroken solitude, a living spirituality, and an astonishing play of movement between the sacred texts and the wind.

In the small towns, simple shops with earth-beaten floors sold surprisingly fine fabric. There were hidden treasures in the piles of brightly colored rolls of cloth, even brocaded silk of gold thread. It was an extraordinary palette for an apprentice painter who by then had been working in black and white for several years. I was dazzled by the quality of the dyes and the weaving techniques that produced varying weights and patterns of all sorts. They were miracles of ingenuity and taste by these Tibetan craftsmen. Penniless, I bartered my watch and jeans for some marvelous rolls of fabric.

The patterns of the fabrics represented fascinating mandalas, "sacred circles" which, according to the Tibetans, symbolize the infinite, the absolute, and the divine. They are a sort of evocation of the universe in its essential design. This representation of life was deeply inspiring to me. I made some astounding mandala sketches and my imagination ran wild before this celestial mapping. I perceived wonders within: from the embryo of a tadpole in its protective sheath to the solar system; from the structure of a molecule or an atom to the rosaces of our Gothic cathedrals; from the mysterious kaleidoscope of a snowflake to the formation of the iris; from the heart of a flower to the weave of a spider's web. Wasn't there a link with the cosmic rhythms in all these creations? For Tibetans and African tribes, philosophers of the Middle Ages or great Zen calligraphy masters, the circle is the central point: the nourishing void, the primary fullness, the birthplace of all that is. This "cosmogram" represents the experience of sacredness, the diversity of the world in unity.

Tibetan women like dressing up. Some of them showed me their jewelry— necklaces of stone or amber, carved in the heart of the mountains by their fathers or their brothers.

We visited a thirteenth-century monastery in the Song and Yuan styles located in the middle of the country. A monk explained to us that it had been looted and not much was left inside. In spite of that, there were still some liturgical objects and a library containing sutra texts, books on Tibetan culture, astronomy, and medical treatises and biographies of famous lamas.

These outings in the shadow of the clouds kindled a true awakening to what Huang Laoshi had been trying to impart: a clear understanding of the unity of the world. Way up in those mountains, my face to the wind, alone on the back of a yak, I became aware of the absolute truth of the teachings I was receiving. Perhaps I had finally found the path of truth I had been seeking for so long, even if it was minus fifteen and I thought I would die from the cold. My professor had never been to Tibet; I spent many hours, upon my return, recounting my journey and sharing my sketches, much to his enjoyment.

One year, I went with Mrs. Liu to Guizhou province. "Come with us, we're going to visit some friends," she said to me. "Afterward, we'll go into the mountains that are home to some extraordinary ethnic groups, including the Buyi and Miao."

Miao dress is splendid. When I asked them how they made their clothes, they explained that first they scrape off the green from tree bark to use as a pigment for their dyes. Then they polish the fabric to obtain a golden-green sheen, like the back of a beetle. Their weavings and embroideries were astonishingly beautiful. The Miao embroidery patterns are connected to their myths and beliefs and are a way to preserve their culture, since they possess no written language. A woman told me that it took her years to complete her daughter's outfit.

Strolling through the villages, I discovered little drawings carved into the walls in houses built entirely of cedar. I copied some butterflies I noticed into my sketchbook. In the evening, dining with the Miao, I asked them what these drawings meant. They burst into giggles when they saw my butterfly, exclaiming, "It's the Butterfly Mother!" before they told me her story. One day, a god found a seed that he planted in the ground. A maple tree grew from it, near a lake. It grew and grew until it became immense. Wild birds roosted there, for it offered marvelous shelter. When the birds ate all the fish from the lake waters, the tree was blamed for the death of the fish and was immediately chopped down. The tree then turned itself into a butterfly and was fertilized by raindrops. When the mother butterfly laid her eggs and sat upon them for a long time, she gave birth to the Earth, the god of the heavens, and the god of the mountains. These gods created the first man, the ancestor of the Miao. This is why the Miao represent the Butterfly Mother in their folk traditions and worship maple trees.

In another village, I came across offerings and little altars covered with red strips of fabric and smoking incense sticks placed between the roots of an old tree. It proved that rituals were still alive. When I made inquiries, I was told that this rite was to pay tribute to the god of the soil, provider of all things. For the farmers, the old tree symbolized fertility and longevity: its roots, extending down toward subterranean rivers, were the link to the water to irrigate the fields, nourish the plants, and give life. The tree was reassuring to the locals. Its vitality was considered auspicious for the crops: it was the village protector.

I did not meet a true shaman but was told the oldest person in the village fulfilled the role. He was the voice of reason and settled village business, but today he was also the Communist Party official. Among the Miao, I saw famine and poverty but I did not sense the Chinese presence as strongly as in other locations. Driven out to hostile regions, they had nothing to attract cadres or immigrants. The Miao detested the political representatives who came to periodically monitor the region, but other than that, the omnipresent weight of the Party was not really felt.

In the 1940s and '50s, the Kuomintang committed massacres: the Miao were pillaged, the women raped and dismembered. During the Cultural Revolution, the Miao suffered further plunder by the Red Guard, who stole their jewels. Displaced yet again, they took refuge in the mountains. Unfortunately, once they arrived, they were not able to feed themselves because their staple food was rice, grown by terrace cultivation, and they could not find enough water to irrigate the fields. There was literally nothing to eat. They suffered catastrophic famines even up until 1995. The Tibetans managed to get organized despite their poverty but the Miao were utterly destitute. Children died from malnutrition; food shortages were truly severe. I was shocked to see them living in houses with beaten-earth floors, almost naked. Not only did they have nothing to eat but also nothing to wear. A woman who hosted me in her home told me, "There is only one pair of pants for all the men to share. When someone has to go to town, he wears them." Women had no contraceptives so they had up to ten children. When they went off to the fields, where they worked like slaves, the children were left to their own devices. They followed me everywhere. Each time I set off by foot with my sketchbook to explore the area, fifty or more children in rags, just skin and bones, tagged along. They had great fun tripping me but it became tiresome. One woman offered me her beautiful three-year-old girl wearing a votive locket around her neck for protection. "I have seven," she begged me. "I can't feed them anymore." The only way to survive was to grow opium. They trafficked in it not for food, but for tools so they could work their fields.

The Yi are another national minority of south-west China. We visited their villages with the figure painting professor so we could study the physical traits of the natives. This professor made no effort to conceal his dislike for me. One other girl, the girlfriend of one of the college students, had been granted permission to come along with us since the journey was to take place during the school break. We were not friendly: she did not say a word to me and kept to herself, with her boyfriend. My other classmates were scarcely any friendlier. "How are we supposed to manage with her along? What a pain!" they complained. It was tough: I was a burden they were constantly having to hide because the Yi lived in a region that was strictly off-limits to foreigners. Permission to enter would have been refused by the authorities so we set off without informing them. The roads became increasingly dangerous. At one bend, we saw a bus in the ravine. As in the high Tibetan mountains, the driver simply told us that there had been an accident two weeks before and all the passengers had died. When we went downhill, we coasted in order to conserve our gas because there were no gas stations. When we were about to enter forbidden territory, the students warned the professor, "The cops are up ahead. We'll put Miss Fa up on the roof and hide her among the baskets, under the geese." They stopped the bus, hoisted me up on the roof, and, pushing aside the geese, put me inside a basket of bird droppings, covering my head with fowl.

At the border, the guards checked people's papers and seemed satisfied that everything was in order. Unlike the urban Chinese who constantly inform against one another, people in the mountains behave differently. Though they all knew I was on the roof, not a single one of the old women on the road to the market turned me in. My classmates all had a good laugh, and prolonged the joke until the next stop, ostensibly because I could be seen from afar. The smell of the geese was revolting and my hair was full of bird droppings. When I was finally rescued from my hiding place, I railed at them in a rage. I had an awful time getting clean afterward as there was no water. The further we traveled, the harder it was to bathe.

The first cities we visited were very bleak. They had been colonized by the army and the government. The mountain Yi hated the urban Yi, who they referred to as "Yi swine" because they were more or less paid by the government to live side by side with the Chinese. The urban Yi had agreed to become Chinese. They were traitors to their culture. As with the Tibetans, you could feel the antagonism between the collaborators and resisters. The army was starting to move into the ethnic group's territories. Yi schools had been closed, and people were banned from speaking their language and practicing their ancestral culture or shamanic religion. Instead they were forced to adapt to the Chinese culture. The Chinese colonizers, miserable at having been exiled to such a remote area, were aggressive toward the Yi. We visited certain art professors who had been assigned to teach in the region's urban schools after graduating from our college. They, too, were bitter at such an exile. They led an infernal existence that was so difficult, they lost their artistic inspiration and even the will to live. In their place, I would definitely have preferred a life in the mountains, but perhaps they would have considered such a sentence even more degrading.

The Yi, who are mountain people, grew corn, wheat, potatoes, and, like the Miao, opium in order to survive. They traded with people from Chengdu who traveled to the Yi, some of whom had grown very rich. It was a feudal system. There were white Yi and black Yi. Black Yi were aristocrats and intermarried; white Yi were their slaves and belonged to a different caste. In one of the cities I visited, there was only one black Yi left. He was a friend of our painting professor and served as our guide and took us into the mountains. He was extremely bright, very handsome, and spoke Chinese.

Our professor showed us a black-and-white film shot when the People's Liberation Army arrived in the 1950s, when Mao's policy was to liberate the mountain people while also using them for propaganda purposes. It showed Yi slaves, chained and treated like animals. Our black Yi host explained that in the past his noble ancestors would collect a tenth of the harvest. Custom granted the black Yi the right of life or death over the slaves, and if born a slave one remained a slave for life. Following the liberation, the white Yi were indeed "liberated," but the Chinese officials and soldiers sent to their territories began a policy overnight of collecting half of their crops. The ex-slaves, numbering about 700,000, discovered that their new masters were even worse than the black Yi, taking half of the crops instead of a tenth. Terrible famines ensued, darkening a situation that had already degenerated.

The Yi language comprises six dialects. It has a written form of one thousand characters, made up of pictograms and beautiful ideograms. The sole person left who knew the written language was a *bimo*, or shaman, in the mountains; only he could pass along the culture of his people, and their knowledge of medicine and astronomy.

The territory had become dangerous since the arrival of the army and the Red Guard, because the Yi, like the Tibetans, had proved unyielding. One night, we heard gunshots in the mountains. The next morning, we asked our black Yi friend about it. "They are officially referred to as bandits," he told us, "but they are Yi who are defending their culture. Increasingly poor, ravaged by alcohol and opium, they are still waging a war against the Chinese Army and the collaborator Yi's. People are killed every night."

According to tradition, when a friend or a guest was to be entertained, a glass of alcohol was passed around; whether outdoors, on the roadside, seated in a circle on the floor of a hut or in a city, this immutable tradition was still observed.

One evening a Yi who had drunk a lot told me, "They are killing us off one by one. Our daughters are forced to marry Han Chinese. We will not survive this."

One day we were invited to the Great Fire Festival, so we set out early in the morning with our sketchbooks for a long walk. The festival was held at a magnificent site in the rolling hills, one of which was completely taken over by Yi. They came from all over with their oxen and roosters, and their daughters and wives in fine costume. Women carried yellow parasols, and in the sunlight, I felt like I was standing in a Monet painting or beholding a swarm of butterflies fluttering about and foraging. People sang, drank, and played games; there were horse races and ox and cock fights, on which betting took place at a steady clip. Suddenly, a procession of young women appeared. A panel of judges was to choose the most beautiful woman in the land. Adorned in their all their finery, the women had an easy grace in their large black hats and embroidered clothes, parasols in hand. The young men were strong, like the Tibetans, with handsome square faces. There were also love song contests: men and women, split into two groups, faced each other and, based on the charm of the voice or the lyrics, the young women would choose their beloved. At nightfall, they would form a long procession to travel across the hills with flaming torches. It was the high point of the festival, intended to drive away the evil spirits that caused epidemics. This rite of exorcism resembled those mentioned in ancient Chinese texts. Arriving from Chongqing to such a place was like entering another world. I understood how painters who first came to the area after the ravages of the Cultural Revolution found it enchanting and were delighted to discover such a paradise of beauty.

We spread out with our portfolios and paintbrushes to sketch women and children. At the foot of the hills, outside their beautifully designed wooden houses, they offered me bowls of food. To thank them, I left a few sketches. Years later, a student from our group visited me when I was a cultural attaché in Beijing. He told me that he had just been in Yi territory and my drawings were still hanging on the walls of some homes.

The Yi's traditional costumes were made of woven lamb's wool, and they wore sheepskin capes that doubled as blankets at night. When I walked among them, they hid their faces behind their capes. They adhered to a strict code in regard to hairstyle. One day, our guide became highly embarrassed when he saw me out sketching with my hair in a single braid. He immediately went to find our professor and asked, "Could you tell your student to do her hair in two braids instead of one?" Everyone laughed at this: a single braid meant one was looking for a husband; two braids meant one was married; and if after seventeen a young woman was not yet wed, her braid was cut off, meaning she could have sex even if she was single. In this way, everyone could easily identify who was unmarried, who could have love affairs, who was married, and who was looking for a husband. The men shaved the top of the head. They were one of the last ethnic groups in China to still wear a braid rolled up in a turban. Blundering my way through Yi-land, I asked a very handsome man whose portrait I wanted to sketch if I could see his braid. When he took off his turban, a braid rolled down to his feet. I was astounded. I had believed that the braid had disappeared in China at the fall of the last dynasty. I was so inspired that I took the braid in my hand. At this, the other Yi rushed forward and pushed me away so violently that I fell to the ground. The Black Yi alerted our professor. "A Yi's hair is sacred. A Yi has the power of life or death over any woman who touches it." Our professor lectured me that what I had done was far more serious than I realized. The very next day, he decided we should leave.

It was difficult to find houses to sleep in. At one, the man of the house ordered his wife, "We have guests. The rooster must be killed." Because I was their guest of honor, the man offered me a little cup containing the warm blood of the rooster to drink. My traveling companions explained it would be an extreme insult to refuse. When we parted, they presented me with a cup carved by the host mounted on a real rooster foot. I still have it in my studio, among my unique objects brought back from China. Their wooden crockery was beautifully crafted, decorated as always with red, black, or yellow patterns.

The grandmother of the house asked me if I had fallen from the sky. Recalling that Huang Laoshi spoke often of the "path to the heavens," I answered no, not yet. She told me that when she was very little, she met a foreigner who looked like me and who had fallen from the sky. Our professor made some inquiries and learned that during the war, an English pilot arrived via parachute. Adopted by them, he started a family but died relatively young due to the harsh conditions. The old woman, who had never seen another foreigner, was convinced I had come from the sky. Talking with her, I realized that for her, the world stopped at the Yi. Even when I traced the outline of the earth on the ground, she remained adamant. If I had not come down from the sky, I could only have come from the mountains to the north.

The Yi had nothing to eat; the further we went into the mountains, the more food became scarce. Nothing much was available at that point beyond a kind of biscuit. Fortunately, there were potatoes, which we cooked in the ashes of a wood fire. I was eating practically nothing. One day, I was passed a bowl containing our hosts' last piece of pork fat. There was no meat left, just a single piece of fat. For them, this was a real luxury. I nibbled a bit of it and then shared it with the others.

Stories of ill-fated love were common, since once the shaman had determined the favorable signs, marriage had to take place within the clan. Many men bore scars; I discovered that these were the marks of the wedding ceremony.

Between the engagement and the wedding day, the young woman was free to take as many lovers as she pleased, so the first child was often not that of her husband. On the appointed date, the groom came on horseback to take his beloved away, but first he received a good thrashing from the family who put him through all sorts of tests. Tradition required that the moment he took hold of his bride, she would violently claw at his face; the deeper the wound, the happier the union and the prouder the groom would be.

We stayed in a house where the wife had just given birth. She was not allowed to light a fire or cook food for a month afterward, for fear of causing offence to the god of the hearth. Nor could she go out for fear of sullying the gods of the doors. Once this period had passed, she would go out and present her baby to her in-laws.

With the Yi, I learned to play the *binayo*, a traditional musical instrument; this helped pass the time after long days out exploring. But one evening, when a young man came to find me, I was very embarrassed to learn that when a woman plays it, it is to call a man.

Upon our arrival in a little village, we were told, "The village elder has just died. There will be a very special ritual. Come with us tomorrow morning." We left the next morning at dawn, heading for the mountains. A bonfire had been readied to burn the body. Mourners started to sing funeral chants similar to those in Tibetan monasteries; a shaman recited incantations. I was afraid our presence would disrupt the ceremony, but the Yi appeared pleased to have us attend since the occasion was to honor the memory of the ancestor. We were simply asked to remain at a respectful distance. The villagers killed a pig and offered me the animal's head, a supreme honor. My classmates were highly amused to see me with the head of a pig perched on the end of a stick. I had no idea what to do with it. I knew I shouldn't attempt to bury it, since for these mountain dwellers, this was a very generous offering. The shaman took the pig's entrails and read the omens in its gall bladder and pancreas.

They told me that long ago, the dead were wrapped in a tiger skin for cremation because the Yi believe they are the descendants of a mythical tiger. This way, the deceased could re-join their ancestors. According to legend, after its death this tiger totem was divided up: one eye became the moon, the other the sun, while its whiskers gave birth to rays of light, its fur to trees, its belly to the sea, and its guts to rivers. This tiger is said to be the source of the universe, the reason why the shaman wears a tiger skin at certain ceremonies. Today, in the absence of tigers, the dead are wrapped in fabric with little black and white strings to symbolize tiger fur.

When the pyre was lit, all of the Yi on the surrounding hills stood up and the women wailed, like in a Greek tragedy. It was very powerful. I cried at the beauty of the ritual, and the sacred fervor of an entire people.

It was then that I committed an enormous mistake. When the cremation was just coming to an end, I borrowed a camera from another student to take pictures. At the very moment I focused the camera, a Yi armed with a knife surged out of the crowd and rushed toward me, intending to kill me. Two Party members threw themselves on the man and disarmed him just in time. Students often took photos but had abstained during the ceremony since it was forbidden: the Yi feared that photography would capture the village elder's soul. To this day, I have no explanation for why I did something so stupid. I had not even brought a camera along on the journey since I was adamant that I was only there to paint. Our teacher, very distressed, tried in vain to convince the Yi that we had come to sketch, attracted by the beauty of the place. I understood at that point that the Party was perpetually present, even in the little villages. They had never stopped watching me. Although Party officials had initially tolerated my presence, they were now convinced that I was a foreign spy and would not listen to any arguments. They believed they had captured a dangerous criminal. I was arrested and taken by car to the local authorities. My professor, furious, was forced to cut the trip short, just halfway through. He was also worried because he had no idea what they would do to me and felt responsible.

Once we got to the city, I was locked up in a cell. The police officers were very aggressive, spitting on the ground and insulting me. I sensed that their violence and contempt was somehow rooted in their desire for revenge. The Jesuits had colonized the Yi at the beginning of the nineteenth century, and the memory of their acts, together with the massacres that they prompted, remained with the people. During the nineteenth and twentieth centuries, the few foreigners who had made it that far had humiliated the native population, so the Yi had a very poor opinion of Westerners.

When I tried to speak to my jailers, I was told to shut up and keep still. They refused to let me send a message to the head of the college or communicate with anyone at all. Our teacher, sensing that I was in real trouble, got his former colleagues from the school to send a telegram to the head—who, once again, proved my savior. He had granted me permission to travel only in the Yunnan province, less dangerous than the very wild place where we now were, since the people were better integrated and assimilated with the Chinese.

He called the head of the district office, who told him his version of the story: I had committed a serious criminal offence, I was a spy, I had no right to be where I was and had taken photos. The head of the college was forced to contact people in very high places in the provincial government. For three days I was locked up and mistreated, sleeping on the floor and eating revolting food. Finally they released me, literally throwing me outside with my portfolio. Our professor resented me terribly. It was out of the question to stay one day longer; our group took the first train back to Chengdu. I had committed a monumental mistake and had the scare of my life. I felt horribly guilty and uncomfortable with my professor and my fellow students. They did not stop attacking me for a moment during the whole journey back: I was a total moron. They lamented having brought me along. But what else could you expect from a foreigner?

Disgustingly filthy travelers were crammed onto the train's wooden benches. Exhausted, I crawled under them, amid all the spit, opened my portfolio, and laid down on it, curled up inside my jacket, like the Yi, to hide my humiliation. I slept that way until the train pulled into the station the following morning. Back on campus, the shocked Party official was speechless. The poor teacher chaperoning the student trip was undoubtedly ordered to undergo self-criticism sessions. He detested me from then on and refused to ever teach me anything again. From that time on, even for the most minor outing, my destination was checked and I had to be accompanied by two college professors who never spoke a word and thus held little interest for me.

My hair had also suffered from the journey: it was so dirty and tangled that I could no longer brush it. I had caught ticks and crab lice. I did not dare go to the health center for fear of being ridiculed. Lying on my bed with a mirror, like the beauties in old engravings, I shaved my genitals and tried to remove the crabs one by one with a pair of tweezers. The ticks were a greater challenge. Ultimately, I turned to the school nurse, who kindly gave me ether to get rid of them.

The Yi and their rich culture so impressed and moved me that I made a second journey to see them with my two government minders four years later, my last year at the college. During those years, an ethnic cleansing had taken place: the Yi were no longer in traditional dress, but army uniforms. For the Great Fire Festival, loudspeakers had replaced the live love songs; ox fights and wrestling matches were now prohibited. The Yi, having been placed under army control, were utterly oppressed. Out in the countryside, Party loudspeakers blared elevator music, a true cultural travesty. One evening in a seedy town, I crossed paths with a drunk Yi. He spat out violently, "Go back home and tell people what's happening to us, what's happening here! Yi culture is gone. We are not allowed to speak Yi or think Yi anymore. We are no longer allowed to *be* Yi."

Celestial vagabonds

There where the gods of happiness caressed my brow.

One day, Huang Laoshi announced he would take an excursion to Mount Emei. It would take at least a month to visit all the temples in the mountain range. I was delighted by the idea of such a long break from the college. Several students had told me this mountain offered some of the most beautiful scenery in all of China. One morning we set off for Chengdu. From there, we took a bus to Meishan, where my professor wanted to pay tribute to one of the great men of letters of the eleventh century, Su Dongpo, a native of that city. We visited his house and the temple built in his honor. The Chinese build temples in memory of their great men: for the Confucians, they represent models to be revered, while for the faithful of the folk religion, they incarnate divine powers. It took a lot of imagination to picture what his home might have been among the buildings in the fake traditional style. They had clearly been recently restored as a museum-like structure. There was not much to see apart from a few modern editions of his writings. As for the temple, it was empty: the statues, destroyed by the Red Guards during the Cultural Revolution, had not yet been replaced. If the poet's ghost still resided there, it must have haunted the garden, since that was the only place where any atmosphere of the past might be conjured. We took a seat there and he told me the story of the writer's life.

"Su Dongpo was born here; his mother was a very cultivated woman and devout Buddhist, and his father a property holder. At first, Su Dongpo was relatively uneducated. It was his wife who gave him a taste for the arts, and it was only late in life that he began his studies. But he was so passionate about them that he became as important a man of letters as his two sons, who were educated from a very young age. So you see, it is never too late to learn, and even if in later years learning no longer sheds a bright light but the soft glow of a flickering candle flame instead, it is still preferable to darkness.

"After his imperial exams, Su Dongpo became a local administrator, like the majority of Chinese writers. His official life was punctuated by hardship. He spent time in prison and twice he was exiled to distant regions and put on half pay. But these painful experiences didn't diminish his wisdom at all. He took pleasure in living a simple life and was not averse to being poor. He wished to serve the government and relieve the poverty of the people, but his exile prevented both. His era in some ways resembled ours. A few ministers imposed reforms; they set up militias and cooperatives, socialized the land and introduced collective responsibility, with the best intentions in the world. Su Dongpo understood that instead of improving the life of the people, the government's grip merely created suffering. He was courageous and showed his opposition openly. This cost him his job, as the reforming ministers were in power. He had a great deal of esteem for Tao Yuanming, a fifth-century poet, whose works he calligraphed. He would have liked to emulate the poet, who chose a life of poverty in the country as a junior local civil servant, and only briefly, because it was a way to procure wine. Tao Yuanming regretted this passing weakness in one of his poems:

All my life, I have been at odds with the world
My instinctive love goes to the hills and mountains
Misfortune led me to fall in the dusty nets
And, for thirteen years, I was far from home
The migratory bird dreams of his native forest
The fish in the pond recalls deep waters

Now I am clearing a few acres south of the city
And I remain a simple man, back on the land.

"I cannot remember the rest of the poem," lamented my storyteller, "except for the last two verses:

For too long I was a prisoner in a cage
Now I have found my freedom again.

"But Su Dongpo never managed to resign: he remained a prisoner of the illusion that he could change society."

Old Huang continued, "I had a friend who, at the end of the Cultural Revolution, also believed that it was possible to change the course of history. He joined the Party. He believed that one should participate in political life rather than criticize and complain, that it was better to reform from the inside and that this was the only way to change the status quo. He had forgotten that it takes time, a long time, to change people's thinking. He launched into proposals that were too radical to be accepted, and very quickly, he was the one who was reformed; nowadays, he no longer dares open his mouth and has to be content with sighing his regrets. Never go into politics: you will not change anything, but politics will change you. It is better to be the turtle wiggling its tail in the mud far from man than the turtle who ends up in the pot."

"I am sure you are right, professor, when it comes to a dictatorship," I could not help replying, "but in France, with the vote and freedom of expression, we can at least prevent certain excesses and fight against atrocities."

"Enough of your nonsense! Getting involved in politics means replacing your ideals with cunning compromises and learning to delude yourself. Politicians, just like those they govern, are pawns in situations that they do not control. Yes, you can change the world, and even profoundly, but not by politics—which can only oscillate between domination by some and submission of others—but by your art. Tell me, what emperor or leader ever transformed society as profoundly as those who invented the saw and the plane, the wheel and the clock, the automobile and the airplane? And yet, you would be quite unable to tell me their names. The Little Red Book is not so old and yet it is already nothing more than a collector's item sought by antique dealers, while Laozi and Confucius are still being read. Scholars and thinkers change the world, as do artists, albeit in a less obvious but just as meaningful way. Leonardo da Vinci changed the vision of the Western world, and Wu Daozi that of the Chinese. You want to help others? Then cultivate your painting, perfect your art. Instead of imposing something on others, you will offer them a window to another place.

"All his life, Su Dongpo believed that he had to remain a public figure. What did the civil servant leave behind? A useless dyke on a lake in Hangzhou. But with his essays and poems, he left a lasting legacy. He awakened us to an art of living imbued with wisdom that teaches us to better bear life's vicissitudes. What more could we ask for?"

The following day we started our ascent, initially amid tourists and pilgrims; very soon, however, Huang Laoshi left the main trail to the summit to follow cross trails where we were alone most of the time. The path constantly rose and dipped through valleys where scattered farms clung to the hillsides of sloped orchards and small terraced fields. At night, we would stay with farmers or in a monastery. My professor had made this journey so many times that almost everyone knew him and would willingly spare us a room for the night, providing a camp bed and blanket for each of us. The meals we were served were very simple but good. After hiking all day, even with numerous breaks, we were exhausted. During our climb, the beauty of the place brought to my mind a few poetic thoughts that I wanted to share with old Huang, including a line from Paul Valéry's "The Spinner":

. . . between them the pure air and a shrub contrive a living spring . . .

I would proclaim it across the mountain, which sent it back as an echo. Or, for the sheer pleasure of it, I hollered my interpretation of Goethe into a rock crevice. "The passing moment represents a whole eternity!" Together, we experienced intense emotions of sheer joy. When the student progresses and becomes bold enough to spontaneously offer a few fleeting thoughts to the master, it means the fruit is starting to ripen. Huang Laoshi would be happy and proud the whole day long. It was as though, little by little, my brain cells were establishing instinctive links between my modest poetic experience in France and my experiences in these high altitudes. I was surprised by the transformation taking place inside me, without my realizing it.

Before going to bed, we always observed an unchanging ritual: my professor would procure two washbasins full of very hot water and we would sit, soaking our feet, for an hour.

According to him, this was an infallible way to get a good night's rest and a proper start the next day. We took advantage of these moments to chat. He never forgot his duty to educate me and often used the time to tell me legends and recite poems that he would then explain. Many times, we revisited certain aspects of Chinese thought.

Our favorite pastime was to spend hours discussing the theme of the microcosm and macrocosm. "There is an eminent astrophysicist of ours, called Hubert Reeves," I told my professor, "who believes that ultimately we are only stardust!"

"He's right."

"Heraclitus, an ancient Greek philosopher, even said, 'The soul is a spark of stellar essence.' Do you believe that is possible?"

"At any rate, it is a lovely idea."

I told him about the images the Hubble telescope sent back from space, from over seven thousand light years away. I told him how striking the similarity between a dream stone and the photographs taken of Mars was. I also explained that when I looked through a magnifying glass at the composition of ink in the washes of the paintings we worked on together, I detected the same matter as in the formation of young stars in space: thick clouds of dust borne by gases, like the mineral dust of China ink born of energy flows most likely obeying the same magnetic forces.

Huang Laoshi gently poked fun at me. "We Chinese have intuited that fact for over two thousand years, but it is good to hear your story and know that we now possess, thanks to technological progress, images revealing the mystery of the universe in movement. I would love to see those images! You should understand this: in the infinitely tiny space of our paintings, we merely reproduce the principle of the infinite greatness of the cosmos."

With renewed enthusiasm I responded, "Ultimately, we could say, and it is a very beautiful notion, that the creation of a painting is identical to the birth of a star . . ." I was delighted by my idea, that had come to me suddenly while sitting there soaking my feet.

As the water grew tepid, he smiled, a cigarette dangling from his lips. We stayed like that, content in the silence amid the mountains, lost in our strange yet profound thoughts.

Anxious to thank him for his teachings, I once again attempted a translation. "When I was little, my aunt often quoted the English poet William Blake:

To see a world in a grain of sand,
And a heaven in a wildflower,
Hold infinity in the palm of your hand,
And eternity in an hour."

"Bravo, Fabi," he replied, beaming. "I will answer with words of the painter Bada Shanren: *Ah, the whole universe, in a lotus flower!*"

Then he launched into a long explanation: "As I've already told you, you don't need to know what the characters you calligraph mean; that's not your concern, for you are a painter. However, to master calligraphy and Chinese painting, you have to understand their spirit, and in that regard, you shouldn't limit yourself to aesthetic texts. There is plenty to be gleaned from Taoism and Buddhism for us artists. Ancient Taoist thinkers never spoke about art and yet they furnished the basis of our aesthetic thinking: you have to learn, then forget what you have learned, finding the organic way until creation is effortless. This sounds simple but it is in fact exceedingly difficult to discover your true nature, especially in an age when family, education, social rules, external pressures, and trends all shape us without our knowledge.

"I want to clarify certain philosophical movements, because they concern you as a painter. When Buddhism first appeared in China from India, the first translators did not know which terms to use to translate the Indian concepts, so they turned to words borrowed from the Taoist philosophy. That is why in China, Taoism and Buddhism so often seem alike. Likewise, many young Westerners, I am told, are interested in Zen; this is a form of Zen from Japan. But did you know that Zen is a pure Chinese creation? We call it *chan*. Its fundamental principle is Taoist: one must rid oneself of thought and belief. If you meet the Buddha, said one of the Taoist monks, kill him. The goal is to be conscious without being conscious *of* something, to empty oneself completely. To do so, Buddhists and Taoists developed breathing practices. This is why every morning, before we set off, I invite you to sit for a while, completely still, before a landscape. This exercise demands a lot of practice, but the day when it finally happens, there is indeed an awakening. You will not live differently from others per se, but you will acquire another perspective on what is around you. Your subconscious will then speak to your conscious.

"Of course these notions are difficult for you to grasp. What are our texts like when translated into Western languages? Just as we translated Buddhist sutras, you Westerners must have found terms in your languages that fail to accurately reflect the original texts and ultimately mislead you. Your concepts come from Greek philosophy and Christianity. I imagine that borrowing from them to translate our writings cloaks them in strange disguises! Wouldn't it be better to transcribe them phonetically in order to preserve their autonomy? Or even explain them using different passages where they are cited, thus providing the context? You would enrich your vocabulary with words like *Tao*, *Li*, and so on. The *Tao* is not your God, or the Supreme Being, or a principle that rules the universe, but perhaps a bit of all three. The *Li* is not what you call reason, or logic, yet it is not completely alien to those concepts. Here's another example: I know that Westerners speak of the 'Chinese Rites Controversy,' when the Jesuits were attempting to convert China to Christianity. There must have indeed been controversy, since the word 'rite' in Chinese has a completely different meaning than yours. For us, rites are first and foremost social rules intended to avert violence and promote respect for others.

"When you find certain texts interesting, try to find different translations. By comparing them, you will get a better idea of their meaning—as long as the translators have not copied each other! Even for us there is a problem, not of geographical distance but of time. The same notions to authors in different centuries do not necessarily have the same meaning; certain words used in different eras fall out of fashion and are replaced by others. For this reason our philosophical texts are always published with commentaries and explanations added by succeeding generations. Maybe Westerners should also translate our texts by including different, or even contradictory, commentaries. That would make it easier for a foreign reader to understand. However, in any case, beware of books: we put too much faith in them solely because they are written. Learn our thinking above all by practicing your painting. You will go much farther that way."

"Of course, China is China," I argued, "but I have been struck by the similarities certain thoughts of our philosophers and poets in the West have with those of your thinkers. And it is precisely in my practice that I perceive their truth."

"I don't doubt that. Although China is China, as you say, man is man everywhere. Otherwise, how could we understand one another? Only distinct historical experiences separate us. But be careful: even if certain isolated phrases seem similar, whether written by Western or Chinese authors, this likeness is often illusory. Placed back in their context, they have a very different meaning, and such differences are often more interesting than their apparent similarities. Bada Shanren is not Dürer, even if both painted blades of grass or a rabbit, because they belong to different cultures."

"Yes, Huang Laoshi, but as a painter, I believe I do not perceive things like a Sinologist or an intellectual. To meditate on a blade of grass painted by different masters teaches me a lot. I am like a worker bee foraging for good sources to nourish her spirit, and every flower is a unique experience involving different essences or subtle scents. Your words bring to mind Victor Hugo's recommendation: listen to the 'winds, waves, trees, rocks, for everything is alive, everything is full of soul,' and he concludes, 'I am the resonant echo . . .' Or Gérard de Nerval, who conjured up the invisible force that penetrated his mind: nature takes on new aspects; he sensed the resonances of harmonies that drove him toward creative folly."

I recently came across a passage that I tried to translate for my professor at the time, from Nerval's *Aurélia ou le Rêve de la Vie*: "Everything is alive, everything moves, everything communicates; magnetic waves emanating from myself or others cross unhindered through the infinite chain of creation; there is a transparent web which traverses the world and whose loose threads gradually connect to the planets and stars."

He would smile at my mad desire to prove to him that sensitive souls also existed in the West. Those who had perceived the pulse of the universe, as the men of letters taught us. Was I desperately seeking an explanation for my own story?

Secretly, even if Huang Laoshi sometimes teased me, I was weaving a fine thread between the East and West and holding on with all my strength to my belief in a timeless universality of poetic sentiment.

I was not accustomed to long hikes in the mountains. I sweated, panted, and, in the wake of the ensuing fatigue, felt as if I were intoxicated. The physical effort triggered a deep reaction, like a drug or purification of body and mind. I was so physically exhausted that I forgot my troubles. Old Huang explained to me that these were the early stages in developing a spiritual and mystical life. I was reminded of the beautiful story of Petrarch, who similarly had scaled Mount Ventoux as a discipline in his spiritual quest.

Scrambling over rocks by day, I recalled the legends my professor told me by moonlight, and the mountains seemed to be alive with spirits. I imagined I could make out monsters in the trees with twisted upraised arms trying to snatch the living; on the mountain ridges I saw the forms of snakes and fossilized dragons. I felt as though ghosts were hiding out in the thickets ready to bar our way, especially when we heard the rustling of the wind or unseen animals moving in the bushes. Sometimes the trails gave way to man-made steps, and when there was a heavy mist or we reached cloud level, it seemed as if these steps led to the heavens, culminating in a kingdom of celestial beings formed out of thick clouds. I recalled the fantasy illustrations in certain books, like the *Classic of Mountains and Seas*, a kind of hallucinatory geography. I was inspired to depict this dreamlike universe in my landscape sketches. I had some fun sketching these scenes one evening, but my professor's somewhat scornful smile made it clear that this was not the reaction he wanted. "At best, these are illustrations for children's books. You deprive the viewer of the pleasure he may experience in your painting if you force him into a single interpretation, suggesting nothing more than a science-fiction universe."

Monasteries have a history of offering hospitality to visitors, and scholars sometimes stay there for long periods to work in peace. The first night we stopped at a temple, the monk in charge of guests quoted us a high rate. Because I was a foreigner he assumed I could pay. Huang Laoshi had to explain that I was a student on a Chinese scholarship. After a long negotiation the greedy monk finally gave in. The dinner was delicious and entertaining—completely and ingeniously vegetarian. The "chicken drumsticks" were mushrooms; the "fish" was made of soybean paste. We were served a magician's meal to remind us that the world we live in is but an illusion.

Before dinner, we visited the sanctuary. The buildings were very beautiful; unfortunately, the statues were greatly damaged during the Cultural Revolution. They had been crudely restored, then coated in garish colors with enamel paint. But what else could one expect from craftsmen who didn't believe in the deities they depicted? The rooms opened onto a wood balcony built over a steep drop. There was a tremendous view. After a cup of tea, we sat out there for our morning meditation before enjoying a substantial breakfast. On the esplanade in front of the monastery, I saw monkeys gamboling. A monk walked by and informed us that they were not dangerous, but it was better to ignore them and not feed them. "If you really want to give them something to eat, put it all in one hand behind your back and dip into it with the other to give the food out slowly to the monkeys. When nothing is left, hold out your two empty hands. Then they will understand there is nothing more to be had. Otherwise, they will think you are still hiding something and jump on you and rip your clothes." I was not reassured and decided the monkeys would have to do without peanuts that day!

One afternoon when it was very hot, we decided to take a long nap. I do not know why, but I began to think about people I cared about and had left behind in France. I wondered if we would be strangers when we met again. In spite of my joy in seeing them again, wouldn't I feel strange? They would be expecting the person they once knew, but I was not that person anymore. My professor noticed a hint of sadness on my face and asked me what I was thinking about. "My friends and family in France," I sighed.

"Just admire the power of the mind: you are here, lying on the side of a Chinese mountain, and your mind can take you to your native land! The mind possesses an infinite variety of possible excursions; you must use it to travel. It establishes connections all alone, it's like a cloud that passes, without any stable state. Follow its endless variations. We have to accept our different thoughts, even when they are paradoxical. Nourish your mind. Observe the morning mist carefully, watch how a branch sways in the breeze, and be present in every place you find yourself, because places cultivate the spirit. Why else would I have brought you here? Feed your spirit, not only with book learning like many people, but also with the reality around you, and your thoughts—train yourself to dream and to remember your dreams when you awaken. Order them up just before you go to sleep, give them a starting point—then you will see the spirit in full force, which produces intuition. Streams of intuition burst forth and then all you need to do is transcribe this poetry of a passing instant. Stop thinking and trying to understand; forget, forget and your mind will naturally understand."

On a stop in a temple, I couldn't help asking him a delicate question. "Huang Laoshi, do you believe in these gods, in these buddhas all around us here?" He appeared disconcerted by my question. He reflected briefly, then answered, "I certainly don't believe in these naive representations whose beauty comes from the spirituality of the craftsmen who created them. I also don't believe what the monks and other priests whose spirit is trapped in dogma say. Some of them, but only some, are cynical exploiters of folk belief. However, religious thought cannot be reduced to superstitions, as the government claims. I believe there is something beyond us that the human brain will never be able to completely grasp. In this, I share the view of Confucius: I don't even know what man is so how can you expect me to know what gods and spirits are, or even if they exist? If they exist, they certainly do not take the form that we imagine. There are some questions we will never be able to answer. We must accept this. What do we know about what happens to us after death? The best thing is to follow your heart. A good man obeys his heart and speaks or remains silent, according to the moment."

"That reminds me of something Gustave Flaubert said, I offered. 'I cannot bear those who claim God exists, or those who claim he does not.'"

"Do you mean the author of *Madame Bovary*? I've read that novel; we have excellent Chinese translations of it. It is no surprise that such a shrewd observer of the human heart should have such an intelligent approach to the hereafter. Believing or not believing in the heavens is not important. The essential thing is that they exist, not in the sense of the vault of heaven but as an order of the universe, the genesis of everything starting from the cosmic egg. Our mind is also a part of this order, and what counts is being in harmony with it. So we have to try to penetrate the secret order of things and model ourselves on the nature of the heavens. It is a model of greatness and emptiness, and a generator of the absolute. Only by following its path may you approach the Supreme Being. As an eighth-century painter once said, 'I took nature for my master and discovered the nature of my heart.'"

"Sometimes I have trouble grasping the deeper meaning of words like these and those of your thinkers when I read them in translation. I even feel that I am not worthy of your teaching."

"Don't try to understand. If you find it difficult, that means you're already on the right path. Learn to know yourself and you will understand the heavens, for it is all a part of the same. There are many ways to get there; they are all just parts of the same path. The heavens offer at least one way you can always follow: sincerity. Don't attempt to dazzle or show off—stay real. But I have said too much; I am only confusing you. There is a fundamental truth I'd like to express, but I can't find the words. The heavens and earth do not speak, nor do the four seasons, and yet they teach us so much better than words do. We babble too much."

At a bend in the path, we met an astonishing being who scared me a bit. He sat on a low wall under a tree. He had very long fingernails, a bushy beard, and a weather-beaten face. He was so emaciated that he seemed to have turned into rock or mineral. Moss nearly sprouted from the straw cape on his shoulders. He wore rope sandals and carried a carved cane. His look was mischievous but his smile benevolent. Although he stank terribly, he gave off an extraordinary radiance. Huang Laoshi was delighted to meet a forest hermit and offered him a cigarette. The old man read palms. With his active interest in the occult arts, my professor encouraged me to hold out my hand. I wanted to refuse, but when he insisted, saying it would make him happy, I gave in. The man took my hand, and after a long silence, stated, "It's excellent." My professor was very pleased. "You have a marvelous destiny," added the soothsayer. "Your path will be very hard and exhausting, but you will be successful and happy. Don't worry at all. You will live from your painting and poetry."

Naturally, I was skeptical. I was a penniless apprentice painter far from the world and my loved ones, following an old master, lost along the misty trails of a sacred mountain. All I had to my name was a little bundle of clothes and a walnut cane. Was I not the hobo of Sichuan instead? Yet, inexplicably, these promising words reassured me. My professor suddenly seemed relieved. I knew that he had been disparaged at the college because the administration had noticed that his teaching had assumed much greater proportions than authorized: the technical subject matter had blossomed into a genuine initiation. Although he had not told me everything, I knew his life must have been difficult due to censure by people whom he never wanted to deal with again, nor owe anything to. This prediction delighted him. In spite of all our difficulties, his and mine—the future looked brighter. When we left the seer, I was light-hearted and old Huang was full of renewed energy.

That evening, he related stories about immortals and hermits. Once upon a time, a member of the imperial family had a brother who had been executed and close relations who were mistreated. Disgusted by the lamentable state of the empire, he went off into the mountains to meditate. One day, two immortals asked him what he was doing there.

"I'm looking for the Way," he said.

"What Way and where is it?" they asked. He was silent for a moment, then pointed to his heart. Satisfied, the two immortals told him, "The heart is the heavens and the heavens are the Way." And they invited him to join them.

My favorite immortal was the one who chased ghosts and demons with a fly swatter. He just had to dust off his head to make them disappear. Then there was Hanshan, the eccentric poet who wrote poems on rocky cliff faces or flat stones. A monk, he refused to bow to the rules of monastic life and went wandering across the neighboring mountains instead. He is depicted as ragged, his hair standing on end, with a beaming face. He was friendly with a lay brother assigned to the kitchen who, also a poet, saved him the leftovers from the meals of the other monks. After his death, about three hundred poems were collected.

Huang Laoshi admired Ge Hong, a fourth-century alchemist who sought immortality through drugs, breathing techniques, and sexual practices. When I returned to France I found a translation of his book: "He passes through the doors of infinity, wanders through marvelous voids, travels to the heart of the unknown, strolls through the dark vastness, walks on rainbows, and strides upon Big Bear. Such is the man who has found the Way." My professor saw Ge Hong as a man who learned how to exist removed from the world without serving it. Honors and humility were all the same to him, and, remaining detached and calm, he adhered to his original simplicity. He did not allow external events to influence his essential being. "If you decide to live from your painting," he advised, "don't be afraid of preserving your anonymity. Of course, it would be more pleasant and beneficial for you to live in the country, but you can be a hermit in a city, in the most hideous of buildings standing amid factories. Living as a hermit does not mean you have to withdraw to a cave deep in the mountains. It is a state of mind that generates a certain outlook on the world, certain relationships with others. It means contriving to become simple, and that is very difficult when you are intelligent."

Then, in his seemingly disconnected way of leading me from one subject to another, he explained the Chinese word *yun* to me. "In its modern sense it means rhyme, but in a broader sense it means rhythm. This is essential in music but also in other art forms, like the art of living. Without rhythm, there is no art. Originally this word had another meaning: it meant refinement. It is no coincidence that we went from refinement to rhythm; the meaning has simply been narrowed. Cultivate refinement in your thoughts and behavior; this will make you more human. What is inhuman and even contrary to life and its evolution is vulgarity and violence. Even animals and plants are not insensible to refinement."

After long detours, we finally arrived at the highest peak: ten thousand feet. A monastery stood there. It was cold but the monks fortunately provided the visitors with long quilted army coats.

What struck me, at this altitude, was the bamboo growing alongside the edelweiss. The bamboo that survived was very thin bamboo, sagging under the weight of the snow all winter. It reminded me of the toothless old man who says to his disciple, "You see, teeth, which are rigid, are worn away by time while the tongue, which is supple, does not age. It is like the water flowing everywhere: it is fluid and eventually wears down the hardest of stones."

A mass of clouds hung over the terrace next to the temple. I heard that if the gods were smiling down upon us, we could catch a momentary glimpse of Buddha's shadow when the sun hits the clouds at a certain angle. Pilgrims made offerings along the edge of the precipice, Tibetans hung multicolored prayer flags on strings stretched between two poles, and tourists took pictures or peered out through binoculars. I stared into the emptiness, this sea of clouds moving toward infinity. Without realizing it, I leaned out to try and glimpse Buddha when I felt myself literally sucked into the ten-thousand-foot-deep abyss opening under my feet. I was about to go over when a pilgrim caught me just in time and threw me to the ground with a shriek. My professor nearly had a heart attack. I experienced a terrifying delayed vertigo reaction and could not get up, to the bemusement of those gathered around. That evening, in our dormitory, he told me, "Did you know that fervent pilgrims come here to throw themselves into the void to join Buddha, and offer their lives to him? At the exact spot where you almost went over. It is a beautiful end, but please, wait awhile. You can come back when you are old, if you want to disappear into the infinite void."

I thought we would be heading straight down the mountain. Instead I learned we were but halfway through the journey. "I want to keep going," declared Huang Laoshi. "There are still some extraordinary places to visit, including a monastery perched on a rocky peak where I would like to stay a few days." This meant another thirty miles of trails and steps. It was exhausting, but sometimes we would stop and pause for a full day. My professor would rest, as each stage was arduous for a man in his seventies, while I went to sketch in the area. At night, over our bowls of rice and vegetables, he often spoke to me of painting and poetry.

"Have you ever seen, in a temple, mediums incarnating a deity? It is a rare sight today since it has been deemed a superstition and forbidden, but long ago it was a part of religious festivals. The deities showed their presence to humans by taking over certain individuals whose souls would momentarily withdraw. These mediums would then enter into a trance. They would not feel any pain and could cut their tongue with a blade or self-flagellate with spiked balls without suffering; they would hardly bleed and there were no scars. In this altered state, they played the roles of spirits or deities with stylized operatic gestures, and naturally, only spoke as the deities with whom they were familiar. When actors play a character on stage, they are also possessed by their role but they remain conscious. You see, the painter has to imitate the medium, but like the actor, remain conscious. He must forget himself entirely, lose himself, in order to become the branch of a cherry blossom tree, a bamboo, or a landscape. He has to feel the bamboo growing inside of him. He will no longer need to think about the form to give it, the form will just appear. It order to reach this state, midway between the conscious and unconscious, where the unconscious speaks to the conscious, certain artists painted by using their hair dipped in ink or holding the brush between their toes. Others used something like a planchette: they held a divining rod to which they attached a brush dipped in ink and allowed the rod to guide them across the paper."

This brought to mind how Victor Hugo would spread ink on a sheet of paper, fold it, and then work from the blots: landscapes appeared, which he would then draw. I also thought of Alexander Cozens, who extolled the same invention for the composition of landscape paintings in the eighteenth century. He introduced the theory of "blot art"; he was audacious for the time and his explorations are fascinating. I told Huang Laoshi about the automatic writing of the Surrealists, but that was merely a point of departure—suggestions to follow when beginning a creation. Perhaps the Chinese techniques would have interested OuLiPo (*Ouvroir de littérature potentielle* [Workshop of Potential Literature]), a group founded by French writer Raymond Queneau.

"Be careful," he warned me. "This approach can lead to madness, and is not without its dangers. Most shamans know how to come back to reality when they choose, but some of them lose themselves in the beyond. We have to know how to control our ability to rid ourselves of the shackles of blind trust in reason. The same is true of wine. Painters and poets drink to liberate their mind but know that, if they overdo it, they will only fall asleep. Yet, in wine there is a taste of profundity. It is still the best drug, if administered in proper doses.

"Have you heard this amusing poem by Tao Yuanming?

Residing in me are two different people who pull me in opposite directions.
One gets drunk all alone,
The other is sober throughout the year.
They poke fun at one another, the drunkard and the abstainer,
And never understand what the other says.
How stupid he is, this narrow-minded man,
The detachment of the drunkard seems wiser.
But a word of advice to the one who gets drunk:
Light a candle when the sun goes down.

"The artist is like a kung fu practitioner who concentrates his energy on a specific point. Once it has been activated, nothing can stop it. An inner alchemy is needed to give birth to a joy inside you that nothing can destroy, even under the worst conditions. Painting is fighting, like in kung fu: he who frees the most energy wins.

"Beware of knowledge. Too much knowledge kills creation—you don't know where to focus, you're overwhelmed by so many things. When you prepare a dish, you put in only the necessary ingredients; you don't buy onions if they are not in the recipe. The same is true in art: don't be distracted by knowledge you don't need to make your omelet. Leave it to academics to follow their desperate race toward knowledge that they cannot even digest, let alone regurgitate. Learn the techniques but go beyond them. Your strokes on paper must be full of life and born of themselves, and above all free of toil or traces of book knowledge."

One day, the sky clouded over; it was not as hot and we were able to advance more easily between the steep slopes. When we made a stop at a farm, Huang Laoshi looked up to the big clouds rolling along with the wind. "Look," he said, "that is a good image of chaos. It is your starting point. In chaos and the dark lies the original mystery. You must also follow the cosmic principle to give life to your creation. Like the heavens, create from chaos.

"Follow your intuition and clear out the formless to finally arrive, through the forms, at a place beyond them. Communicate the *spirit* of things and don't forget that the spirit also lives in mountains and plants; they have a soul, and it is the heavens that gave it to them. Form arises from the absence of form; we must not be afraid of chaos. Take a pot, for example: it is the emptiness that it encompasses that creates the pot. Form of any kind merely serves to limit the void in order to pull it out of chaos."

I have explored chaos ever since. For certain paintings, I use the gesture delineating a circle, for all things are born of the circle. In the chaos of ink that I erase and recreate—in this vortex, this maelstrom—suddenly and mysteriously, the form appears and the object of my intuition is born of itself. I am left amazed, as if beholding a magical event.

"The act of painting must be the action of non-action, natural action, free of desire and not turned toward the self. It is in forgetting oneself that the fusion with the heavens, with the whole, takes place. Stop thinking, wanting, calculating. Introduce into yourself a total absence of constraints to be in harmony with the source of your heart. Flee what is rational, what is conventional. When that spring from which you drink the best of your work dries up, do not force it, do not try to extract passing inspiration, for it is as fleeting as desire. Go outside, go for a walk, talk to your bird. And have no regrets: you would have merely created a dead work.

"Consider Buddhism: it requires reasoning that is foreign to a peasant who toils the land. Yet Buddha Amitabha will save him: the peasant only needs call upon him once with a pure heart to be welcomed in his paradise. Of course maintaining a pure heart is easier for a simple being than for an intellectual. For you, a painter, it is a necessary condition if you wish to enter into the paradise of art. Be generous and uncompromising, keep ambition in check and success will come. You won't have cause to regret later."

I knew that the socialist-realist art style reigning in China repelled him. During a stop, to tease him and see his reaction, I posited the following. "It's different from traditional Chinese art," I said, very naturally. "But isn't it art just the same, on a par with Western or African art? Giacometti said in all earnestness that he admired those statues of farmers holding a sickle or workers wielding a hammer, for the artists had succeeded in something he himself had tried but failed: colored sculpture."

"Of course, it could have become an altogether valid art in its own right. The mistake was subjecting art to politics; the result was didactic works. As I have told you, the criteria in art is not beauty, a subjective notion that varies according to time and place, but sincerity and authenticity. Socialist statues are a failure not because they are commissioned works, but because they claim to represent the spirit of the workers yet are created by people who are not workers. The same goes for the contemporary art inspired by folklore or carved tombstone rubbings; it claims to be the successor of folk art. How presumptuous to speak in the name of the farmers and workers when you know nothing of their way of life! How pretentious to assert that we know better than they what they want, and even what they think! Our woes are in large part due to the fact that the Party leaders claim to have a monopoly on what is good for the people.

"However, even if art is incompatible with politics, it still assumes a moral aspect. The stroke on the paper is the imprint of your heart and reveals, for those who know how to read it, your moral character. How many times have I told you appearances only fool the blindly ignorant; vulgarity is easily discernible. When we judge a painting, we also judge the personality of its creator. If you fail to cultivate detachment and restraint, your painting will reveal their absence, and no amount of words will manage to conceal that. In art, the point is not to say, but to suggest. In addition to a landscape, you suggest your mind and its quality; you reveal, through a branch of hazel tree or a mountain, your innermost being.

The remarkable thing is that you suggest them without saying as much, in the same way that poetry suggests emotions, while in prose emotions can quickly sink into sentimentality or indecency."

Huang Laoshi thought we should end our journey by visiting the area's most ancient site, the Temple of Ten Thousand Years, founded in the fourth century and built at the top of a steep slope. In the center of the sanctuary there was a statue of Buddha seated on lotus flowers.

At a certain time of the year, a ray of sunshine passes through a hole in the dome and shines light upon Buddha's brow, as if to emphasize his wisdom. My professor was keen to let me admire the treasures still housed in the temple—a well-deserved reward, for we had walked a long way to get there. The monks showed us illuminated manuscripts of sacred texts copied onto palm leaves, an imperial seal dating from the Ming dynasty, a small jade Buddha, and the crowning glory, one of Buddha's teeth.

"So we traveled thirty miles to see a tooth!" I exclaimed.

"Don't forget that it is sacred," he answered, laughing. "A pilgrim earns this reward only after a long inner journey."

The walls of the sanctuary were covered with magnificent frescoes that unfortunately had greatly suffered the ravages of time. Their subjects were religious but in a style that was very different from the one I was studying.

"In China," Huang Laoshi told me, "there are two sorts of painting: that of the painter-scholars or men of letters that you are starting to understand and that of the craftsmen-painters, a very good example of which you see here. In the first, as Su Dongpo observed, it is easy to create an illusion: the water of lakes or rivers, or mountain summits, constantly change appearance, and the artist can argue that what he paints exists. However, when it comes to figures, buildings, and objects, the slightest blunder is easily identifiable. The art of the craftsmen-painters includes some masterpieces, especially in their use of color. It is regrettable that our art history has been reduced to only paintings by men of letters. But there is an explanation for that: painter-scholars alone wrote about art. The painting by craftsmen-painters is easily understood, even if, to appreciate the subject matter of the religious paintings like these, one would have to know the stories of Buddha's life and the bodhisattvas. The art of the painter-scholars, however, is abstract: the painter does not work by setting up his easel outdoors, like Monet or Cézanne; he *creates* it, and the viewer not only sees but also understands the mountain or the old pine tree, because the artist has gone beyond the landscape. He has merely rendered the structure necessary to embark on an imaginary journey. Regardless of the style or subject of a painting, meditate on what is before you: its ephemeral trace imparts eternity."

Throughout our journey we lived like celestial vagabonds, and from this way of life I retained at least one important lesson: I can be content for months on end with bamboo shoots and rice soup!

This pilgrimage remains one of my most beautiful experiences in China. I spent the whole journey as happy as a lark, and so did my master.

The damned of China

Since time immemorial the wise and the good
Have been abandoned to their solitude.

For my final two years at the college in Sichuan, I obtained a grant from an American foundation. My aunt the ethnologist had filed the application for me; she believed that my stay in China qualified as an ethnographic experiment and that a written account of it might prove valuable. This meant that I could buy books and carry out more systematic research. I decided to visit the former centers of Chinese culture where old calligrapher-painters still lived. Huang Laoshi and other professors who knew them personally or by reputation gave me the names of the survivors of a world that had disappeared. It felt important to meet them. As a Chinese proverb goes, one can learn more from a conversation than from a cartload of books. And if I wanted to tell my story, it was also to make these last of the great masters, keepers of an ancestral tradition, known.

During the summer holidays, I set out for Shanghai. I stayed for some time with the parents of a professor from the college. They lived in an old district that had not yet been razed by bulldozers. Their home consisted of one large room with a little courtyard in the back. Three generations lived there: the grandmother slept in a deck chair next to the fan, the grandfather on a mattress on the floor; the couple had one bed and the children another. The heat and snoring kept me awake. There was just one washbasin for taking a sponge bath. A bucket in a corner served as the toilet; every morning it was put out on the street when the sewage man loudly announced his arrival. The whole neighborhood stank. I was unable to go to the toilet in front of the family and they all laughed when I asked if we could hang a curtain in front of the bucket. But they were very kind and did as I asked.

The neighborhood teemed with life. Because of the heat, windows and doors stayed open and some people slept on camp beds out on the street. At night, there was such a racket that you could not hear yourself think: televisions and radios turned up full volume broadcasting interminable Chinese variety shows, people trading insults, couples quarrelling . . . The atmosphere in Shanghai was mellow and friendly—much more relaxed than in Chongqing. People did not live in constant fear of criticism, unlike when I stayed with the family of a professor in Sichuan and I had to inform the local police station. No one seemed preoccupied with the authorities, but this did not mean I was no longer under surveillance— something I quickly realized when I met the old scholars.

In the home where I was staying, the grandfather, father, and little boy, an eight-year-old nicknamed Little Monkey, were all great cricket-fighting enthusiasts. Little Monkey and I became friends. He lent me a bicycle so I could ride around the city. When I returned from my trips, I would go explore his universe, a cricket farm he had set up in the tiny courtyard in back of the house.

Little Monkey was fully occupied tending not only his own cricket but also those of his father and grandfather. In the yard, I stretched out on the ground to put myself at the level of his Lilliputian world, trying to understand his attachment to these tiny creatures. He said his cricket was a warrior who enjoyed music. He liked to hear singing; it cheered him up when he was down. "If he is trained properly," explained the little boy, "he will become brave and bold, capable of fighting to exhaustion; he will win many fights and become the honor and pride of our family."

Thanks to my young friend, I learned a lot about crickets. "Our crickets should not be confused with green crickets," he gravely explained to me. "Those are prized for the variety of their songs and are raised in a little woven-fiber cage. You often find them in the markets. People like their chirping, which augurs good luck. My old uncle, a peddler in the country, carries around his musical cages of crickets hung on a stick to present them for sale. Our crickets are different; only this kind can fight. They are nicknamed 'ringing horses' or 'musical caterpillars,' but my grandfather likes to call them 'celestial dragonflies.' I hate my cousin," he went on, tirelessly, "because he feeds them to birds. My father and I raise them to earn money—lots of money. Training them is hard and their daily care is delicate. Like with great athletes, you have to spend endless amounts of time building up their muscles, strengthening their bodies and spirits so they will perform well in combat. There are many ancient techniques to raise them, and the Chinese have been practicing this art form for over a thousand years. There are even books on strategies and training methods used on cricket farms."

Poets and scholars are all passionate for these little insects. Pu Songling, a seventeenth-century writer, related that cricket fighting was immensely popular at court under a Ming dynasty emperor. Government officials were ordered to collect crickets, so much so that people everywhere started to hunt and raise them. Prices escalated: a good cricket was worth more than jade. When a poor scholar-bureaucrat, the head of his district, was beaten because he proved incapable of collecting taxes from residents, he decided to turn to cricket hunting. After many adventures, he finally caught one that was small and ugly but was able to beat any opponent. It could even challenge a rooster by jumping on its head and biting its comb. The poor scholar presented the cricket to the emperor and garnered such a reward that he was able to buy land, many houses, and a large herd. Pu Songling concluded, "An emperor's every action has an effect on people's lives, so any negligence is unacceptable. This poor man of letters, at first subjected to the greed of other local officials, acquired such a large fortune thanks to a cricket that he paraded around on fine steeds, covered in magnificent furs. The heavens had decided to reward an honest man."

Cricket owners got rich from big bets. The winning cricket would be crowned army general. Sometimes, following a brutal fight, the hero would devour the body of his exhausted opponent. The grandfather assured me that the winners were without doubt reincarnations of valorous warriors of old. Some Chinese positively worship this fascinating world of insects. It is a living and entertaining world offered by nature, featuring complex and admirable creatures, a microcosm of their world. Little Monkey had an earthenware pot decorated with a warrior deity that provided shelter for his insect, a dark and cool room for him to escape the unbearable heat of Shanghai. He would take him outside in a small cage with wood bars, a kind of miniature birdcage, with a sliding door and all the creature comforts to make the cricket's outing enjoyable in the fresh air. On the top of the cage someone had written: "Everyone has his reason to rejoice."

In mating season, the general needed a wife. Long pots made of gray clay acted as rendezvous spots. They were an ideal place for nuptial festivities. The crickets also had decorated porcelain feeding dishes and delicate accessories. Thin bamboo rods, painted in different patterns depending on the region, with two rat's whiskers at the ends, were used to tease the insect. A cricket could also be roused by tickling various parts of his body. The language was very codified. The owner tapped the edge of the pot, and depending on the vibrations, the cricket understood and obeyed the orders. It was a fascinating spectacle! This breeding of purebred miniatures was a beehive of activity in the house. Special dishes were prepared for the general: cucumber, lotus seeds, and finely chopped lettuce. When I brought in a blood-filled mosquito that had just bitten me, Little Monkey jumped for joy: blood, he told me, made his cricket stronger and more aggressive in combat. At the market, Little Monkey and I would buy beans and fresh fish which I would grind to make a choice dish of the general's.

In the summer, the crickets were trained for the fighting season, a favorite autumn event in Shanghai. Entry in the grand prix of Shanghai required membership in the Chinese Association of Cricket Breeders. Officially, betting was forbidden in China, but there was a cricket market on East Terrace Road and enthusiasts would meet up there or in gardens, hidden courtyards, and reputable teahouses for this clandestine activity. Before the fight, each insect was weighed on a tiny scale to decide if the future champion qualified for the heavyweight, middleweight, or lightweight division. With extraordinary seriousness, the referee would list the titles won by the warrior of each family, prepare and excite the fighters with a little rod, then place them into their combat positions. At this point, the manager of the place would go around collecting bets. The fighting would be fierce and the ambiance impassioned around the tiny arena. When a warrior decapitated his victim a cry of admiration would go up in the crowd. Little Monkey explained to me that his father bet big but could not honor the debts when he lost. There was no reasoning with him, and more than once, he ruined his family. His reckless betting made his wife hysterical and sometimes he did not dare come home.

After a fight, the exhausted general earned the right to be bathed in a teacup. If he caught a cold or a chill while out, Little Monkey would prepare a special brew with his own urine. A child's urine was a radical remedy that supposedly would heal a cricket and perk him up right away. If he was injured, he had to go on a special diet prepared for him by the family. To rebuild his strength before the next fight, he was given slices of bread with honey. We all lived in the general's shadow, so much so that at night, on my straw mattress, lulled by the snoring of the clan, I could not stop dreaming about him.

During the day, I tried to track down the great painters and calligraphers of Shanghai. A young professor from the local art academy accompanied me, helping me arrange appointments and providing introductions so that they would agree to see me. From one house to the next, I retraced the history of these artists, students of great masters whom I had studied. I started to connect what I had learned from books, my old professor's teachings, and what survived with these heirs to a lofty tradition. It felt like I was entering a chapter of art history.

I first went to visit master Zhu Qizhan, the centenary doyen who enjoyed an official status. He was an adorable little gentleman, modest and very British, with a strong personality. He was exceedingly kind when I told him I wanted to collect information on his art and how he had been taught, adding that I had brought along a few of my scrolls to show him. But his wife, who must have been fifty years his junior, was another story. I understood immediately by her haughty attitude that she was with him for money. She abruptly broke in: "You have five minutes. It is out of the question for you to stay longer. He's very busy." She was a real policewoman.

I entered his studio and admired a few paintings he unrolled. He had just started to enjoy telling me his story when two communist officers, summoned by his wife, arrived and demanded: "What are you doing here? Your papers, please. You are a student at the Sichuan Fine Arts College, right?" The atmosphere was very tense and it became difficult to continue the interview. They ordered me, politely but firmly, to leave the premises. On the landing, the old painter bowed repeatedly from behind his door and told me, "Above all, keep painting and, please, forgive me . . ."

Next, I met Li Tianma. I had no problems with him. He was the first and last artist I met in China who lived in a magnificent house that he owned, located in the old concessions district. All the other artists I had visited lived in remote, concrete buildings in miserable conditions. Li, however, enjoyed an official status and lived like a nineteenth-century man of letters, amid dream stones and rosewood armchairs. He did not seem to have suffered from the changes brought on by the Cultural Revolution. Calligraphy was an art form that was far more respected in Shanghai. Li was a member of the Shanghai Calligraphers' Association and gave lessons from his home. He was an expert on aesthetics and a great master of small regular script. The author of numerous essays, he possessed an extensive library containing precious works and rare copies I had never seen before.

During this visit an unexpected event transpired which drastically transformed my own painting technique. His wife served us tea, a ritual that differs according to region in China. The tea was prepared Chaozhou style: brewed in small earthenware teapots and served in tiny cups. This woman was quite elderly but exceptionally refined and elegant. Her traditional dress was so remarkably beautiful that I asked if I could touch the fabric. It was ochre on the outside, shiny black on the inside. Worn by time, it reminded me of an animal skin or a landscape painting from the Song era. "It's a very famous silk in Shanghai," she told me, "we call it 'fragrant cloud silk.' There is only one place left in China that still makes it. Hand-woven, it lasts a lifetime. The more it is worn, the more pleasant it is to wear. The Shanghainese like to make clothes out of this silk because it is extremely light, does not stick to the skin, and is a good insulator from the heat.

"Look, Miss Fa, I have been wearing this dress for sixty years and it has no holes, it is indestructible. Every time I wash it, new patterns appear. The ochre color that you so appreciate was obtained by a dye made from riverbed sediment. Once the fabric leaves the weaver's workshop, it is first dyed using yams, giving it a tobacco-red tint, then dipped in the river where the sediment gives it this very particular ochre color."

The old calligrapher was taken aback to discover that I was more interested in his wife's dress than in him. I asked the woman to take me to the shop where this silk was sold. I had been unhappy with the paper used at the college, as I found it too white. White is not inspiring to me as a basis for creation. However, I was fascinated by the paintings of the Song and Yuan eras, whose ochre-brown backgrounds made me dream. In the end, I experimented with this silk, wearing it down artificially, trying to recreate the mysterious life contained in the fabric. Was it the forces of the earth, rising morning mists along a lakeshore with thick cloudy passages suddenly clearing into an emptiness that prompted reverie? Years later in my Beijing studio, my housekeeper Auntie Xu and I would put yards upon yards of silk into the bathtub to soak in dyes. I obtained the backgrounds I sought and my first paintings were born of this dyed fabric. I used the same pigments and technique Li Tianma's wife had described. Then I tried other pigments, such as tea, but I never obtained such fine results. I don't know if this "silk of perfumed clouds," a national treasure of savoir-faire, exists still.

I had not come to talk fashion with his wife, however, so Li Tianma led me to his studio upstairs, where he taught. Steeped in Confucian morality, he sought to impart his knowledge with great precision. He decided, after seeing my exercises, that my regular script still needed practice. According to him, I learned intuitively and was drawn to the natural and spontaneous flow that fascinated me—but without having sufficiently trained in the architecture of the characters. He criticized the teachings of my old professor harshly: "What kind of Taoist is he? He hasn't even taught you the essential structure! You don't know the fundamentals."

This was followed by a long dissertation on the subtle composition and proportions of the strokes of a character. His analysis of writing was purely formal, his method very rational. He made a point of reciting all of the technical terms. That first day was dreadful. Li Tianma assailed me with disdainful remarks on the rules of composition and character forms, putting me in a cold sweat. He kept returning to a study of the methods that I had not sufficiently practiced. His logical approach, without the slightest bit of poetry, failed to convince me. Never had Huang Laoshi disparaged me in this way; he had always used poetic metaphor to make his meaning understood. My belief was that if I succeeded in practicing the principles taught by my professor—to experience in my brushstroke the infinite transformations of forms of the universe—I would embrace at the same time the rational rules. Bolstered by Huang Laoshi's teaching, I listened to the dry lectures of Li Tianma with a certain detachment. He sensed this and became annoyed. In the end, though, I decided his comments merited my attention and I resolved to become more demanding of myself.

Perhaps he sensed my distress as he invited me into his library. It was a veritable forest of calligraphy rubbings from stone carvings and old manuals. He excitedly showed me an exquisite example of the small regular script he particularly prized. We spent the rest of the afternoon going over it with a magnifying glass.

I returned to see him several times, contemplating in detail the absolute ideal attained by the great masters he so admired. Curiously, each master had his own master. To me, Li Tianma's own compositions were like an army of well-aligned and well-equipped little soldiers, harmoniously built, marching in distinct lines. Despite their apparent severity, his characters were remarkable: their structure had body; each of them was perfect and yet different. The work emanated a powerful and impressive rigor while still conveying a clever and disconcerting approach. I recognized the beauty in it but eventually concluded that it was dangerous for a free spirit like mine to delve deeply into his work. Torn between Confucianism and Taoism, the Chinese culture draws its richness not from a single synthesis of these two philosophies, but from the thousands of possible syntheses that each individual may choose to compose as he sees fit. I practiced this style of calligraphy for several months until I realized that its spirit was foreign to my nature. To continue would have buried me in a quest for the perfect regular script.

I adored wandering around Shanghai. I biked with the young professor who accompanied me to visit the artists. Compared to Chongqing, a very harsh city, Shanghai was enchanting. In the old concessions, cultures and religions intermingled. We would suddenly come upon a Japanese temple, or an Orthodox or Catholic church. At night, we listened to jazz at the Shanghai Club, inside a big hotel. Life there was very different from what I experienced elsewhere in China. There were stately Western buildings on the Bund, old districts where people lived on their doorsteps and in summer slept out in the street. At dawn, people practiced tai chi outdoors, under the shade of a tree, to tango or disco music. We often dined on fried dumplings and bowls of noodles from food carts. But modernization projects were beginning to destroy the old ways of life.

I wanted to acquire my first ink stone, so I went to explore the traditional painting shops. Shanghai was full of treasures for a painter. Entering one of these shops was like entering a violinmaker's workshop or a boutique with musical instruments of all kinds. I was ecstatic to discover all the wondrous materials of a painter:

- cabinets full of dragon- or phoenix-headed brush-holders carved in camphor or rosewood;
- woven mat brush-holders for rolling up and storing paintbrushes;
- small sticks of ink from countless provinces, molded from pine wood residues and fish glue. They continued to give off fragrant scents of hibiscus and musk; the most opulent were decorated with gold leaf;
- paperweights engraved with poetic maxims;
- carved water spoons in bronze or copper;
- rinsing jars for paintbrushes, water jars and ceramic palettes for colors. In common blue-patterned white porcelain in fake Ming style, they had lost some of the charm of the past. But, a few paintbrush pots in *huang-huali*, a dense and dark wood with pure zebra stripes, could still be found in the shop windows;
- plain and unadorned brush rests. One was so precious, strange, and fantastic that it still haunts my memory: three milky green jadeite mountain peaks with transparent veins of ochre-brown. Just placing the paintbrush in their valleys or deep gorges would transport you;
- on each side of the shop, there were reams piled up of Xuan paper, rice paper, bamboo fibers with their immortal virtues, and palettes of exercise scrolls tied together with hemp yarn. The "Red Star" manufactured in Jingxuan was famous for its "raw" absorption, which was so sensitive that it spread the ink marvelously;

- on the back walls, from floor to ceiling, were a whole range of paintbrushes made of animal hair hanging upside down. It was magical.

Some painters use brushes made of rat's whiskers or fox hair. The *langhao*, with hair of the hare, is often selected for painting landscapes. This brush is also the stiffest and the most responsive for lively strokes. Sheep's wool is very sturdy, but one of the most difficult to use because it is so supple. *Yanghao*, or gray goat, lends itself to flower-and-bird painting. Wild boar, otter, *shihuanbi*, or stiff-haired badger, and marten (preferably the winter coat) are also revered for their robust touch. Hog's hair, but also the coarser horsehair, allows heavy inking for large paintings.

I also found paintbrushes in rooster and pheasant feathers and duck down, which are ideal for washes.

The handles had different diameters and lengths, which also affected technique. For example, it is easier to paint the heart of an iris with a long handle! Some were in buffalo horn, others in varnished wood and bamboo stems with carefully chosen knots.

A humble painter could leave these magical places inebriated, delirious and pale with envy or rage at not being able to indulge in such wonders and utilize them.

The Confucian calligrapher had asked one of his students to help me choose an ink stone. We found one that represented the "eye of a blackbird," which I found fascinating. The traces of plant fossils that the sculptors showcased when cutting the stone were, it was said, intended to ward off evil spirits. It felt auspicious: I chose that one and still have it, precious as it is to me.

My third visit, to a famous calligrapher, proved disappointing. He was aged seventy-five and apparently wealthy, with a well-established shop. He charged a lot to see his calligraphies. He was considered something of a public letter-writer and only worked on commissioned pieces, provided he was well paid. He could afford to be selective because he had placed sixth out of ten thousand candidates in the international calligraphy competition. He was very accomplished in the cursive script.

His great-uncle had introduced him to calligraphy and by the age of seven he was already producing an astonishing twenty calligraphed characters per day.

The gentleman clearly had a solid foundation. He had developed his own style, but it lacked personality because he stuck too closely to the rules. What a strange character he was! Hunchbacked and dressed in a suit and tie, he was grumpy and moody, and constantly had a handkerchief in hand to wipe away his perspiration, perhaps due to poor health. He only thought of money and was often unintelligible. When I showed him my exercises, he asked me how much I sold them for. I had never thought of selling my work. When I replied that I was still just an apprentice, he immediately lost all interest: I was not famous and didn't count on the art market. He told me that I was disturbing him and that he had a lot of work to do.

In Shanghai, I met two women painters—rare in this field, perhaps due to the extreme difficulties. One of them, Li Guoxiang, told me her life story:

"I was born in 1915, in Zhejiang province. I am descended from a family of scholars who had sunk into poverty: my father had to leave our little city to earn a living; my mother was illiterate so she could not read the letters he sent. She had been raised in a society where an educated woman was a bad thing. Even so, she wanted me to get an education, so I was sent to a traditional school. The primary school teacher, a very cultivated man, had a great interest in calligraphy. He taught me to write characters, and when I went home I spent hours and hours practicing with a brush that was too large for my little hand.

"One day when I was practicing on my sheet of paper, my mother, who was looking over my shoulder, took me into her room and pulled a trunk out from under her bed. It was full of calligraphy rubbings inherited, she said, from her family. She told me to practice copying them. These works were by the great artists my teacher had mentioned. When I showed them to him, he encouraged me to persevere. 'Calligraphy is like a river,' he told me, 'it will not turn into a mighty torrent overnight; but through its steady flow, it will eventually trace its path over rocks, and when it has become a majestic moving force of water, nothing can stop it.' Since then, I have never stopped. When I was thirteen, my mother enrolled me in the secondary school of our city, where art classes were given following Western methods. The drawing teacher had studied in Japan; sometimes he took us out into the countryside to study nature and I began to paint flowers, birds, and insects. At home, when I wasn't practicing calligraphy, I was painting. My mother excused me from having to learn sewing and embroidery like other girls.

"My father wanted to marry me into a wealthy family so that I would never be poor, and arranged an engagement. The idea of living with a man I did not know terrified me. I told my mother that I did not want to marry, that I preferred to study, but she tenderly answered that my father was imposing this marriage upon me for my own good. I went to beg him; he loved me very much and was swayed: he allowed me to finish the three remaining years of secondary school. However, a relative who had seen my calligraphies undermined me: 'Girls will always be just girls. Your characters lack force.' My fiancé's family was growing impatient: 'A girl should know how to do women's work, serve her in-laws and bear children. Why does she need to spend her days studying?' My deadline was approaching but I did not want to become a caged bird forever forbidden to fly. I secretly wrote to my fiancé, begging him to break our engagement. My letter was returned to my father who, furious, immediately set the date for our wedding.

"Thus, at seventeen, I found myself in a decorated palanquin led by a great procession to join my in-laws, prosperous merchants who owned several shops. My husband ran the money-changing business. He often went drinking with friends, ran around with women, and threw money away. With me, however, he was the opposite. He was very miserly and I had to account for every penny. It was impossible to buy paper and ink. When I ran out of the money I had brought with me, I continued to practice by writing characters on stones with water. One year later I had a daughter, and two years later a son. I did not want any more children and tried all sorts of tricks to avoid getting pregnant again. My husband often came home very late, completely drunk, and made use of me while pouring out insults: I was no better than a plank of wood compared to the other girls he knew. Finally, one day I said to him, infuriated, 'If you want other women, go to them; in any case, it is calligraphy I love, not you.'

"At the end of 1937, the Japanese occupied our city and we fled to Shanghai. I saw an advertisement in a newspaper offering calligraphy lessons by Li Zibai. At the end of the first lesson, I shyly asked if he would accept me as one of his students. He asked me to write a few characters and I calligraphed, in regular script, a poem by Du Mu called 'Autumn Evening':

The cold light of my lamp and of autumn on the folding screen,
My small gauze fan chases away the evening moths.
The color of the night which climbs the steps to the sky is as fresh as water.
Reclining, I gaze up at the stars of Herd-Boy and Weaver-Girl.

Surprised, he asked me with whom I had studied.

"With my schoolteacher, and then I practiced alone for ten years."

"You have talent. If you had studied with me, you might have been successful, but now it is too late."

"It is not too late!" I begged him, taking his hand. "Please accept me. I promise to devote myself to my studies."

"He gave me a rubbing from the Wei period to copy, and from then on I went to see him once a week so that he could correct my exercises. Every week he wrote three characters that I had to copy every day as many times as I could. After two days, I would be fed up: I had already studied for ten years; why should I start from the beginning? When I took him my three characters at the end of each week, he would find lots of mistakes. After two months, he increased the work: now I had six characters to copy. In a few more months, I acquired a solid base. He didn't want me to copy too many different rubbings but to limit myself to three. A year later, his tuberculosis had worsened and he was bedridden. I went to his house every ten days and took him fruit and vegetables that he liked, for he was very poor. When he sensed his end was drawing near, he told me: 'Guoxiang, I don't have much more time. Carry on. I have only had two students like you. I'm going to send you to my friend Gu Kunbo.' And in his bed, with a trembling hand, he wrote this note: 'My brother, I am entrusting Li Guoxiang to your care . . .' I fell down on my knees at his bedside and cried. I will never forget this master who devoted his life to his art.

"Gu Kunbo was a rich and famous artist who trained hundreds of students. He asked me if I knew his terms: forty dollars in Mexican silver per year. I didn't have that kind of money. But when I got back home, I thought of the money that was in the bottom of a trunk of clothes: over the years, my family and friends had given me money for my children for various holidays. I withdrew the necessary amount for my lessons. A few days later, my husband went looking in the same spot for money to buy a gift for a girl and discovered the missing cash. When I came home, he punched me and kicked me while insulting me: 'A woman's role is to look after children, not do calligraphy. You should be ashamed of yourself! The truth is that you're out looking for men!' Then he left, staying out all night. I went to my work table and wrote this poem:

> When the calm returns, the past comes to mind.
> As I think of my children, I weep in anguish for this night.
> The man to whom I am bound seeks nothing but pleasure and smiles.
> Who can understand my pain?

"In 1941, Gu Kunbo organized an exhibition of his work, including a few pieces by his students. It was the first time I exhibited. I was twenty-seven. I sold the ten canvasses that I showed and made two hundred yuan. I took the money to the widow and child of my old master Li Zibai, to whom I was so indebted. In 1946, I participated in a show by Chinese women artists. The most famous painter at that time, Zhang Daqian, noticed my work and asked to meet me. Despite all the kindness well-known painters like Gu Kunbo and Zhang Daqian showed me, they would never fill the same place in my heart as my first master, Li Zibai.

"I also knew Tang Yun, who entrusted me with a few of his works to copy. I do not know why, but my husband was very jealous of him. One day, I took advantage of my husband's absence, to copy a painting by Tang Yun depicting branches of cherry blossoms. I didn't hear my husband when he returned and silently entered the room. When I turned around, he was standing just behind me, glaring at me with hatred. He was about to rip up Tang Yun's painting but I managed to save it by convincing him that all the money he had would never cover the price of such a work of art. Instead, he vented his fury on my work, which he proceeded to tear to pieces, and on my painting materials, which he threw to the ground and smashed.

"In 1949 the Liberation came, and in 1952 I was able to get a divorce. But my freedom was not to last long. Starting in 1957, for thirty years, my life was very hard. There was the Anti-Rightist Movement and the Great Leap Forward. We were just starting to move past this when the Cultural Revolution arrived. I was attacked. The rubbings I had so painstakingly collected were burned and my work shredded. My daughter was locked away in a dark and humid studio, and one evening the police came to arrest my son. For twenty years, I was not allowed to sell any of my work. I lived on twenty yuan a month from my daughter, eight of which went to rent. That left about forty cents a day to eat. When my son was freed, he got married and I gave him my only room; I slept under the staircase, even though there wasn't enough room to stretch out properly. I had no money to buy paper; I would gather old newspapers and children's exercise books from the garbage and continue to practice calligraphy. In 1979, my situation improved and

I started to live again when my daughter was killed in a car accident. I fell ill. My hair turned white overnight, I developed a hunchback, and my eyesight began to fail. But my painter friends helped me: they got me into the Institute of Art and History. There, I met Wang Ziping and, in 1984, we were married. So you see, the heart always triumphs. You must never despair, and if you have a vocation, you must follow it no matter what the cost. I am not very agile but my husband is sturdy; he will show you a few of my works."

I left her feeling utterly distressed and sad. With a bitter heart, I understood that my own path, hard as it was, was minor suffering compared to the painful life of this woman painter-calligrapher.

I often visited Suzhou gardens. What a marvel! A recreation of utopia, it was an attempt to understand the principles of the world's transformation, and who knows, perhaps to find again the primordial wholeness that can lead us to an awakening. I walked through a surreal landscape among raised, inclined, and reclining stones that evoked cloud races, lightning flashes, splashes of gushing water, the footprint of a Buddha, the head of a roaring tiger, a dragon sleeping at water's edge, and caves of immortals. The site emanated peaceful harmony, a kind of hide-and-seek between the mineral, vegetable, earth, sky, and water. Visions of paintings or rubbings appeared in fragments through openings as round as the full moon—perfect compositions for revealing a cosmogonical perception. I discovered dream stones hanging in the various pavilions scattered throughout the heart of the gardens. In the Master of the Fishing Nets Pavilion, they were presented on the walls in the entry to the residence. The milky white of the marble evoked cloud formations creeping into the landscape, and the gray-and-brown-toned veins suggested some long-forgotten celestial world perfectly. An old master once told me that these living mineral elements invited conversation about truth.

I felt some hallucinogenic shocks, like blows on the shoulders that Zen monks give with bamboo rods to hasten an awakening—these true visions that I attempted to transcribe with my paintbrush while studying the spirit of landscapes by masters of the Song period. Here, I had a sudden, fundamental insight: if the landscape painters succeeded in reproducing their visions so powerfully that they seem almost real on paper, it is because they understood, with absolute humility, that they were the little brothers of the stones and trees on this Earth and that we are capable, through our inner alchemy, of giving life to a mineral presence just as nature gives life to us. I had moved beyond figurative painting based on a motif, or even painting from memory, as taught in the West. That experience helped me to comprehend why I had spent so many years practicing the brushstroke and to finally grasp the fundamental link between man's act of creation and that of nature.

Every time I went to meditate in those contemplative spaces, my thoughts would ricochet off the subtle wonders they offered. At times, this meditative state would help me along in my quest. So they were lucky days, pure joy, when I would set out to explore the streets of Suzhou by bicycle with a song in my heart.

I visited the Hangzhou Fine Arts College, still the most famous art school in China and the one which produced the greatest painters. It is located along a lake. At the time, it was the only school that still had the calligraphy and traditional painting departments I had searched for in vain in Chongqing. These classes had just started up again since, in Hangzhou as well, the students had only been taught oil painting. The calligraphy professor who met with me was eighty-five years old and knew the history of the college by heart. He told me how the old masters had suffered under the Cultural Revolution, particularly the great painter Li Kuchan. Li had obeyed the instructions of the Great Helmsman and ran the school as the government required, but his work still betrayed his political beliefs though he never voiced them. He was a disciple of Bada Shanren, the great seventeenth-century painter whose works conveyed his resistance to the Manchurian occupation: he would draw a rock with considerable refinement in the great Chinese tradition, but on the rock he would place a fearsome vulture that kept watch over everything about him as he gripped the stone; he also painted vicious, terrifying cats in a floral universe. Li Kuchan was persecuted by Jiang Qing, Mao's wife, who had him beaten so severely that he died.

In Hangzhou, I also paid many visits to a man called Sha Menghai. Aged ninety-two, he was one of the last great calligraphy masters in China. His writing, in the crazy cursive, exuded a powerful vitality. I had trouble communicating with him because he was nearly deaf and I had to shout in his ear. He was gravely ill and often in and out of the hospital. He was extremely polite and refined, and would always see me to the door despite his advanced age. He was impressed when I showed him my exercises. Unfortunately, after two or three meetings, I learned that he was in the hospital dying. He was very touched when I visited: "We'll keep up a correspondence," he told me. "Above all, continue to paint. I have rarely seen a student like you and I have taught many years. There is something in your calligraphy—you must continue." Sadly, not long after, I heard that he had passed away.

In Hangzhou, I met another kind of painter. Dressed Mao-style, master Xie Zhiliu had skillfully managed his career. He lived in a magnificent old house and collected antiques. Officially recognized, he had no political troubles and earned a lot of money as a dealer.

He had sound knowledge of the art of landscapes, calligraphy, and aesthetics. A historian, he had written several works on ancient art and was sought out as a great specialist in Chinese antiquities and old paintings. Our meeting was amusing because his wife, also a painter, was present. More talented, her paintings were more interesting than those of her husband, which maddened him.

Lu Yanshao, eighty years old, was the last landscape master in southern China, and the greatest living heir to Shitao, whose spirit he had perfectly assimilated. Exuding intelligence, he was entirely self-taught. He was a colorful character, a bohemian with shaggy hair down to his shoulders, with a caustic sense of humor.

His unexpected and extravagant reactions were dazzlingly accurate and acute.

From our first meeting in his grimy building, it felt as if we were old friends. He treated me like his own daughter. Having spent so much time alone, he had difficulties expressing himself and drooled when he spoke. He confided to me that he had no more friends as they had all died. He preferred to live and paint in the mountains and told me about his pilgrimages to marvelous landscapes. When he spoke, I couldn't tell if he was describing real life or his paintings: the memories of his experiences and the experience of his creation had merged into one.

"My father," he told me, "had a rice shop. He had a very beautiful regular script. My mother was his second wife: she was thirty when they got married. After several boys died at birth, she had a girl who died of illness when she was barely a year old. Then I was born, exactly the same day of the same month as my sister. My mother believed my sister should have been born a boy but was born as a girl by mistake so then was reincarnated as me. This belief was a comfort to her. Thus she brought me up as a girl, letting my hair grow, dressing me in floral fabrics. Older kids made fun of me. One time, they caught me and wanted to pierce my ears and hang earrings in them, but I managed to escape. The rest of my family also treated me like a girl and forced me to urinate squatting. My mind was so confused. I thought I was abnormal. Because I didn't feel like a real boy, I buried myself in painting and calligraphy. I loved to go with my mother to visit my maternal grandfather. There I would see my uncle, a true man of letters who had passed the imperial exams. He died young, at thirty-six, leaving behind a little girl my age, six at the time. When she was twelve, my grandfather decided we would marry. After that, we were so shy when we met that we did not even dare look at one another. My teacher, who knew I was engaged, would tell me: 'The period before marriage is that of the greatest love; it is the most enjoyable and delightful time, the golden age in life, and you two, you don't dare even approach one another—what a shame!' Looking back, I realize he was right.

"I studied painting and calligraphy by watching the masters work. I also learned to carve seals and copy paintings. In secondary school, I got up at four in the morning to practice. My guiding principle was that changing models provided the best possible education in order to absorb the qualities of each, to understand their distinctive characteristics and then to develop my own style. People cannot identify the masters I use as inspiration with this approach. I started with the calligraphy of the Wei period, then the Han and Wang Xizhi, but what is important is not academic study but recreating what you learn. My paintings are more accomplished than my calligraphies.

"In 1955, the director of culture of the Anhui district pressed me to take over the fine arts college of the province. He offered me two hundred yuan a month, a large sum compared to the eighty I was making at the time. However, I declined the offer. I was living in Shanghai, where an artists' center was to be established; I had been given the opportunity to organize it with a friend. I have never been interested in money and I felt that this artists' center, which would house the studios of sixty of the area's best painters, would be an ideal place to study, compare creations, raise the overall artistic level and contribute to the culture of our country. At the beginning, I was very happy there. Full of hope, I believed that art and politics could come together for the greater good of all. But this was a dream. One day a painter said to me: 'I create a certain genre of painting and those who pay money to buy my work demand that genre; if I changed my style, they would say that it was painted by one of my students, or a fake, and refuse to buy it. You, you're different: you progress, you can do what you like, you're free to search for novelty.' He lamented his lack of audacity and wished to escape the repetition of traditional painting.

"Neither of us noticed the dark clouds gathering over our heads. In 1958, the Party decided that we should express our ideas freely. The slogan was: 'May a hundred flowers bloom, and a hundred schools compete without constraint.' I believed in this freedom and openly expressed my opinions about the art world. However, a trusted friend said some things against me and caused me terrible trouble. When the winds changed, I found myself labeled with 'rightist' tendencies and made an outcast, my right to free speech withdrawn. In the artists' center, I was assigned to menial tasks until 1961. Still, I was consoled by my belief that had I accepted the position in Anhui, I would not have escaped the political upheaval.

"The Hangzhou Fine Arts College absolutely wanted to hire me to teach landscape painting, but the Shanghai authorities refused to let me go because I was suspected of being a rightist. Finally, a compromise was reached: I would go to Hangzhou to teach for two months, then return to Shanghai for two months. In 1963, during a medical check-up in Hangzhou, I was diagnosed with tuberculosis. Rimifon, the miracle drug of the time, didn't work on me, but I was saved by a friend who got me another drug, Dibaifen.

"The Cultural Revolution took place in 1966. Despite my denials, I was accused of belonging to the large landholder class. Having painted every single day of my life, I was forbidden to touch a paintbrush and my materials were destroyed. Sick with worry, my wife wondered every night if I would return home from struggle sessions where I was attacked. This torment lasted for ten years. My wife repeatedly comforted me, trying to hide her own tears. Without her, I'm not sure I would have survived. Five of us lived in the house. Besides the two of us, there was my mother-in-law, my son, and my daughter. We received fifty yuan a month and our living conditions were very difficult. We lived in two rooms—three hundred square feet in all—and only the front room had a window. It served as our living room, bedroom, kitchen, and my studio. My mother-in-law and my children slept in the back room. The sole table served in turn as a kitchen table, my worktable, and my children's desk. In the winter, there was no sunlight in the house. The ceiling was made of boards, and when it rained hard, water seeped through. There were insects and rats. I felt guilty: it was because of me that the family had to endure such hardship. For many months, a comrade tried to get me to confess that I was a member of the large landholder class. At one struggle session, he hit me so hard over the head that I nearly fainted. I got on a bus, planning to drown myself in a lake, but on the way, I realized I had no right to leave my wife to face everything alone, so I returned home. At the next struggle session, my torturer asked me why a bastard like me hadn't killed himself yet. He organized another session where he forced me to wear a dunce's cap announcing I was a large landholder and made me walk out on a slippery plank over a river to draw water in a bucket, hoping that I would fall in and drown.

"In 1978, at the age of seventy, my name was reinstated. It was acknowledged that I had been falsely accused of rightist tendencies and I was paid my salary of eighty yuan. In 1979, I was a member of an artist delegation sent to Osaka. I was also selected as a representative of the sixth session of the National Popular Assembly. I was so moved that I could not sleep for several nights. Finally, in 1982, I was given my dignity back. On my return from Beijing, in June 1983, I moved to Hangzhou where I was provided accommodation. I was so happy that I did not know how to thank the Party enough for its consideration. The occasion arose when the government commissioned me to paint a large fresco for the government headquarters."

Lu Yanshao showed me a part of his oeuvre, painfully unrolling each painting with trembling hands. He explained details, pointing out the evanescent mist shrouding the top of a hill or an old, partially uprooted pine tree desperately clinging to a sheer rock face, indifferent to the terrifying gorge over which it perched. Then he would turn to me and smile. I could not mask my emotion. He was happy.

One day he announced he was on a treasure hunt. He tripped over his papers and dusty boxes of documents. He was on all fours in front of his cupboards when, suddenly, he let out a cry of joy: he had found his treasure wrapped up, Chinese-style, in newspaper. He gave it to me. When I eagerly opened it, I discovered it was a dream stone. "Believe me, if you want to paint landscapes one day," he said, "you should study as closely as possible the profound kinship of destiny between the work of nature and that of man. I would be proud if you would meditate on this stone. It will open the doors to inner landscapes for you." It was my first dream stone; I was elated and immensely touched at the same time.

This gift did indeed bring about a powerful awakening in my explorations. At the time, I had difficulty believing that the beauty of the stone was natural: its veins suggested a sublime landscape of simple and harmonious composition. I rubbed it and vigorously polished it, unable to convince myself that it was not painted. Since that day, I have built a collection of dream stones; they never cease to teach me about the mysteries of the living.

I never tired of meeting such exceptional characters, ghosts of times before the Cultural Revolution, products of what Chinese culture could offer at its most refined, living in the middle of a pseudo-modern environment where generations of social classes had been destroyed, terrorized, or branded with a red iron by the Mao era. In this new China of corrupt brutes, venal Party officials, and conceited illiterates, how could these old men of letters who had survived a tidal wave manage to endure? They had flirted with madness and were worn down by unimaginable daily aggression, beatings, and torture, often misunderstood by their close relations, viewed with shame by their own children, relentlessly criticized for years while their belongings, old scrolls of paintings and scholarly libraries, were burned, all for what? Because they painted? Because they wrote poetry? Because they were bold enough to speak of the intangible, and through art, free themselves of their chains? In the big "Open China" of that time, they were left behind, banished for maintaining their love of painting, poetry, philosophy, and the tireless contemplation of nature's marvels. At each visit, I always found old Lu Yanshao all alone, lost in thought, the last survivor in a place that had forgotten him.

How can I express the profound feeling of helplessness I felt in meeting these final surviving links in the chain of the history of painting, bearers of eternity, heirs to mankind's heritage? How can I explain that at their level of knowledge, of absolute detachment imposed by the totalitarian regime, they had attained a powerful universal reach? In their presence, I completely forgot that they were Chinese, even though I was at the very heart of what is characteristically Chinese. With them, the cultural barriers, the very same ones with which I had painfully collided, instantly fell away.

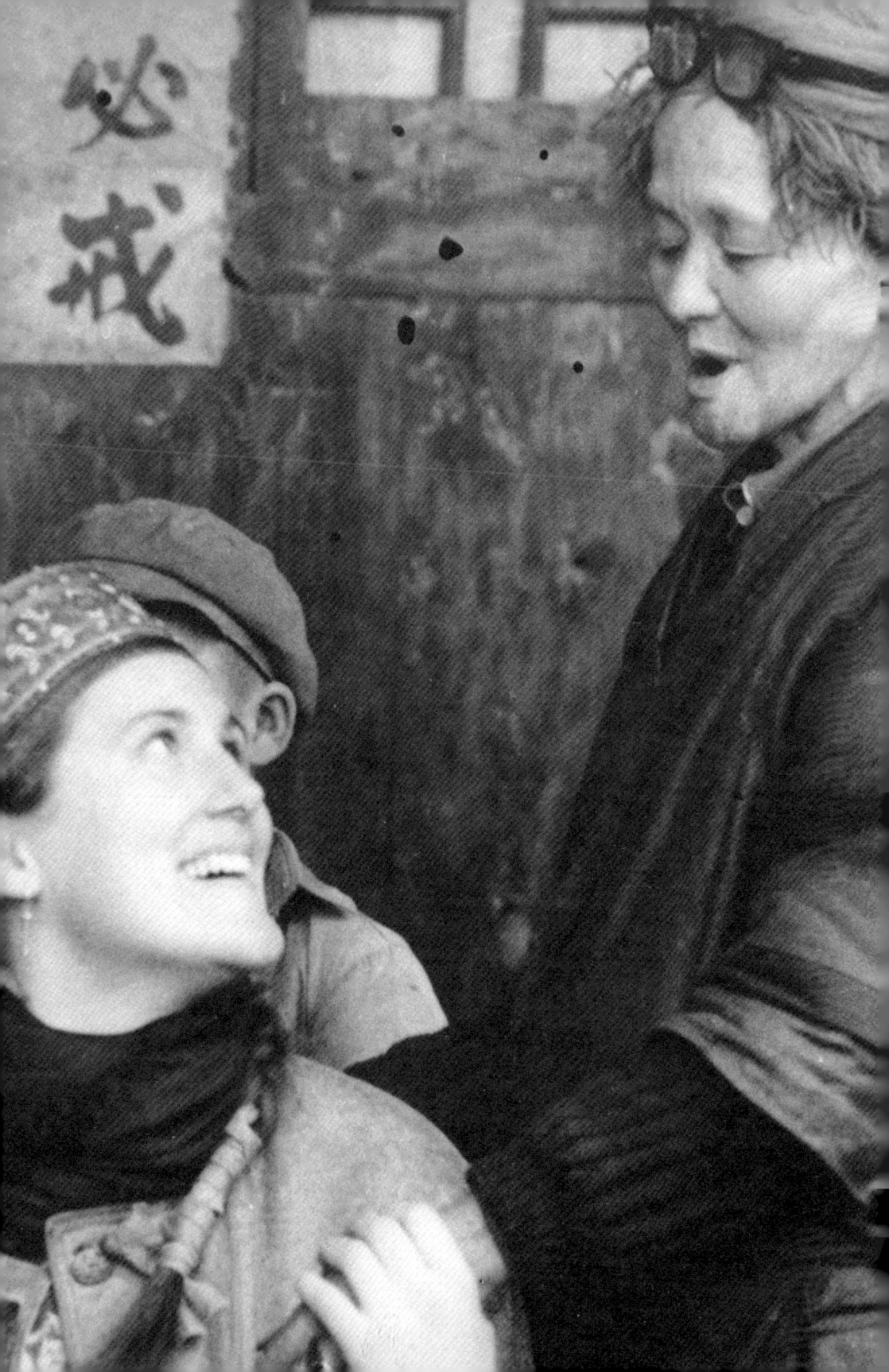

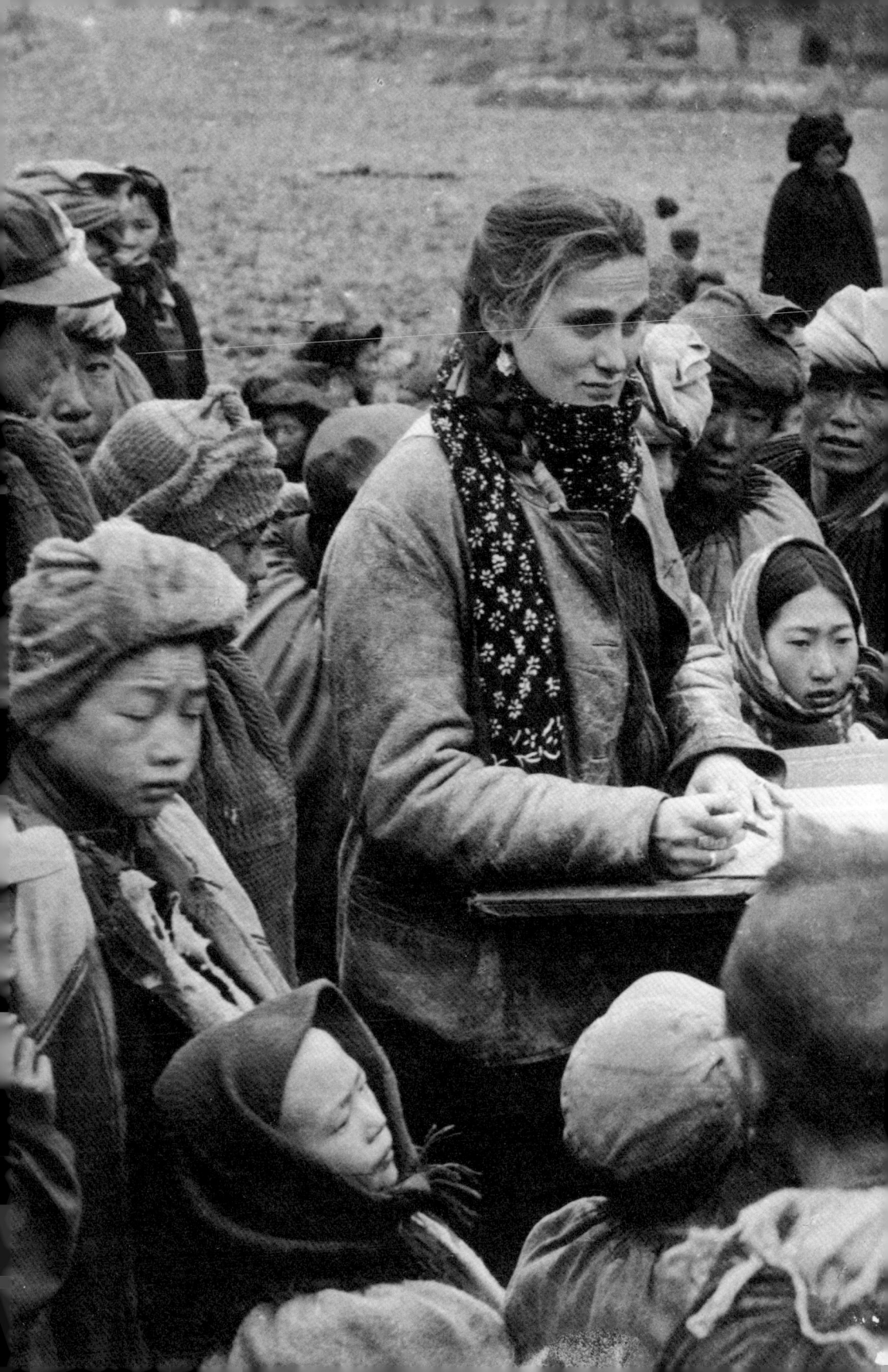

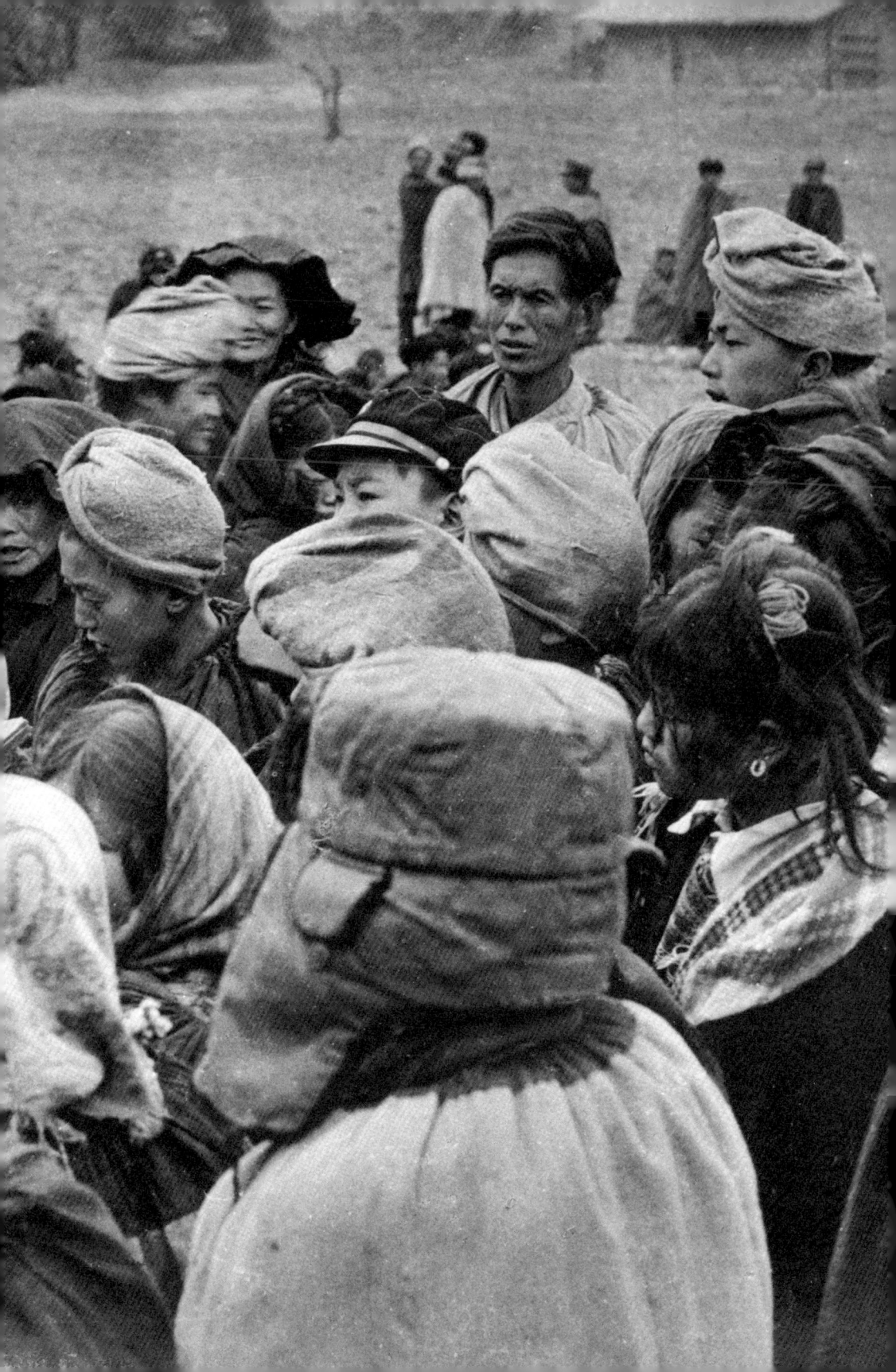

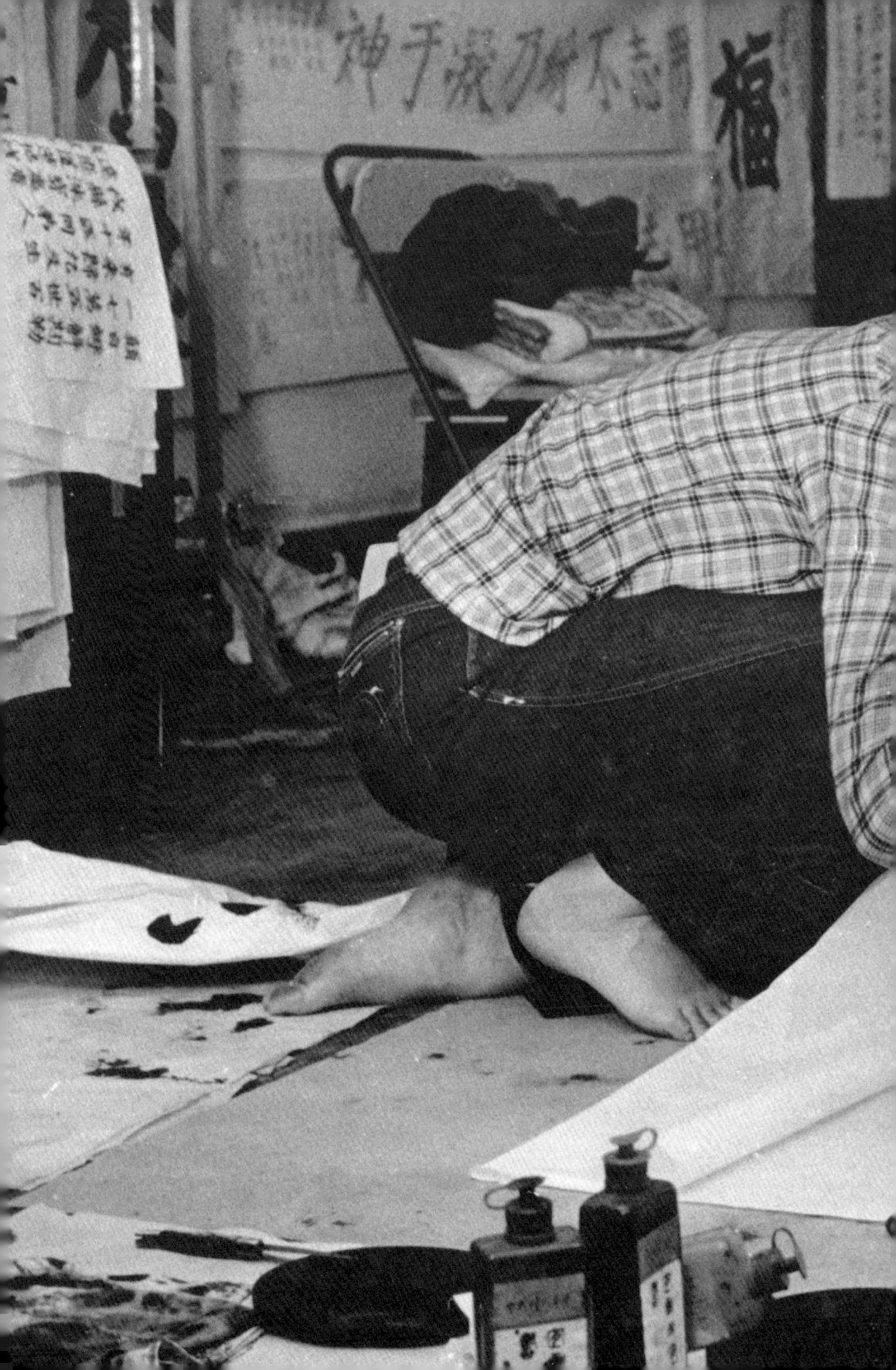

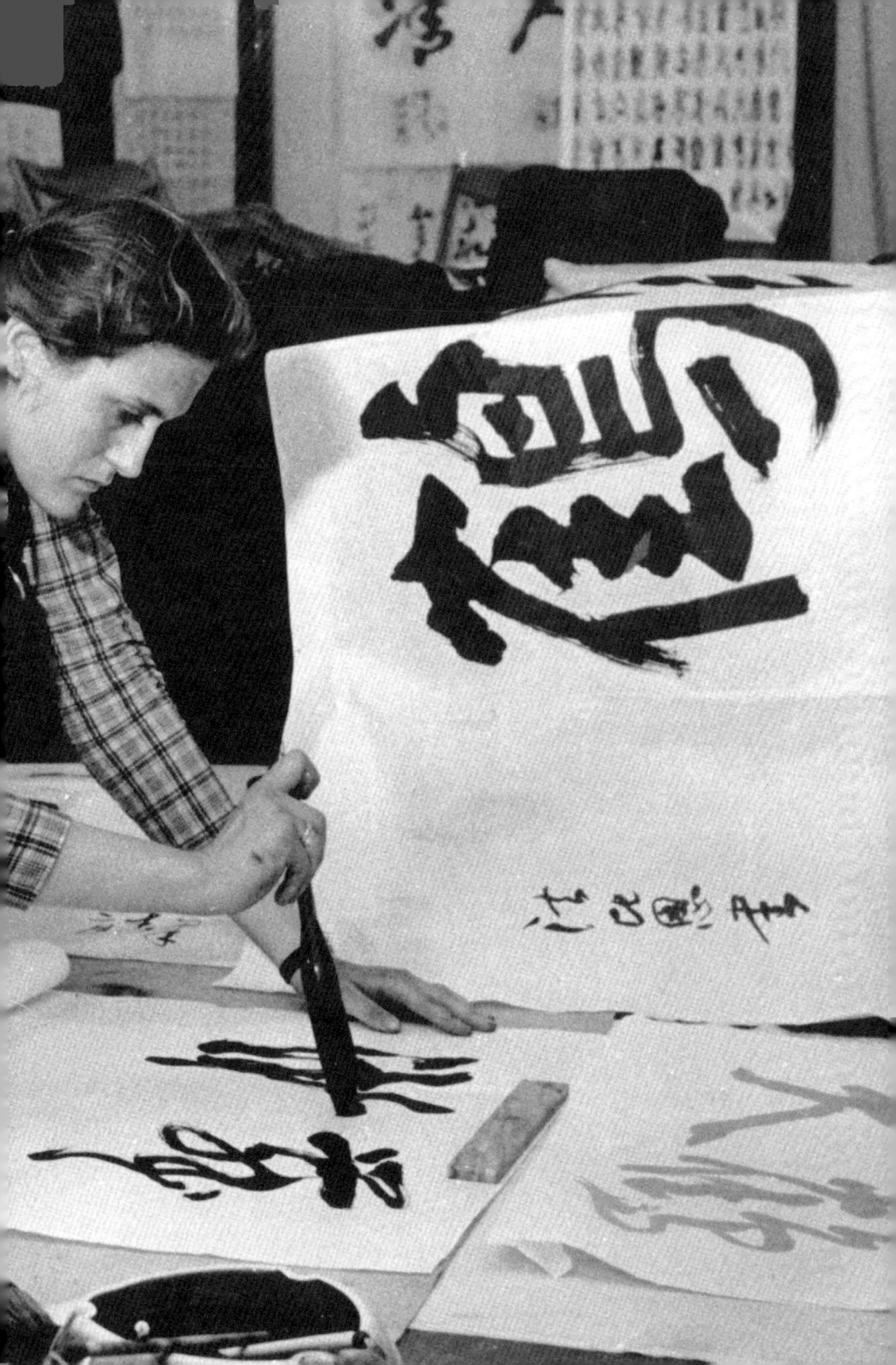

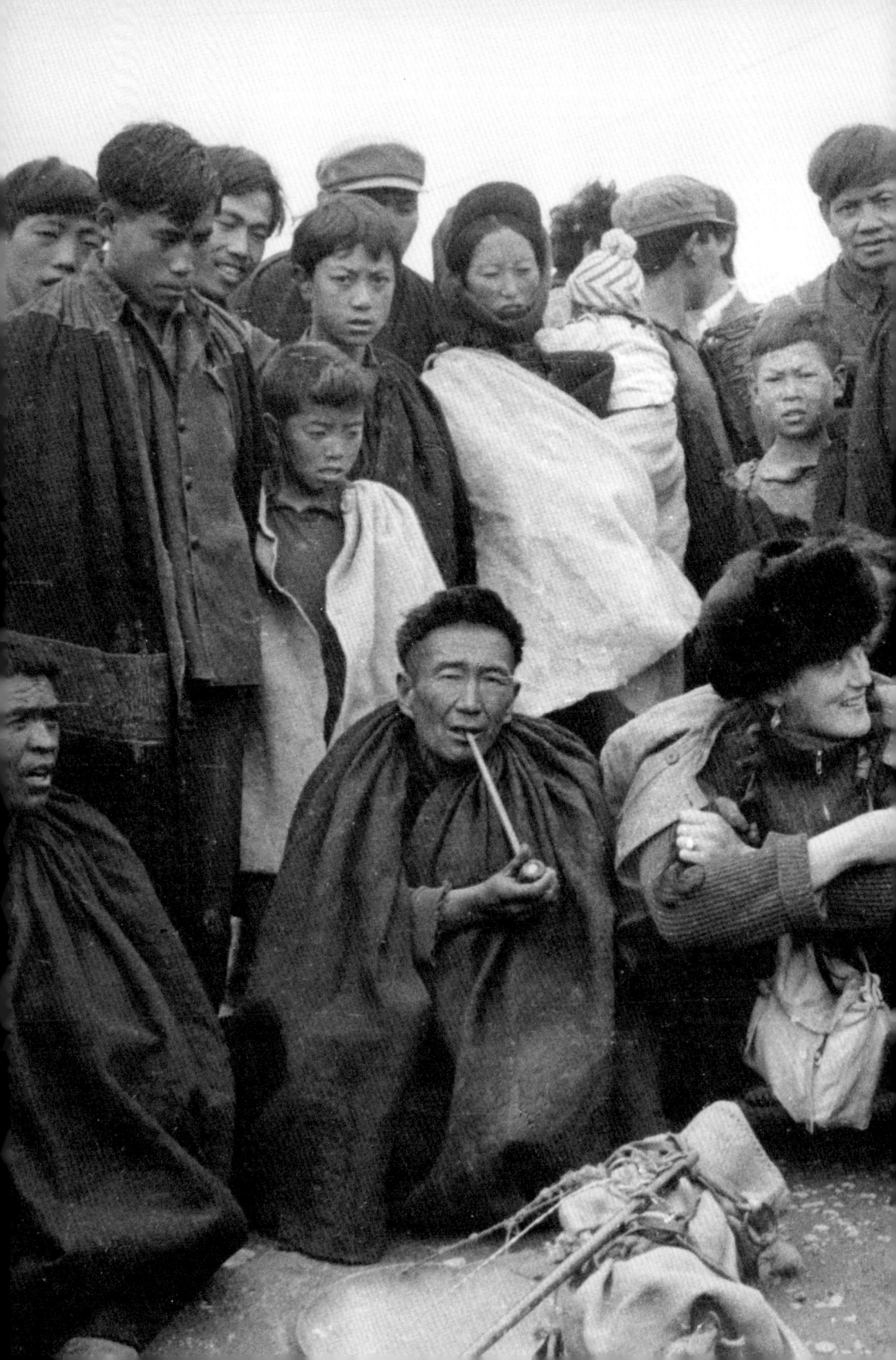

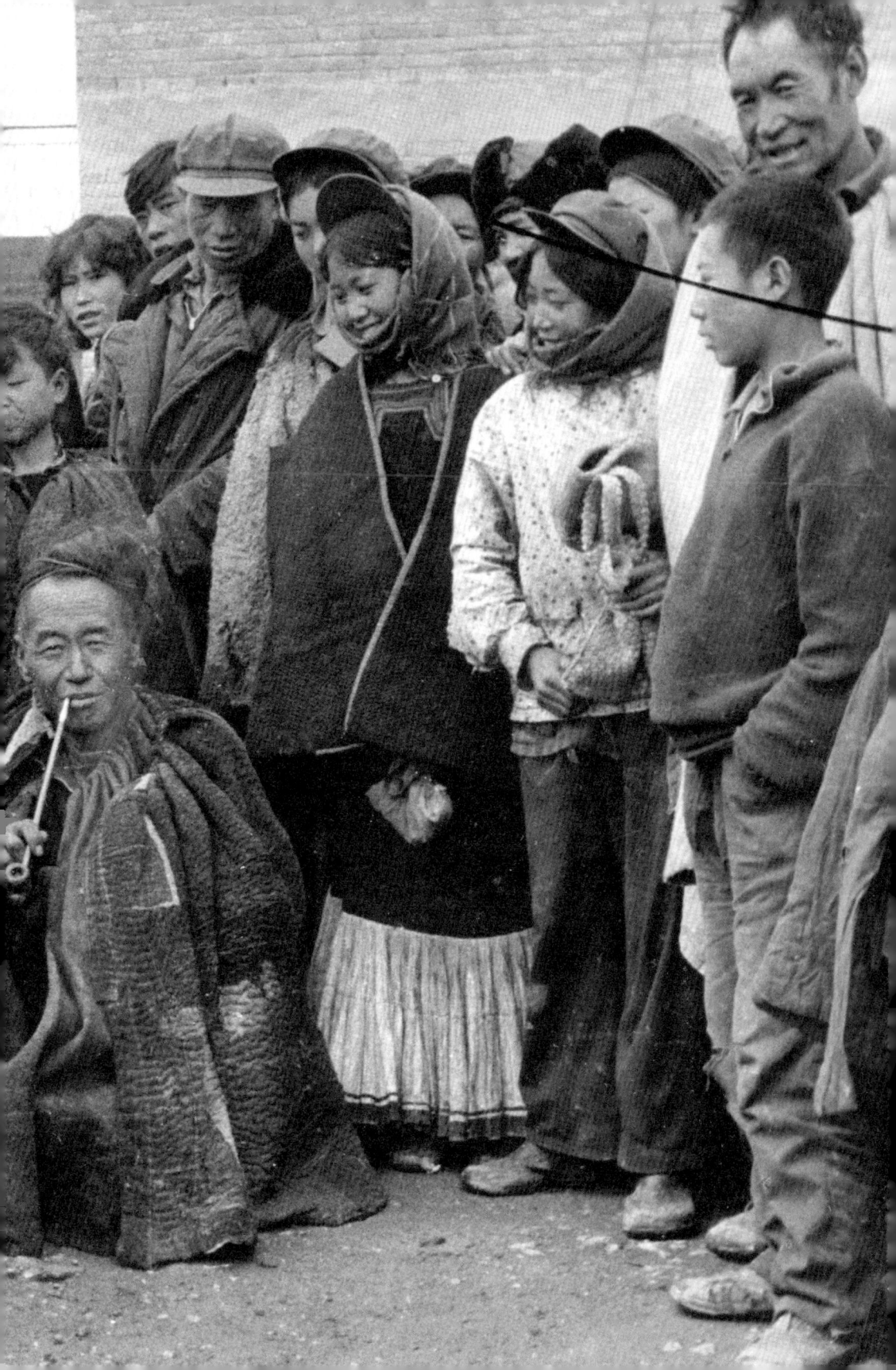

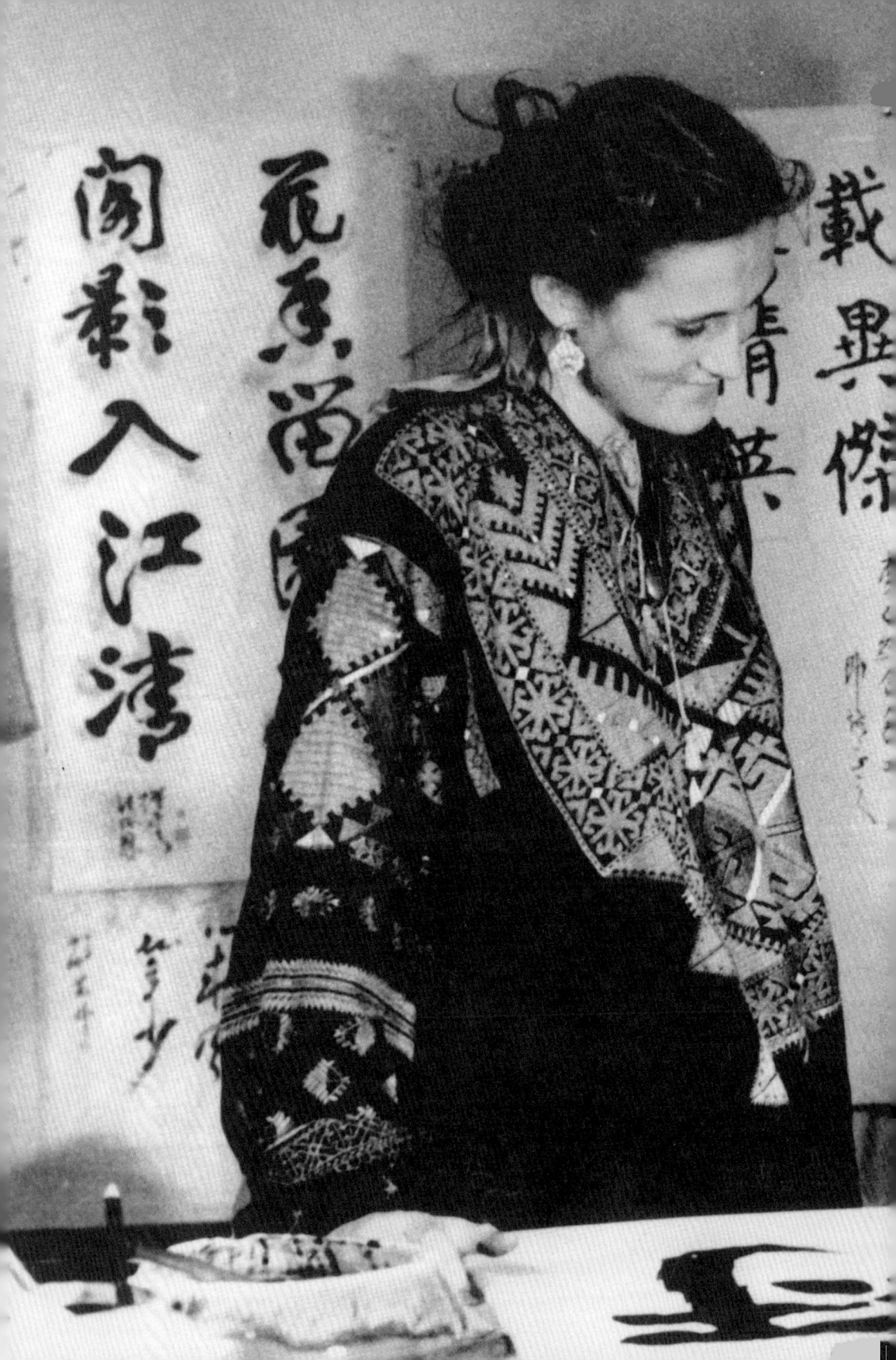

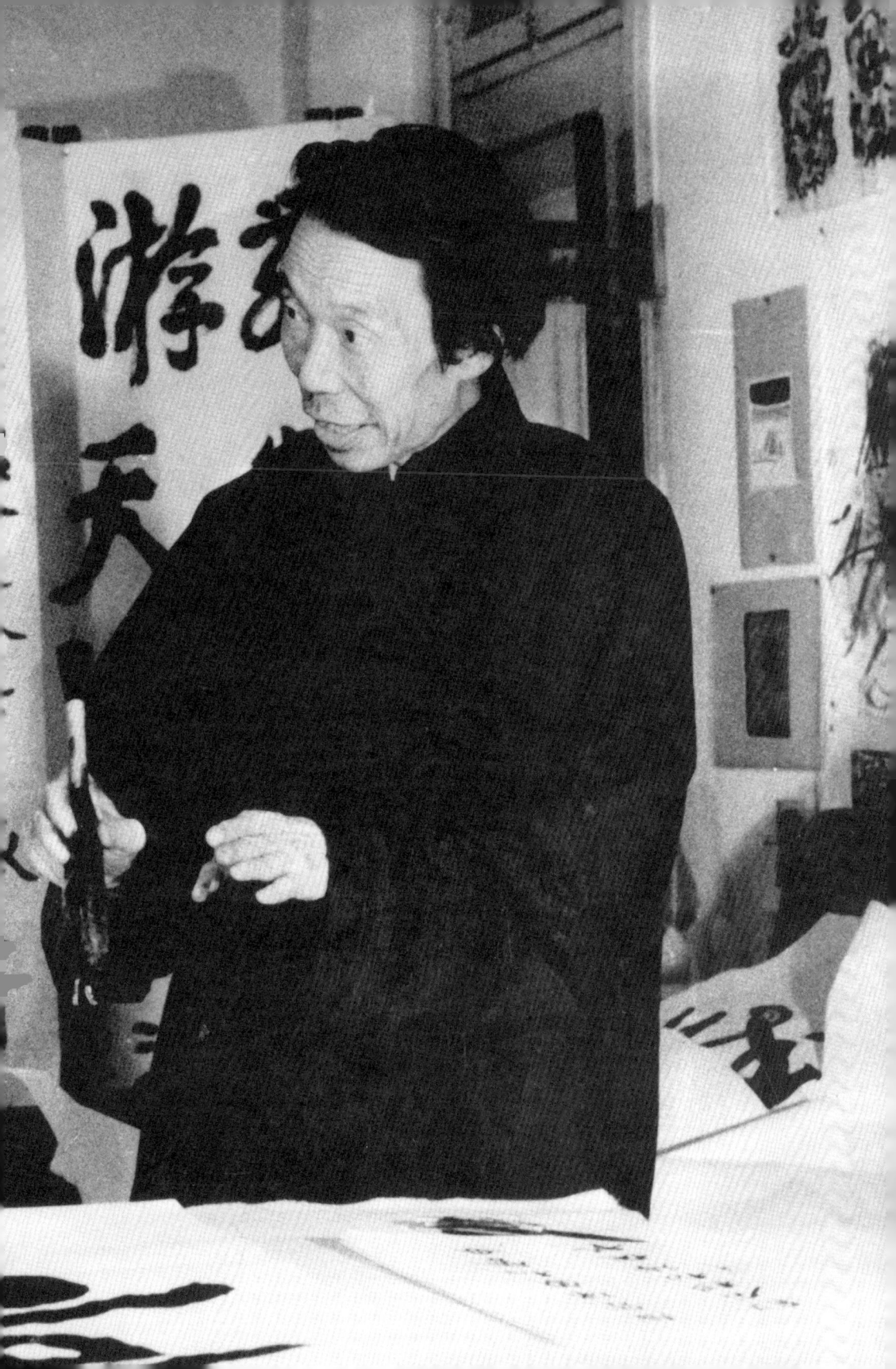

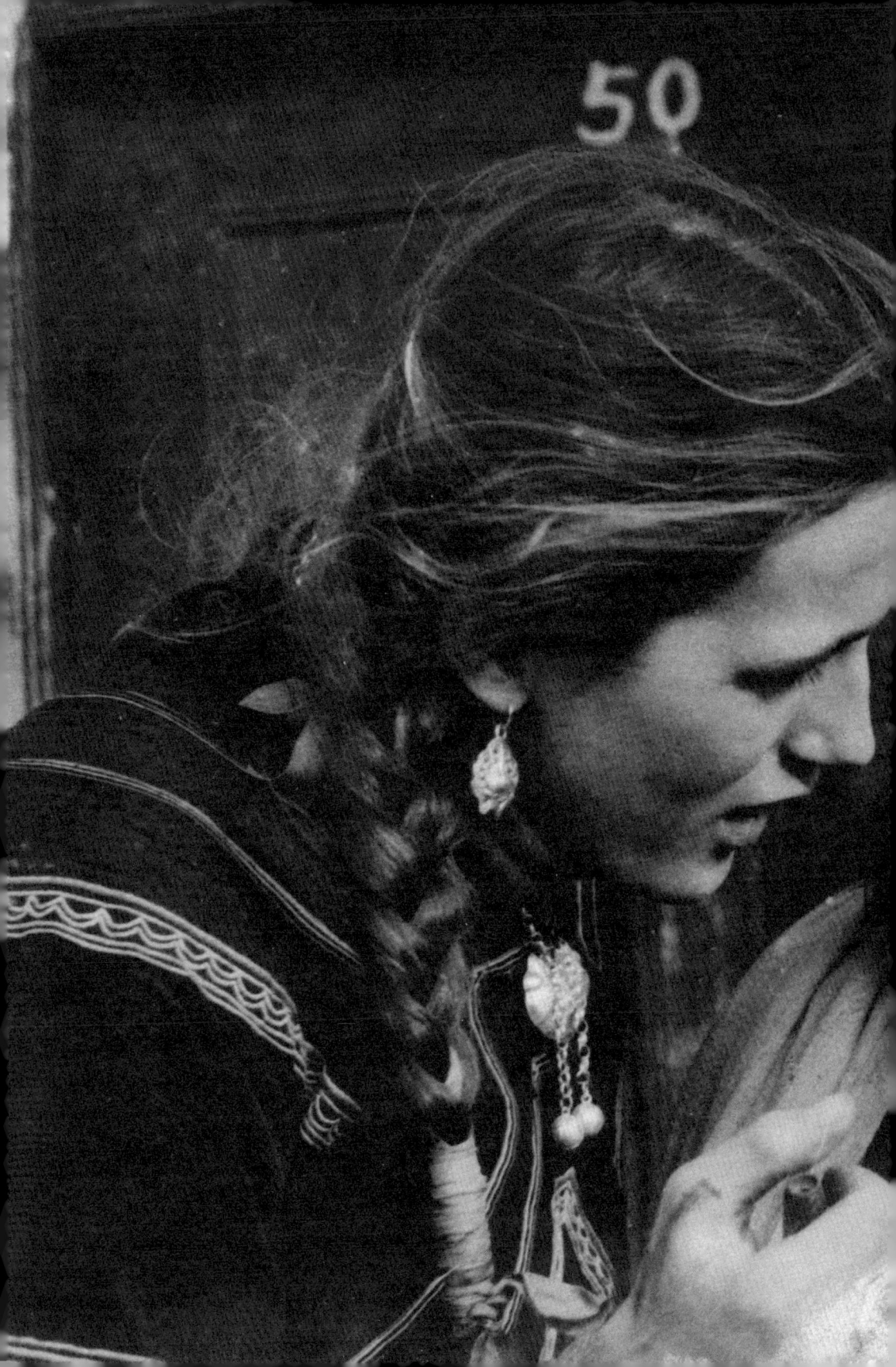

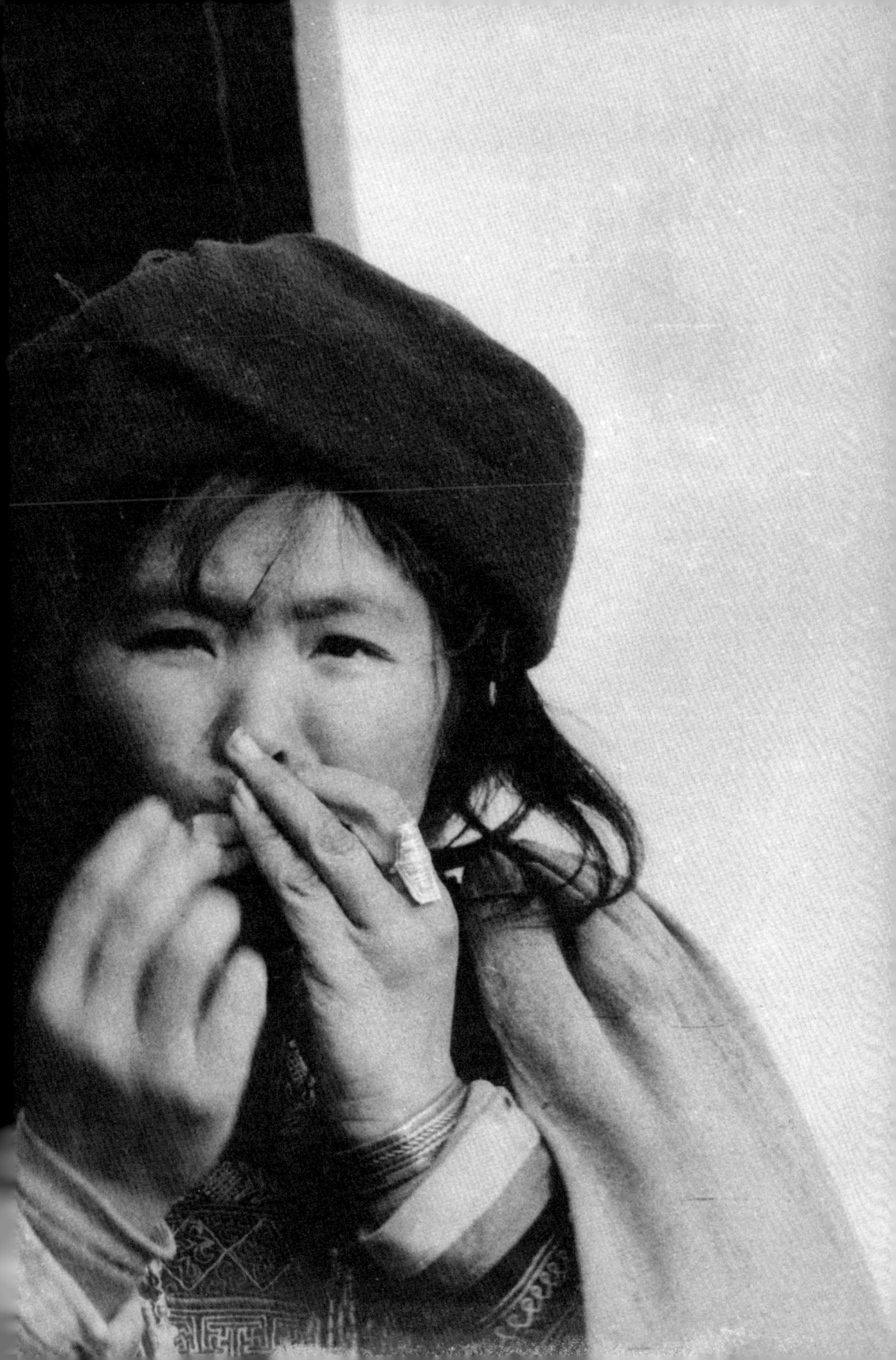

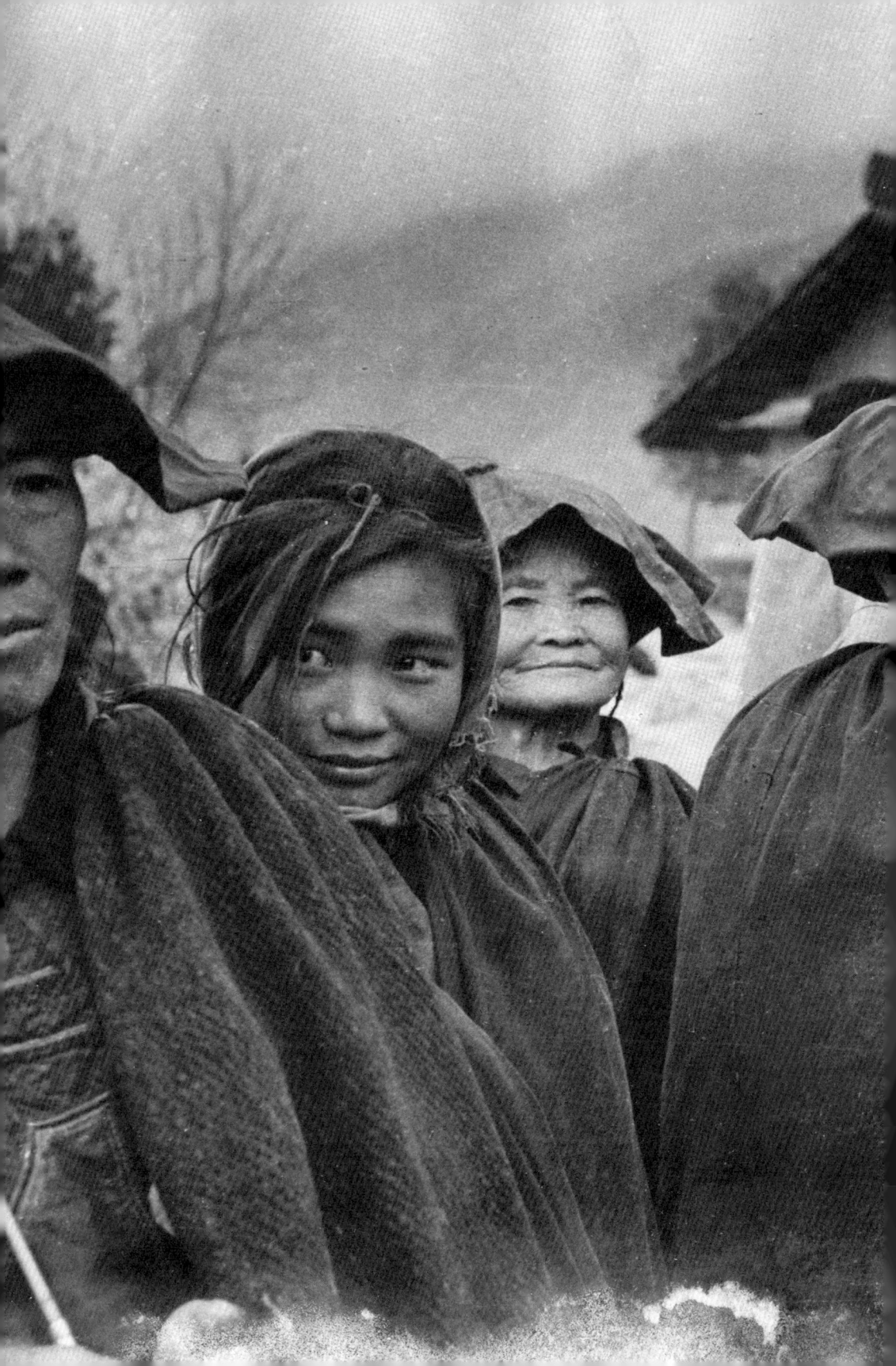

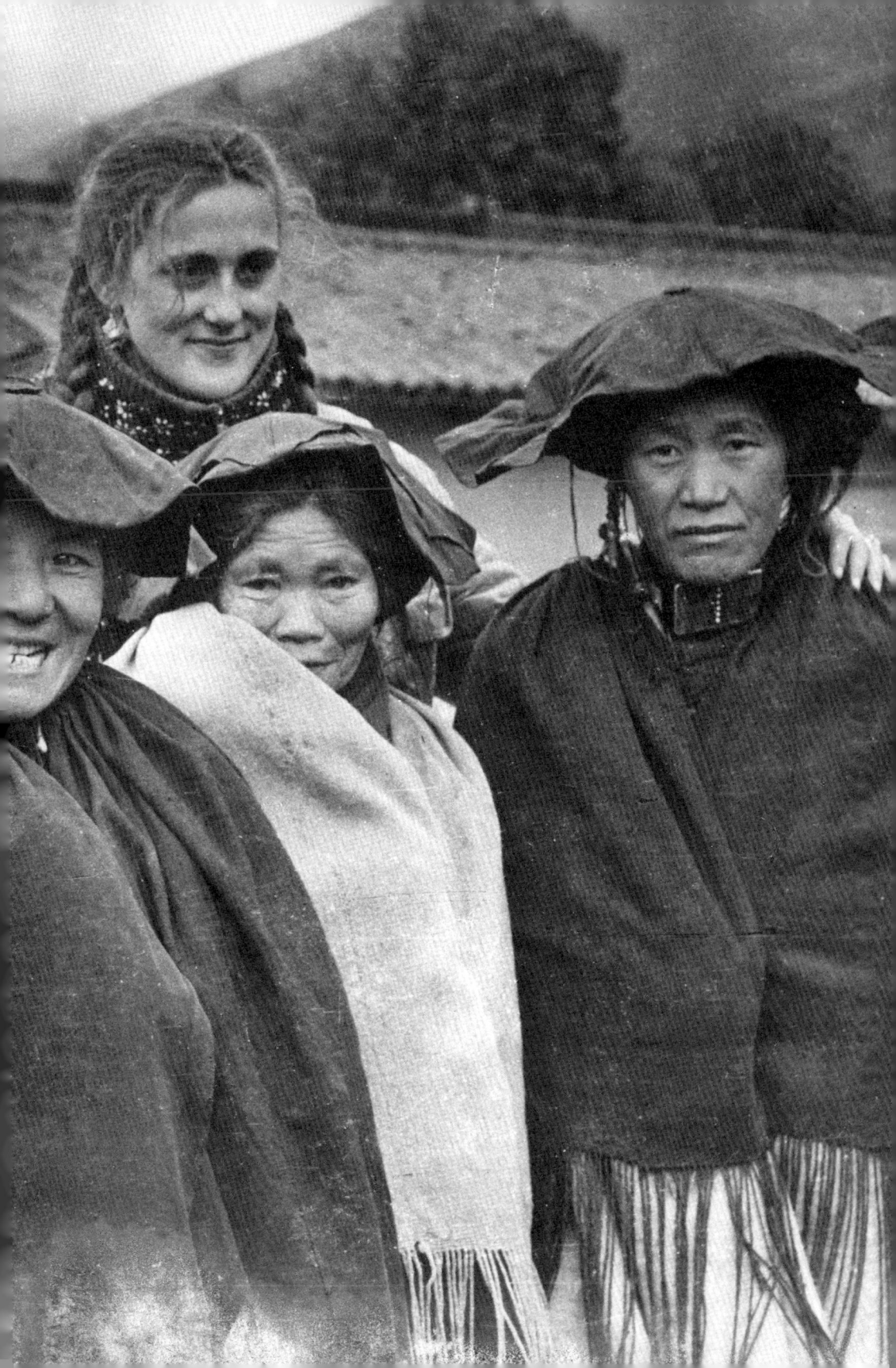

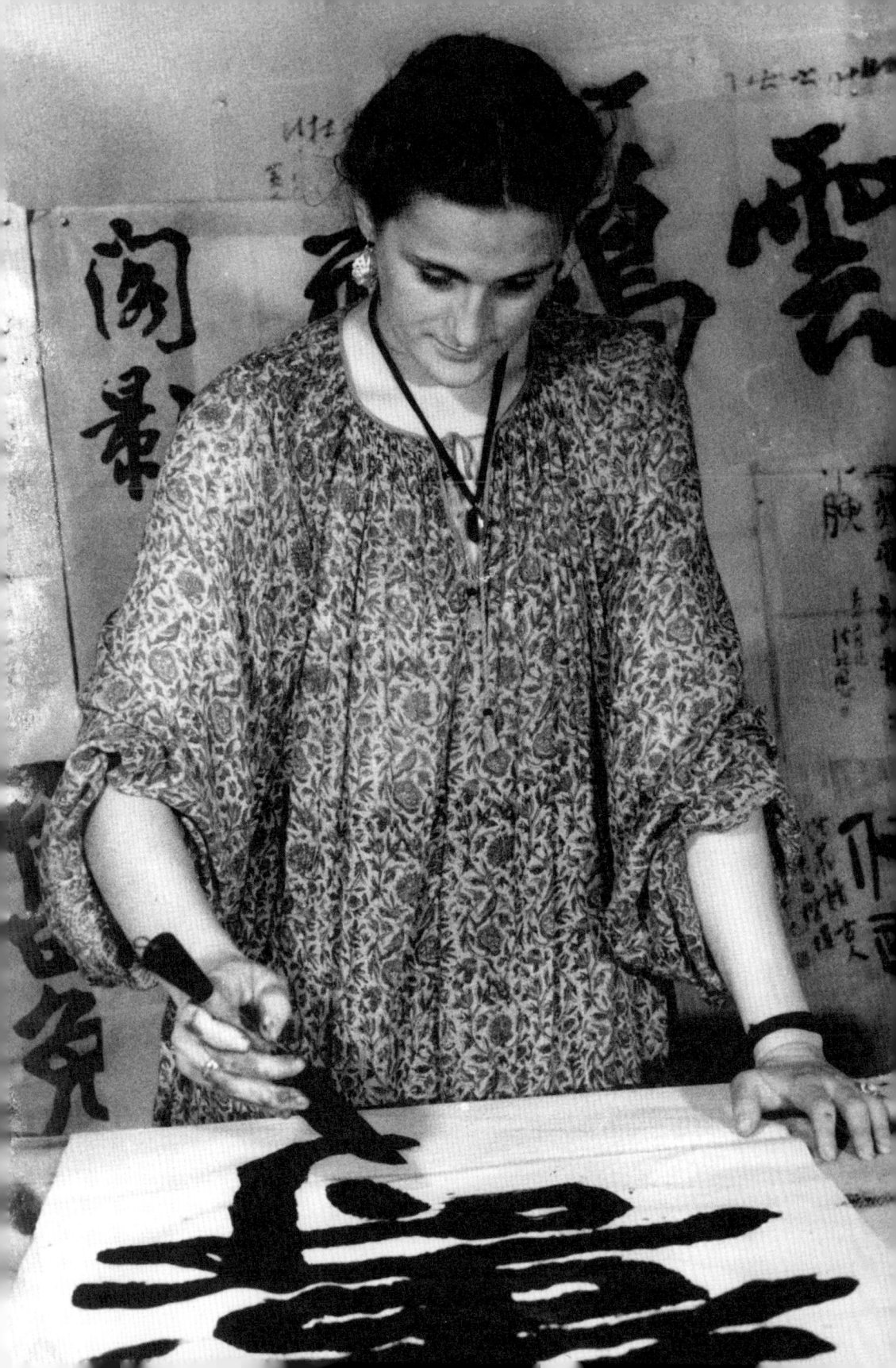

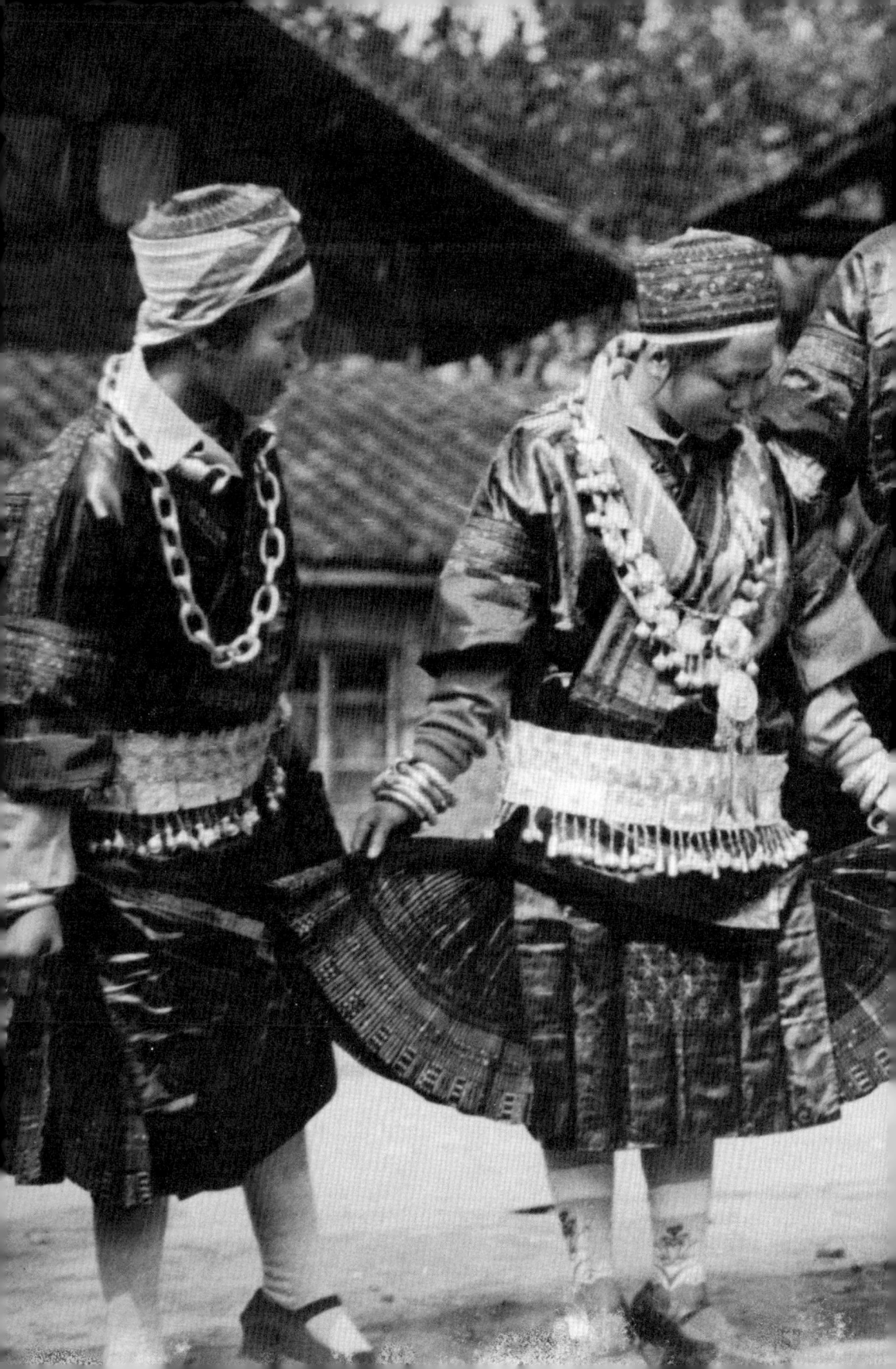

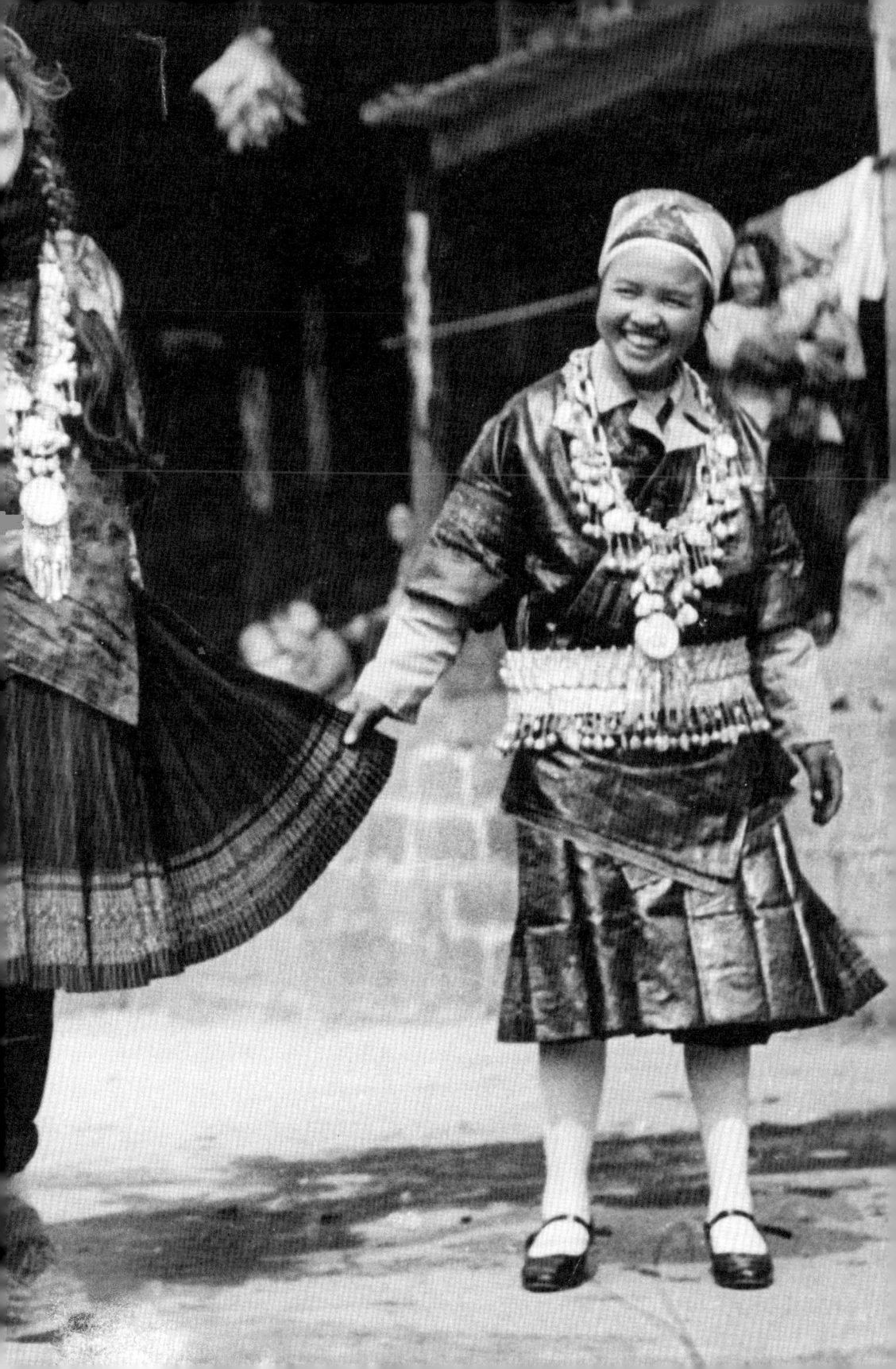

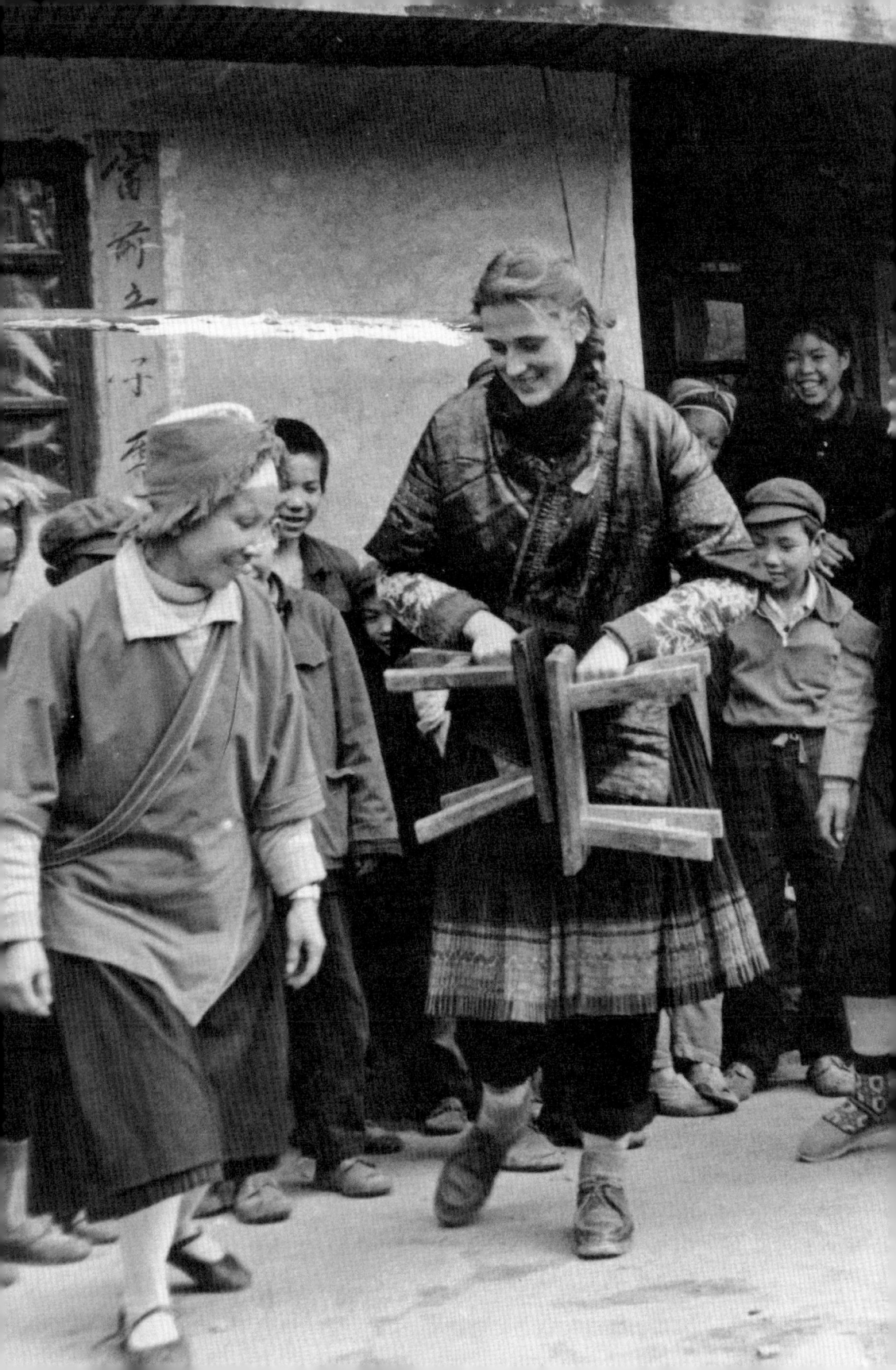

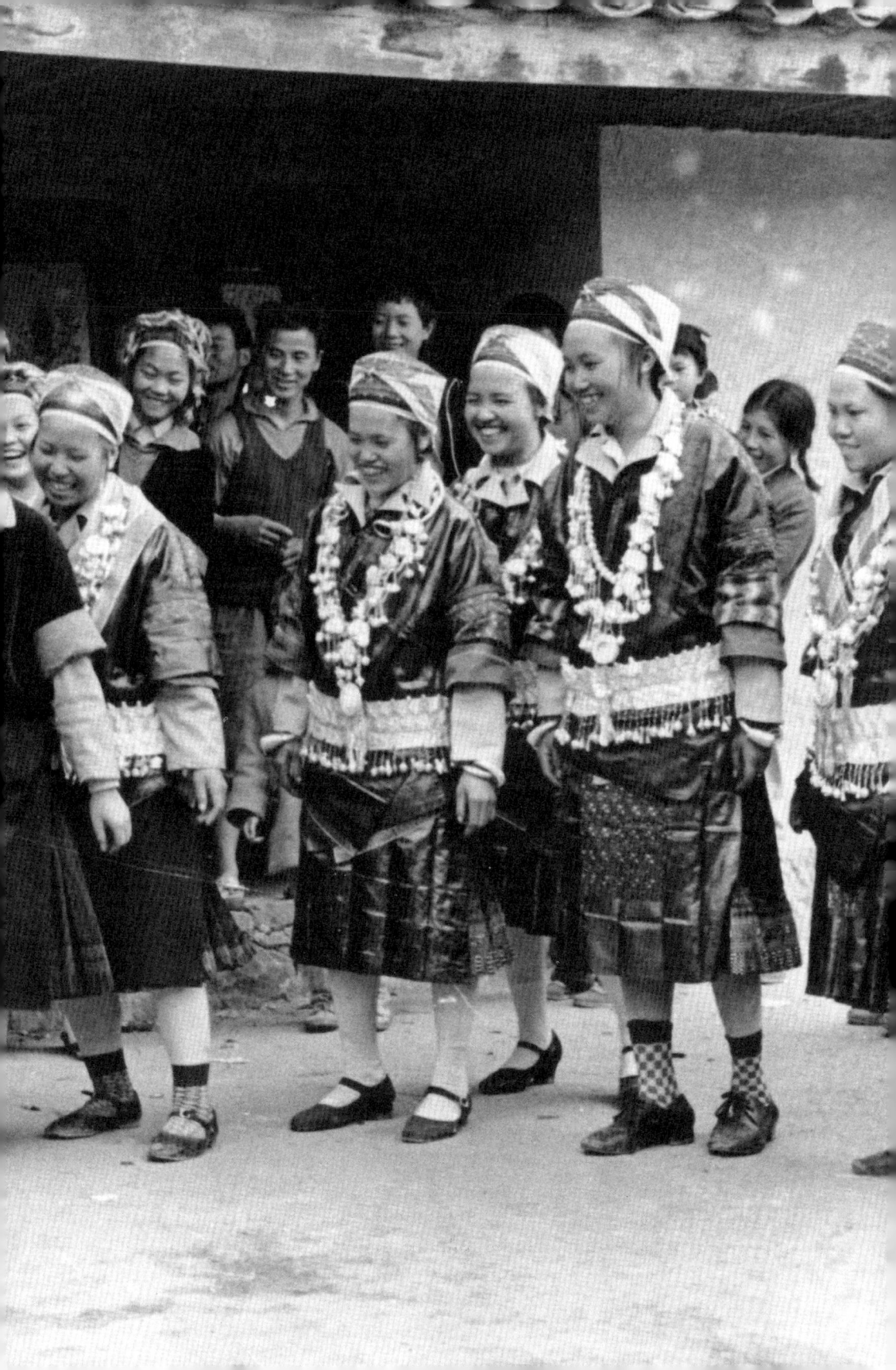

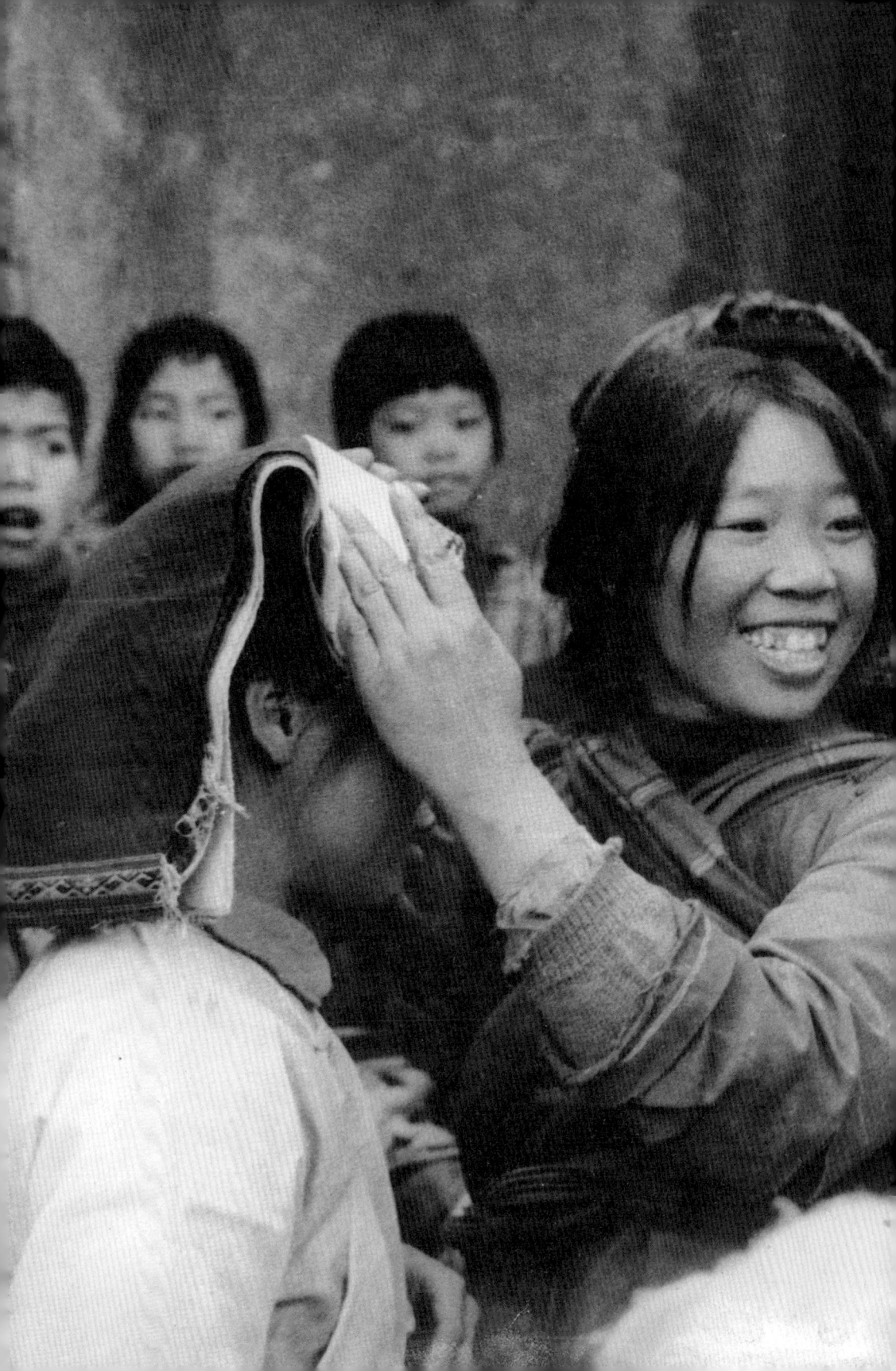

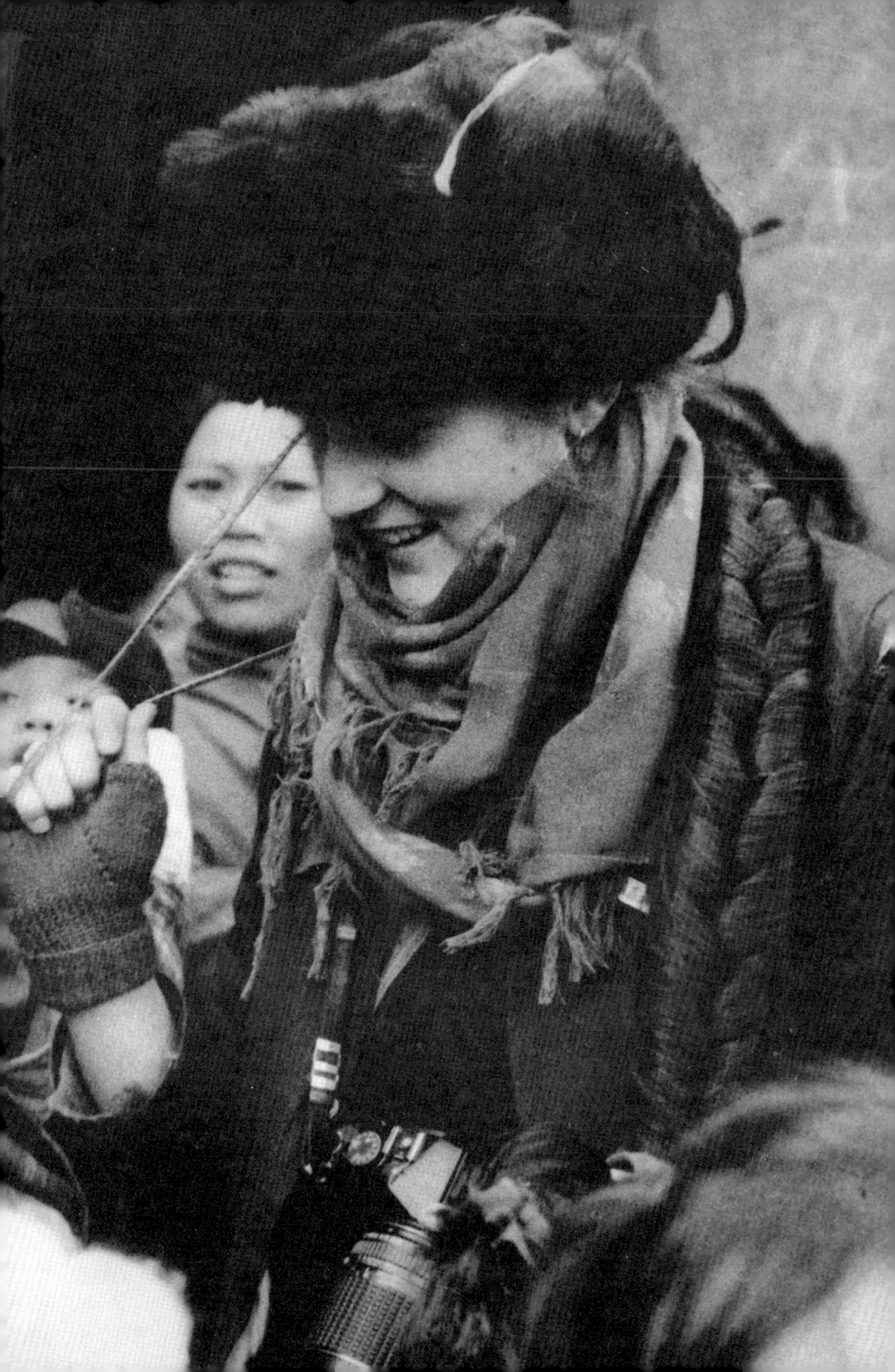

204-207
  Learning the "stool dance"
  with Miao women in the
  village of Huangping
  during the local festival.

208 Meeting a group of young
  Buyi girls on a study trip to
  Guizhou province in 1985.
  They wear a huge braid
  made of their own hair
  along with their mother's as
  a kind of headdress on top
  of their heads.

211 In the company of a young
  Yi who often helped me find
  my way. My only meal was
  a bowl of pork soup and
  a crust of bread.

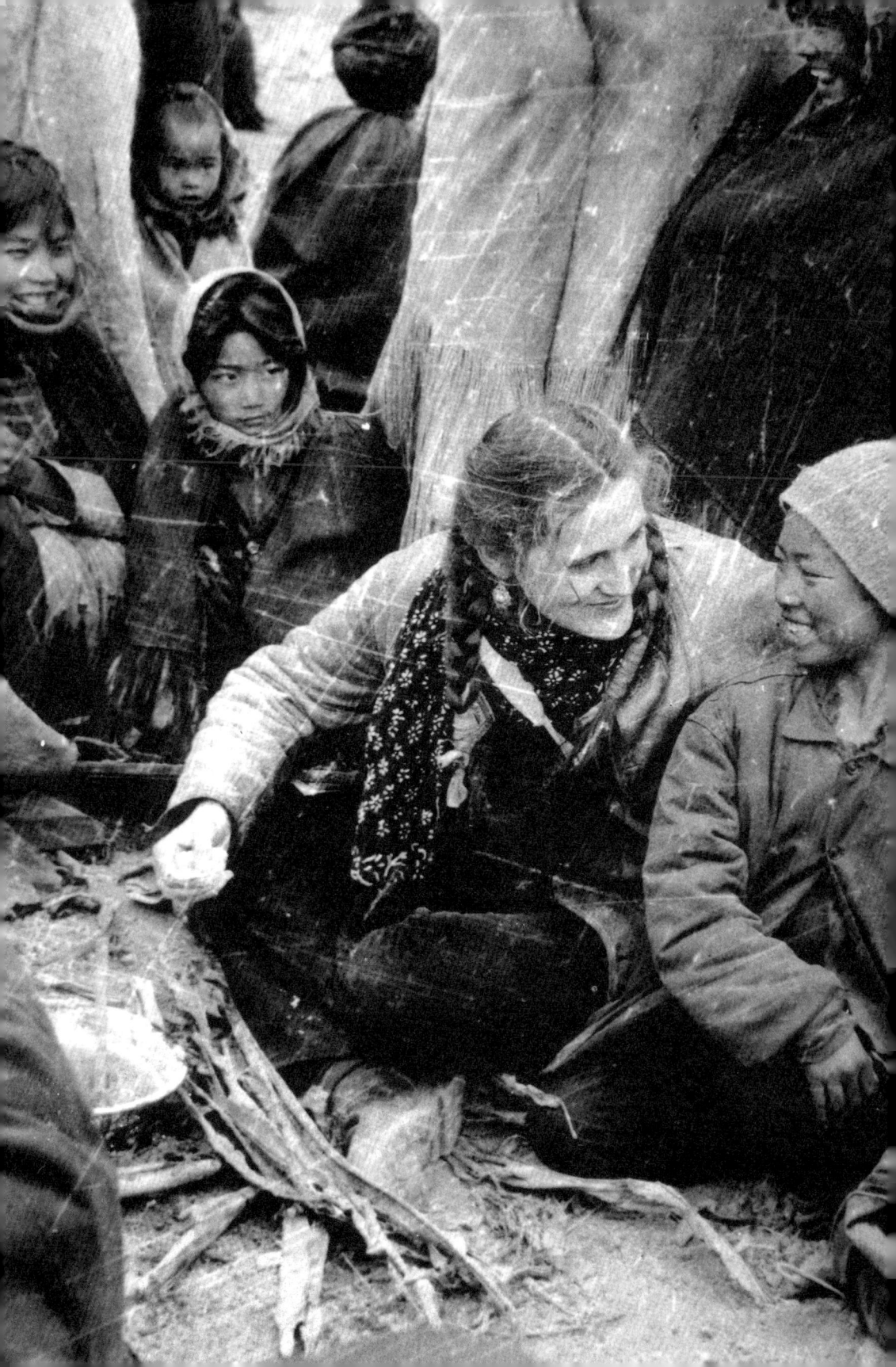

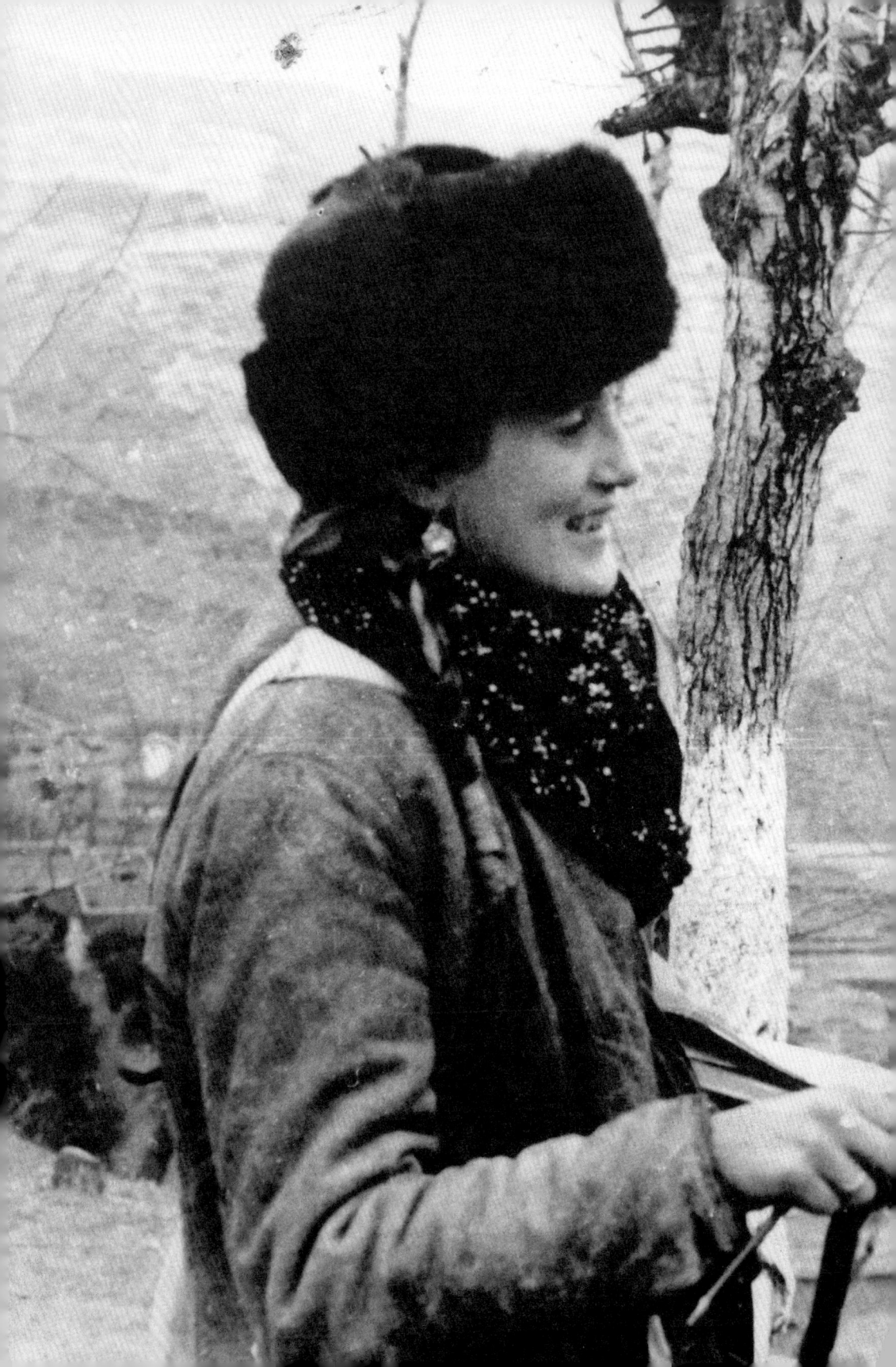

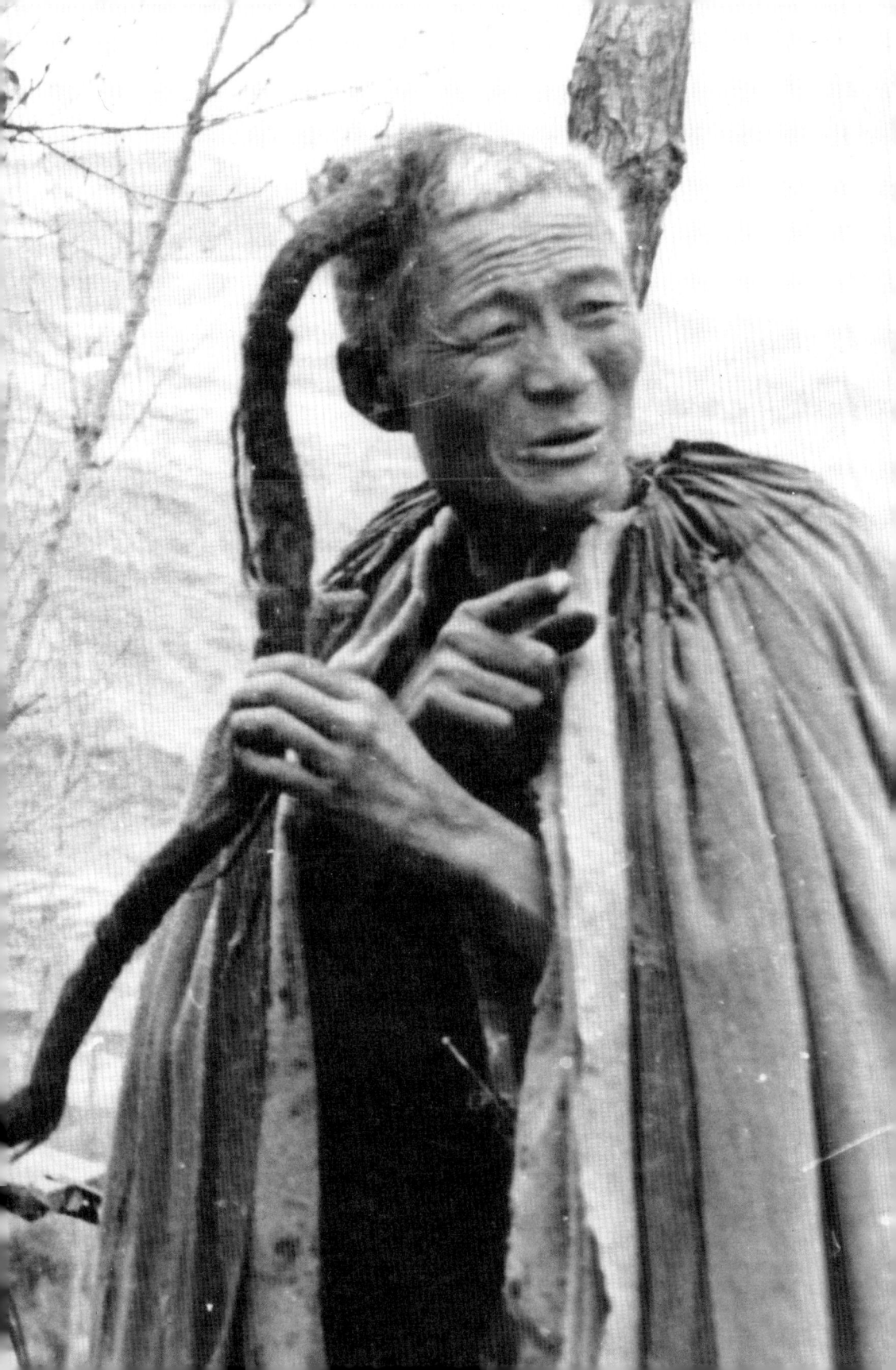

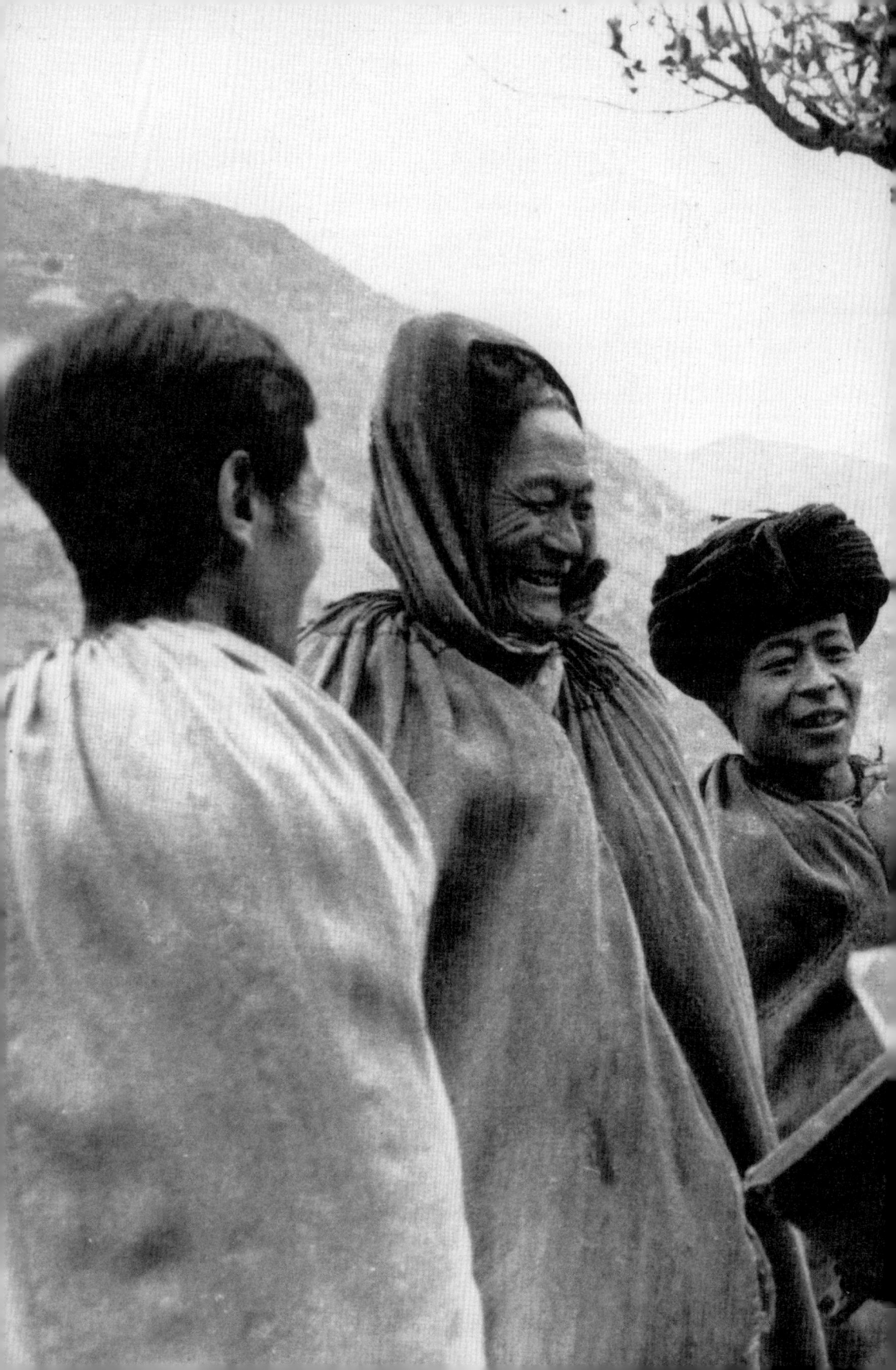

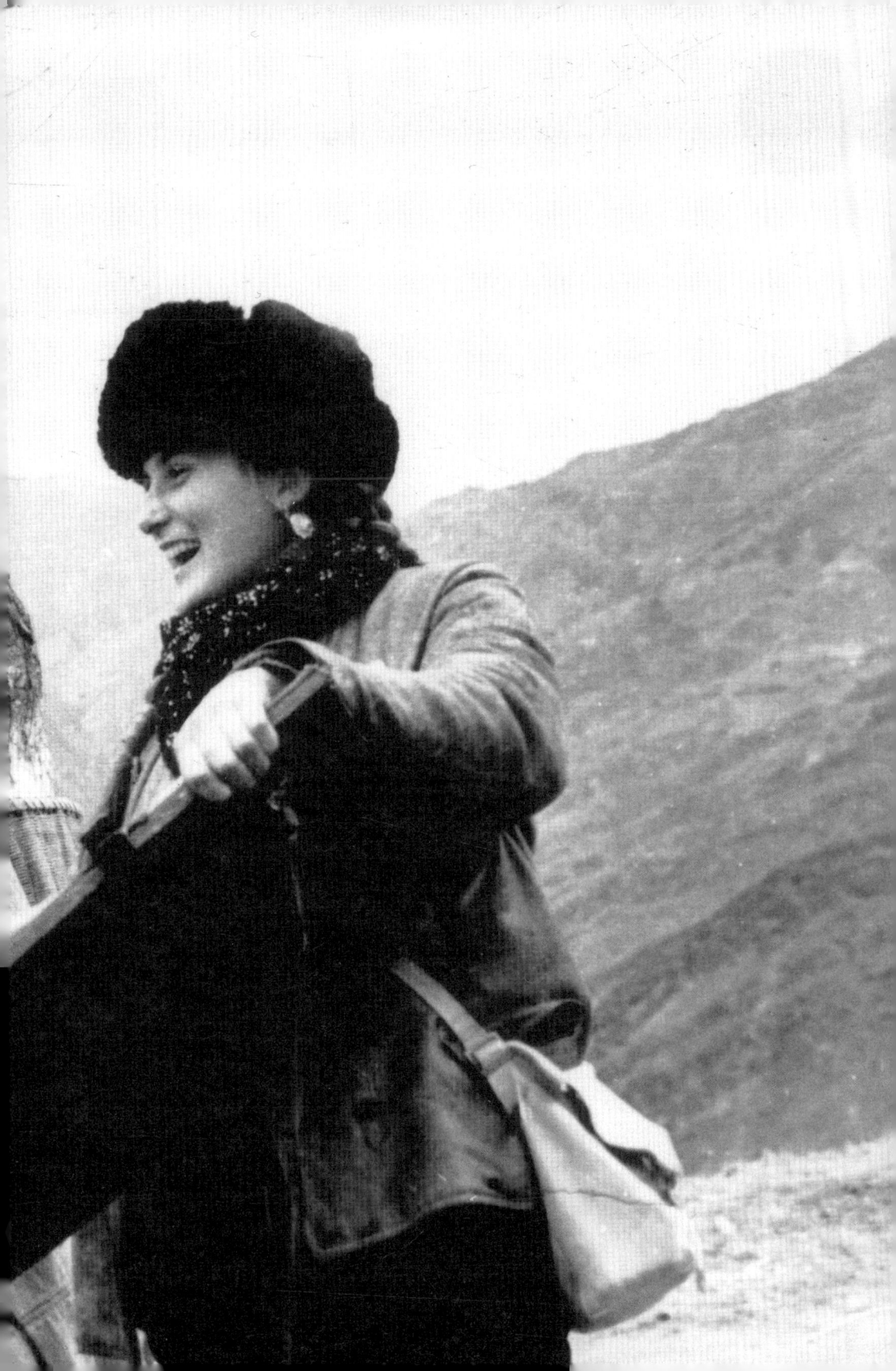

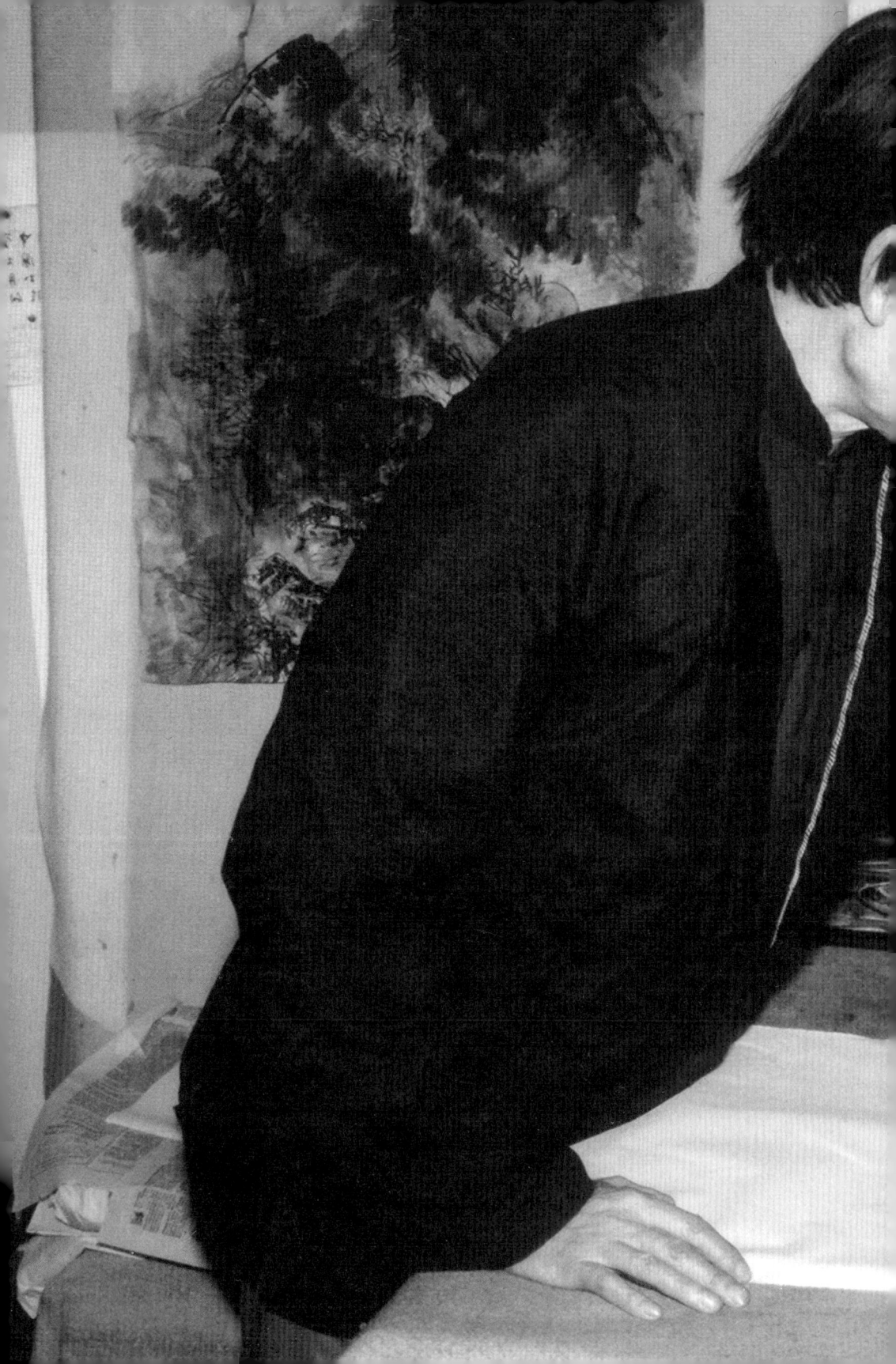

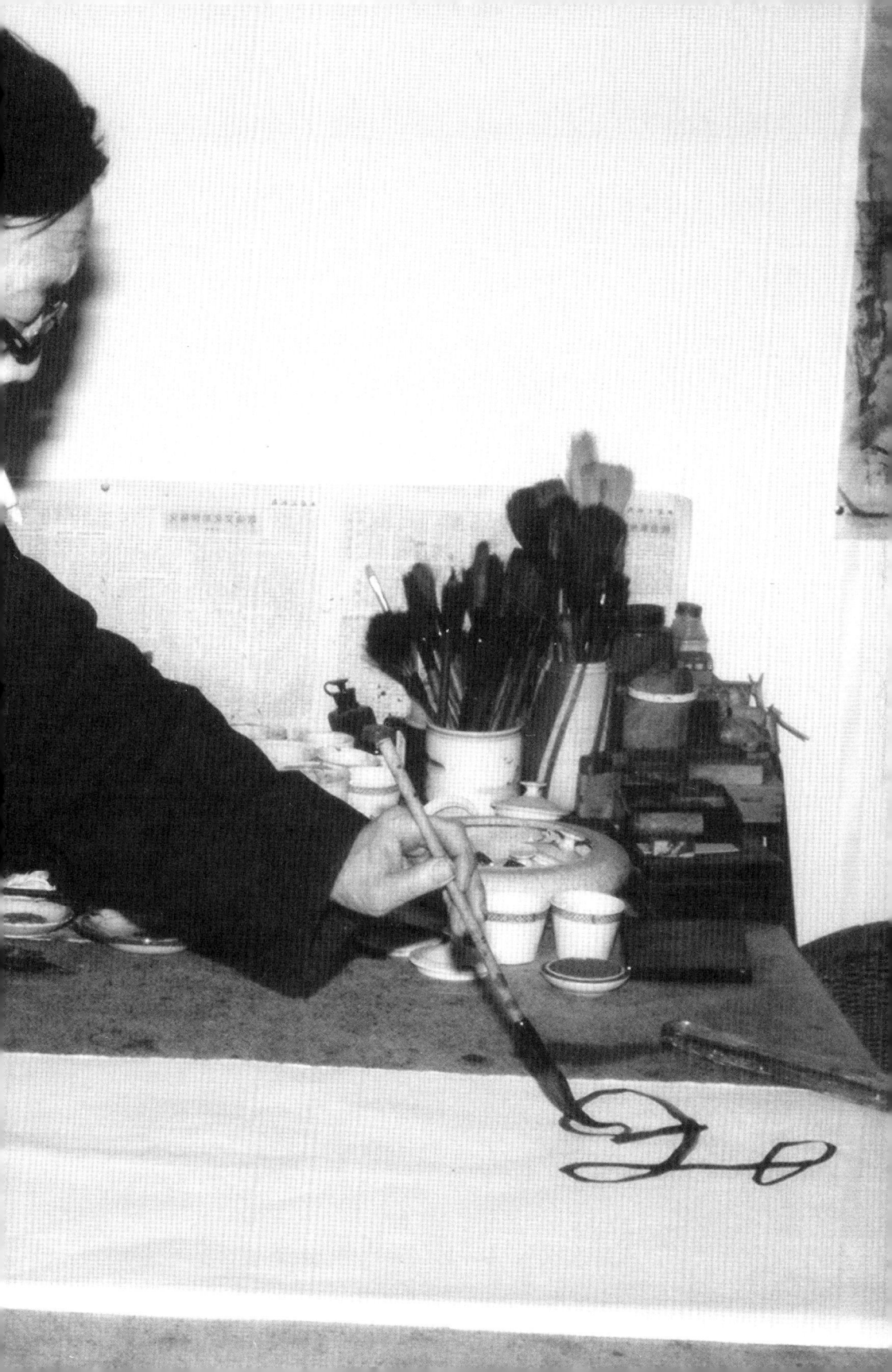

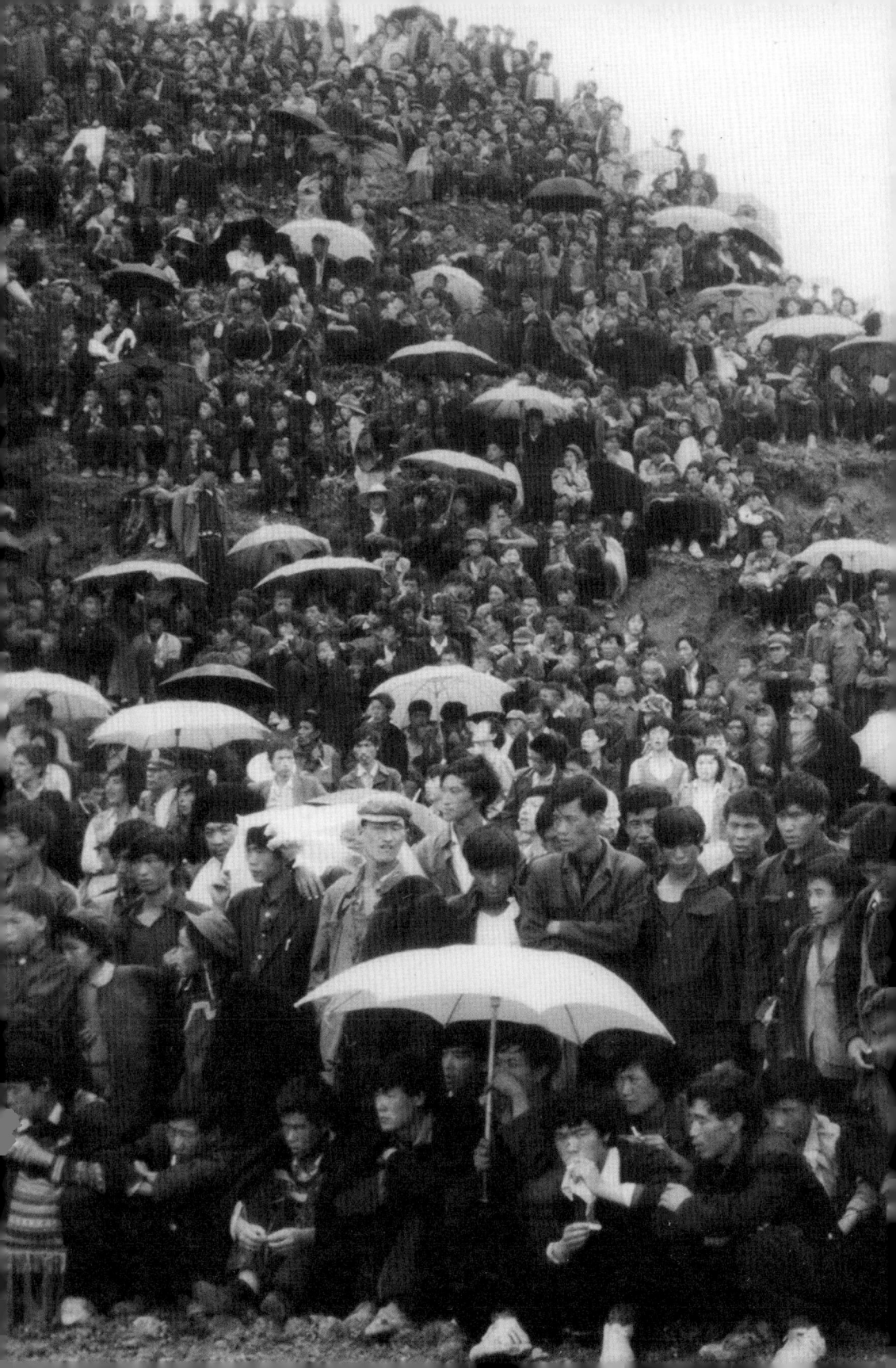

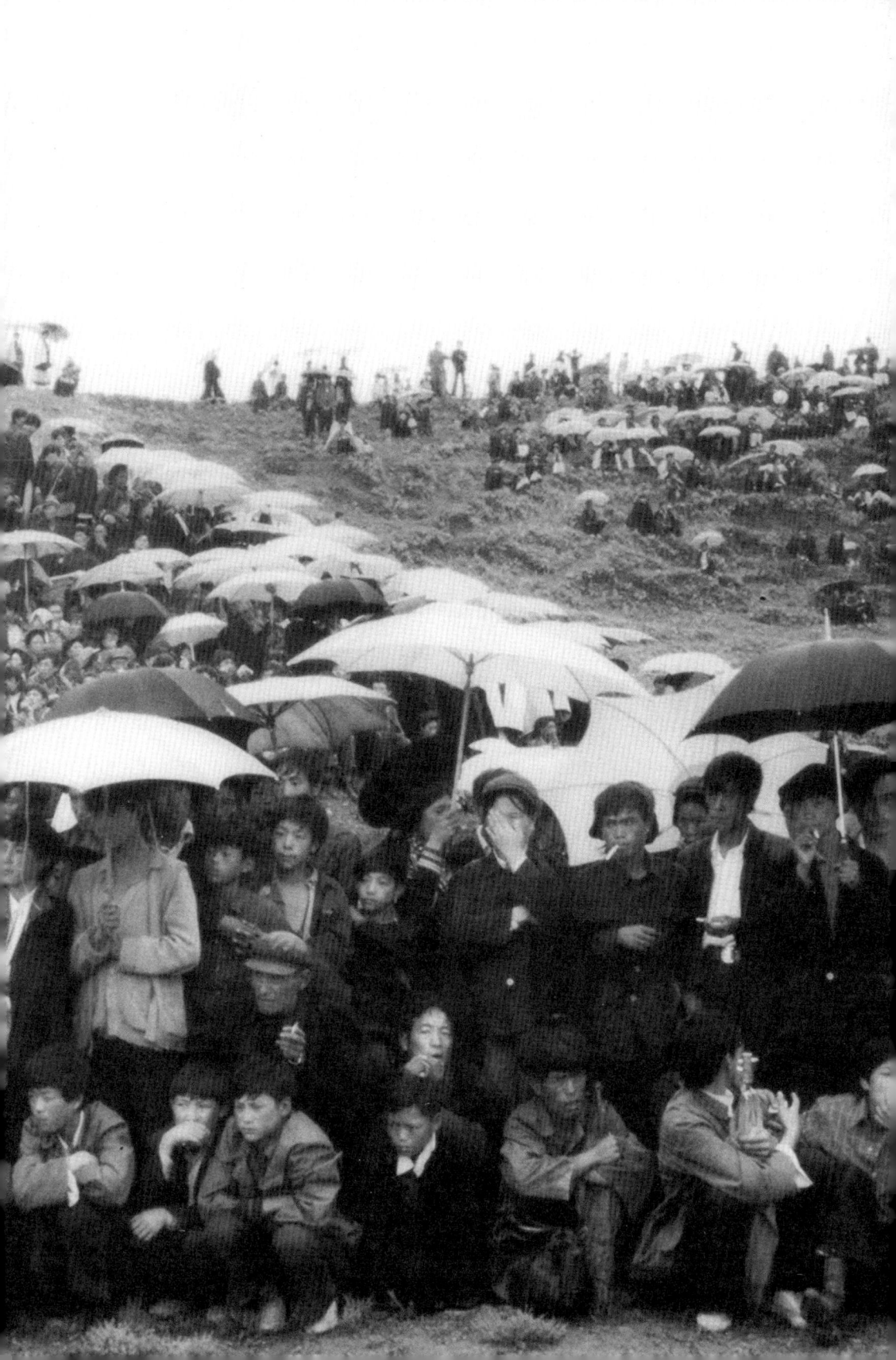

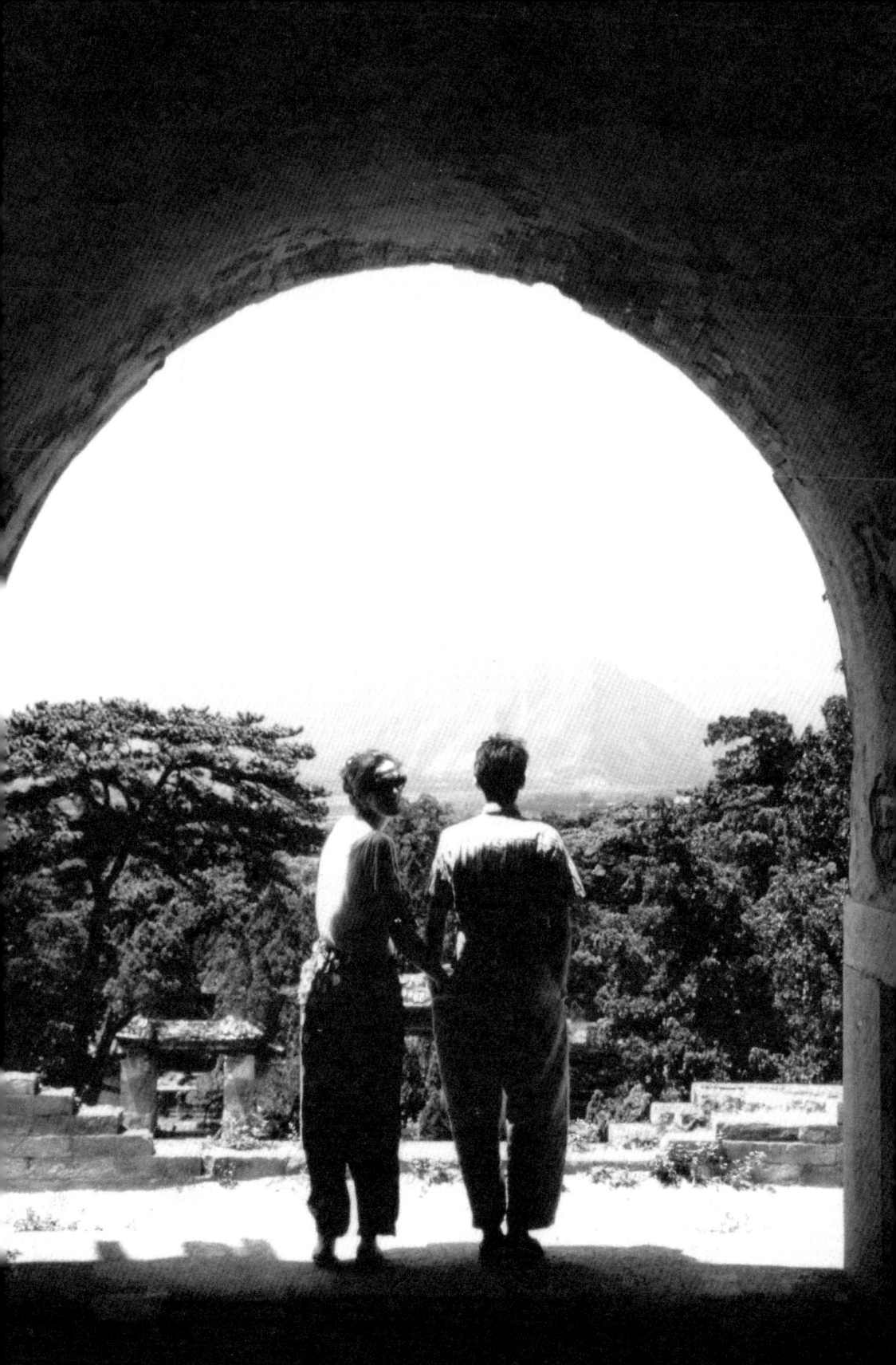

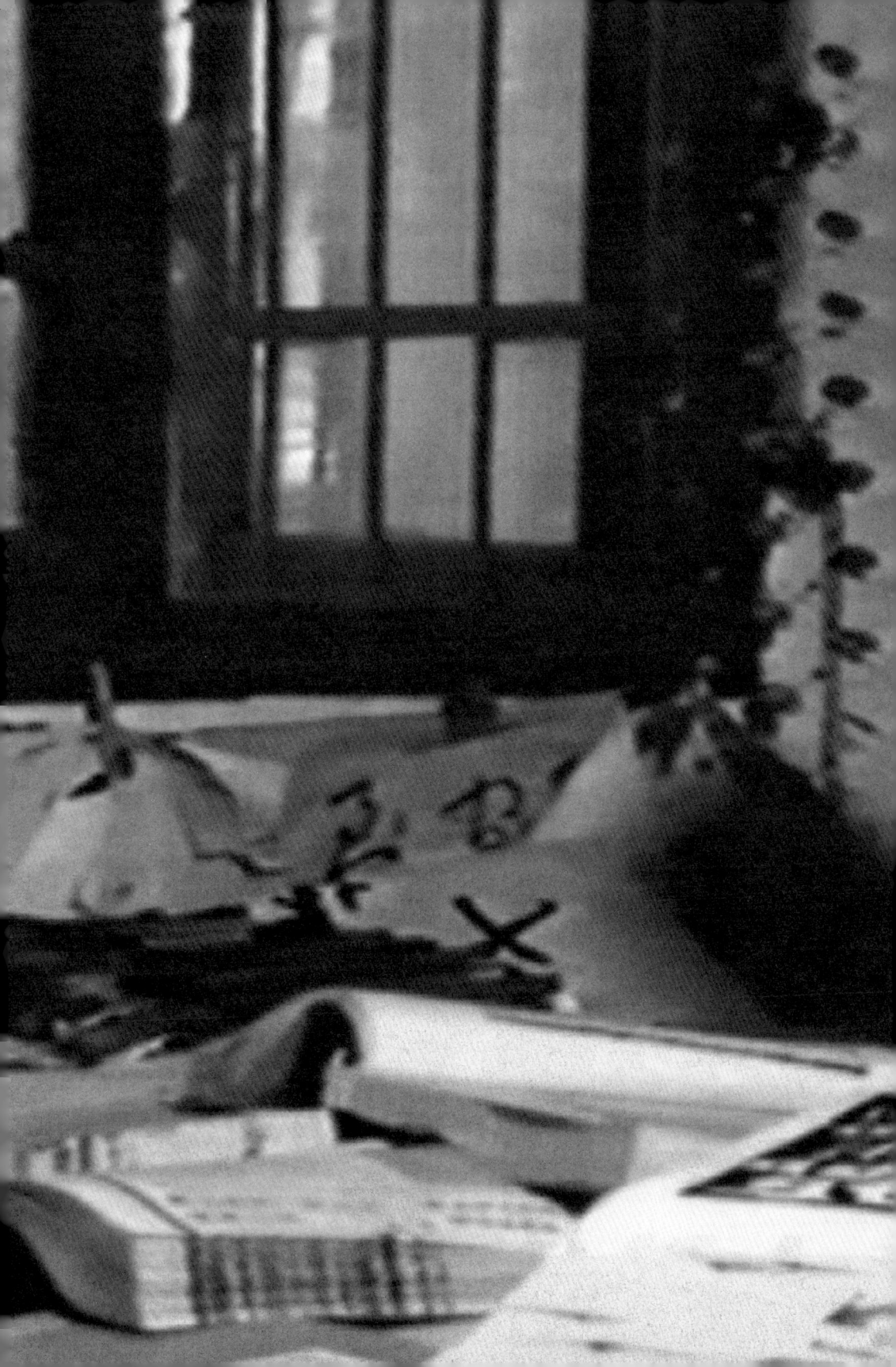

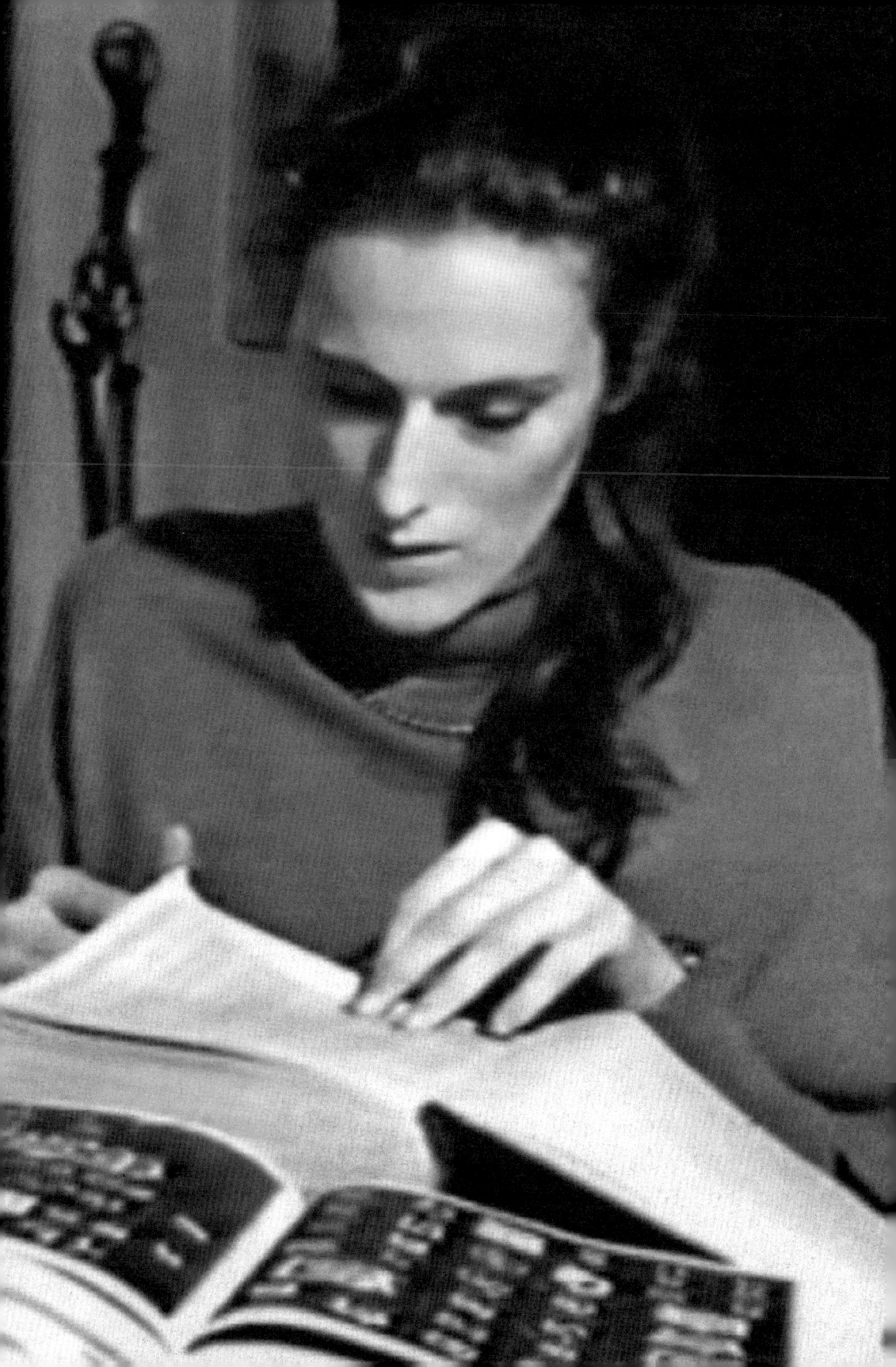

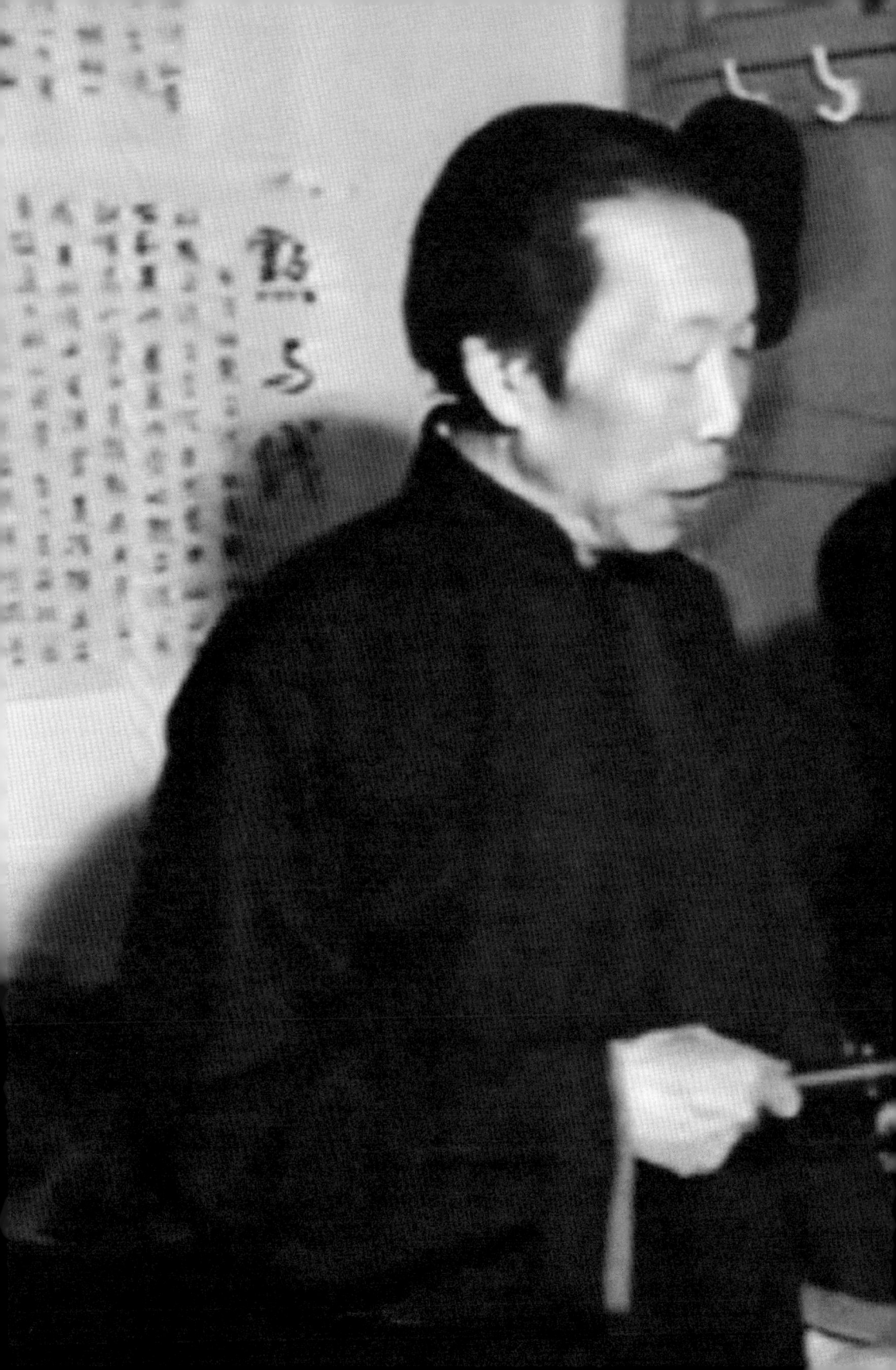

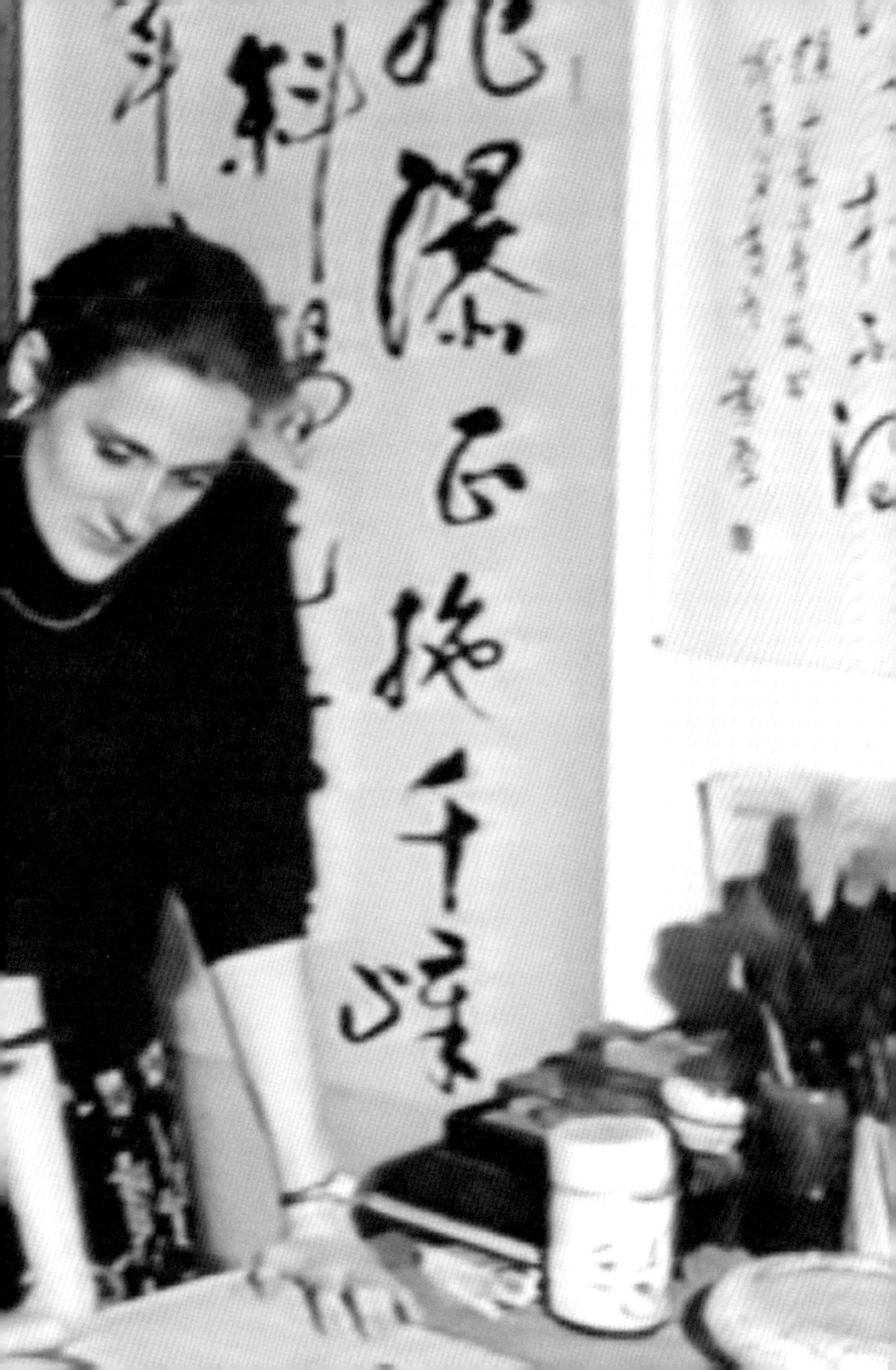

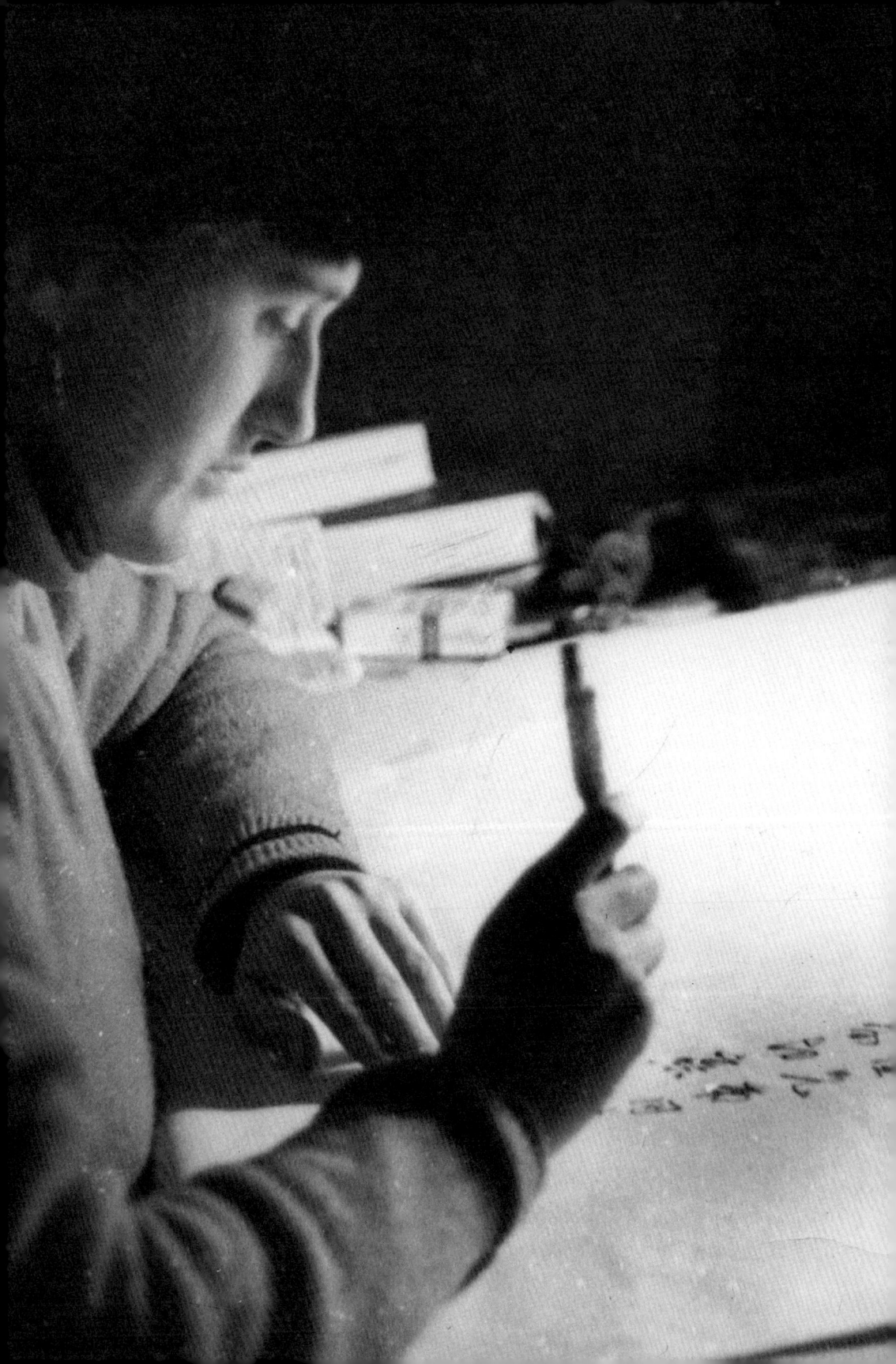

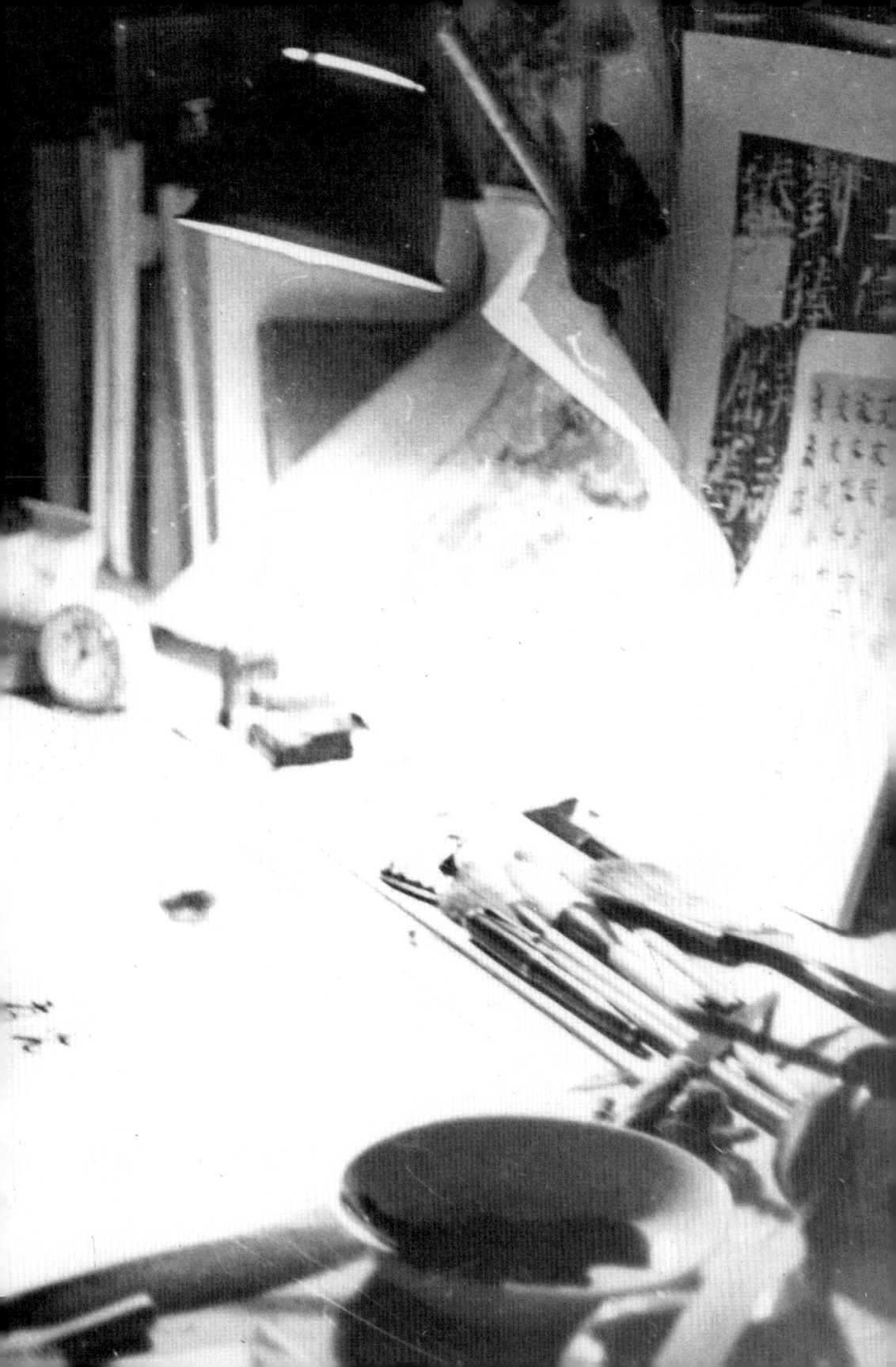

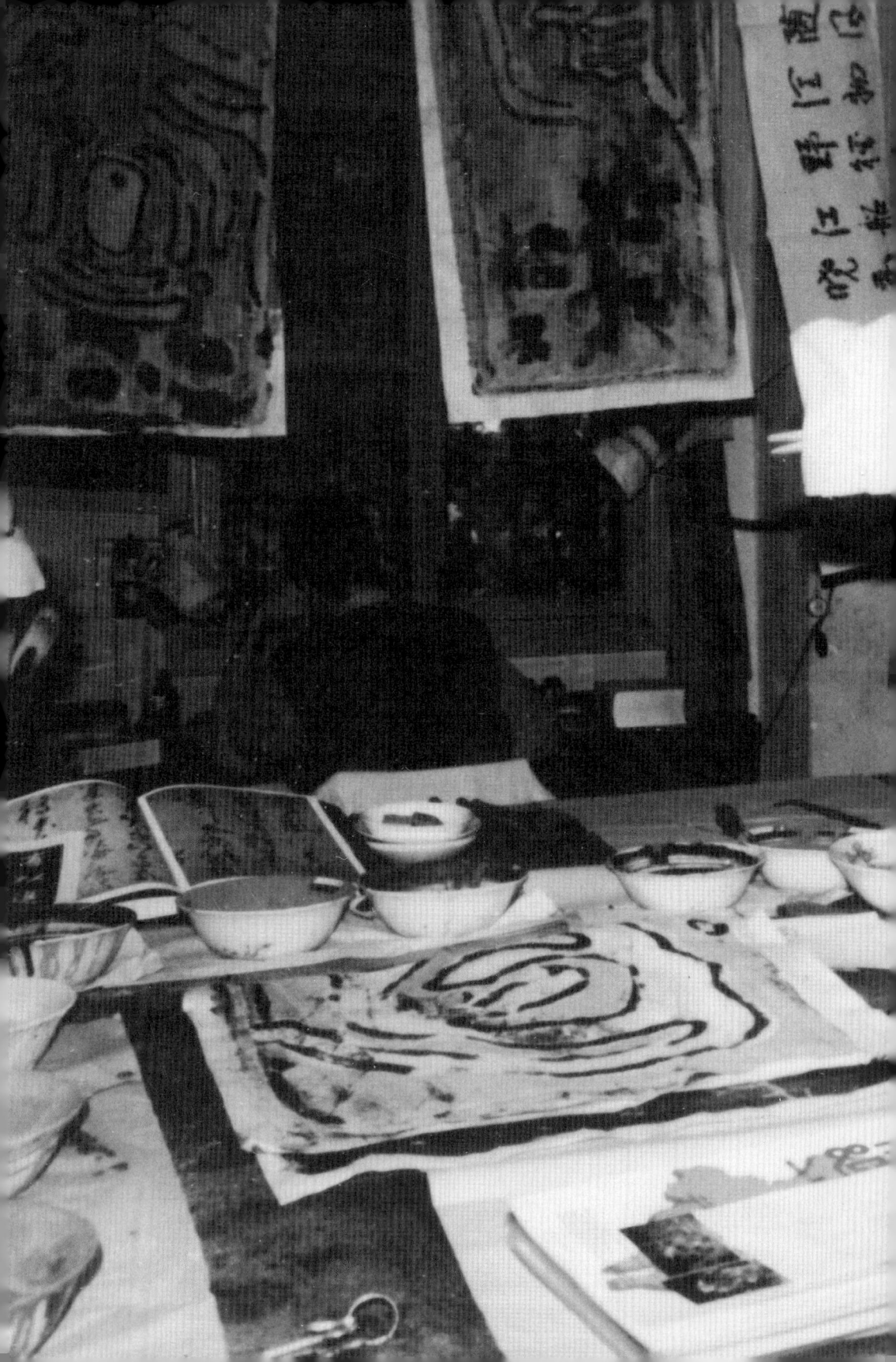

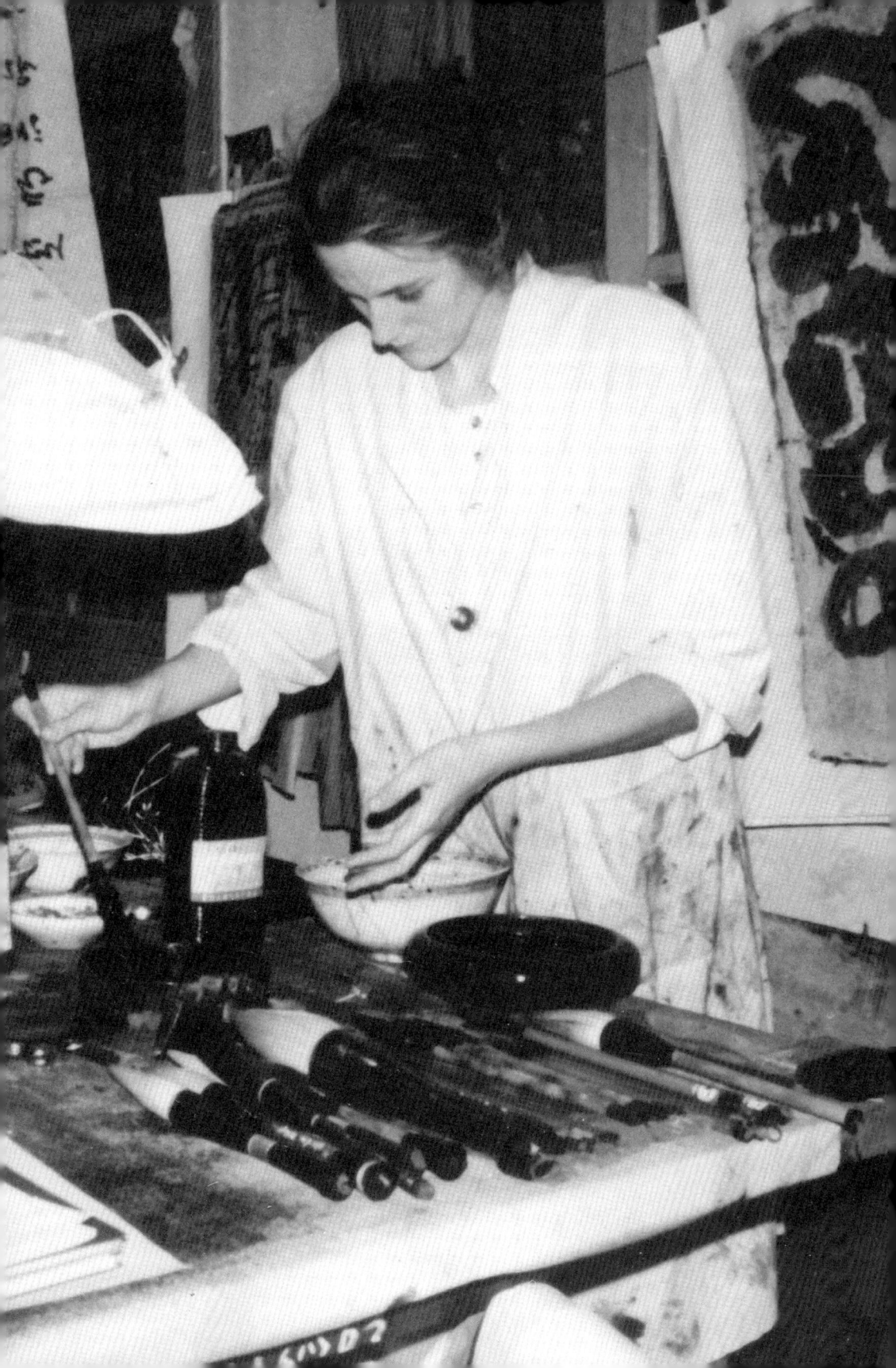

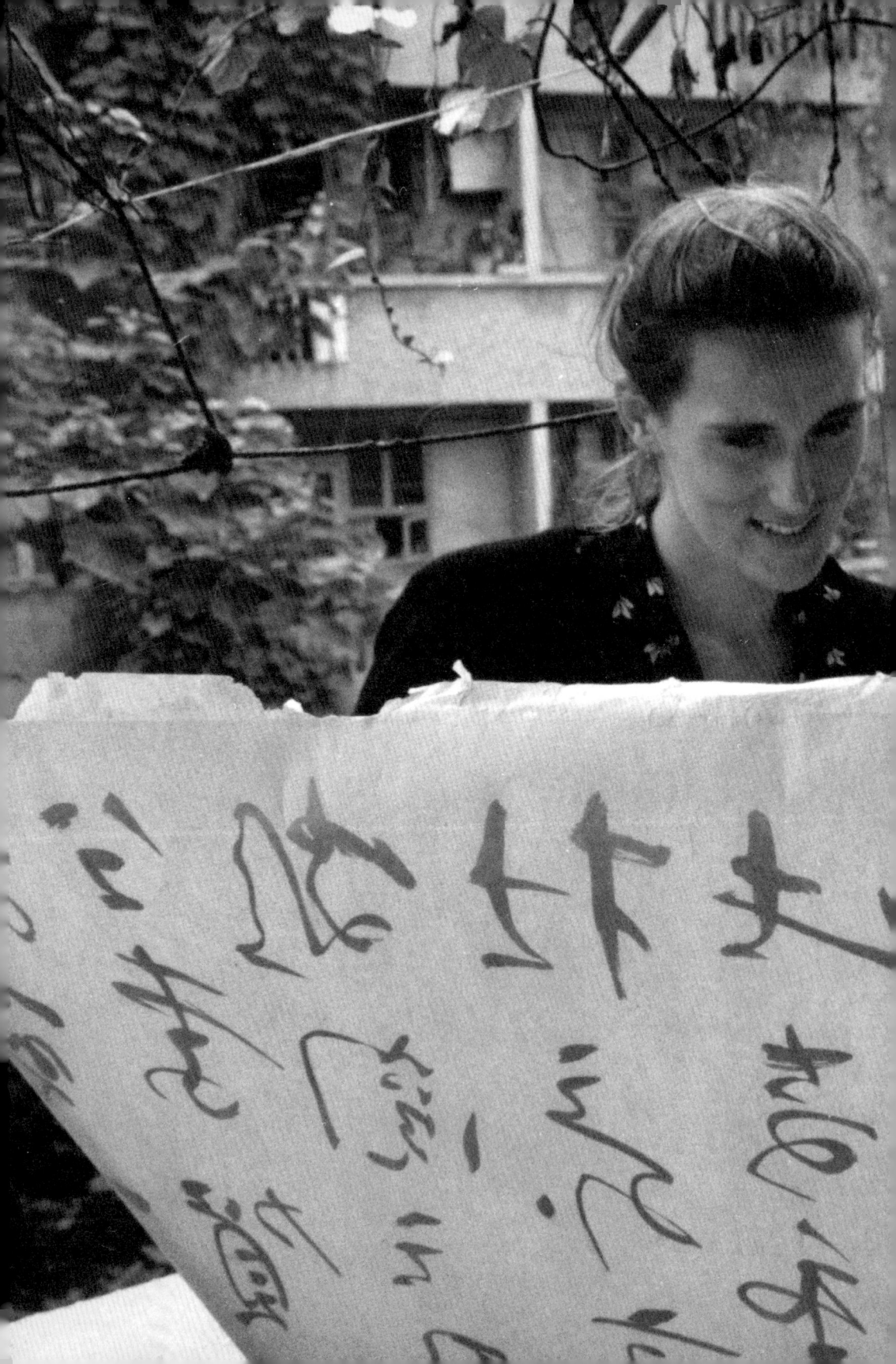

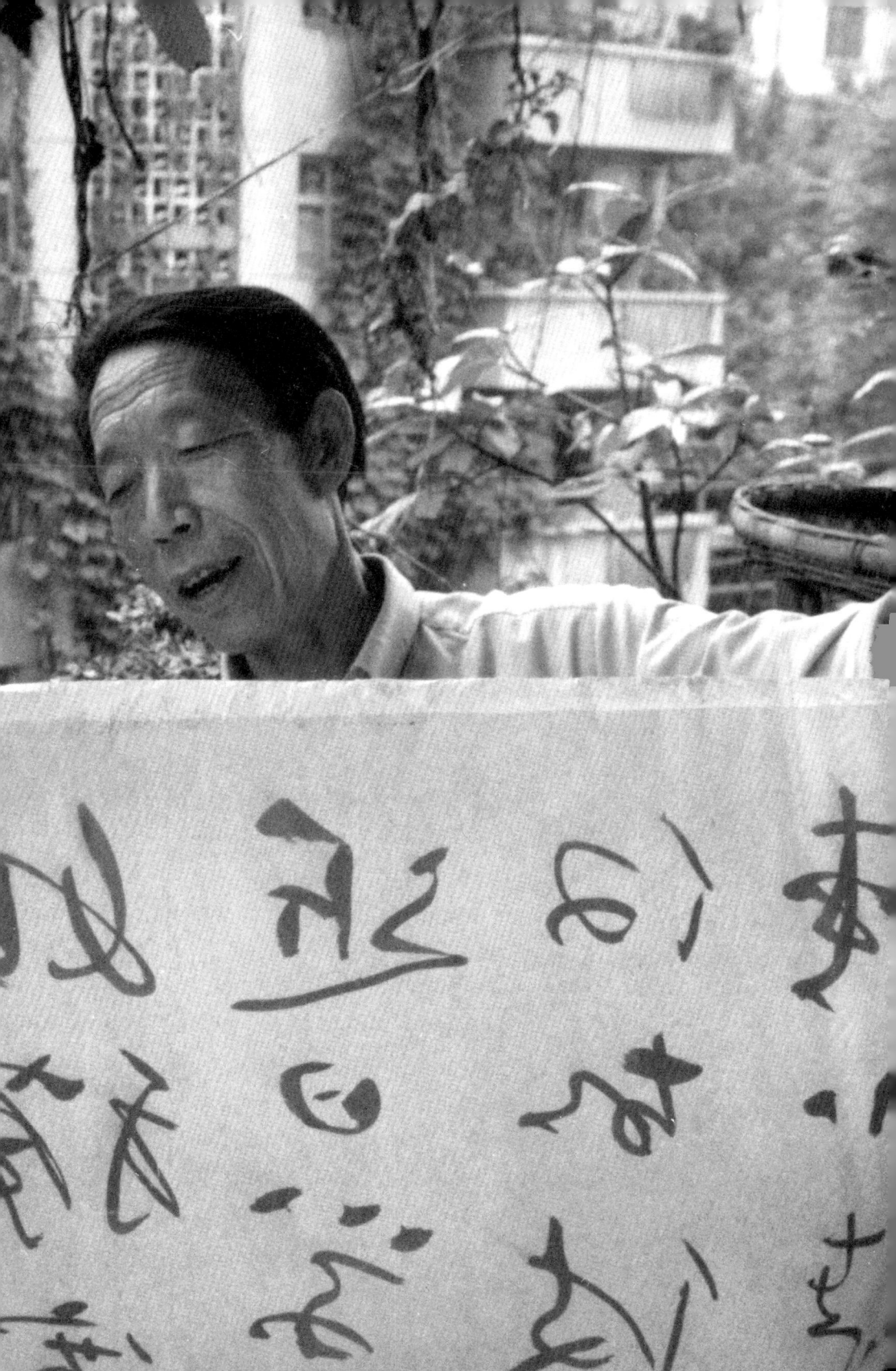

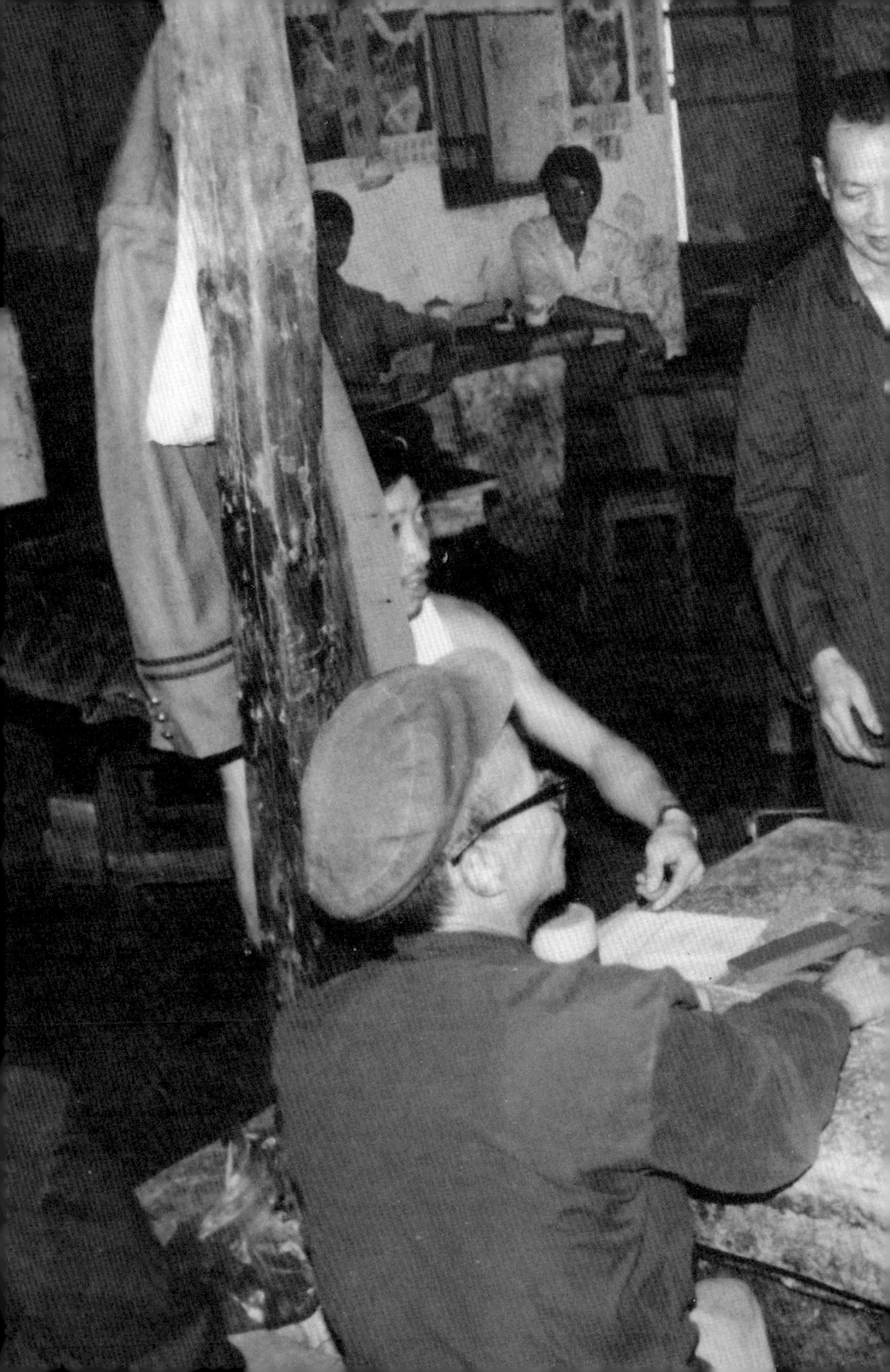

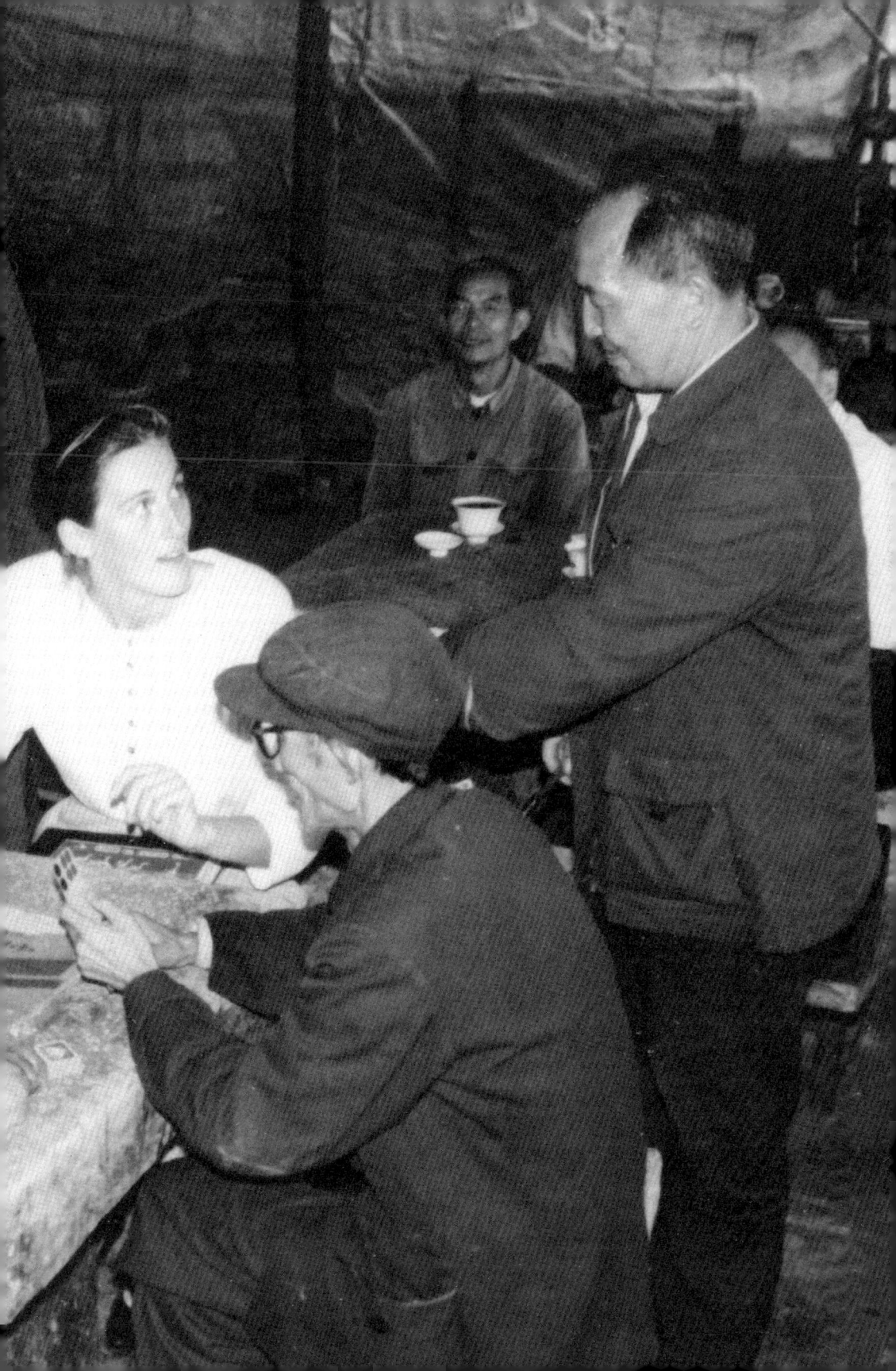

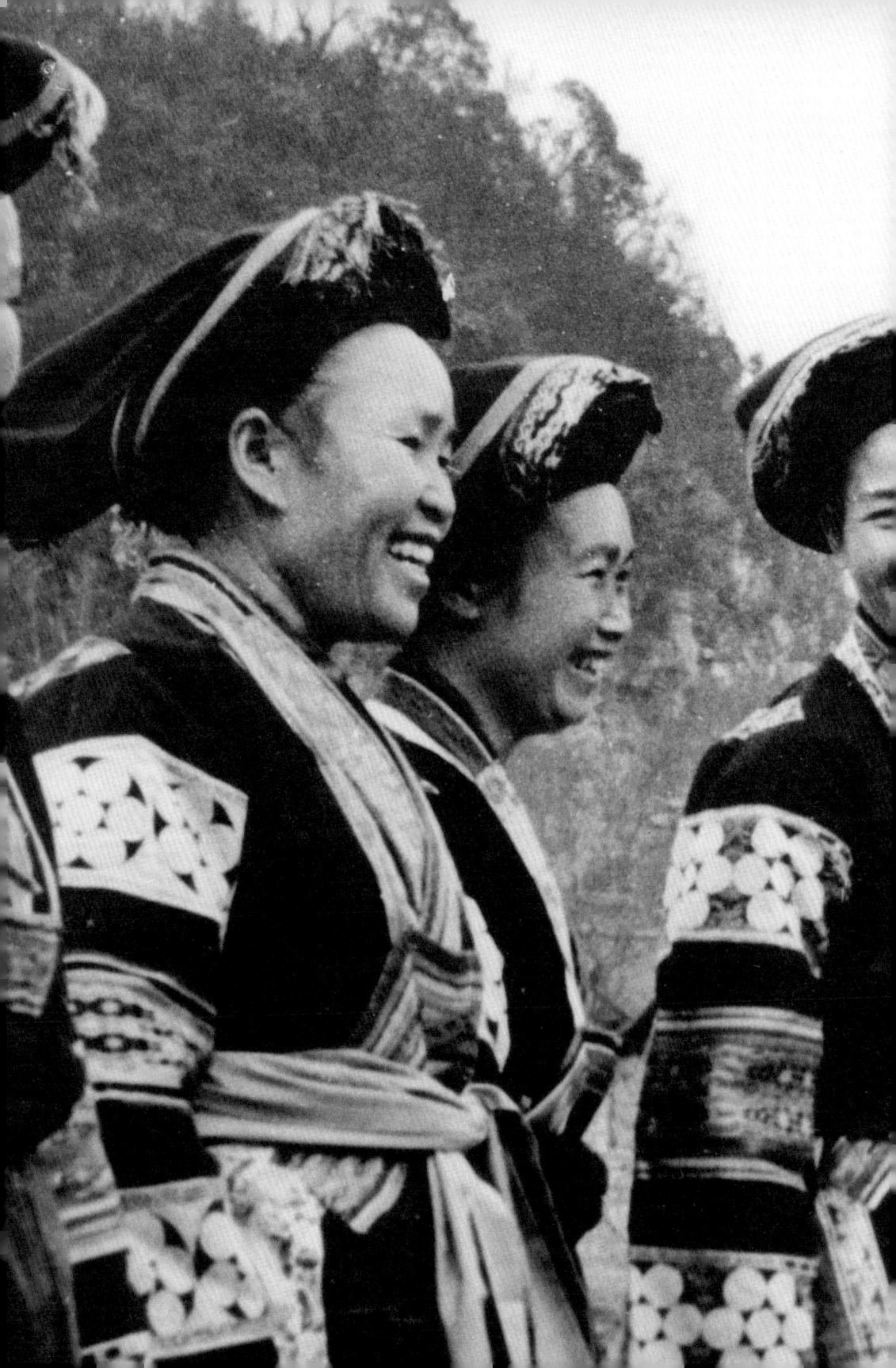

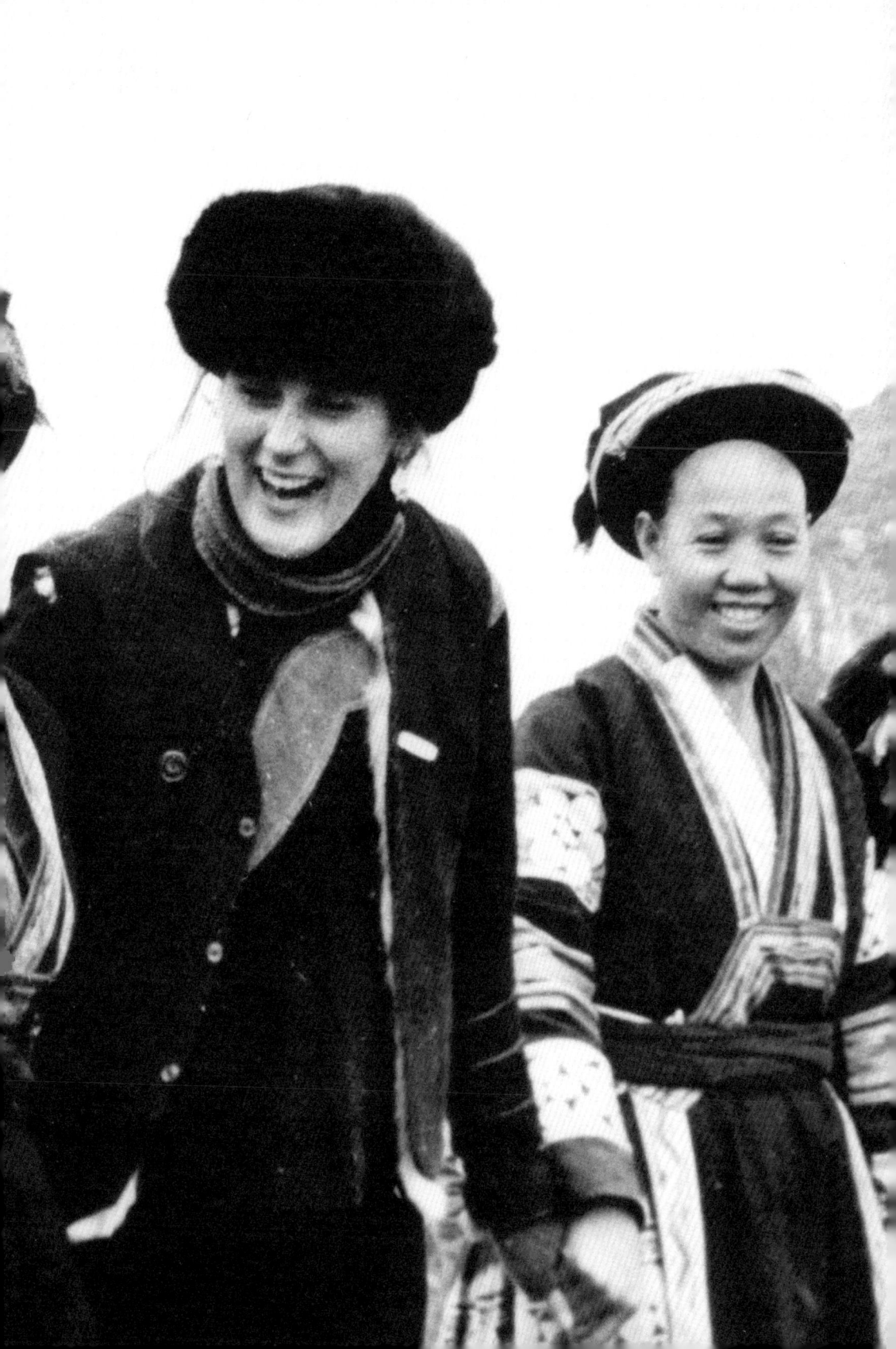

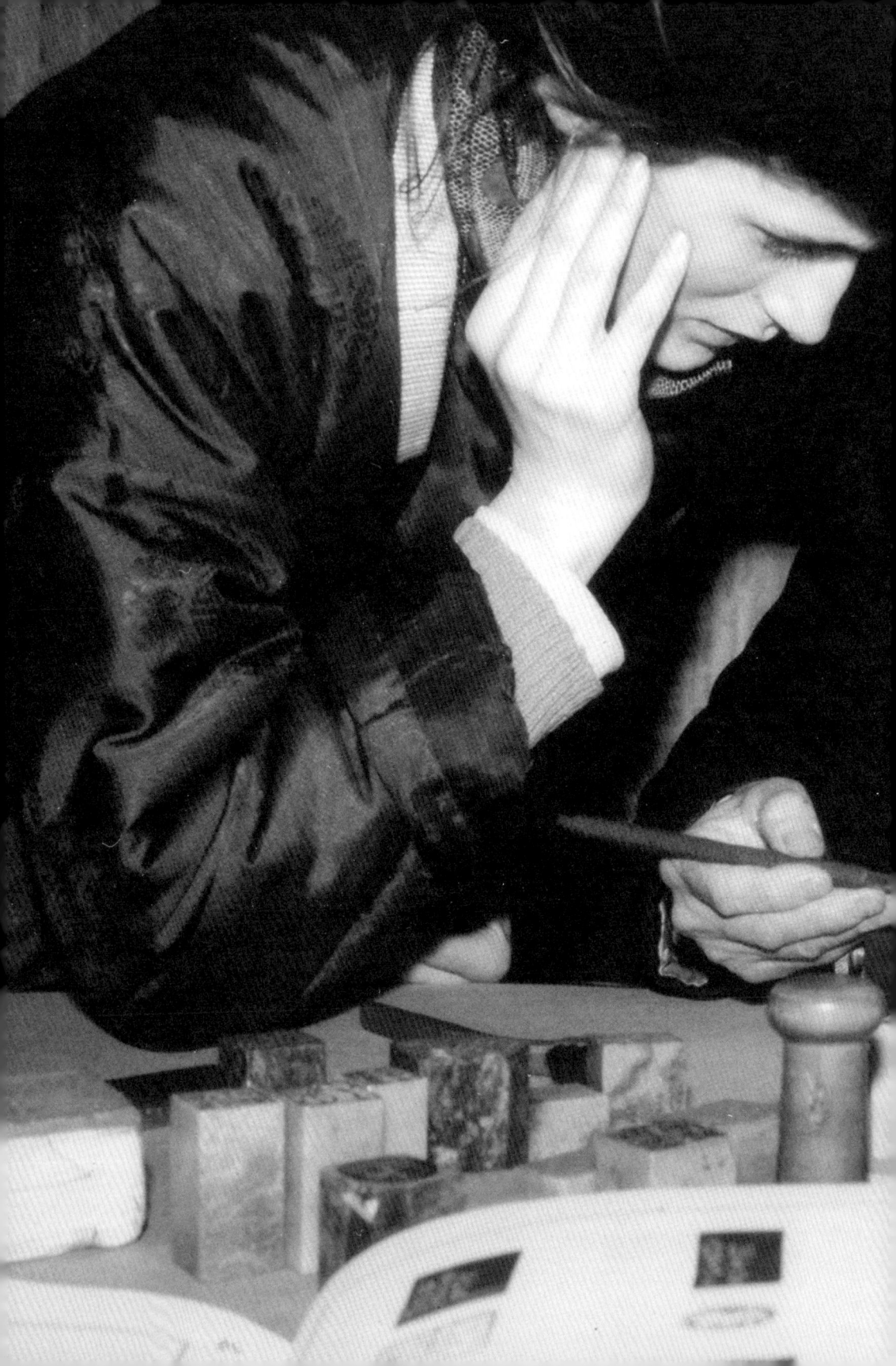

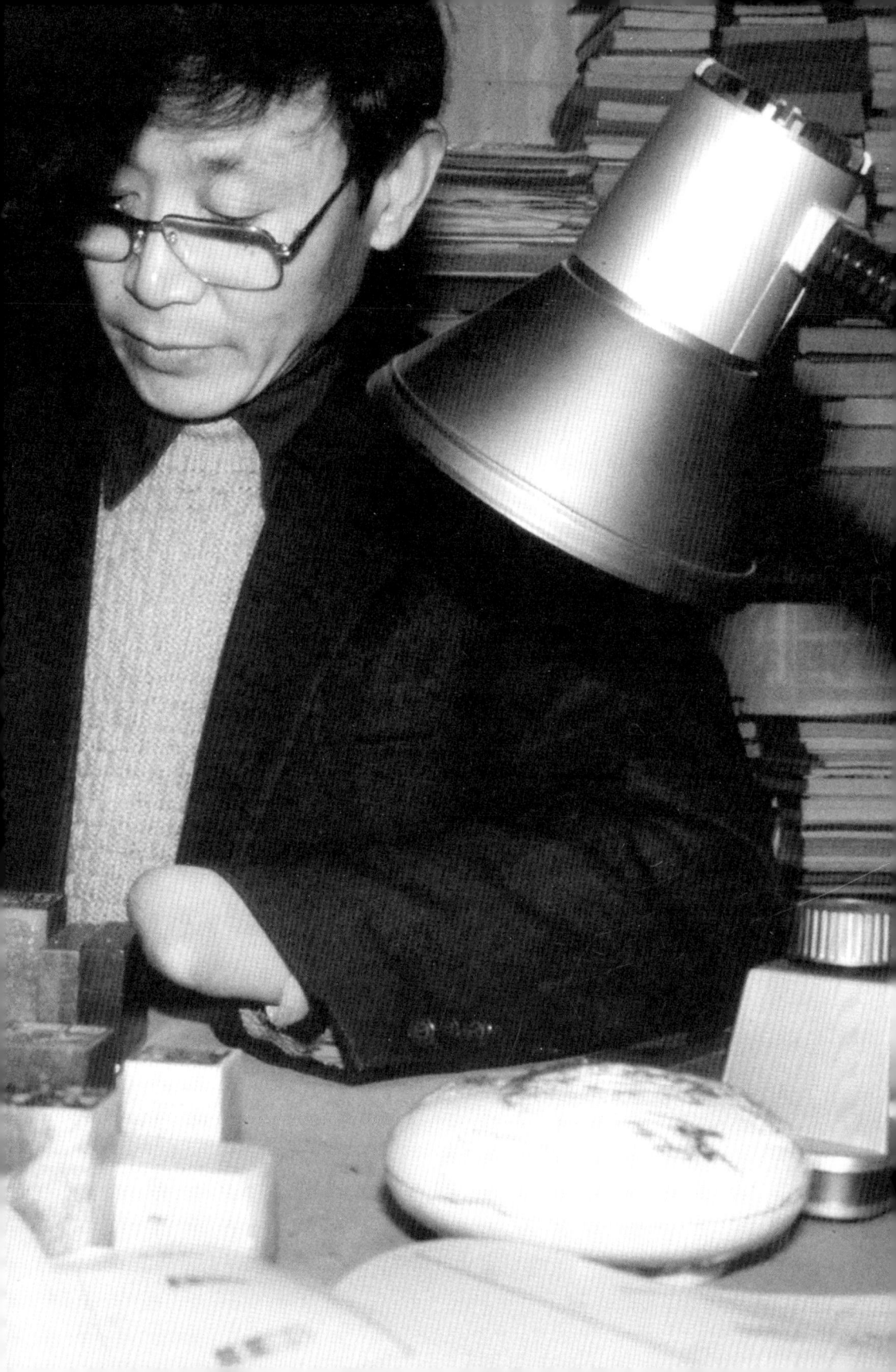

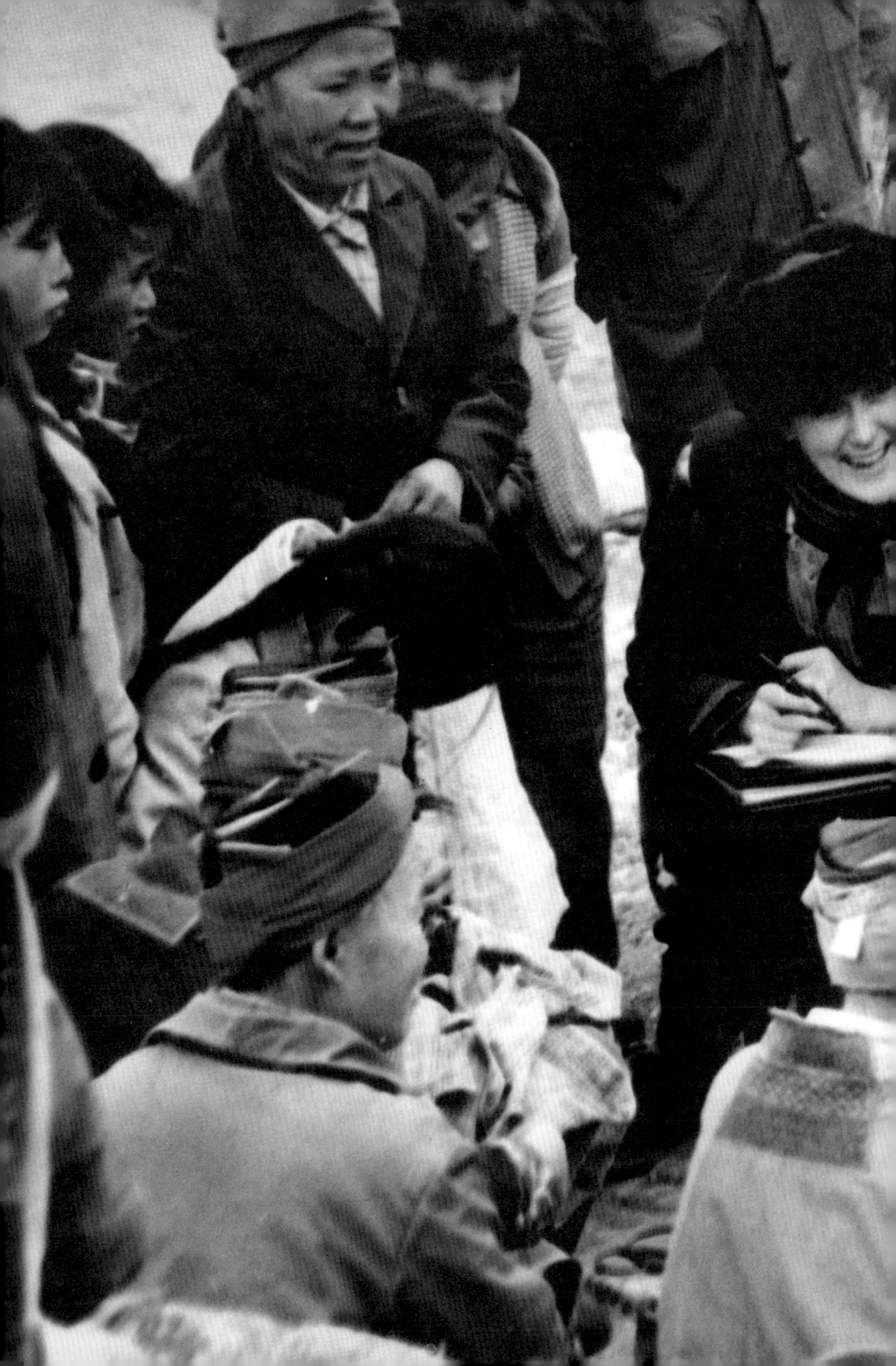

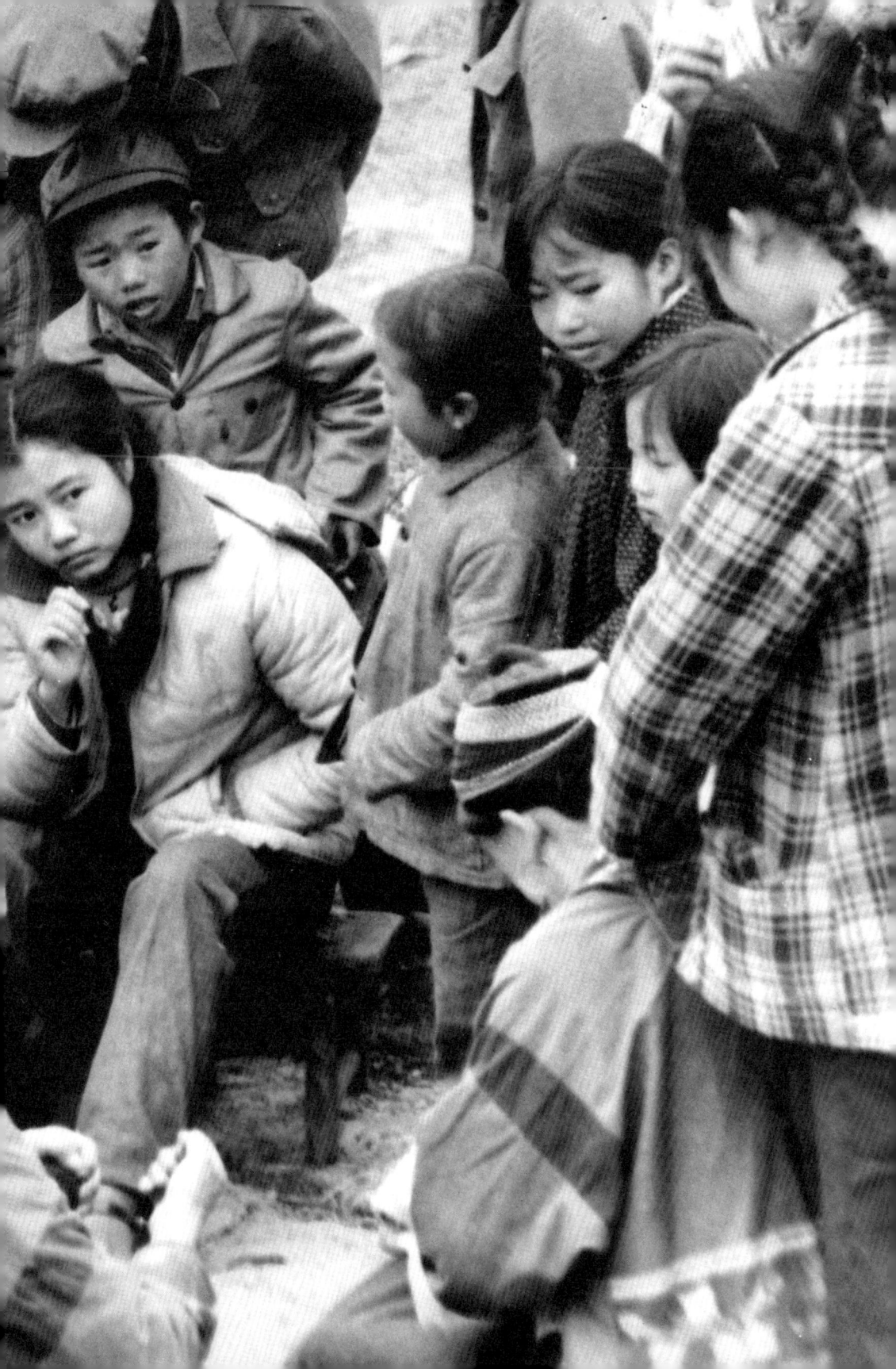

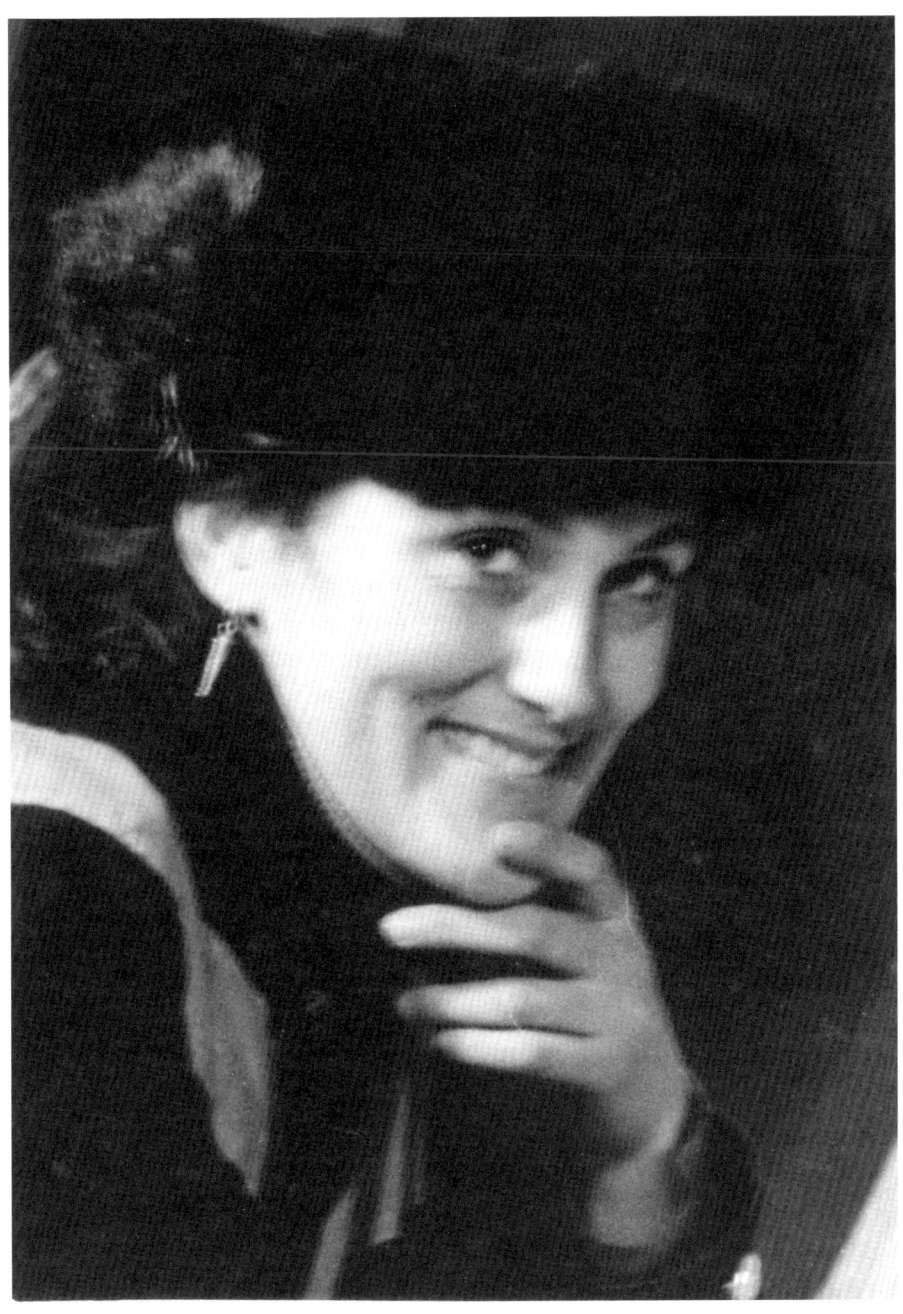

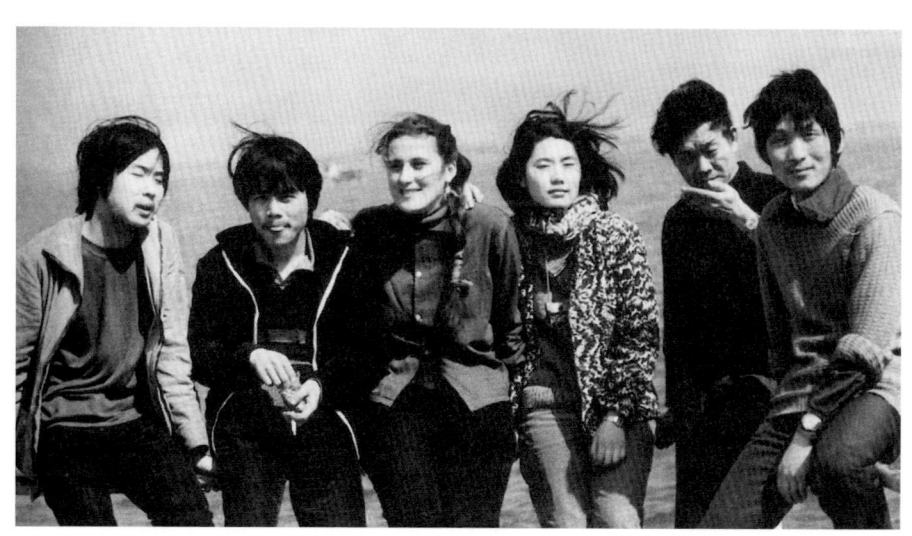

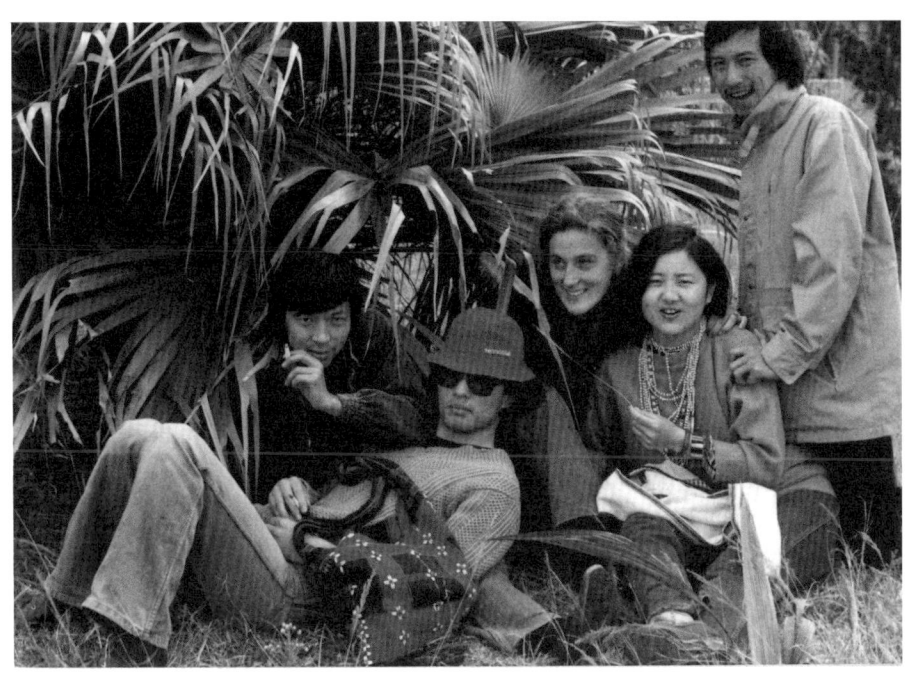

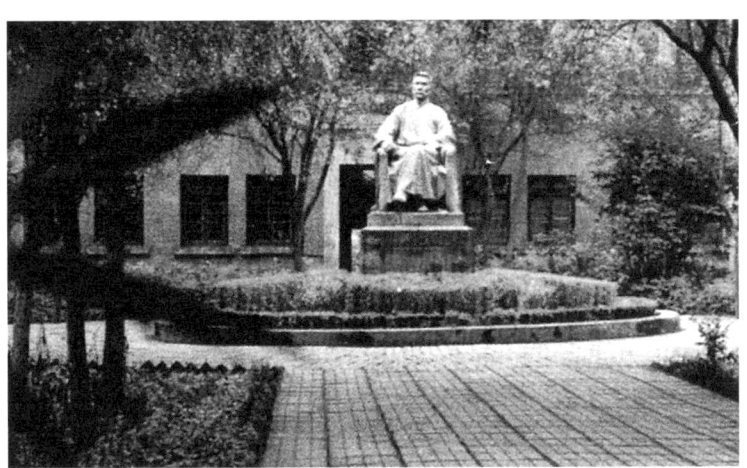

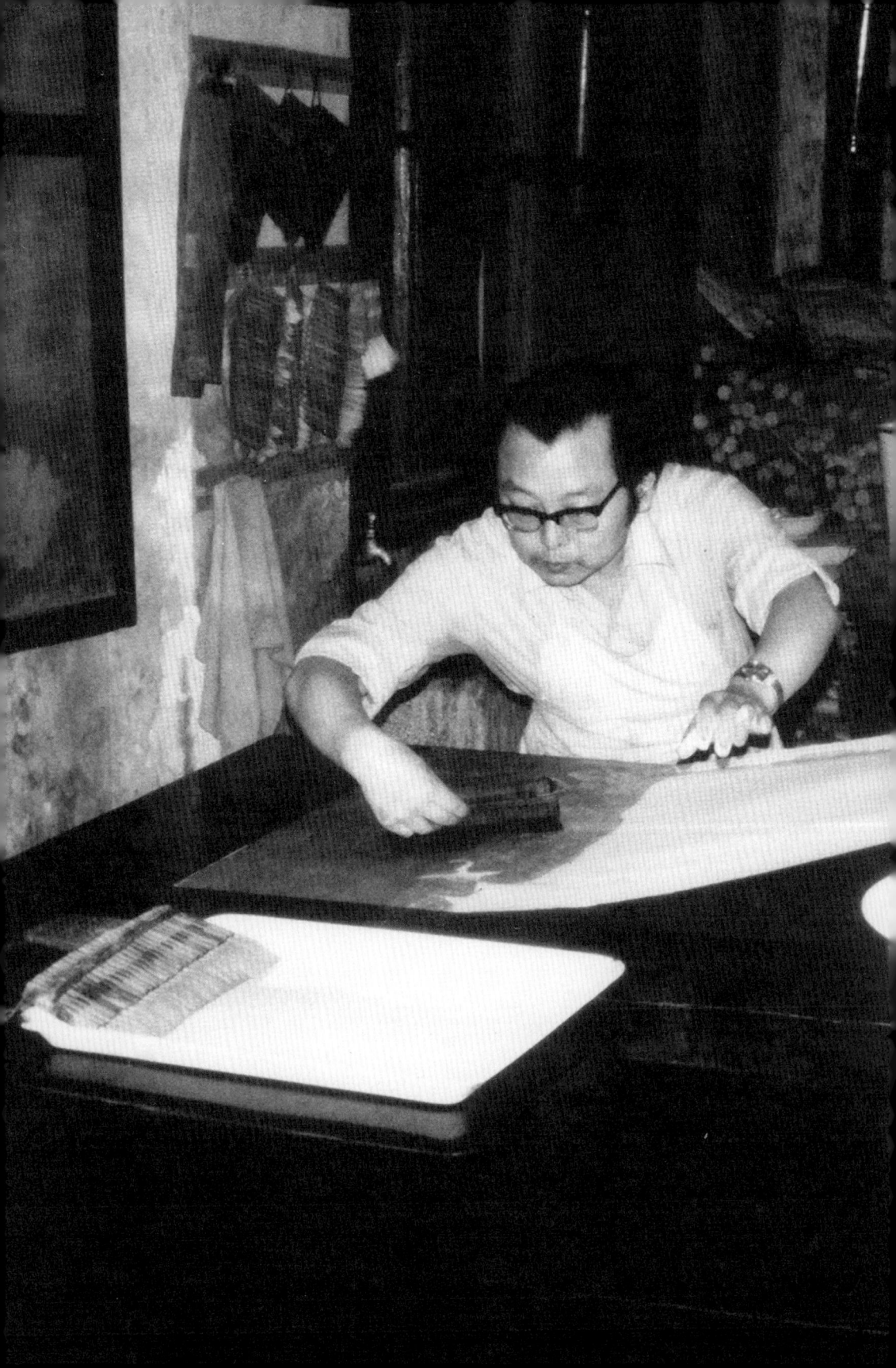

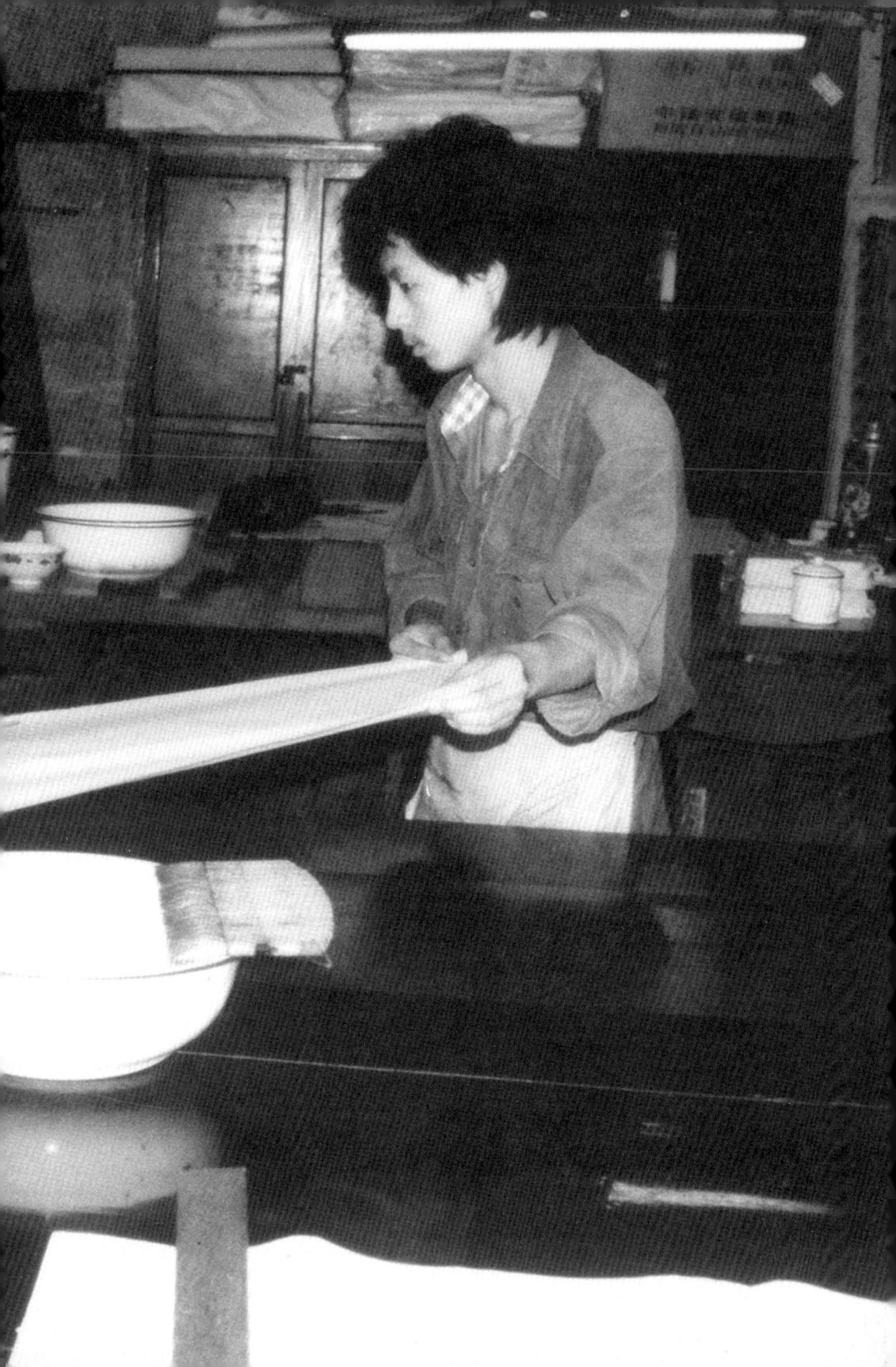

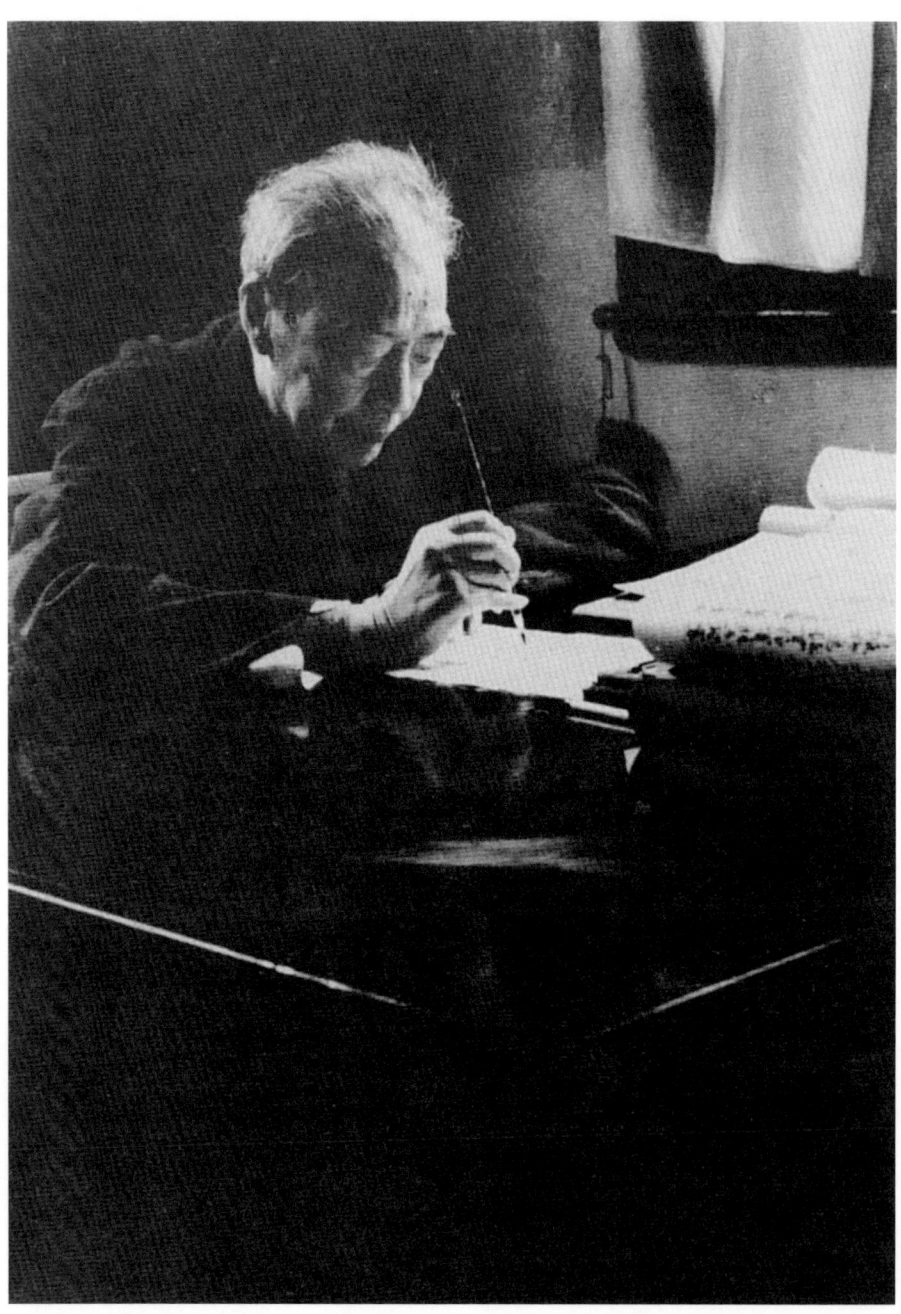

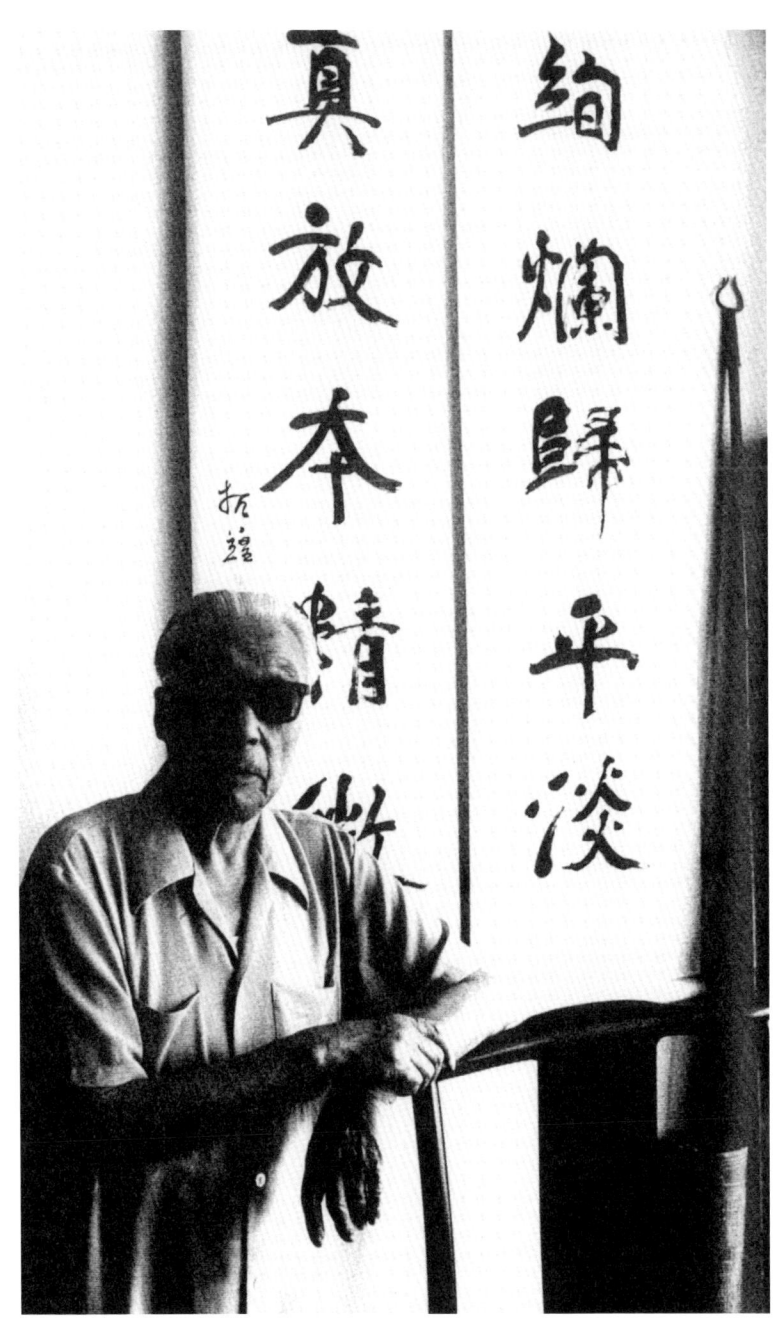

242 With my classmates and
Professor Bai (second from
right) at the start of our
study trip to the Yi, in the
Liangshan territory on the
borders of Sichuan, Tibet,
and Yunnan in 1985.

243 Top. From left to right:
painters Ye Yongqing,
Pou Li ya, Zhang Xiaogang,
and the friend from Yunnan
who received us during
a convalescence trip to
the Anni family, after my
hepatitis in 1987.

Bottom. My dorm room
studio in the administration
building (far right window)
overlooking the Lu Xun
statue, in the center
of the Chongqing School
of Fine Arts campus.

244 Marouflage class with
master Li and his assistant.

246 Sha Menghai, calligrapher
in Hangzhou.

247 Xie Zhiliu, painter
in Shanghai.

249 Lu Yanshao, painter.

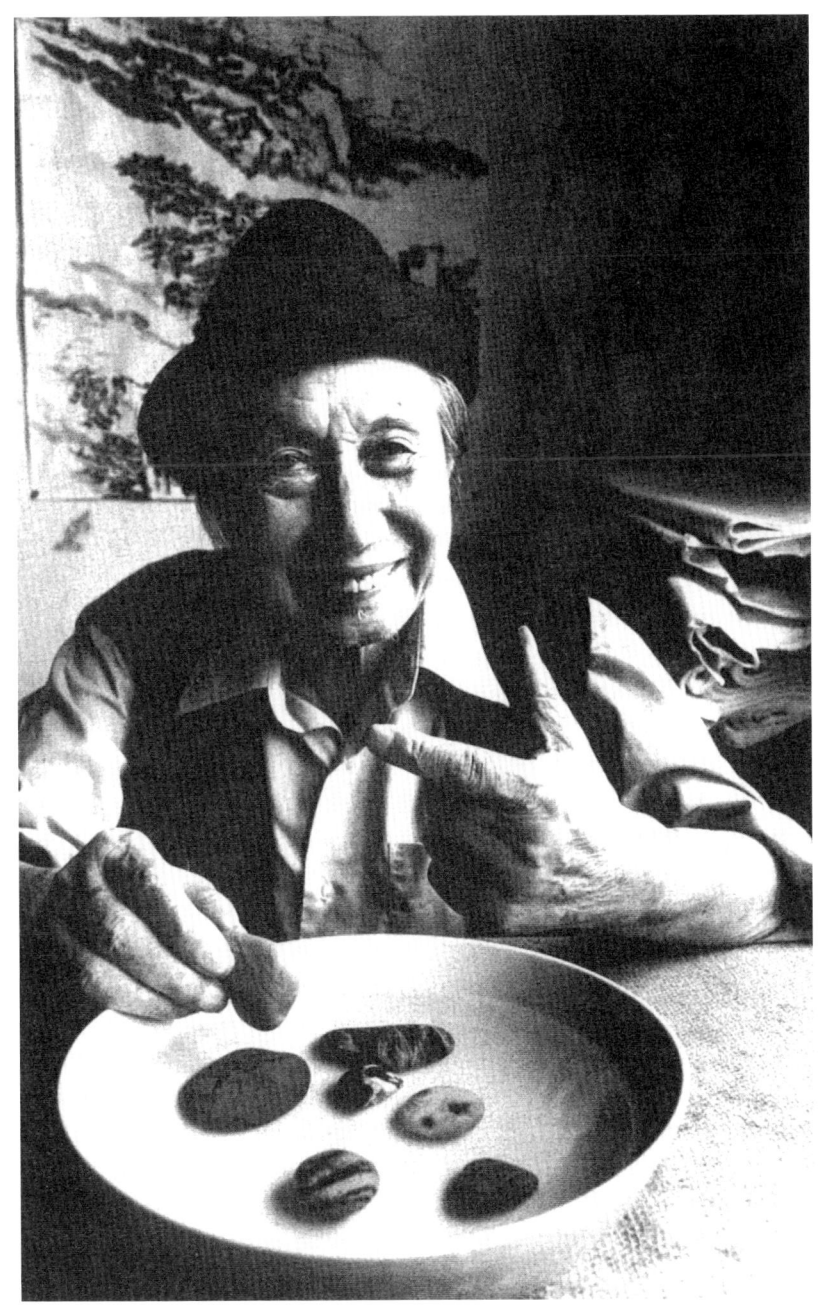

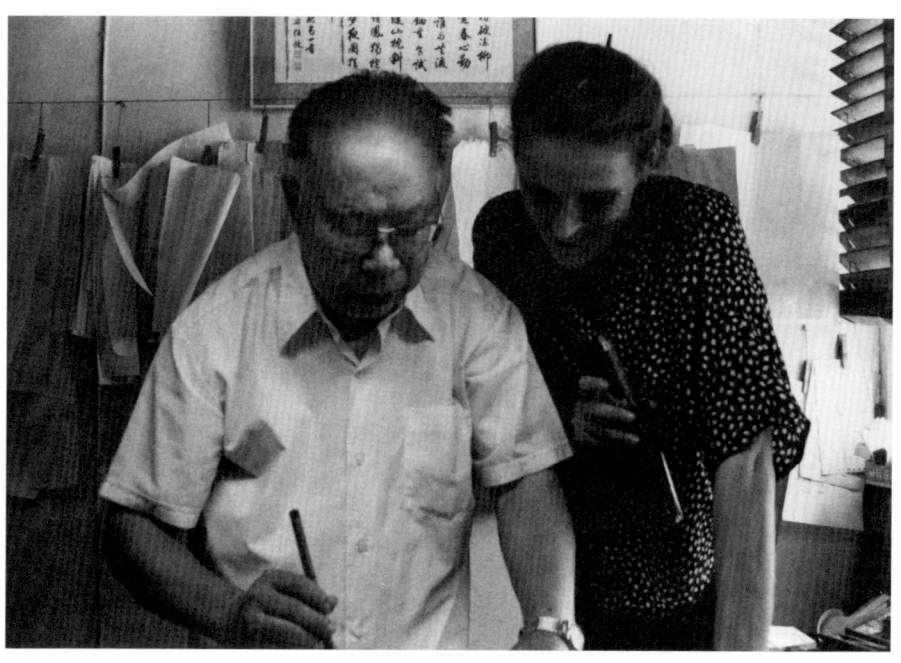

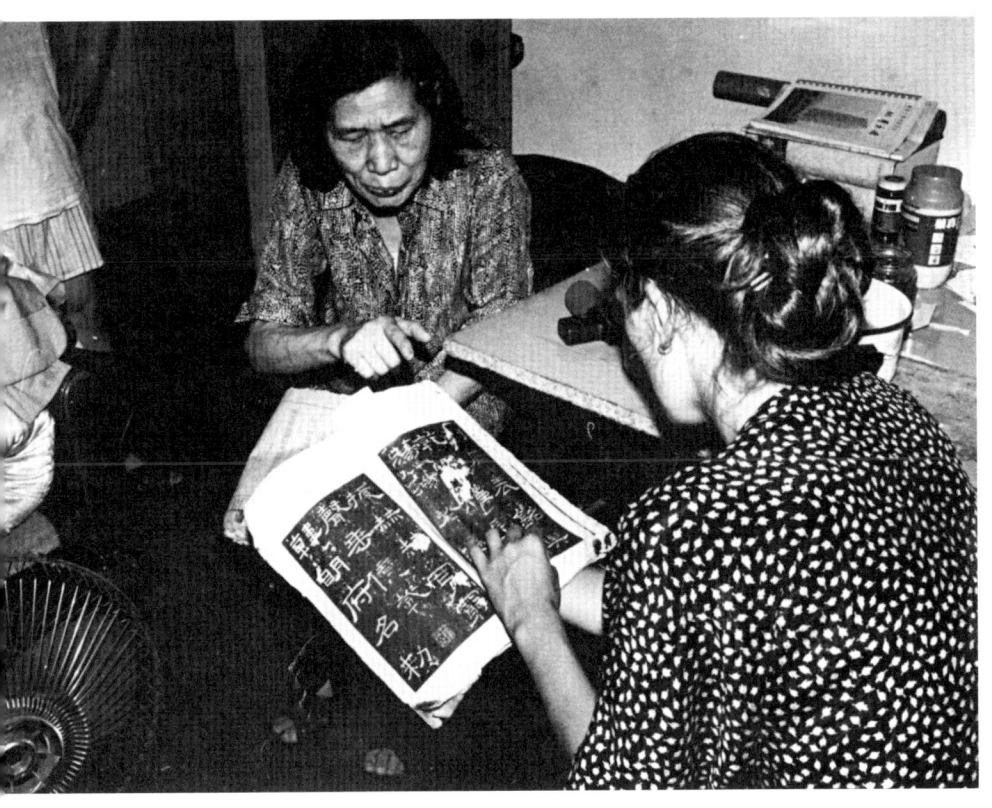

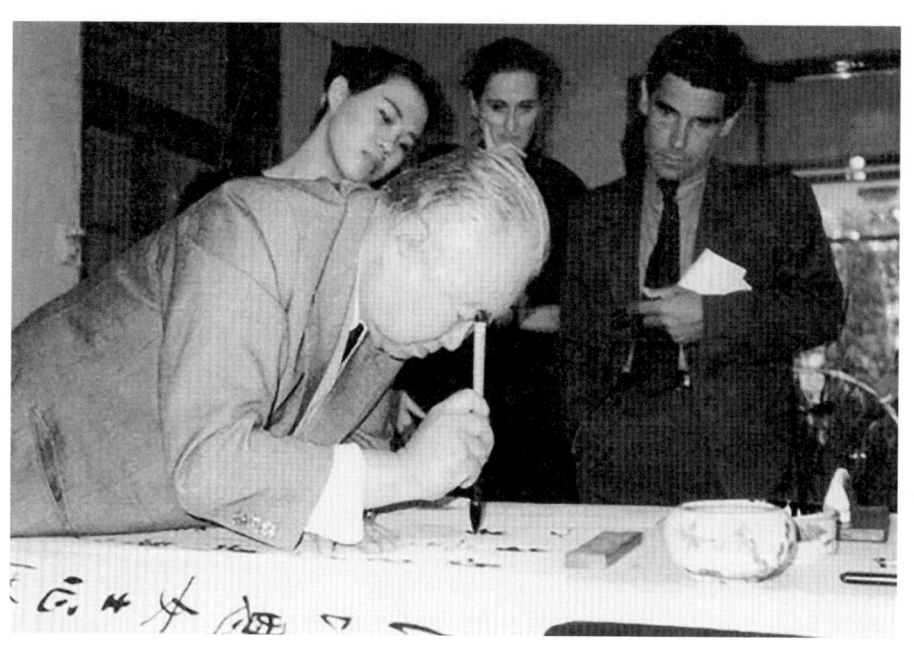

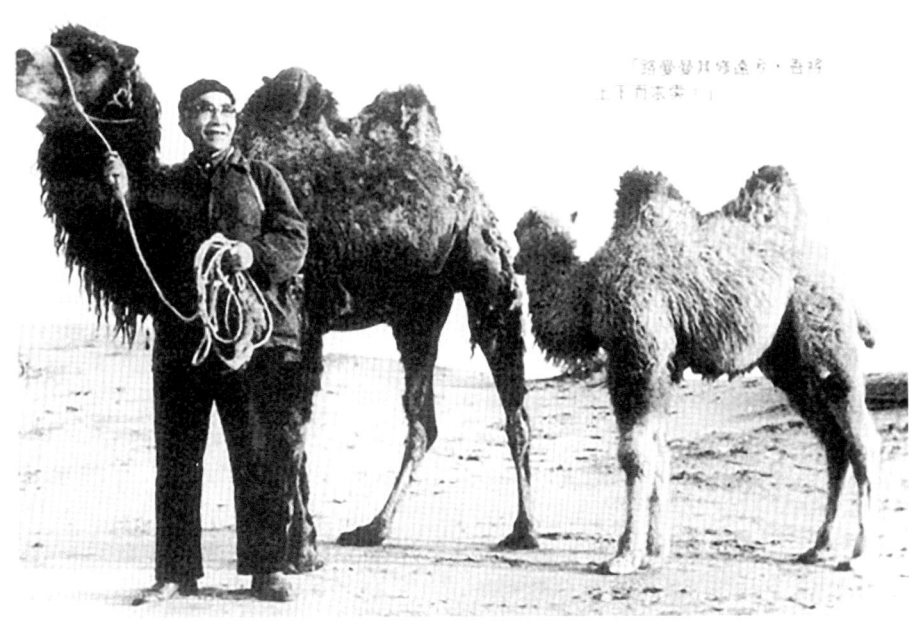

「路邊照张遗念吧，那時
上下不靠的。」

Farewell youth, farewell China

Ask the river which lasts longer, its flow toward the East
or our feelings when we part?

The end of the 1989 academic year was approaching when I had to submit my work to graduate like my fellow Chinese students. I worked very hard to make the deadline. "You'll be obtaining our doctorate degree," my classmates told me, "and you'll soon be leaving us, so we should celebrate these two events. We'll clear the gallery so you can exhibit your work and invite some local figures." The exhibition was planned for June 1989, but June 1989 was to go down in Chinese history for other reasons entirely.

My friends had told me about the serious events going on in Beijing. The atmosphere at the art college grew tense. People were anxious, and agitation was mounting every day. It was difficult to get any information; we met in the evenings to glean what little we could. One morning, I saw strips of white cloth hanging everywhere in the trees. I asked old Laopo, who took care of my room, what the strips meant. "It's the students," she answered. "Apparently the military has moved in; tanks ran over the demonstrators in Tiananmen Square. People were killed. The students are upset and tied these white cloths in the trees in tribute to the dead since white, for us, is the color of mourning."

People from the college who had children or cousins in Beijing were claiming that family members had disappeared. Overnight, the atmosphere became serious. There was an uprising, a revolution within the college. The Party official did not know what to do. We learned that in Chengdu there were huge demonstrations on the big square where Mao's statue stands—a popular nighttime meeting spot for homosexuals—behind the old Helmsman. People had set fire to a police station and the crowd was fired upon. I felt sure that the tiniest spark could trigger the settling of scores after the violence of the Cultural Revolution. Suddenly, I was terribly afraid that people seeking revenge would pour into the streets and proceed with the massacre that they had been dreaming of for so long. The government had always been sitting on a volcano—hence its authoritarianism—and now the volcano was stirring. We could get no information: the television was silent, as was the radio. All we had were rumors that spread from city to city. We could not reach anyone by telephone. I had trouble believing everything I heard. I thought there must be misunderstandings, which happened so often with problems between the officials and the foreigners or the populace. Each had their own story. Those with access to foreign television broadcasts, in particular CNN, passed on alarming news. But the Chinese people realized very quickly that no one was telling the truth. The foreign press was exaggerating, turning the situation into a kind of western, with the good and the bad, trying to get a scoop, while Chinese television, forced out of silence, ludicrously labeled the demonstrators as terrible enemies of China.

With revolution looming, I prepared for my student exhibition. The Party official had called in reinforcements, and soldiers were stationed around the campus. I was worried because the school officials feared student protests and destruction. The Party official said we had to cancel, but once again, the head of the college intervened on my behalf: "She has been studying here for six years; we should pay her the tribute she deserves. The exhibition will be held in the presence of officials." Later, I heard of his efforts to free some students who had been arrested for wanting to demonstrate. He was sent to a detention center and subjected to struggle sessions for having supported the protestors.

The day of my opening, many visitors arrived from the city center. All three floors were packed. There were even staff and patients—some in pajamas—from the small hospital where I had stayed at when I had hepatitis. It was as if the only way these people could express their hope for change was to attend the exhibition. A strange atmosphere reigned: the white cloth tributes to the dead fluttered in the trees, while loudspeakers barked out warnings nonstop to students to remain calm if they wanted to graduate and avoid being sent to the country for reeducation.

In the end, there were no serious incidents, save a few acts of vandalism. The perpetrators were quickly arrested. The Party official had done her job very well: the authorities were not overwhelmed by events as in Beijing.

My graduation ceremony was very moving. It took place in the presence of guests from everywhere, including many unknown to me. It was a happy surprise: my work and also the antiestablishment value of art was recognized!

I thought I would be able to organize my move calmly and spend the summer packing what I had accumulated in China. However, as the situation worsened in Beijing, the Party official received a telegram one day from the French Embassy: "Request French national Fabienne Verdier, student at your institution for many years, to call the embassy." When I phoned, I was told: "We don't know what China will be like tomorrow. It may close its borders. We have received instructions concerning you: you must leave immediately. A special plane will stop to pick you up in Chongqing tomorrow." I tried to protest: my paintings were still being exhibited at the college. I was not ready. Couldn't they postpone my departure? Their response frightened me. "Impossible. Events are happening very fast. Overnight, you could be trapped, and then who knows what might happen to you."

The Party official was jubilant and told me: "Pack your bags and get organized. We'll help you, but you're leaving tomorrow." The decision came as a bombshell. I would never have imagined that it would be so hard to leave, in this unreal atmosphere. I had a ton of things, including notes and notebooks that I had accumulated over six years, but I was limited to the plane's baggage allowance. That evening, my friends came to see me and advised me to leave nothing behind, adding: "And be careful. If you took notes about your stay here, even about old Huang, you should get rid of them before going through customs." I had broken a good many rules over the years and was worried about what would happen to others if my notes were confiscated at the border. After many tears and much bitterness, I decided to burn everything. I took only a few works with me. That night, friends brought me many gifts—most of which, to my great regret, I was forced to leave behind. Everyone was worried about the future, but they still sought to reassure me. They told me they had already lived through similar situations and were expecting struggle sessions. Huang Laoshi was taken ill with grief, but in my presence, carried himself with extreme detachment.

The next day, a special bus came to drive me to the airport. The head of the college, my friends, teachers, and their spouses all rode the bus with me. I tried to put on a good face, but when I had to part with everyone at the airport, I felt miserable. I had no suitcases, only cardboard boxes containing paintings, painting supplies, and a few personal belongings. It was especially hard for me to tear myself away from those I was leaving behind. I had become attached to my prison-like universe and to these survivors of the totalitarian system who had become my friends. When they left, I wandered exhausted in the waiting room not knowing what to do with myself. The experience was heartrending, though I knew I should be happy to escape the madness.

I arrived in Hong Kong in a pitiful state. The customs officers in Chongqing had opened all of my boxes. They had not been properly resealed so they had come open in the baggage hold. An official from the consulate was waiting for me. She recovered the sorry wreck that I had become and kept me at her house for a week. With access to the press, I finally learned what had really happened in Beijing. I saw the photos of the tanks, the injured and dead. It was such a shock that I fell into a deep depression. The woman who took me in was extremely kind and even ran hot baths for me. But I could not adjust to living in a normal apartment with carpets and a functional kitchen; I had forgotten how to use everyday objects and even how to speak French, sometimes responding in Chinese. I felt completely lost, incapable of telling my story. My hostess, who had followed the events, understood my state. I was put on a plane to Paris, my scrolls under my arm and without a penny to my name. I wondered what to do with my life.

When they saw me, my uncle Jean-Louis and aunt Yvonne took me in hand. "You haven't finished your apprenticeship in China," my aunt told me. "You'll go back." How her words comforted me! "Wait a few months to see how the situation develops. Your first priority should be to recover your health. Don't forget I got you your ethnology grant. You have to settle down and write your report on the teachings of the old masters. I'll help you." She was correct, writing was excellent therapy. My aunt's ethnologist friends Hélène Clastres and Tina Jolas were also very supportive during my depression. They helped restore my self-confidence and encouraged me to continue to paint and find my path. I had survived the hardest part.

But not long after, my aunt and uncle left for the weekend at their house in the Cévennes region and were killed in a car accident. After the shock of leaving China, this loss was almost too painful to bear. They had believed in me.

My uncle had been a researcher in mathematics. We would compare mathematical notions with the teachings of my old masters. He was surprised that studies of aesthetics gave me access to aspects of Chinese thought that overlapped to a certain extent with his research in random mathematics. He had proposed to take me back to China with him for a meeting with important Chinese mathematicians. My aunt's field of research was the English poets. She also had fascinating interpretations of *Little Red Riding Hood*. We would spend long evenings together exchanging ideas. It was tragic that they died before they could complete their research.

My aunt and uncle had suggested that I offer my services to the French Foreign Affairs Ministry in case an artistic attaché position should open up. I had met Mr. Malo, the French ambassador, on a trip to Beijing, so I had asked him how I could return to Beijing once I completed my studies. I knew Sichuan province well. I had met the great masters of Shanghai and Hangzhou, though I did not know much of the north. He was one of the rare Frenchmen to speak the Sichuanese dialect and answered me in Sichuanese. He even asked me if a certain peanut shop, the Number Twenty-Six of Chengdu, was still there! I answered in kind and felt a certain affinity grow between us.

I went through the proper channels in Paris and obtained a meeting with ministry officials of foreign affairs. An intimidating interview followed before a panel to assess my personality and reactions and to determine whether I was capable of representing France abroad.

When I left that meeting, I felt I had no chance: I did not fit the profile they wanted at all. I knew there were at least ten other candidates who were more attractive, with experience in the cultural departments of several countries who knew the job. However, a few days after the deaths of my aunt and uncle, I received a response from the Ministry: "You have been assigned to Beijing. You leave in three weeks. Meanwhile, you are to take a training course and meet with representatives from the various French cultural organizations you will be dealing with."

And so I returned to China, Beijing this time. The ambassador was still Mr. Malo. I went to thank him, as he had supported my candidacy. "We need people like you who know the lay of the land," he told me. "We have to maintain contacts with the Chinese intellectuals and art world. Unfortunately, there is no funding, and diplomatic relations have been at a standstill since Tiananmen Square." My assignment seemed impossible. How could we do anything without a budget?

I went from the life of a Sichuanese beggar to that of a diplomat, complete with an apartment, cook, and housekeeper I affectionately called Auntie Xu. Such material comfort and having to manage staff made me uncomfortable, but I was told that the staff went with my job description. I was expected to entertain regularly, and I could not be both at the office and in the kitchen. From the moment I arrived, I was overwhelmed. In addition to my work at the cultural center, I had to do the accounting and keep to a budget, tasks for which I had absolutely no training.

At midnight, I could often be found in my office trying to figure out the machinery of the administration. This was my day job since I was not advanced enough as a painter to earn a living from it. In the beginning, I hoped to have enough time to continue to paint, but I soon put that idea aside. Furthermore, the French Foreign Affairs Ministry made it clear that they were sending me to China to work as a cultural attaché, not as a painter. I had to forget my vocation and concentrate on my job.

I discovered a new hierarchy: not that of the Chinese Communist bureaucracy but that of the French administration. Here too there were rules to follow, behaviors to adopt, and tasks to achieve. The first criticism I received concerned my friendly relationship with my cook and Auntie Xu: they were supposed to serve me, not keep me company. Then I was admonished for having Chinese friends. It had taken me months of struggle in Sichuan to be allowed to meet other students freely. Now, in Beijing, I found myself on the fifteenth floor of a high-rise (where the elevator was often out of order) in the diplomatic district under military protection. Dogs were free to enter but not the Chinese! They had to provide proof of identity and be registered. The attendant would draft meticulous and detailed reports on all the visitors.

Since I had this job, I decided I should try to be useful and help artists, whose hard times I understood very well. From the files I realized that those in charge of the cultural department knew almost nothing about contemporary artists. I would be asked to organize a concert, for example, but had no information on the best violinists or conductors in the area. No attempt at cataloguing information concerning the Chinese cultural milieu had been made, so I met with artists from the China Central Academy of Fine Arts where I ran into friends. I was supposed to look after musicians, actors, directors, dancers, choreographers, and photographers as well, so I requested official appointments at each university to meet with specialists and the finest virtuosos. I was happy to discover Beijing, but I quickly realized that the miserable conditions in which the great painters lived were the same for other artists and writers. Official visits were always amusing. At the music conservatory there was a sign: "Welcome to the new French cultural attaché." I met with many talented people, from three-year-old pianists who played Chopin to a great conductor directing Beethoven and Mozart. It was touching to see how zealously they worked. I could figure out the situation straight away because it was the same as in Sichuan. I immediately understood who was a professor or a Party official. I knew how they thought, what to say to them, and what their reactions would be.

I was invited behind the scenes at the Forbidden City thanks to friends who knew the curators. The latter had been driven to despair. They had no financial support to conserve the collections properly, and the painted scrolls were deteriorating in cases that were not always lined with camphor. I subsequently visited the museum of Taiwan. Fortunately, the most beautiful objects had been transferred to Taipei before the Liberation. There they were, perfectly conserved, in conditions that would have been the envy of many a French museum.

When visiting the Forbidden City, I would always take a detour through the Garden of Tranquil Longevity, Ningshougong, to pay tribute to the rock formation of Lake Tai. It was magnificently hidden behind a sacred door tucked between two lanterns.

Another of my pleasures in Beijing quickly became a habit: I loved to stroll through the Imperial Garden, Yuhuayuan. There was a magical tree there, a cypress standing like a cathedral and dating, it was said, from the Ming period. To those who contemplated that tree, it told our history. An old man often meditated on a bench beside it, as if he were charging himself with its energy—the vital breath emanating from its very core. It had strange and unusual contours: the old knotted trunk had been shaped by telluric forces, winds, erosion, and the human touch over many centuries. In certain parts of it, one could imagine the movements of a sea agitated by thousands of waves created by a storm. The old man appeared to be feeding in some way on the longevity of the cypress. He meditated as if he were before a sacred temple, a microcosm revealing the history of matter.

One day, both of us were sitting on the same bench. Looking at the tree, the Chinese man said to me in a low voice: "Young lady, we learn to live and grow old with what nature has given us at birth, just like this tree." After a long silence, he went on, insistently: "Young lady, we must cultivate the principle of life within us." I never saw him again, but I often returned to salute the tree and ponder the old man's words.

I had a cook so I invited artists over and tried my best to help those who were interested in France and sought information. Word quickly got around that there was a French woman who was different from the civil servants one usually encountered in diplomatic circles, someone who seemed to know China well. I was rapidly inundated. There would be twenty Chinese lined up in front of my office every morning. It was impossible for me to respond to so many requests, which were also varied. I felt sad and frustrated: I had met the greatest Chinese artists and I knew how to help them in a way that few could, yet I could decide nothing.

However, I was able to help some photographers who had published photos of the Tiananmen Square tragedy to escape China, and for some filmmakers to go to France to participate in festivals. With my colleague and superior Nicolas Chapuis and the Chinese Minister of Culture, I organized a large exhibition of Rodin. I tried my best, but I was stymied by the attitude of certain foreigners and the backwardness of some mentalities. Sometimes I felt that the colonial period had never ended. Women who had worked in offices and did their own shopping and cooking in Europe didn't stop complaining about their servants.

Meanwhile my requests to fund worthwhile cultural projects were met with refusals, though there was enough money to put up vacationing politicians and officials in grand hotels. We hosted cocktails and dinners in their honor, where I was asked to invite important Chinese artists so that they could boast of having met them. (They would have forgotten their names by the end of the evening, but appearances were all that mattered.) Sometimes we even had to procure prostitutes for them!

Huang Laoshi had recommended that I pay a visit to his close friend, Lan Yusong. He was not only one of the greatest musicologists in Asia—having authored two dictionaries on traditional Chinese music—but also an outstanding calligrapher, painter, seal-maker, and historian. He was an all-round man of letters, the likes of which China would never see again. When I asked to meet him, I was told he no longer received guests except for certain specialists from Taiwan or Japan who came to work with him. I had to get special permission to visit him.

He lived in a kind of cell which he never left. When I entered his room for the first time, I saw stacks of documents reaching the ceiling everywhere. The bed was covered with piles of books and scrolls of calligraphed documents. There was not an inch of space in which to sit. He had a phenomenal constitution and slept just four hours a night in his armchair. The music academy students had told me that at night they would navigate by Lan's studio light, which also served as their clock.

 In this oppressive place, his smile expressed a mischievous calm which was disconcerting after his years of undergoing self-criticism. He was supremely intelligent and so wise that every discussion with him, no matter the subject, left me enchanted. Of all the Chinese intellectuals I met, he made the deepest impression on me. His thoughts were lively and often inspired. When I arrived, he would take up his paintbrush and calligraph for me his poetic feelings of that moment.

He had worked ceaselessly since the age of fifteen, which he claimed was the reason for the baldness that made him look like an old monk. At eighty-five, he told me he owed his survival to the tasty dishes his complaining wife (who constantly railed about the hardship of their lives) cooked for him. Although repeatedly invited by the greatest American universities, he had never been allowed to leave China. More than once, Harvard had wanted to bring him to the United States. We became close friends and I maintain an immense admiration for this extremely refined man. He could recite Verlaine and Lamartine in French and launch into comparisons of Chinese and European poetry and landscape painting.

As with Huang Laoshi, we enjoyed studying reproductions of old works of art together. Generally, the anonymous works were our favorites. When we admired *Pier at Dawn,* a painting by Xia Gui, he asked me to study the graphic expression of the foliage in the trees which were so light and yet so dense. One day, he mentioned the *Adoration of the Magi* by Leonardo da Vinci and spoke of two trees, his favorites in the top left corner of the canvas that were absolute marvels. He teased me when I was too slow to follow him. "I'm trying to picture them," I told him, astounded at how alive these trees were in his mind. Searching desperately in the modest pictorial recesses of my memory, I finally found them: a few strokes of the brush, lively and ingenious. They had also made a strong impression on me when I was a student in France. Old Lan opened new doors for me, helping me make new connections and embark on new journeys that I had carried inside of me without ever being able to bring them to life.

On another occasion, he drew out a little landscape by Shitao from under his bed. It was an original that he had managed to save during the Cultural Revolution by burying it. He had also saved some other treasures that way, including a piece of mural painting from the Dunhuang Caves: he had wrapped the fragment in a blanket and hid it under the floor tiles of his cell. His great pleasure, when he was feeling low, was to take out these objects and contemplate their uniqueness. He explained to me that their creative force had helped him to endure his miserable destiny. He played the *erhu,* a kind of Chinese violin. When he had a bit to drink, he would invite me to be seated and then improvised fascinating music, expressing autumn gusts of wind or raging rivers of the high mountains. I would be carried away very quickly.

He was delighted when I showed him my work, and in many aspects of Chinese culture he continued Huang Laoshi's teachings. He introduced me to ceramics and antiques. He would tell me to meet him at five o'clock in the morning on a little bridge, and we would go to discover what the farmers had brought to the Beijing markets where the antique dealers also sourced their wares. "This is an old dish," he told me once. "Observe its admirable lines. You must learn to appreciate this art form. Buy it, you will live with it until the end of your days. It will bring you the purity that you must uncover in your spirit in order to work." Another time, when I made a face at a bowl, he burst out laughing: "You obviously don't know anything about this: it is a ceramic piece of rare quality from the Song dynasty." He pointed out a speck on the surface: "That is the 'stardust' technique— it suggests the cosmos." He explained to me the representations of Chinese myth notated by the little characters on the sides, and how to identify the period in which ceramic pieces were made. Their presence in the world, though humble and modest, became a source of contemplation. It was not the illusory resemblance to reality that the object represented which we found interesting, but its living presence. Old Lan continued: "Try to feel the plenitude of their being in the space of silence. They are full of the void that gave birth to them. How serene they seem, and yet they were born of the chaos of molten matter. Notice the reserve, the restraint with which they tell their story. Decipher it, describe the relationship that they maintain with the world. Recognize the pure intelligence of their internal shape. Try to penetrate the organic universe of their matter; it will bring a cosmogonical dimension to your work. You must perceive at the tip of your brush the ebb and flow of the matter that gave them life. Do not forget, Miss Fa, the perfection of their form in their clumsiness. It is pure knowledge. It has the power to restructure us internally. No words can describe the joy that it brings. In the clearness of a glaze or the luminous brilliance of a piece of porcelain, our troubled thoughts disappear without a trace. The object is serene. It truly possesses a magic power over the person contemplating it. Unconsciously, tirelessly, perhaps we are seeking the original mind.

"You must know that these objects so admired by the men of letters are an inexhaustible resource for the painter. They are the starting point for all meditation, for all creation. You will need to have such objects around you, in your studio. I'm not speaking here about 'still lifes,' as you call them in the West, but 'living lifes.' Just like us, these objects bear the moving patina of time. They are the keepers of secrets. Don't suppose that they divulge them easily! What mysterious breath gives them life? Imagine what this lotus-shaped dish of jade and amber dancing on a twisted base may tell us. Imagine what secrets these other objects may hold: the light glaze on a footed Ming bowl; these camphor-scented tea caddies; this tripod incense vase engraved with dragon veins; this celadon jar whose mouthpiece represents the Supreme Being; this glass dish flecked with patterns of the constellations; this stoneware basin whose marbling represents the fire of vital energy; this dish shaped like a water chestnut; this massive but refined Tang bulb planter; this black bowl, gleaming like the Milky Way, designed to bring out the clearness of the tea; this bronze incense burner incrusted with golden 'sunspots'; this mallet vase of rare porcelain, with smooth 'tea powder' glazes; this collection of ox-blood vases; this heat-retaining bowl with lobes in the form of a Song lotus flower; and these cracked alcohol pots, living memories of dry nature. For me these objects are islands of tranquility where the soul can go, every now and again, to extract a few serene, hidden thoughts."

As I listened to the teachings of Lan, I thought of the painter Giorgio Morandi and his automatic writing. The Morandi paintings that lived in my memory and the words of Lan went together perfectly. I heard a eulogy to simplicity in his interpretation of a few pots—a kind of "neutral intention" or clear revelation—brushstrokes entering into a dialogue with the object's spiritual presence.

My favorite pastime in my years as a diplomat was to meet Lan on the weekend. One Sunday morning, we were walking together when he asked me: "Do you hear that?" I only heard the din of traffic. "Don't you hear the pigeon musicians in the sky?" I looked up but saw nothing. "Let's go have a cup of tea," he suggested, "and I'll tell you about them. In Beijing there are people who raise pigeons and fasten tiny whistles to their feet. When the cages are opened, they take off, and depending on the shape of the whistles and the patterns they fly in the sky, a veritable symphony results. Each whistle is like a different musical instrument. The pigeon breeder-conductors hold competitions to determine whose group of pigeons produces the prettiest melodies." Afterward, I learned to recognize these sounds amid the noise of the city, and each time I became aware of them I would stop to listen. When I visited the museum-home of the great operatic actor Mei Lanfang, I learned that he also raised pigeons, but for another purpose: he followed their flight in the air to train his eye muscles, for an actor must express his emotions first and foremost through his eyes.

Besides hosting pigeon-musicians, Beijing was also a kite paradise. Over Tiananmen Square, which had witnessed so much tragedy, children and adults flew them: butterflies, phoenixes, bug-eyed dragons, centipedes spanning more than ten yards, and other fantastic animals dancing in the sky, at the mercy of the wind, thumbing their nose at the portrait of Mao still hanging above the entrance to the Forbidden City.

When I got annoyed with the French Cultural Center, Lan would tease me: "Forget about that; run up and down the long flight of steps to Coal Hill and you'll feel much better." Sometimes when I went to visit him, we did calligraphy together. His writing was incredibly beautiful; one could sense, looking at it, that he was a musician. He had perfected a musical style of calligraphy recognized by the great masters. His grass script, best loved by calligraphy enthusiasts, corresponded to a fast musical tempo; each note in the form of ideograms remained connected to the others, and the differences in the thickness of the stroke and the size of the characters brought rhythmic variations to the composition as a whole. These characters were similar to old styles but had a quickness, finesse, and great refinement. Everything was born of the restraint from which rivers of thought would gush.

"You with your vast knowledge, here you are, alone, writing, forgotten by the world. What will become of your manuscripts?" I asked him one day.

"If I could buy a computer, I would record everything. I would find someone to help me. It would be ideal. But don't worry, it is not essential."

I put in a request for a computer at the Embassy, but in vain.

Like Huang, Lan maintained that one needed to spend at least ten years with him to truly absorb his teachings: "I've had three students," he told me. "They all left after five years, thinking that they had learned enough; they took notes and disappeared without so much as a thank you or a goodbye. That was the end of our studies together in musicology. In Hong Kong and Taiwan, they became respected, highly paid professors. I was very disappointed by these young scholars who were only interested in money." He was horrified by what the contemporary world represented, and maintained a complete detachment. He would smile as he told stories about his working conditions:

"Some people have tried to help me but I was not allowed to benefit from it. Once, an American ambassador wanted to meet me. He requested special permission and we met one time, under surveillance, at an official banquet. We talked about music because, rare among diplomats, he had an interest. He asked me what equipment I used to listen to my recordings. When I admitted that I did not have any, he promised that during his next trip to the US, he would arrange to get me some. I never heard from him after that meeting. A long time after, when we met again, he asked me, in a highly displeased manner, if I was satisfied with the equipment he had sent me as promised. I apologized for not having thanked him and added that I would make inquiries, for I had received nothing. I discovered that my institute, the Central Conservatory of Music, was indeed equipped with an extraordinary high-tech stereo system. I had never been informed."

Lan's calligraphies were fruits of a unique spirit in China that brought a new resonance to the art form. His theories on ancient musicology fed his astonishing, delicate, and inspired art. He was as capable of creating a harmonious melody with his paintbrush as he could with his erhu. One day, he told me an art dealer from Japan had come to see him, promising to introduce his work in his country by organizing a large exhibition. Lan trusted him and gave him forty of his best works on paper. After no news from the dealer for many years, Lan heard that the thief had made a fortune in Japan by selling off his original calligraphies. This broke Lan's heart.

Tragically, the saddest part was the end of his life, which was related to me by the great pianist Zhu Xiao-Mei, his student. I ran into her in the autumn of 2002, purely by chance, in the stairway of a Parisian building. Two years earlier, Lan had experienced serious health problems from poor blood supply to his brain. He went in and out of the hospital several times. During his absences, his wife lost her mind. Affected by her martyr's existence at the old master's side, she sold the Shitao and her husband's treasures for a few dollars and burned his personal diary. Was this out of spite? On the Party's orders? How could such an insane act be explained? Destroying the memory of a man she had loved all her life? When he returned home after yet another hospital trip and realized the terrible things his wife had done, Lan died. A famous American musicologist recently deplored the loss of Lan's journal. The contents would have enlightened us on China's history over the last eighty years. I will always treasure the memory of our friendship and the smile of this benevolent monk.

In Beijing, I met another exceptional man, master Jin Zhilin, the greatest Chinese expert in folk art. My friend Jean Leclerc du Sablon nicknamed him the Champollion of Shaanxi, a title that suits him perfectly. He was originally a painter and a student of Xu Beihong, whom he continued to admire greatly. His best work dates from this early period. When teaching came under the iron rule of the Soviet experts, his art became academic. Unfortunately, he did not have the chance to paint for long. He was relegated to the Culture Ministry in the isolated villages of the Yan'an region of north-western China for more than twenty years. However, there, he set up a rural painting studio where, instead of teaching farmers the new genre of falsely naïve painting, he let them find inspiration freely in cutouts and folk-art woodcuts. The result was some highly original work.

When the situation stabilized a bit in the 1980s, he invited women from distant villages to Beijing to exhibit their paper cutouts and surrealist paintings made from colored sticky labels or bits of fabric sewn together. He even organized several exhibitions in France. He became quite the Francophile, often sporting a Basque beret brought back from Paris. He also started painting again. When he had time, he liked to go to the countryside with his oil painting materials. In his old age, he sought to integrate certain aesthetic theories on traditional Chinese painting into his work, yet he remained very nineteenth century. Following the classic Western approach, he took his easel, like Cézanne, outside and set it in front of landscape he found inspiring and worked. He could have painted *The Gamekeeper in Fontainebleau Forest* by Sisley. With horizontal strokes of boar's hair, he rendered foliage or the play of light in a lively and subtle manner. Up close, they have a clear and transparent freshness that could have come from a Chinese brush, although they are done in a Western oil technique. Jin Zhilin has the finesse and clarity of an Eugène Boudin and the inspiration of a Camille Corot. It was astonishing and moving to discover this sincere and authentic approach by a Chinese painter applied to this inspiration. We spent some marvelous times together, discussing painting.

During the Cultural Revolution, he endured the worst physical and emotional suffering imaginable. Afterward, he traveled across much of China. He also visited several European countries as well as India to study the connections between the various folk arts. He wrote a book on paper cutouts from Shaanxi province to show how this art form is endowed with an original aesthetic based on religious beliefs, some of which date from antiquity. Another work, on the tree of life, draws parallels between resurgences of the same theme throughout time and across Eurasia. In certain regions of China, he discovered ceremonies that are veritable surviving archaeological vestiges, as well as sculptures that are most likely relics of ancient totems. He fought hard to protect folk art from ignorant local officials who were determined to destroy all religious rituals by labelling them superstitions. Today, these same cadres have realized that they can make a lot of money from them by organizing performances for foreign tourists.

China was modernizing at great speed. The poor were getting poorer and the rich were getting richer or, as one Chinese told me, "Western Europe is becoming socialist while China is becoming capitalist." Some Chinese became billionaires almost overnight. One big star, famous before Gong Li, had invested in real estate and now lived in opulence. Sons of high officials got involved in all kinds of trafficking, even arms.

During this same period, unemployment started to surge while schools and hospitals started to charge. Auntie Lu had to pedal two hours to come to work, and the same in the evening to return home. She was living in a district that was scheduled to be torn down and would later face an even longer commute. The poor were being chased out of town. "Imagine," she told me, "they are going to house us in a tower block; no neighborhood, no market! We will be lost, isolated, uprooted. Plus, with the power outages, the elevators never work." The way of life with people living on their doorstep, taking their birds outside and meeting up with friends at the teahouse, was coming to an end.

A growing gap was forming between the guardians of Chinese culture and the youth of China, who were becoming Americanized. The moneyed could be found in new malls and Las Vegas-style discos, while their less wealthy counterparts visited KFC, hundreds of which had already sprung up in Beijing alone.

The big bookstore on avenue Wangfujing made way for a McDonald's. Certain painters, astute at adapting to the new economy, were by then earning a substantial living. To prevent allegations of corruption, leaders accepted paintings instead of cash and speculation across the art market began.

One day, there was a scandal at the embassy and I was called urgently. Stationed in front of the gates, a Chinese man was screaming insults at me. When I rushed there very upset, I discovered it was my old master Huang. He had learned that I was back in China, and had taken a train to Beijing to find me. He was ranting: "Fabi, come out of that hole. I didn't teach you everything you learned just so that you would become a moronic civil servant!" It was clear that he had drunk a bit too much, to get his courage up. He was happy that I had returned, but was outraged by my working at the embassy. "I've got something to say to you," he told me authoritatively. Fortunately, he was speaking in Sichuanese, so no one understood the foul language he was using. I took him to a little restaurant to explain my situation. He fired questions and disparaging remarks at me: "What are you doing here? What are you doing with your life? We spent six years together working night and day. I tried to give you the essentials. And here you are, playing a bureaucrat!" Even my own father and grandfather had never lost their temper and taken such a vehement tone with me. I admitted that I had gotten off-track but tried to defend myself: "You are right, master, but I am a single woman and I have to earn my living. I can't continue to live like a vagabond my whole life. But I promise I will soon devote myself to my painting once again."

"No, it's all over! Your ambition, the work that we did together, preparing for the act of painting, all that is finished. You will be devoured by political concerns.

Your career in the diplomatic service will leave you dissatisfied. You can't take on this kind of career lightly. I told you never to get involved in politics, didn't I?"

"But at least I can help certain artists."

"How presumptuous you are! Have you forgotten that helping makes no difference? We are just ping-pong balls."

"I met your friend Lan. I can help improve living conditions for artists like him."

"You're joking! All your efforts will be in vain. Artists have been starving since the dawn of time. You would serve much better with your paintbrush. If you continue along the path that I taught you, instead of acting the fool to earn money, your life will have meaning. With the level that you have reached in painting, you could earn your living more intelligently by selling your work from time to time and accepting odd jobs when necessary. You're either a painter full time or else not at all. Continue bustling about in an office and you'll get married and end up deep in pots and pans and dirty diapers, wondering if your husband still loves you, if you should take a lover, and other trifles. Family life and emotions only get in the way."

When I admitted that I had a boyfriend, he was even more infuriated. He left in despair, growling at me: "I've wasted my time." I suddenly felt horribly bad.

When I told this boyfriend about my conversation with Huang Laoshi, he sided with him. At a society cocktail party I had met Ghislain Baizeau, a Frenchman with a deep interest in Chinese culture. He was working for a French company with offices in China. He spoke Mandarin so well that it was impossible to tell what country he was from. Our second meeting was at the home of mutual friends, the de Villepoix, who always gathered an interesting mix of artists and intellectuals in Beijing to generous meals. I could not stay long that particular evening as I had accounting problems at the office to resolve for the next morning. Ghislain very gallantly offered to accompany me and help me with this work, assuring me that he was an expert. We spent a lovely evening together trying to balance the French Cultural Center's budget. The next day, I proudly submitted my accounts to my boss. That same afternoon, he summoned me to his office. He was livid: all the figures were wrong! It was very serious: I could have lost my job. I called Ghislain at once, furious at the mess. He admitted that he had pretended to know about accounts in order to spend time with me. I stayed angry with him for some time.

One evening, my girlfriends from the embassy wanted to go to a party on the other side of Beijing. They did not have a car and asked me to take them. I agreed, even though I had a huge amount of work. When we arrived, I found myself pleasantly surprised by the tranquility and refinement of our host's flat; there was a Han deity of great purity, dream stones, and piles of interesting books, while a melody from *Pelléas et Mélisande* played. The apartment, a rarity in Beijing, was part of a complex overlooking a lovely garden inhabited by Chinese families, artists, movie stars, and the great painter Wu Zuoren. In the course of that evening, I realized that I had landed at my famous accountant's! I was suddenly affected and overcome by shyness. That evening, while driving my friends home, I realized I had lost my head. One of them started to scream: "Fabienne! You're driving in the wrong direction!" Cars were coming at us fast, honking all around. I was heading straight into them. My mind was elsewhere; I had found the man I had been looking for.

The next morning, I called to tell him that I nearly caused several deaths and was not in my normal state of mind. I needed to see him as soon as possible. We met up again one evening at the frozen Lake of Beijing. After dinner in a restaurant near the Drum Tower, we walked for a long time on the frozen Lake of Ten Buddhist Monasteries under a starry, brilliantly clear sky. To move my plan along a little more quickly, I pretended to slip so he would catch me in his arms. That was heaven—blissful days of shared happiness such as I had never known in all those long years of lonely study.

We often went for walks in the gardens of the Summer Palace, Yiheyuan, not far from Ghislain's flat. There I discovered fascinating cosmic axes mounted on large concrete pedestals. We spent time in Beihai Park, in the garden of the "Room of the Tranquil Heart," Jingxinzhui. In these peaceful surroundings, we would talk for hours on end, making happy plans. He had lived in Beijing much longer than I had and introduced me to places steeped in history, as well as Taoist temples deep within the city, not yet restored but offering perfect harmonies of proportions and materials. Sometimes we went on pilgrimages to the White Cloud Temple, Baiyun Guan. I immediately gravitated to the inscription over the door: "Marvelous Domain of the Grotto of Heaven." This temple resembles a sacred mountain in the heart of Beijing, with its deep and dark worlds. We went there half believing we could uncover a key to the mystery of the universe. Very early on Sundays, we loved hunting for antiques in the second-hand stalls of the little markets. Invariably, we would end up in bed with a bad cold and a hot toddy!

Some months later, a Chinese man I had done a favor for wanted to thank me and invited me to dinner at a cheap restaurant. He was poor and I did not have the heart to refuse him. The pork was bad and I got food poisoning. In two weeks, I lost twenty kilos. I was so sick that I believed I would not survive. I was transferred to a hospital in Hong Kong because the doctors in Beijing did not think they could save me. The virus destroyed my whole immune system, and even today I still suffer the consequences. Other diners who ate the same pork died from it. I was ordered to rest for three months when I returned to Beijing.

Ghislain moved me into his home and took care of me with touching devotion. I felt ashamed and embarrassed to find myself in such a pitiful state after we had started out so well! However, I was in no condition to protest and from his art of living, I sensed a pure heart. So I set down my suitcases and let myself depend on him entirely. His patience and tenderness saved me.

After my convalescence, I tried to return to work at the cultural department of the embassy but it was absurd. How could I honestly believe that I could help

Franco-Chinese relations? I was eating next to nothing and had regular fainting spells, after which I would have to be taken to the hospital and placed on a drip. The ambassador ordered me to stop work. My body was giving up, and I fell into a serious depression. The virus was the cause, but also these ten years spent in China, fed by too much hope and despair.

Ghislain was admirable: he managed to persuade my old master to come from Sichuan and live with us. The two of them set up a studio for me. "You need someone to protect you after what you've been through these last few years," Huang Laoshi told me. "You have suffered too much, you went too far and now you are very ill. Shut yourself away and paint. It is the only possible way to recover your health and your taste for life." I might have died if I had not taken up my paintbrush again.

We began our four-handed exercises once more. Ghislain would be surprised to find a new painting or two on the wall when he returned home at night. When I started to recuperate, I decided to exhibit in Beijing my old works from Sichuan as well as my recent works, as a farewell to China. The embassy helped me. Many visitors and artists came. A friend published an article in a French daily: "Art to the Rescue of Diplomacy!" When Qi Gong, master calligrapher and president of the calligraphers of China, saw my work, he asked for a sheet of paper, and, in front of Huang and me, wrote a poem. Then he expressed gratitude to my professor for having found a way to pass on the subtleties of this scholarly form of painting. He hoped that I would blossom in the art form that I had chosen. He sensed I might succeed in opening new doors and innovate. I received a number of tributes for which I felt very gratified. My old professor was deeply pleased to see my work recognized by the officials and painters of Beijing, thanks to the training that he had given me.

"We're going back to France; we have to for your health," Ghislain told me. "But first, let's get married here, so we can have a nice big farewell party with our friends." We booked an entire hotel in the Perfumed Hills, close to Beijing, a magical place designed by I. M. Pei. There was a sublime garden with centennial pines, standing stones, and a small lake. We spent our savings and invited five hundred people, three hundred of whom were the most celebrated artists in China. Everyone came. We hired acrobats and musicians from the music academy; one group played traditional music, another classical. Our friend Cui Jian, the Chinese rock star, came to sing. There were well-known actors, stars from the film world and young designer friends we wanted to thank. A group of men of letters, including the writer Shen Dali, gave me a long scroll on which they had calligraphed my adventures in China.

His Excellency Claude Martin donned his tricolored French sash for the first time and married us officially at the embassy. Ghislain insisted on a religious ritual to mark our union, so we also had a very moving ceremony at the Catholic Church of Beitang. The Chinese priest who gave us his blessing had lived the life of a martyr in the work camps during the Cultural Revolution. He was very weak—thin and unable to swallow anything but soup and yogurt. He told us that when he was in the camps, he was reduced to eating soup made from paper pulp. Despite his suffering, he had a rare fervor and kindness. During the mass, army guards posted around the church kept us under surveillance. The situation was strange given our reasons for being there, experiencing such intense spiritual feeling.

We had amassed many things since we had both spent so many years in China. We sent some of our possessions by boat, but there are certain objects that a painter never lets out of her sight: paintbrushes and seals. Certain seals, very old, were given to me by old men of letters. At the airport, the customs officers searched my belongings and confiscated many of them. I had promised myself that I would save some of these objects that were links in a chain of ancient knowledge, but they were taken from me, as if I had stolen bits of Chinese heritage. Meanwhile, at that very same moment, officials were destroying historical centers of priceless value in China's large cities. The systematic destruction of the jewels of a civilization, begun during the Cultural Revolution, was continuing with China's opening to the West where "modernization" was its watchword. "These objects will continue to belong to you but must stay in China," the customs officers informed me. I never saw them again and was strongly advised not to speak of the matter as it could damage Franco-Chinese relations. In late 1992, as our plane left China for Paris, our hearts were heavy from the very bitter departure. We flew over an already disfigured Beijing, with building sites of destruction and reconstruction as far as the eye could see.

Passenger of silence

With the strokes of my inspired brush I shook the five sacred mountains.

Ghislain and I moved out to the countryside, in the Île-de-France region near Paris. I needed sanctuary, a period of silence to learn to live again and revive my ascetic practice of the work of a painter. A son, Martin, was born to us.

Since my return to France, I have drawn upon what I learned during my years in China and tried to create. I became a painter as others become furniture-makers, bank clerks, or cattle breeders . . . In a few years, I had my first show in Paris, then a large exhibition in Hong Kong at the Museum of Contemporary Art. These were followed by others in a gallery in Paris's Palais-Royal and a famous foundation in Taiwan. In 2002, I published a book of my work.

If in China I was captivated by the mineral world that can be contemplated in paintings and dream stones, it is because I found in that world what I had been missing since childhood—the landscapes I discovered as a little girl in the Ardèche region. It is the source of what I love. What I seek in painting is probably inspired by this.

I recently returned to that untamed place to rediscover vast stone deserts and the sweet, powerful scents of nettles, juniper, boxwood, thyme, and goat droppings that made such an impression on me in my youth. On the high plateaus of the Beaume, celestial gardens still exist, glowing in the moonlight, with their stones, twisted olive trees, and centennial oaks struggling for light between two giant rock walls. There I could see primordial tablelands dug out of ancient moss-covered slabs concealing subterranean water and hermits' caves—maybe druids still live there. As a child, I was awed by this mineral universe, the rocky paths, little timeless stone bridges and dead trees in tormented shapes.

I want to show this feeling of a union with the universe and its beauty in my canvases. For many, there is the world of art on one side and the mundane world on the other—that is, the ideal but artificial world versus harsh reality. I wanted to achieve a balance between the two. My painting does not come from a desire to compete with the ancient masters or to distinguish myself, but from a yearning for exquisite delight, bliss, and a refuge against sadness. Beautiful landscapes have given me my most intense moments of joy and serenity since childhood. I have learned that ecstasy, whether arriving with an explosion or in complete silence, is not a gift from the heavens that we sit idly by waiting. It must be earned and tamed. Intelligence also plays a role.

I wondered why I couldn't transform the teachings of the old masters. I thought of Giotto, who dared to decorate the Basilica of Saint Francis of Assisi in 1279. At the time, paintings were banned from religious surfaces because the Cistercians forbade any "decoration" of sacred spaces. How could you not admire Giotto's audacity in recreating the harmonies of the Gregorian chants with his paintings? He was not interested in likeness, but in the resonance of the spirit. He understood the expression of beauty through simplicity. Transformation is a risk worth taking! Only through ceaseless transformation can we invent new languages. I believe that it is also by virtue of transformation that we can profoundly experience our way of being in the world.

For twenty years now, I have been seeking out and inventing special surfaces to host the poetic thoughts expressed by the stroke of my brush. I am painfully aware of the importance of the background. I spend weeks and even months constructing these varied structures. I feel compelled to transform the ancestral technique I have learned, but it was many long years before I managed to transition from paper-backed silk mounted on a scroll to a linen-cotton canvas mounted on a stretcher.

Modern physics has finally challenged Einstein's theories by proving that the void is not empty. For enlightened poets, the void has always contained life. This depth, this emptiness where the supreme vacuity resides in a constant movement of millions of invisible cells has always been a source of deep inspiration to me.

Mark Rothko spent his whole life searching for the archetype of the "mother house" that is nothingness. In his paintings, those elusive, subtle borders, the blurred, luminous, vertiginous passages from beyond the time of man, have always fascinated me. In his tireless quest for silence, to find the fundamental unity of the universe, there is a mystical beauty.

In the same way, for many years I studied works by anonymous painters from fifteenth-century China. I'd immerse myself in the backgrounds of landscapes by Guo Xi, such as *Autumn of the River Valley*, or Fan Kuan's *Travelers Among Mountains and Streams*. I stood before these paintings for hours in the National Palace Museum of Taiwan, and found them truly enchanting, a brilliant lesson on the manifestation of the void.

So I have recently taken my Chinese training and blended its techniques with the equally fascinating principles of Flemish and Italian primitive painting. Glazes, transparency, and depth of varnish: all are mirror reflections of the life of emptiness/fullness. I am discovering paint matter that is still uncharted territory, preserving the sacredness of form, to which I add the brilliance of light. Once these backgrounds are created, I stand before them, and after hours of meditation, I find the path to inspiration and finally travel with my brush into distant infinity.

For ten years, master Huang insisted I transcribe color through a range of monochromes, most often black, using washes and India ink. It proved a difficult exercise to identify the subtle richness of the colors of the universe in the intensity of the blacks. The neutral wash feeds the essence, and its self-effacement creates an intense presence within. From time to time, I leave the asceticism of black and white to dive into the heart of color. My stay in China brought me into contact with an endless variety of colors: spiritual thoughts calligraphed in gold leaf in Buddhist temples or the cobalt pigment used by the Tibetans. There was a period when I was crazy about cinnabar red, a color traditionally reserved for stamping seals in Chinese painting. This natural mercuric sulphide, a sort of soiled vermilion, is found in the works of Rogier van der Weyden. I decided to transform its original use by using it in my contemporary work, creating new fields of emotion.

I am often asked how I managed to endure such a difficult existence in China over those many years. Why did I not return home like most? Read stories of important artists working in every medium. They didn't confront difficulties in the beginning due to some kind of biblical curse exacting pain in exchange for creation. The quality of a work of art does not stem from any innate talent of its creator, even if it is necessary at the start (which is not certain.) The difference lies in an artist's perseverance, her tenacious will to press forward. Some artists, satisfied, stop before reaching their destination; some are content to learn a few tricks from their painting or calligraphy classes, and believe they can fool others. (That delusion is short lived.) Others continue to search until they find what they seek.

When I arrived in China, I understood that my time there would only have real meaning if I experienced rigorous instruction. If my wish was to master the brushstroke, then I would have to paint horizontal lines for months on end, following in the steps of the great painters. Once I began to acquire the technique, I realized very quickly that in order to go further, I had to study Chinese philosophy. I owe much to my master, who never dissociated painting from Chinese thinking, and insisted on teaching me both at the same time. In China, I was taught a style of painting, but, more importantly, I trained my spirit and learned to guide it and mature. Perhaps I have learned how to calm and control the thoughts and desires that race in my head like a group of crazy monkeys.

I learned, by the light of Taoism and Buddhism, that it is possible to direct one's mind along a chosen path, and not merely let it be formed by society around us. The star that seemed unattainable is within reach: a grain of wisdom that fortunately also carries a spark of madness!

The calligrapher is a nomad, a passenger of silence, a tightrope walker. She delights in wandering intuitively over infinite expanses, stopping here and there, exploring the universe in its movement across space and time. Her desire is to confer a taste of eternity on the ephemeral. My large works of calligraphy are like "poetic plateaus," a kind of architecture of intuitive thought. I bring to life a space of meditation in fiery movement.

My quest? To seize and distill the spirit of life. An atmosphere of strength and plenitude emanating from within, as though serenity is born of incessant movement, like the regular cadence in a Bach fugue or the chanting of monks—interpretations that blend movement and stillness by an endless recitative and succeed in transcending our earthly concerns to reach the beyond. Even a novice may follow the psalmody of the script if his mind is receptive. There is no need to understand the Chinese characters to appreciate the beauty of the movement and reach what Seneca called the "tranquility of the soul."

These days, in my seclusion, I experience a profound communion with nature. Every interior space contains an opening toward the exterior. Tree sap, the fleeting passage of the seasons, the richness of the light and its endless variations are intimately linked to one's inner life. I treasure my fishbowl of serenity and its permanent relationship with the garden surrounding our home.

Monet found his stability as a painter in Giverny. I, too, experience a kind of beatitude in inhabiting a magical place where I can work while contemplating the natural universe. In some ways I live like in the nineteenth century, with a wood kitchen stove and an active mineral spring between the house and the studio. The geomancy of the location is perfect, and I have taken root here.

For many years, I have harbored a secret temptation to address the plant mystery in my painting. I had to wait for the necessary maturity. "The botany of a dream is not," wrote Gaston Bachelard in *L'air et les songes* (Air and Dreams: An Essay on the Imagination of Movement, 1943). Celebrating the living, discovering the plant mystery—the hidden substance of the world— bears no resemblance to the naturalism of my early art studies when I drew botanical plates. Rather, it is a visible translation of the invisible structure of things. The great Chinese master venerated for this art form was called Chuta. He was able to transpose into his paintings his inner reverie, capturing the plant soul. In them, one can perceive the manifestation of a vital force that transcends us. Gaston Bachelard understood, like the old Chinese sages, that a deep and living unity exists between certain plant images and ourselves. And then there is the modesty that sparks our curiosity for the infinitely small . . . Absolute beauty is as present at the top of a high mountain as it is in a leaf of rhubarb or a turnip from the kitchen garden.

Carried along by the breath of the paintbrush, I am now engaged in exploring the genius specific to every living being: the rustling of bamboo, the discrete modesty of a blade of grass, the fervor of young daffodil shoots reaching toward the light, the skeleton of a tree bent by winter gales, a private conversation between two flower buds, the destiny of a black-hearted flower, the stem of the common bramble in search of water, the blooming of cherry blossoms into a Milky Way, the smile of a primrose or the capriciousness of dead wood.

To hone my concentration, I have withdrawn from the world. Moments of vacuity and intimate perception favor detachment. The further I move forward, the more I seek a kind of ordinariness in daily life that offers me joyous solitude. This search for simplicity awakens in me a profound receptiveness to the living, even the most minute. It is only in such a serene state that we can connect with the source of our heart. It took me a long time to grasp and truly practice this discipline. The training between theory and true awakening to life's mysteries is so long that it is difficult to stay the course. One thing is certain though: it is the daily practice of the awakening that allows access to true knowledge. It would take twenty years of contemplation before I could fully understand and appreciate the teachings of my old master.

I am only an apprentice painter in the world of art. My work lacks the necessary maturity. It is too young and too green. I only recently understood the internal principle, the alchemy that brings things to life. To attain this more sublime, even more divine painting, I have to touch an intimate, inexpressible truth. This means curbing insipidness and continuing to cultivate humility and freedom as regards any sort of acquired mastery. I have to become *bendan*—an idiot—as my bird used to call me—according to the great theory of the Taoist masters. Who knows? With time, I just might get there.

Little by little, I have come to know this life, this circle of silence and the presence of the unsaid. I understand the need to forget time, myself, and all acquired thoughts, opinions, and culture. This way, I can transform myself into "grass in the wind" or a "spring breeze"—a light spirit that is fluid and mobile. External limitations are cast aside—not to be trusted. "Emptying the mind" is no simple exercise. The unique brushstroke, the "painter's ritual," is born under the stamp of inspiration through a spontaneous act, a primary impulse, a primordial osmosis with the creative essence. Through this practice, I attempt to experience "one mind" in its absolute reality. Behind the apparent emptiness of silence, life is teeming all around, and so it is with modesty and wonder that poetic thought can be captured.

My hermit's existence painting in the country has led me to recognize the sublime music of the world in the sprouting of a flower bud. What power, what learning, what complexity can be found in that meager little bud! This carnal communion with nature, like a tune that returns over and over, more beautiful and profuse with each passing season, teaches us that life never dies. For me, the act of painting offers all the possibilities of creation: to be at my doorstep, greeting the world's beauty, freely, in the buoyancy of the moment . . .

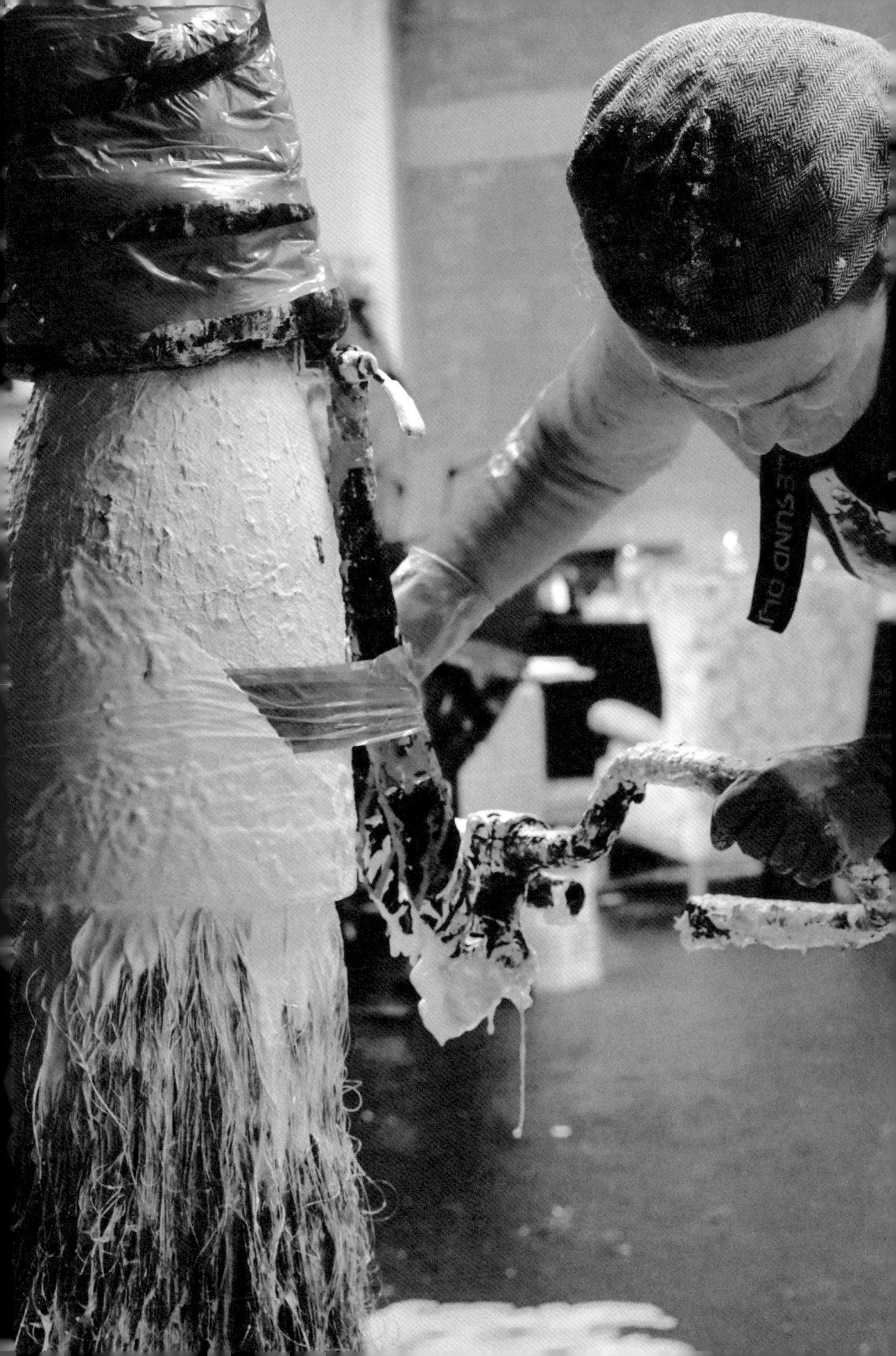

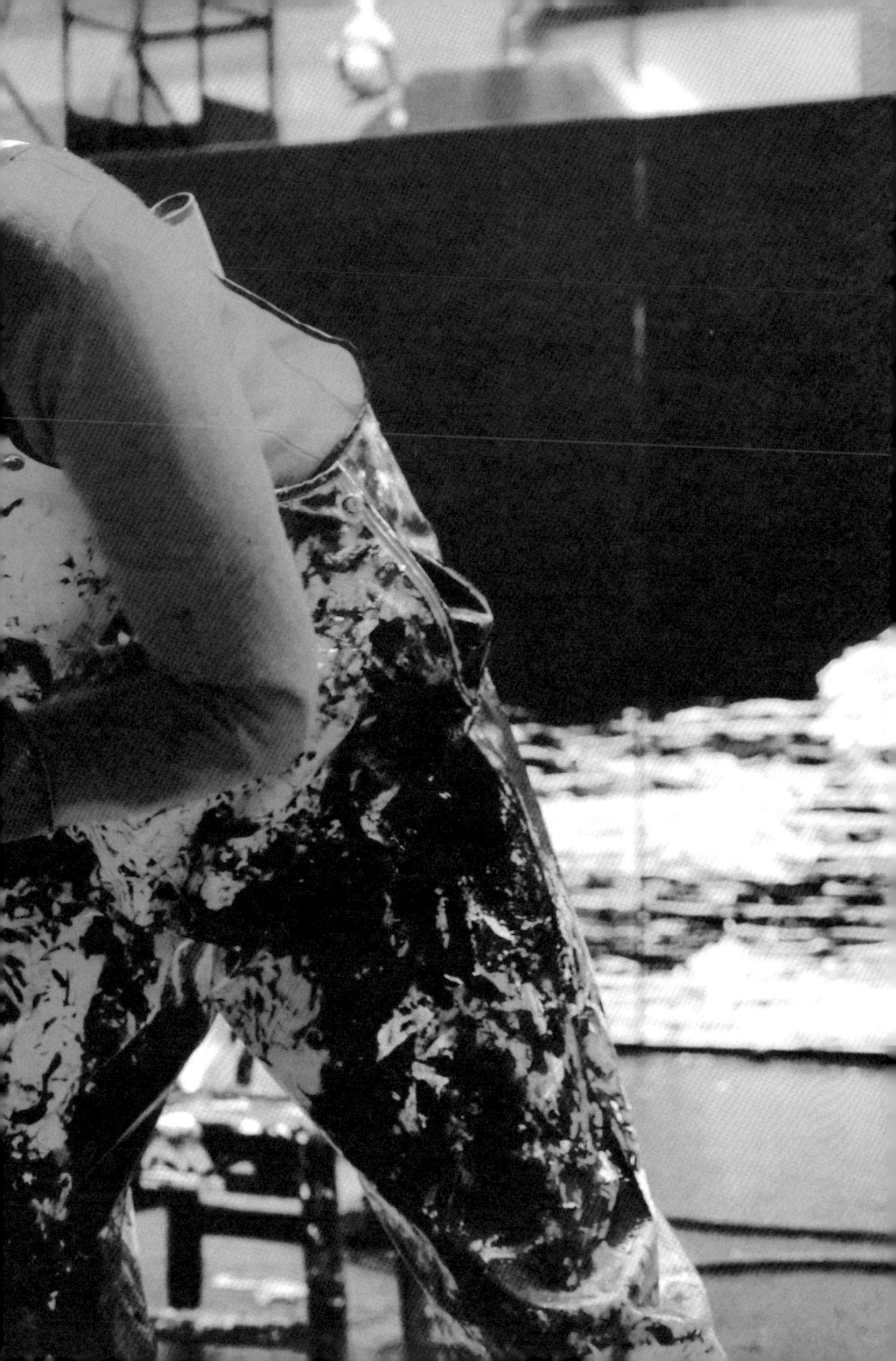

Transposing and Inventing

Corinna Thierolf

". . . new journeys that I had carried inside of me without ever being able to bring them to life."
—Fabienne Verdier[1]

It is said that Marco Polo's[2] family did not recognize him upon his return from China. Like this great Venetian traveler of yore, Fabienne Verdier (b. 1962), who left for China in 1984 at the age of twenty-two to study traditional painting and calligraphy, no longer knew which culture she was most at home in when she returned after almost ten years abroad. Her unique interaction with the country's aesthetic traditions both past and present had fundamentally expanded her ideas of what art could be. After that experience, how could she explain to the art world where she had come from and who she had become? The two worlds were far apart, and she had explored both so deeply that it took a giant leap to get from one place to another and to develop a language of her own. A testament to Verdier's attempt to bridge the worlds is her book *Passagère du silence. Dix ans d'initiation en Chine*, published in 2003, almost a decade after her return. It is now available in English under the title *Passenger of Silence*, having already been translated and

---

The references to Fabienne Verdier's biography in this text are based on *Passenger of Silence* and have been supplemented by sources from the artist's archives and Daniel Abadie, "Fabienne Verdier: Her Life and Work," in Abadie, *Crossing Signs*, exh. cat. (Éditions Albin Michel, Paris; Hong Kong: City Hall, 2014), 12–142.

1   Verdier, *Passenger of Silence* (in this volume), 265.
2   Born in 1254.

published in six languages and in as many as three editions in certain countries.[3] Verdier's book provides detailed insight into a chapter of historical and contemporary Chinese cultural history that is little known in the West. It is also a stirring biographical document of a powerful and unique young woman who is equally gifted in both the rational and the intuitive. This gripping and profound account is an invaluable reference for understanding Verdier's work. Her search for centuries-old artistic traditions in China, which were almost annihilated by the Cultural Revolution, grew into a unique wealth of experience that went far beyond merely being "inspired" by East Asian art. Whereas many Western artists, such as Vincent van Gogh, Franz Kline, and Brice Marden, incorporated isolated stylistic elements from the East into their work, Verdier's long stay in the country and the radical nature of her research left her with a profound understanding of Chinese culture. Not only did she study this culture from a distance, but she also struggled, with the greatest sincerity, to access and experience this culture firsthand. Initially those traditions were completely closed off to her, while her experience of everyday life contrasted starkly with those rarified pursuits.

The knowledge that Verdier sought during her courageous journey to the Sichuan Fine Arts Institute in Chongqing was not part of the curriculum of that or any other university in China at the time.[4] Verdier was interested in "literati painting," an art form of the classically educated Chinese elite, with a far-reaching impact on personal development that encompasses the mastery of the "four great arts": poetry, calligraphy, painting, and music. Its roots go back to the seventh century. But the Cultural Revolution (which began in 1966 and only started to be

3   French: Editions Albin Michel, Paris, 2003 and 2005, ebook 2009 and 2014; German: Edition Spuren, Winterthur, 2006 and 2017; Italian: Casa Editrice Ponte alle Grazie, Milan, 2004, and Casa Editrice Tea Libri, Milan, 2007; Polish: W.A.B., Warsaw, 2007, 2012, and 2017; Spanish: Publicaciones y Ediciones Salamandra, Barcelona, 2007; Hebrew: Editions Asia, 2009 and 2014; Japanese: Sayzansha, Tokyo, 2010.
4   For more detailed information on this, and in particular on changes in the curriculum since the second half of the 1980s, see Verdier 56, 58.

dismantled with the arrival of Deng Xiaoping in 1979) fought against the "Four Olds"—old ideas, old cultures, old habits, and old customs. It almost completely eradicated this "discredited" art as counterrevolutionary and categorically expunged it from students' consciousness.

In the subsequent anti-intellectual campaigns, masters of these forms were humiliated as "stooges of feudalism," cast out from society, and often even maimed. A hand could be cut off not only as punishment and a permanent stigma, but also to prevent the artist from continuing his or her practice. The artifacts of this culture, which in other political circumstances would have been called relics or national cultural treasures, were looted and destroyed in temples, libraries, and collections. As a result, the memory of this culture was virtually erased, and only a few techniques, those that were considered "self-evident," including the skilled use of ink, the production of paper, and the mounting of pictures and scrolls painted on paper, were saved. However, they remained mere bits and pieces to be used pragmatically and out of context, as the full spectrum of techniques and content was consistently excluded.

While literati painting was used to depict fleeting atmospheric moments that simultaneously revealed fundamental philosophical questions to the sophisticated viewer, the style taught at universities in the early 1980s, which Verdier encountered, continued to be dominated by the style established during the Cultural Revolution, which followed the guidelines of Socialist Realism: bold strokes and striking colors intended to glorify the people, especially workers, peasants, and marginalized social groups. Ironically, the mission of promoting ethnic minorities highlighted the double-edged nature of the program: Verdier reports that during her stay in China, artists were probably "the ones who were the most familiar with the reality of their country and knew that an immense disparity existed between the official Party line and the truth."[5] Because artists were sent to villages

---

5   Verdier, 29.

292   PASSENGER OF SILENCE

to study the people, they saw not only the folk art they were supposed to celebrate but also the often miserable living conditions of these peasants, who rarely had the opportunity to express themselves publicly. In the case of ethnic minorities such as the Yi, Miao, Naxi, Buyi, and Yao, artists had the dubious freedom to witness the destruction of unique long-standing traditional cultures in the course of "ethnic cleansing," which not only targeted language, dress, and daily rituals but also led to temples being looted.[6] As a result, Verdier, who actually wanted to learn from these rich and diverse cultures, became a critical witness to their continued erasure even after the Cultural Revolution. However, "Chinese authorities didn't solely use force or censorship to check dissent, but somehow imposed self-censorship."[7]

The story of Verdier's idiosyncratic path also includes an account of numerous aspects of Western painting that enjoyed great popularity among her Chinese peers. Surprisingly, this influence dates back to the reign of Mao Zedong, when Soviet teachers were appointed to schools to teach their concept of art. In their wake came teachers who taught oil painting and easel painting, both of which were foreign to China, where painting was done on paper lying flat. Such Western imports were not taught in a broader cultural context, nor was China's own history. Instead, only individual elements were extracted by government commissions for teaching in art academies. The opening up to the West was not a continuous process but took place in disjointed stages.

In Verdier's *Passenger of Silence*, the reader is taken into the official events of the time, as well as into the dark corridors of the university campus at night, where one can follow the often violent and confusing movements and counter-movements at close range. She vividly recounts how until the late 1970s, the

---

6   Verdier, 47, 57, 141.
7   Verdier, 45.

appreciation of Rembrandt was promoted, while Henri Matisse and abstract painting were considered decadent. During Deng Xiaoping's policy of reform and opening in the 1980s, which she witnessed, the values changed. Verdier's fellow students passionately explored the henceforth officially sanctioned French modernism of Paul Cézanne and Pablo Picasso or Vincent van Gogh, and starting in the second half of the 1980s, American Pop art.[8]

Verdier rejected the direction of these movements for herself: "At heart, I wanted to take the exact opposite course to theirs."[9] She wanted to follow a path in which she was almost completely alone. In 1985, she was finally clandestinely given the names of two elderly masters. They had not been reinstated, but they lived secretly on the university campus. The first of these was an embittered calligrapher with whom she discontinued contact. The second master, Huang Yuan, dismissed her, explaining he no longer existed and no longer wanted to teach.[10] Despite this rejection, she was inspired to persevere. In this stranger's house, she had come into contact with the spirit she was looking for at last. Encouraged, she remembered reading that a master would test the seriousness and determination of a potential student.[11] So she obtained reproductions of China's most famous stone-carved calligraphies, made copies based on them for her own study, and regularly left them at the master's doorstep uninvited. She was undoubtedly aware of the importance of copying within the traditional Chinese aesthetic, which differs from the modern Western definition. The term "copy" has a pejorative undertone in the West which suggests a distance between the activity of the artist and that of the imitator: one work, thanks to technical skill and imagina-

---

8   See Verdier, 58, 60. After Verdier's years in China, the most significant steps in opening up to Western art came during the 2008 Beijing Olympics and the 2010 Shanghai World Expo, where the first Picasso exhibition in China was held in the Chinese pavilion; see Caroline Boudehen, *Le boom de l'art contemporain en Chine* (La Tour-d'Aigues: éditions de l'Aube, 2022), 11–14.

9   Verdier, 59.

10   Verdier, 65.

11   Verdier, 65–66.

tion, is the original, which has relevance in terms of style and content; the other, at best, is a reproduction for study purposes, or, at worst, a forgery. In China, however, copies have traditionally been favorably viewed as an exchange between an accomplished and beginning painter, focusing on the "extraordinarily vivid brushstroke." Master and student are attributed the same creativity: both are artists; both devote themselves to the same subject and submit to the discipline of similarity. They can be compared to two wild geese flying in the sky. Despite the similarity of their paths, the individuality of each bird remains clearly recognizable. There are varying degrees of technical skill, but there are also characteristics beyond technique and form. The calligrapher's stroke, for example, reveals more than technical ability. It reveals the artist's personality: whether he or she has a powerful and perhaps impulsive character or is flexible and malleable.[12]

After six months of unwavering perseverance in carrying out her exercises, Verdier passed the first test. Impressed by her dedication, the master visited her and made a surprising pronouncement: "I can discern the moral and spiritual worth in your brushstrokes. [. . .] There is a resonance inside of you [. . .]. It is the source of works to come."[13] He agreed to teach her officially. Such an assessment of a "qualifying examination" may sound strange to Western ears. However, it is based on the idea of the "naked truth" of the brushstroke, which reveals the creative and human qualities of the artist and thus makes them legible.[14] With just one brushstroke, everything can be said.

With the help of the university administration and governing institutions, Verdier finally obtained the necessary official permission to take lessons. From then on, Master Huang Yuan was allowed to give "the foreigner" two or three

---

12   The image of the flight of two wild geese and its connection to the art of copying is taken from: Nicole Vandier-Nicolas: *Art et sagesse en Chine. Mi Fou (1051–1107). Peintre et connaisseur d'Art dans la perspective de l'esthétique des lettrés [Annales du Musée Guimet : Bibliothèque d'études*, vol. 70] (Paris: Presses Universitaires de France, 1963), 111.

13   Verdier, 69.

14   Verdier, 46.

lessons a week to introduce her to the "use of the Chinese paintbrush."[15] The program was soon expanded to encompass all aspects of the art. Unfortunately, Verdier had barely completed her official studies in 1989 when she had to leave China abruptly, at least temporarily, due to the political upheaval arising from student and popular protests in Tiananmen Square.

During her studies, Verdier explored many techniques and subjects, but the basis was the brushstroke, which has become the core of her practice. The brush is a reservoir of ink that is emptied during writing or painting by the artist's deliberate movements. The gestures, which must not be too slow or too fast, must be in harmony with the person as a whole, including the person's breath, to choreograph the expressive possibilities of the tip of the brush. These depend on the particular position the brush is held over the paper. The posture of the brush, like the posture of the body, should always be upright, because this vertical line represents the axis between heaven and earth. As a result, the artist does not paint primarily as "I" and by the power of his or her will, as is common in Western practice, but is placed in the context of the universe. Verdier describes in her notes how she learned to root both feet firmly in the ground, "drawing the earth's energies upward."[16] This position is extremely demanding, but she nevertheless mastered it and made it the irrefutable foundation of her painting. She consciously submits herself to the invisible and immeasurable axis. This requires both a willingness to take risks and a blind trust in the chaos and emptiness[17] that are at the origin of everything. In this vertical line between heaven and earth, the abyss, abandonment, and despair are just as much a given as the ecstasy of creation. Those who fully surrender themselves to these forces and are willing to forget everything

---

15   Verdier, 70.

16   Verdier, 75.

17   Chaos and emptiness are core concepts in the wisdom teachings of Daoism, as well as of Buddhism and Confucianism, which have fundamentally influenced the spirit and aesthetics of literati painting: the chaos at the beginning of the world is transformed into emptiness through the techniques and energies that man possesses within himself.

they have learned can reach a state of total liberation and thereby capture forms in a flash with the brush—and thus life itself at that very moment.

Verdier has combined her unique knowledge of Eastern and ancient cultures with Western culture and the present to produce surprisingly diverse work. She gradually created special tools and material to be able to create larger works, even wall-sized, which require the use of her whole body.[18] Thanks to her inventions, she can work with brushes suspended in the air like a pendulum.[19] Today, many who picture her painting think first and foremost of the unforgettably large brushes that she guides in an upright movement over a canvas lying on the floor [see fig. on page 288, 318]. No matter how much her technique evolved, she always respected her training by preserving the vertical axis of painting. To appreciate how far she has developed her technique, we must remember that the vertical painting technique she learned in China is practiced on paper and usually from a sitting position. It is an activity that is of a manageable scale and therefore much easier to control.

While Verdier can produce monumental paintings, she has not lost her ability to sense the most discrete emanations of energy. In her "Vortex" series (2020) [see fig. on page 315], her seismographic brushstroke catches the voice of a singer as it expands and disappears in space. A spiral-shaped movement floating upward is suggested by a compelling artistic interpretation in the way color is applied to a canvas spread on the ground. The titles of these works refer to famous arias, including Mozart's "All'eco, all'aria, ai venti" from *Le Nozze di Figaro*. This line is

---

18   To this end, Verdier has developed natural hair brushes that can hold around eight gallons of ink. Thanks to the ingenious technique of combining shorter and longer hairs to form a whole, the ink does not immediately flow onto the floor in a huge mass but is gradually released in a controlled manner through the fine tip of the brush.

19   Verdier's desire for larger paintings was accompanied by the challenge of physically controlling the increasingly heavy equipment. See the description of the moment when Verdier cut off the handle of her brush in order to replace it with a pulley attached to the ceiling. In ancient China, the brush handle was considered the irrevocable center of painting because of the symbolism of the axis. Verdier dared to cut it off because, as she herself said, over the decades, her body had become a handle. See Corinna Thierolf, "On the Works of Fabienne Verdier in the Palazzo Torlonia," in *Fabienne Verdier. Palazzo Torlonia* (Paris: Editions Xavier Barral, 2011), 13–14. See also an excerpt from the documentary film by Philippe Chancel made in this context: https://fabienneverdier.com/db/video/palazzo-torlonia/ (last accessed June 19, 2024).

a poetic expression of her desire to devote herself entirely to what the Greeks call *pneuma* (breath, air, spirit, soul) and the Chinese call *qi* (energy, breath, aura, ether) in this series.

Throughout history, there have been artists who have been inspired by drops of paint randomly landing on the canvas. However, none have focused on making this natural force—gravity—visible like Verdier. Verdier started to harness the power of gravity when she began a group of works in 2013 titled *Walking Paintings*. She freed herself from the brush and concentrated on the effects of falling paint. In this series, she trickled paint from a container onto a canvas spread on the floor while walking at a measured pace. In this way, she dispenses with the direct, gestural application of paint, and gravity becomes a co-creator of the works. On closer inspection, one can see that the lines on the canvas are formed by a multitude of successive dots, some of which overlap. The energy of the impact can cause the emerging drops of paint to bounce back from the center of their first landing point, only to be displaced outward and land in a circle that is empty inside.

A fascinating film by Ghislain Baizeau takes a close look at this phenomenon[20] using an extreme macro perspective to demonstrate Verdier's efforts. Thanks to magnification, her painting offers an experience similar to the zoom effect we use every day on our cell phones. In Verdier's paintings, the viewer can now—and this is the real purpose of the large formats—not only observe but literally penetrate the power of the forces of nature.

This brief review of some key aspects of Verdier's development explains how her art has always flowed toward externalization. Undaunted by any challenge, she is constantly in search of the unknown and the invisible. She reveals what can be captured in the colossal vertical expanse between heaven and earth that she

---

20   https://fabienneverdier.com/db/video/walking-painting/ (last accessed June 19, 2024).

learned to be conscious of in China. Beginning with *Passenger of Silence*, we see a body of work spanning more than four decades, crossing cultures and eras, different arts and sciences. In all her work, she demonstrates the infinite resonance of a painting: how each person can journey beyond themselves and finally bring to life that which they carried inside of them.[21]

---

21   Verdier, 265.

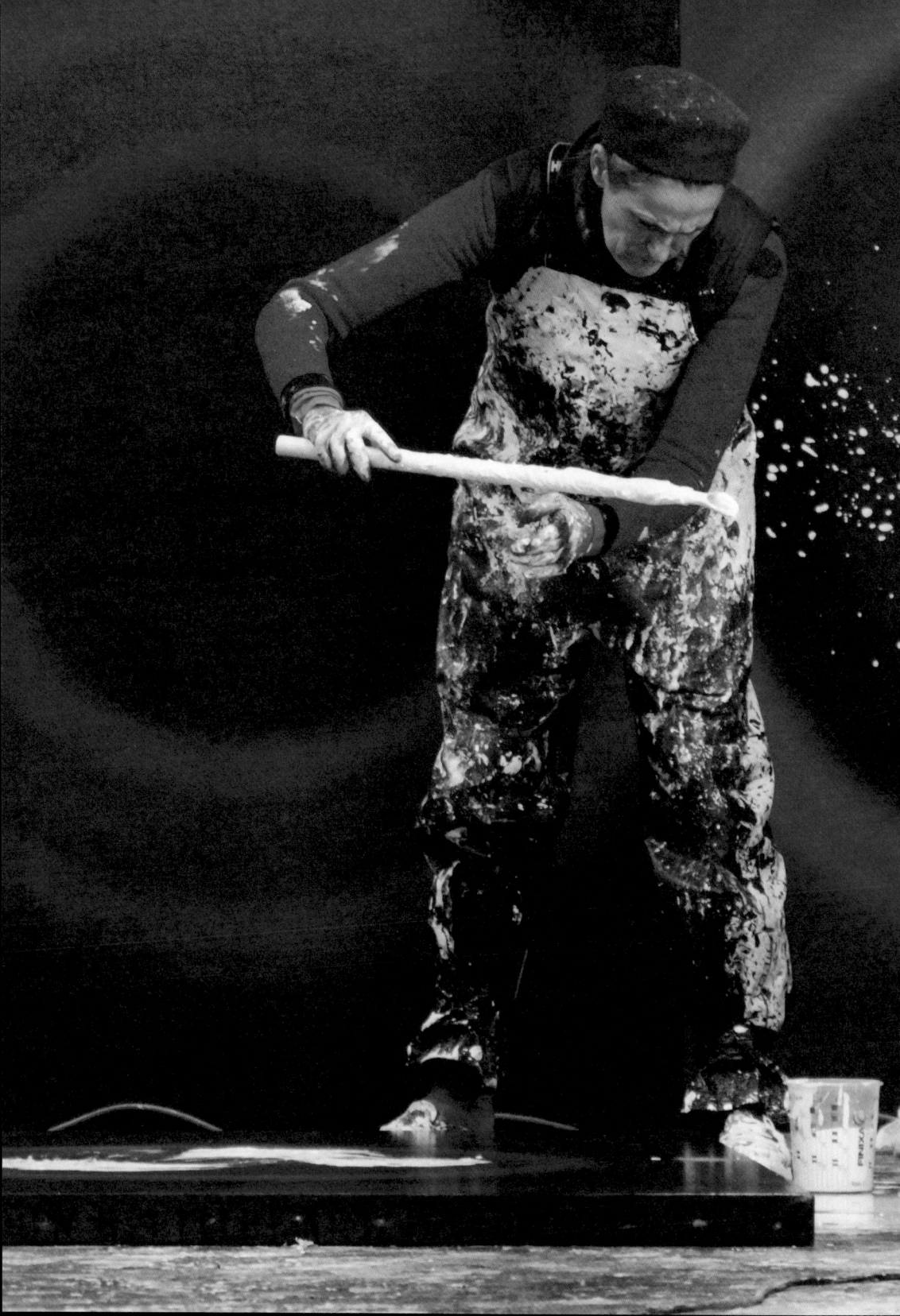

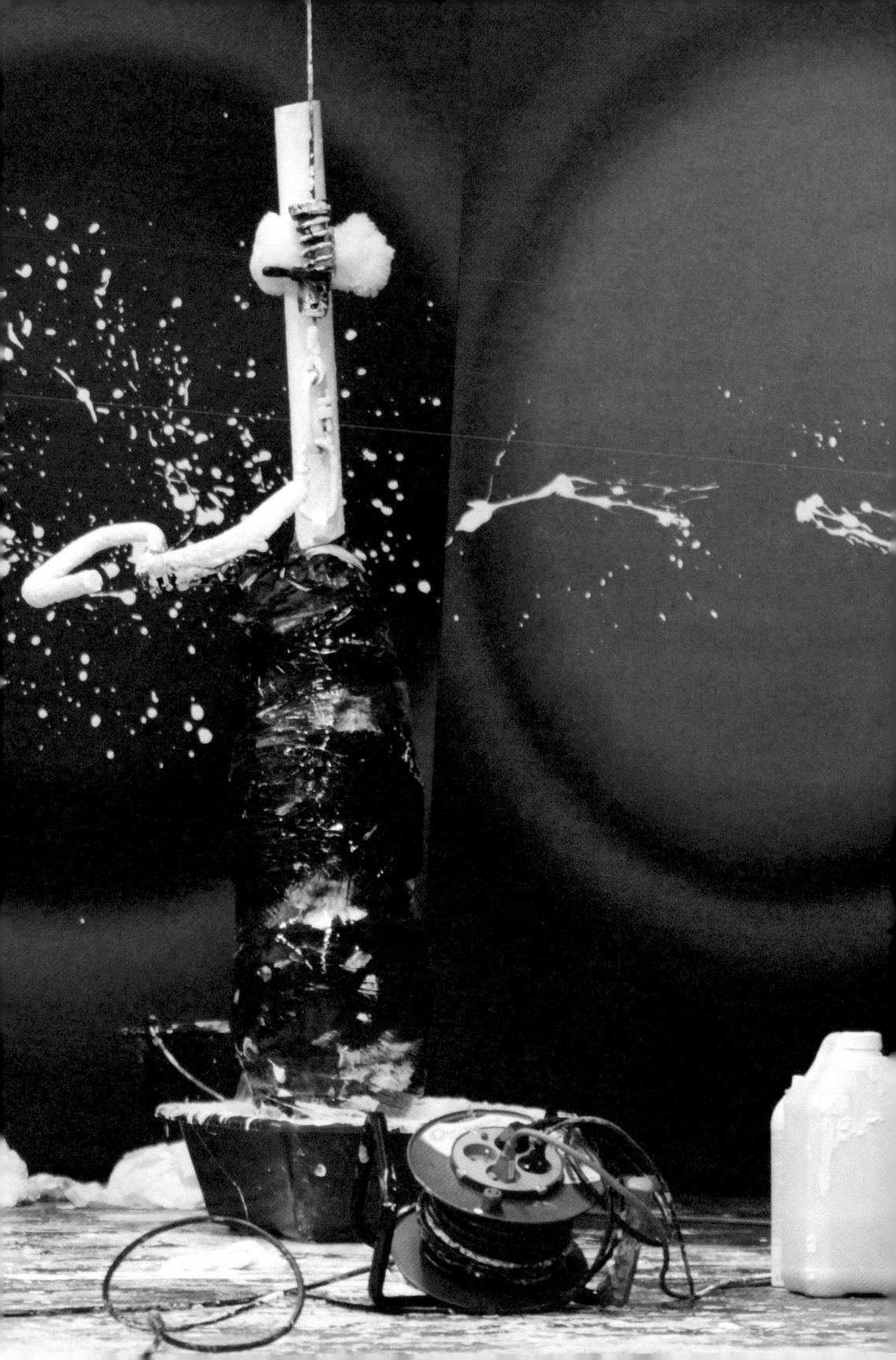

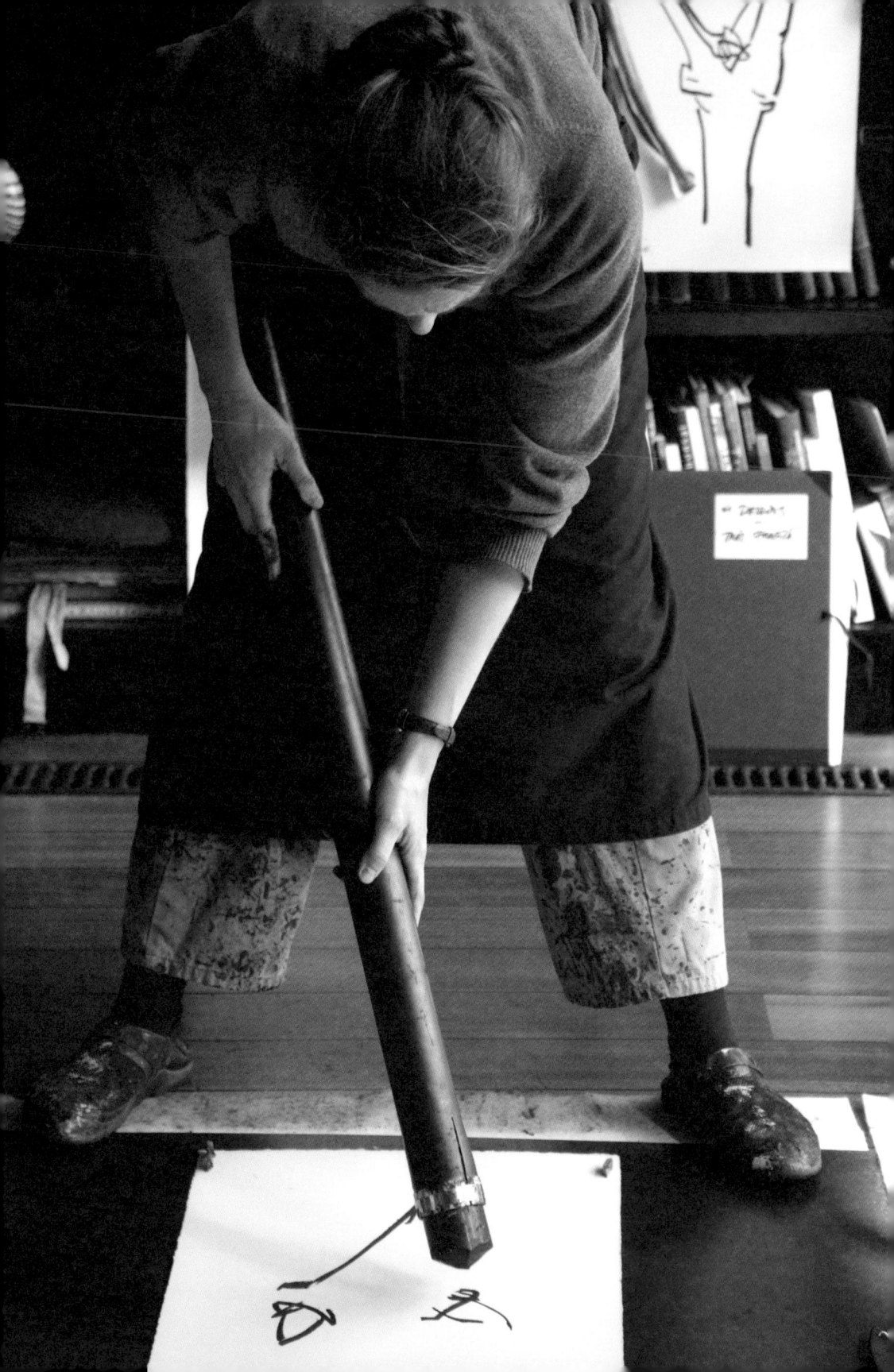

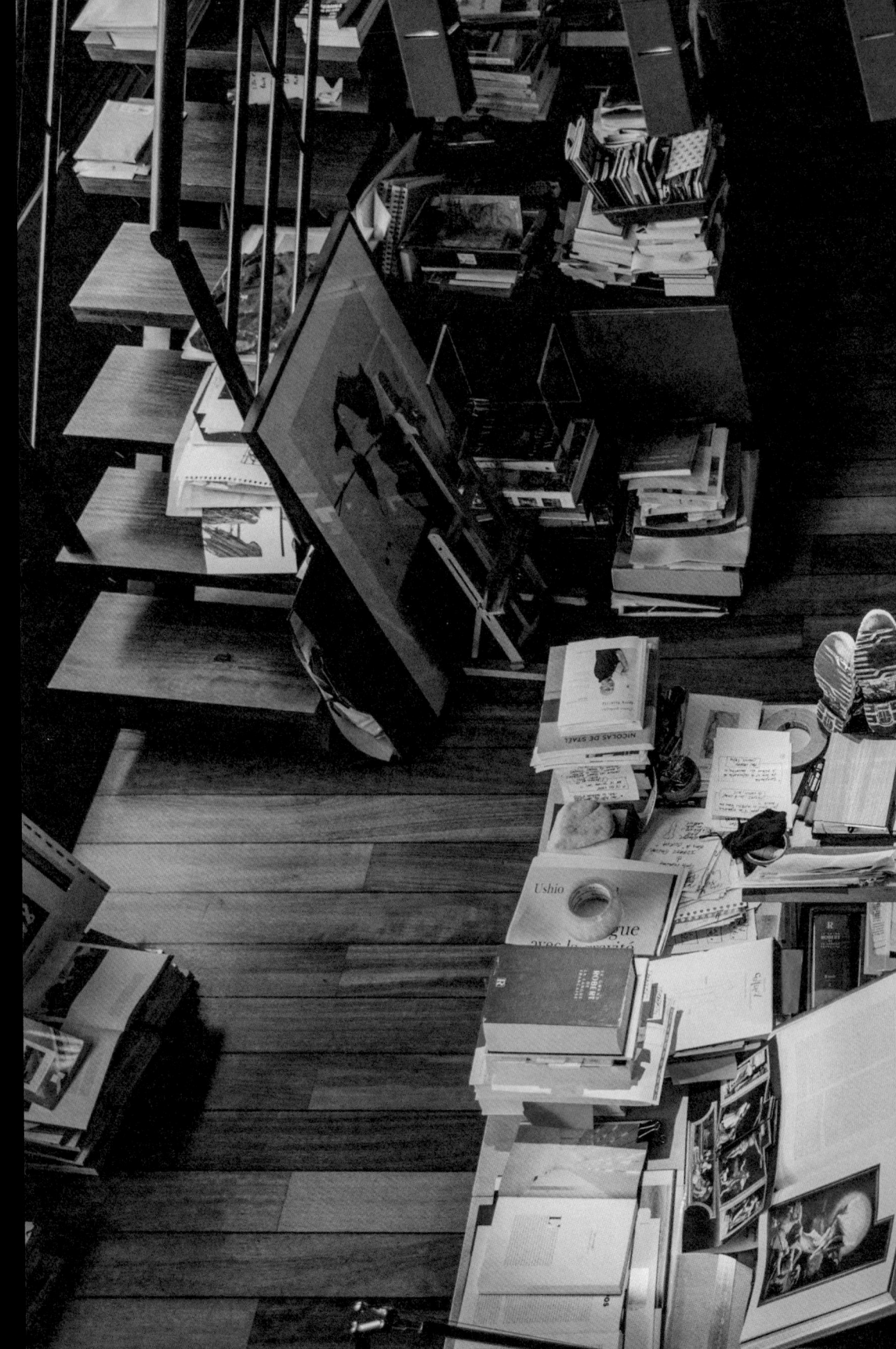

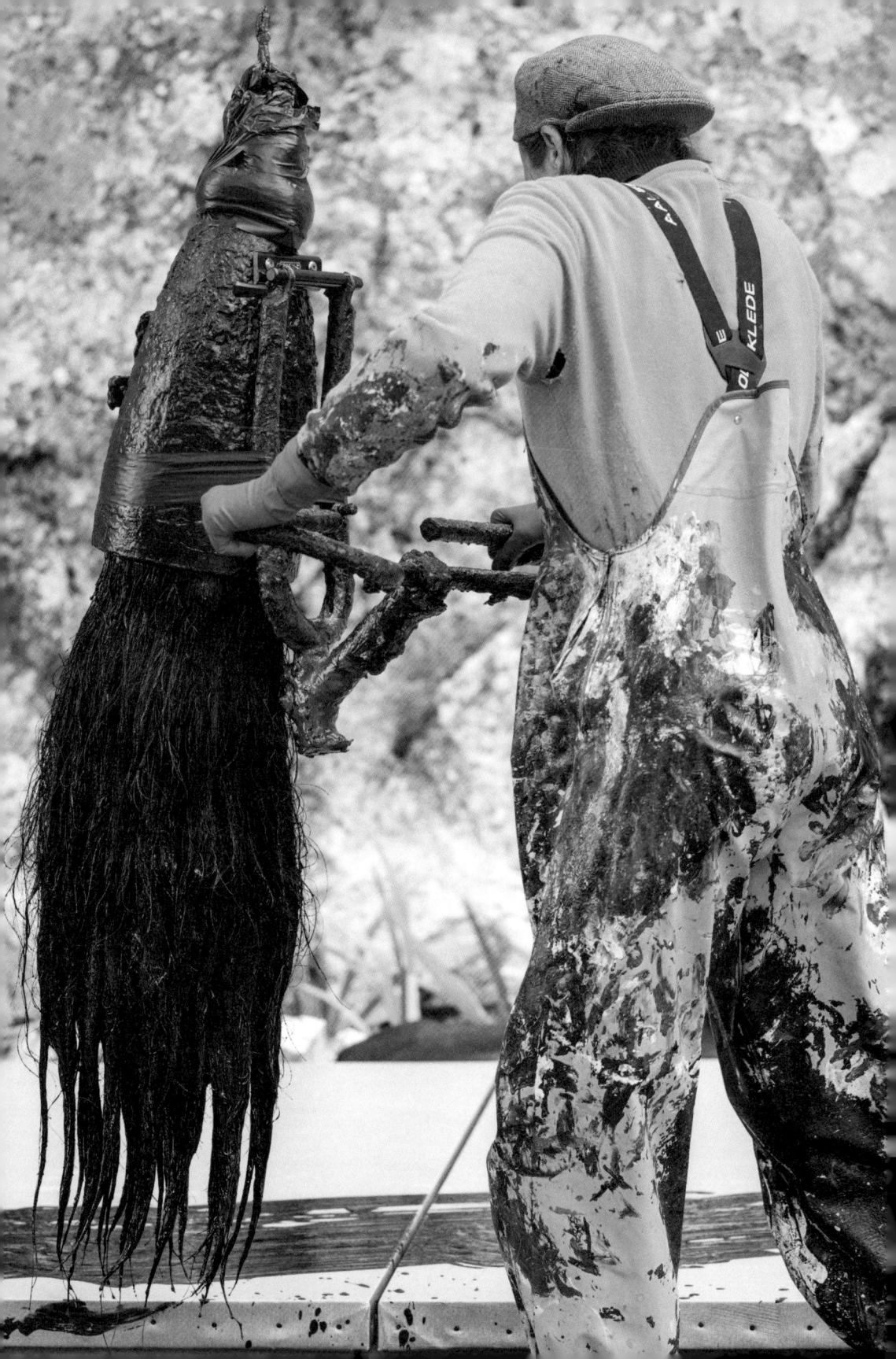

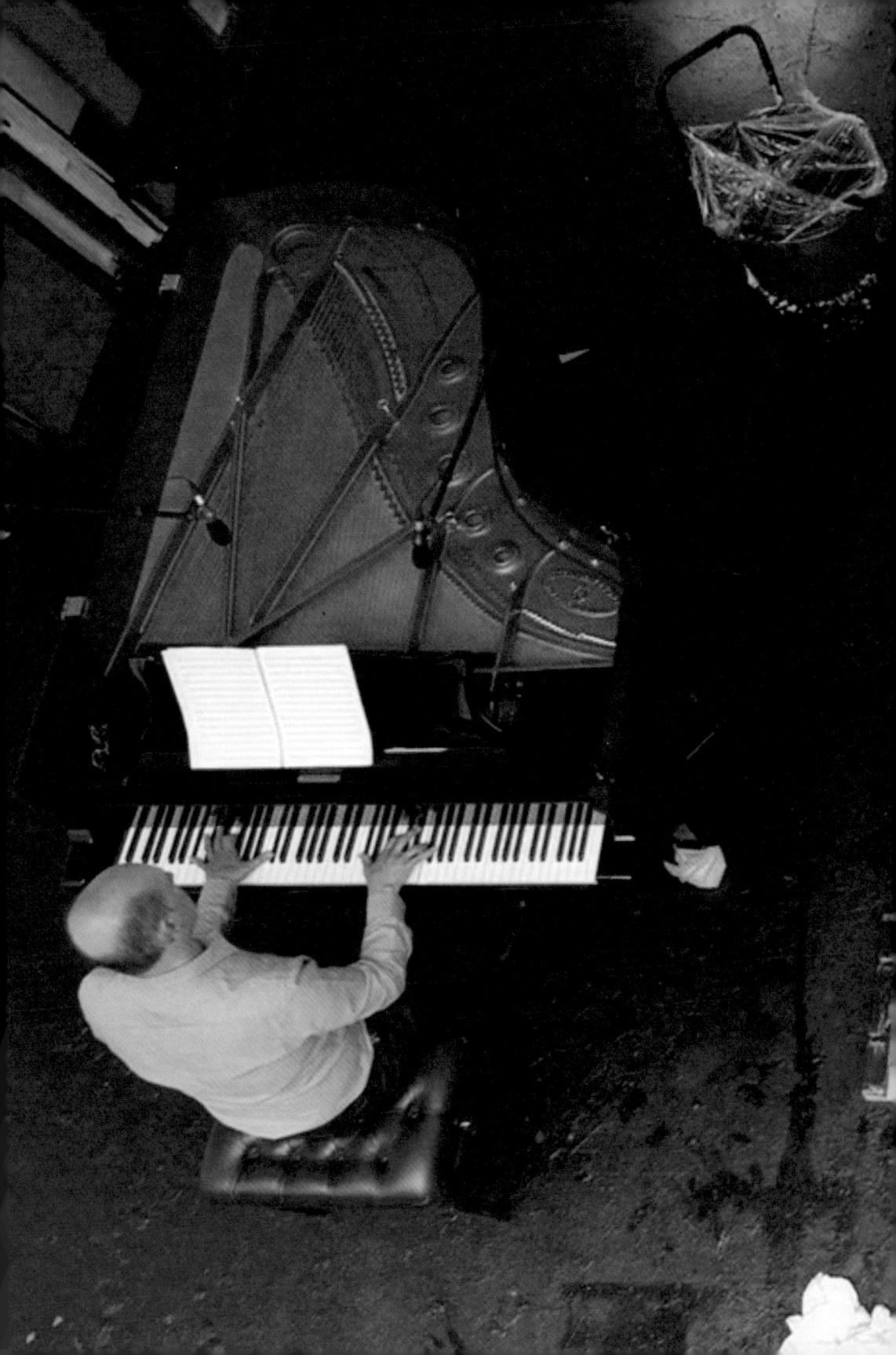

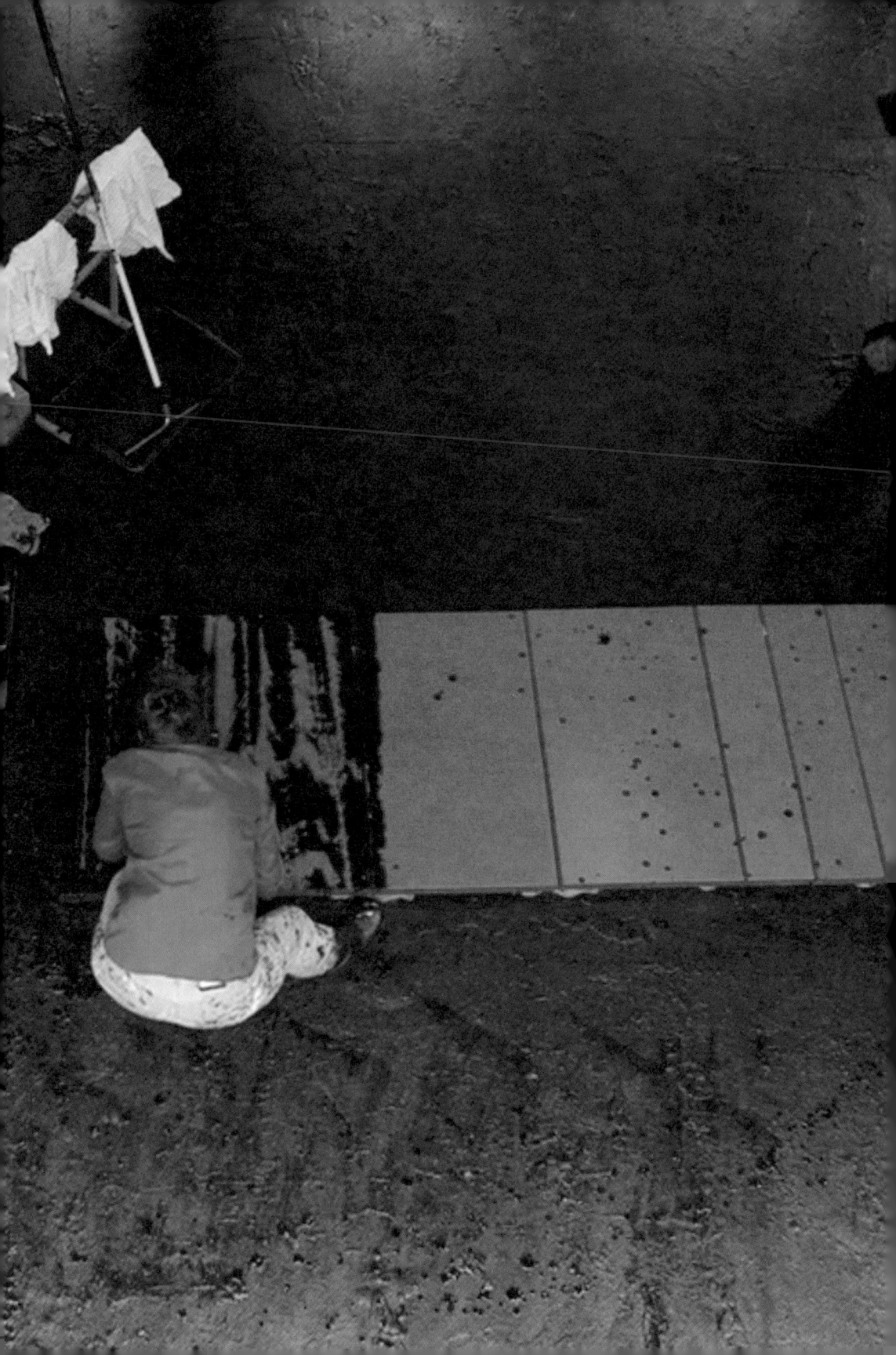

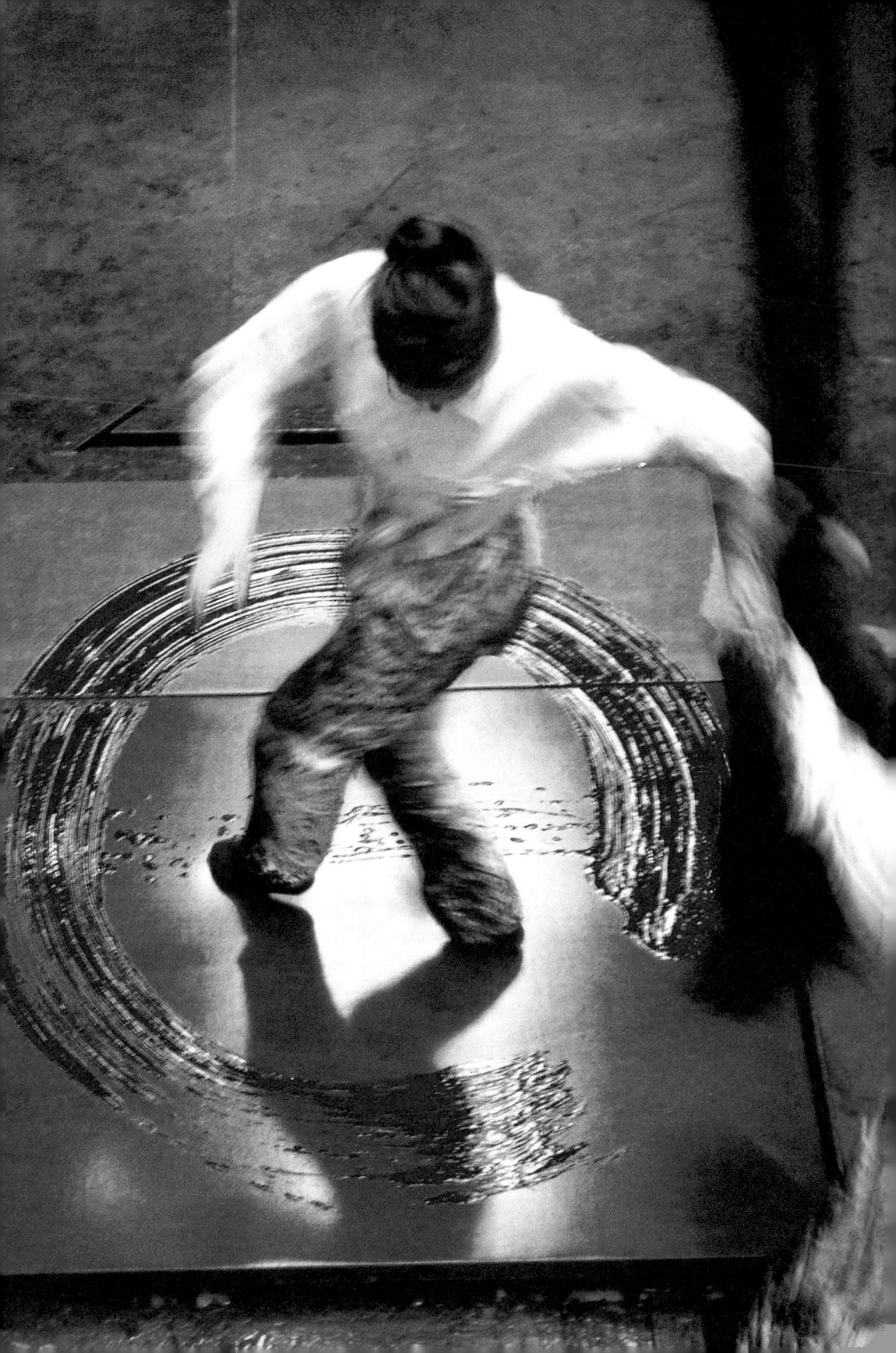

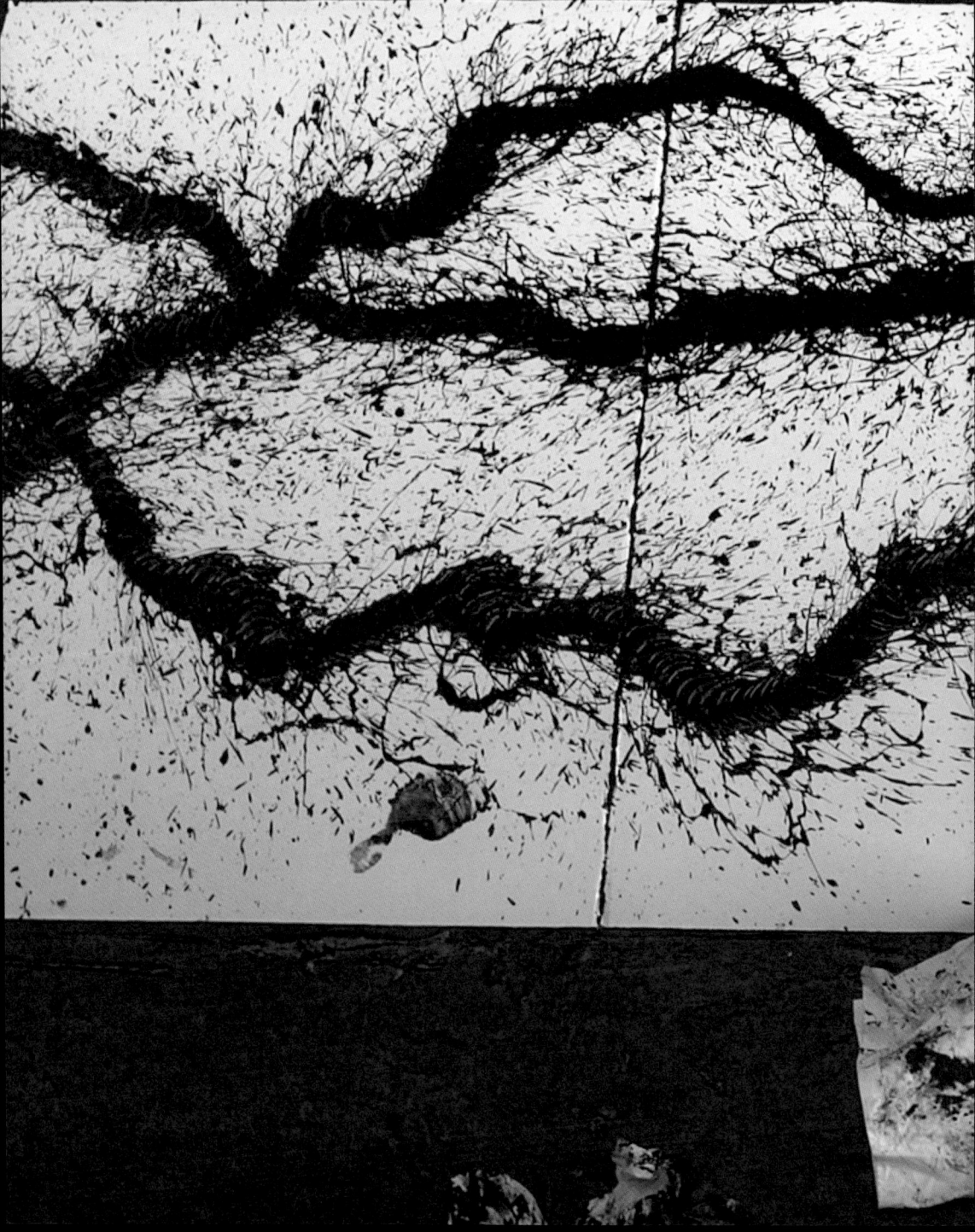

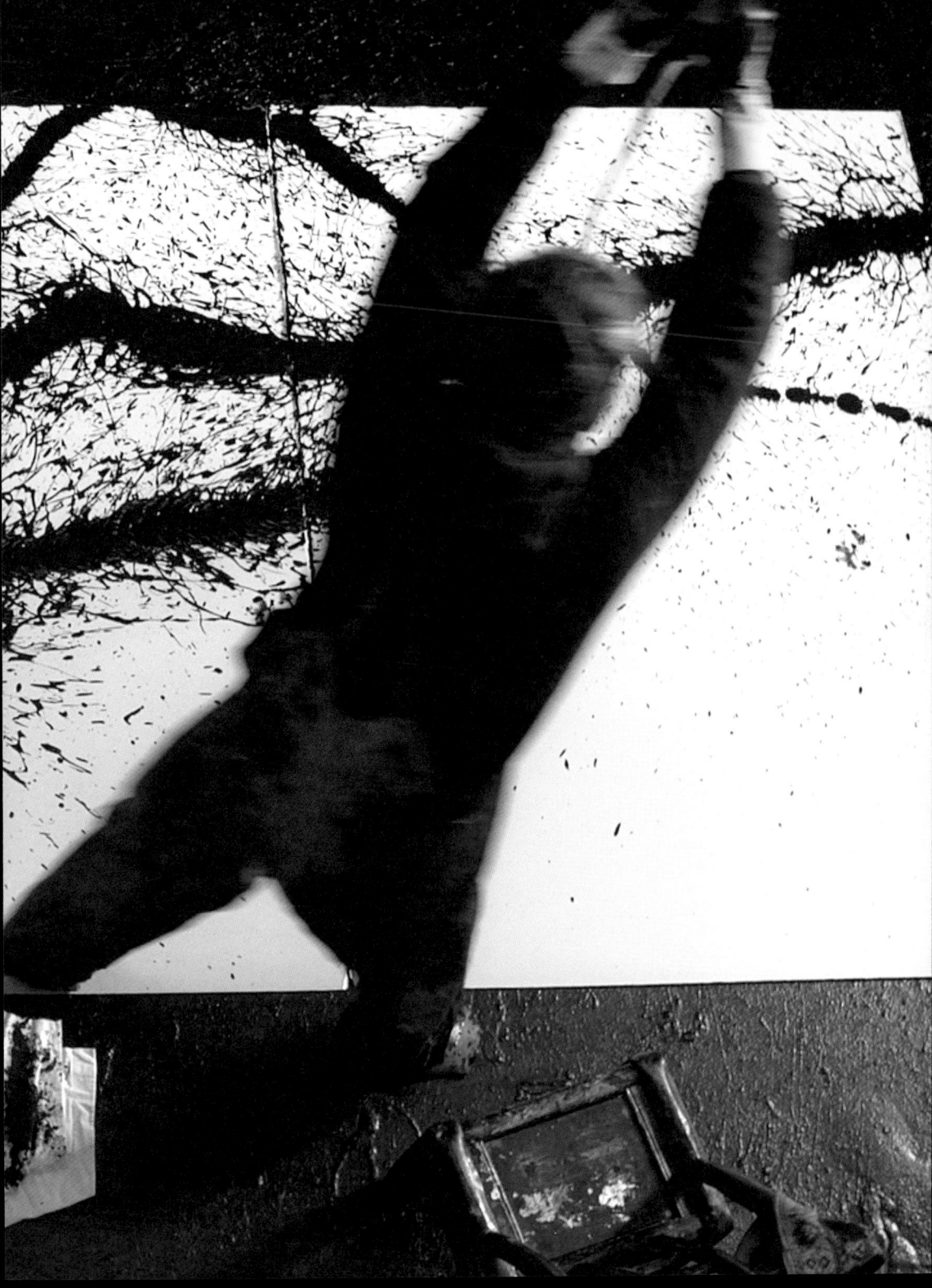

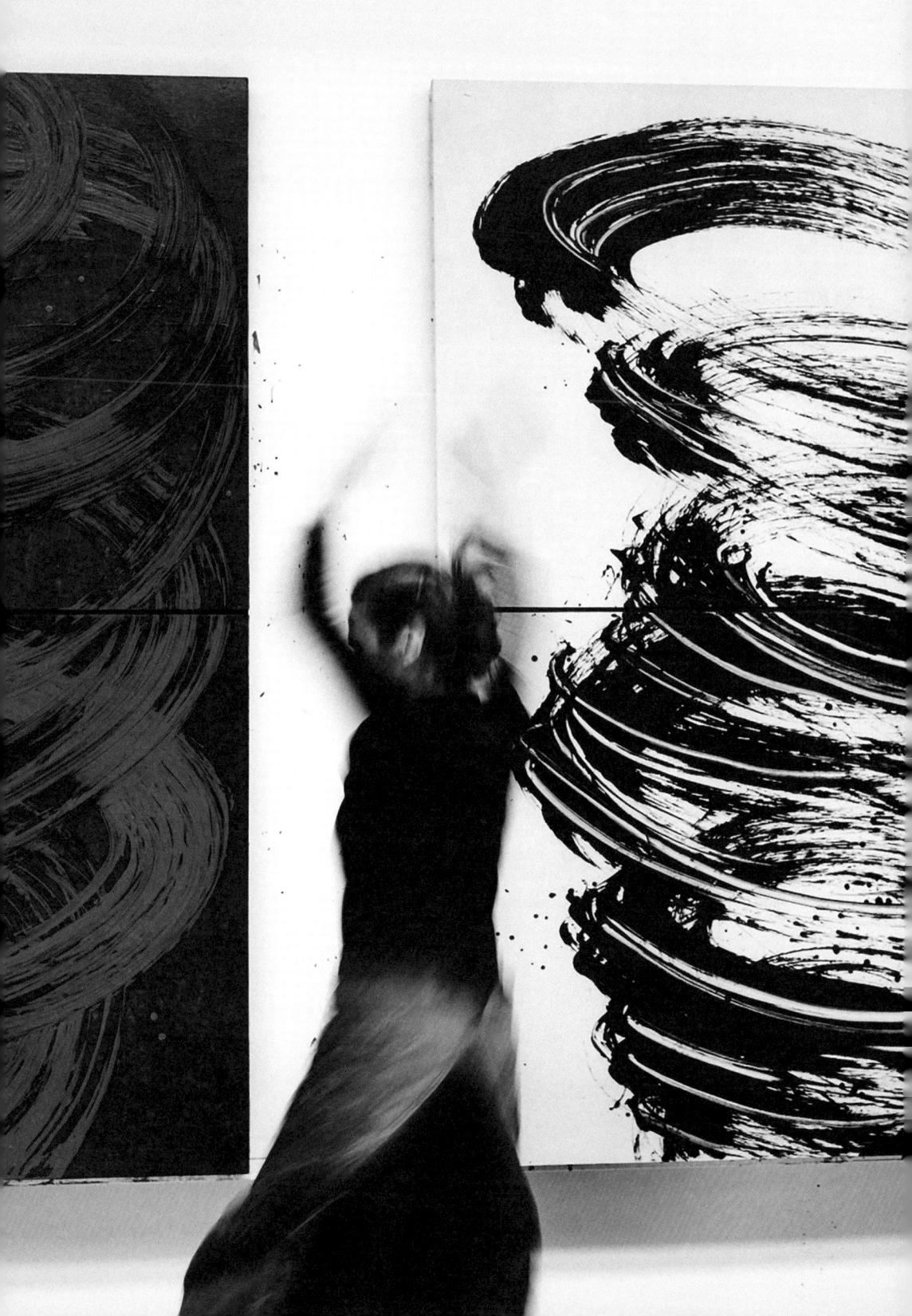

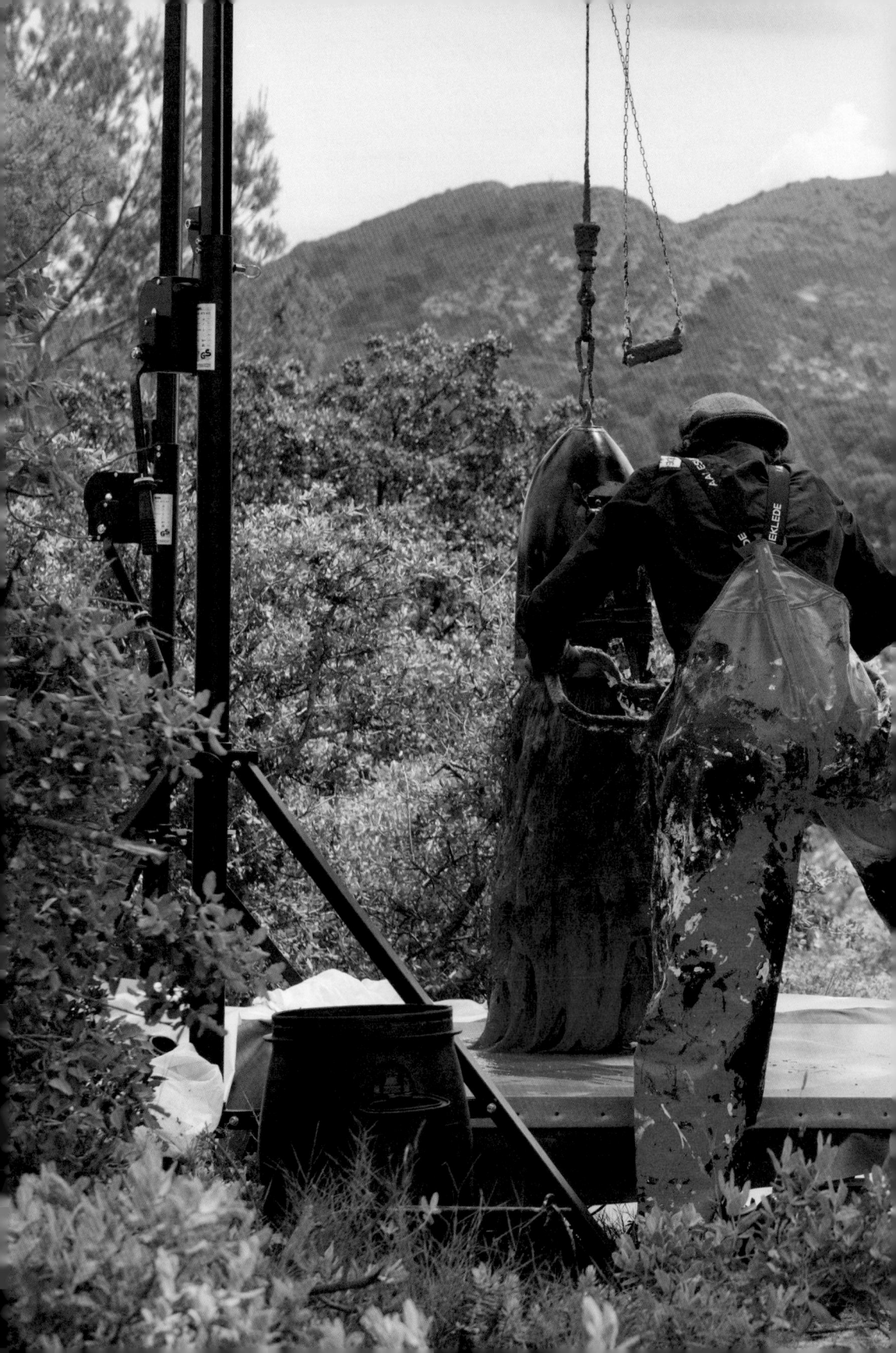

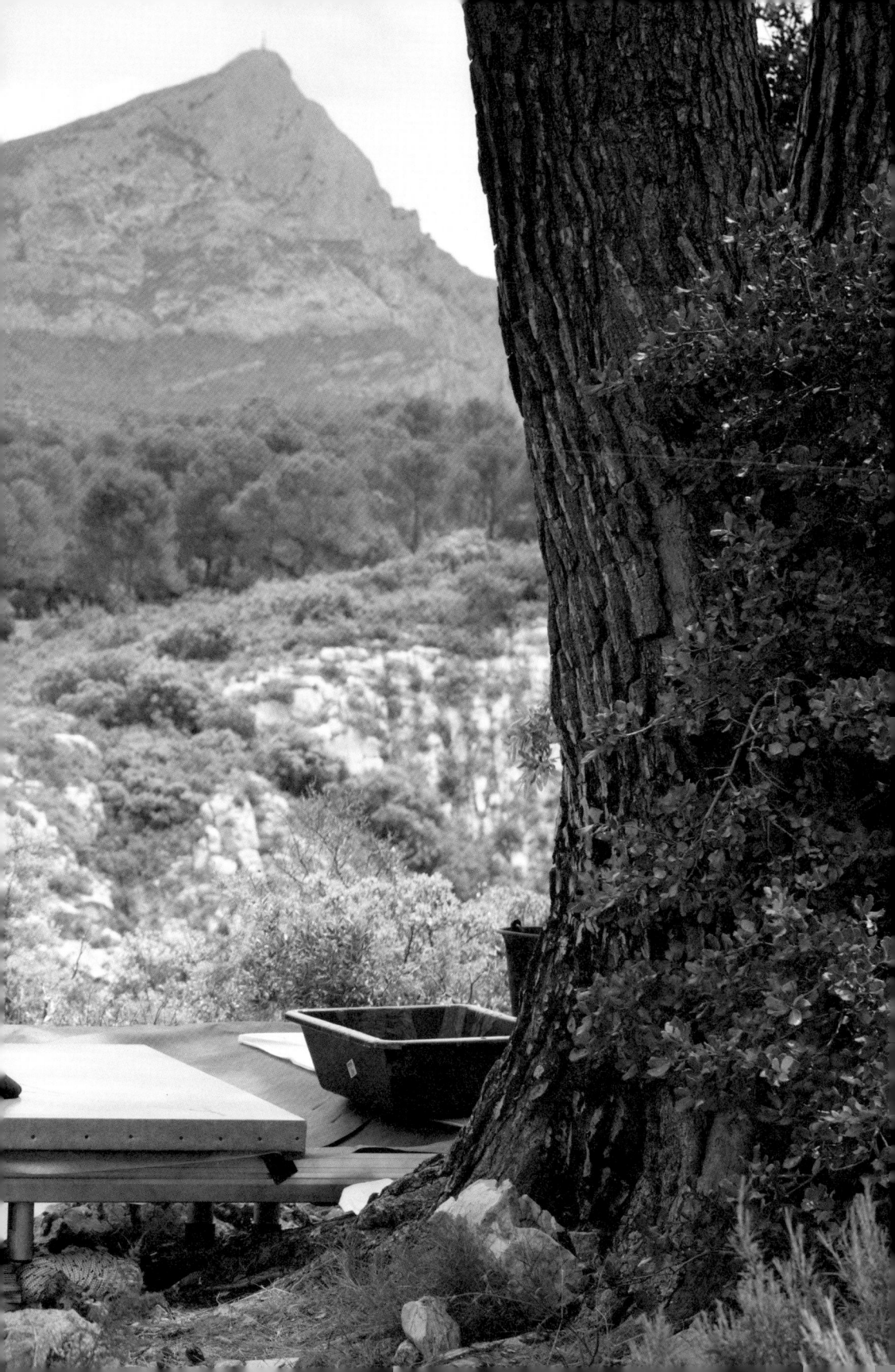

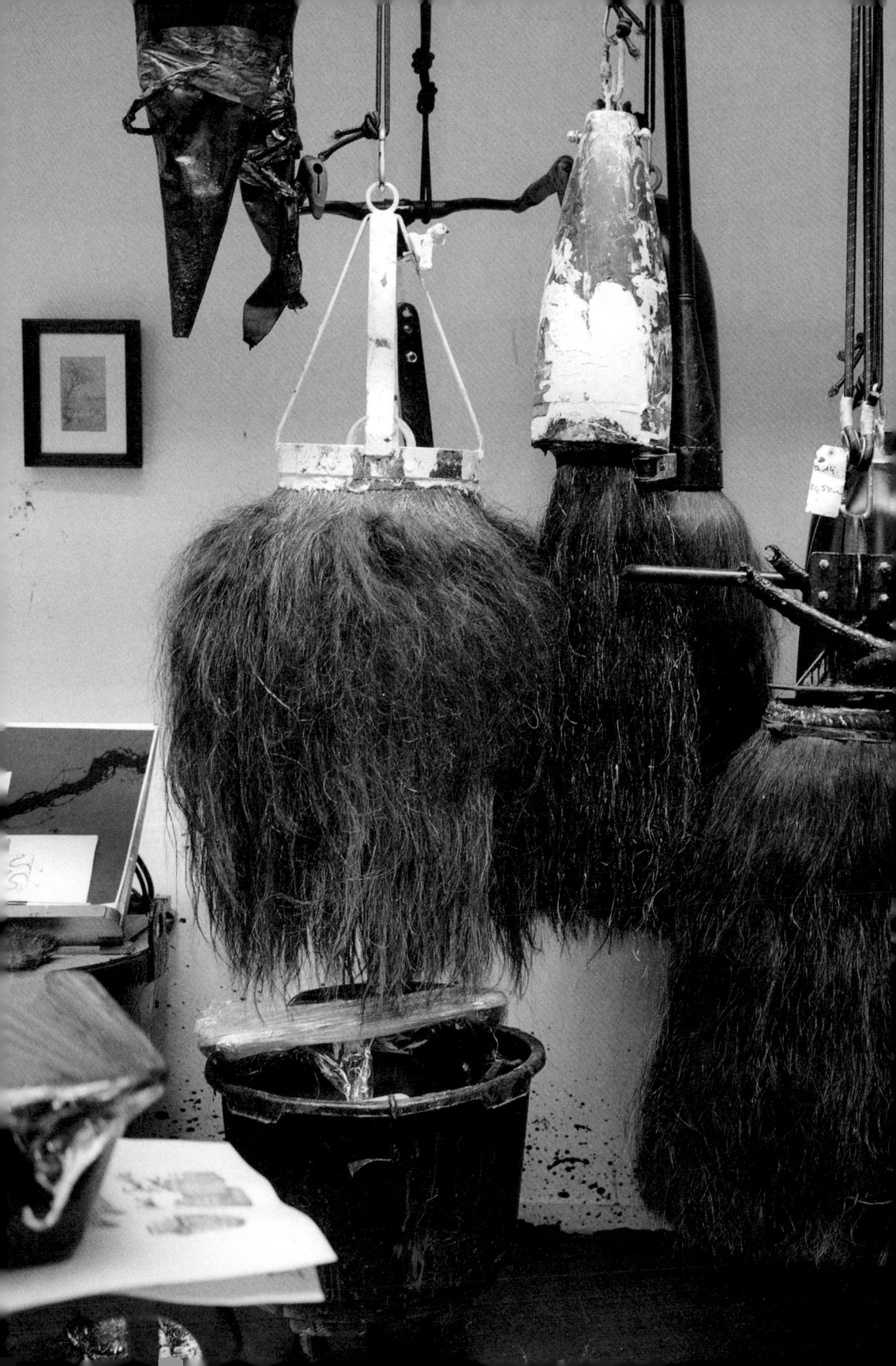

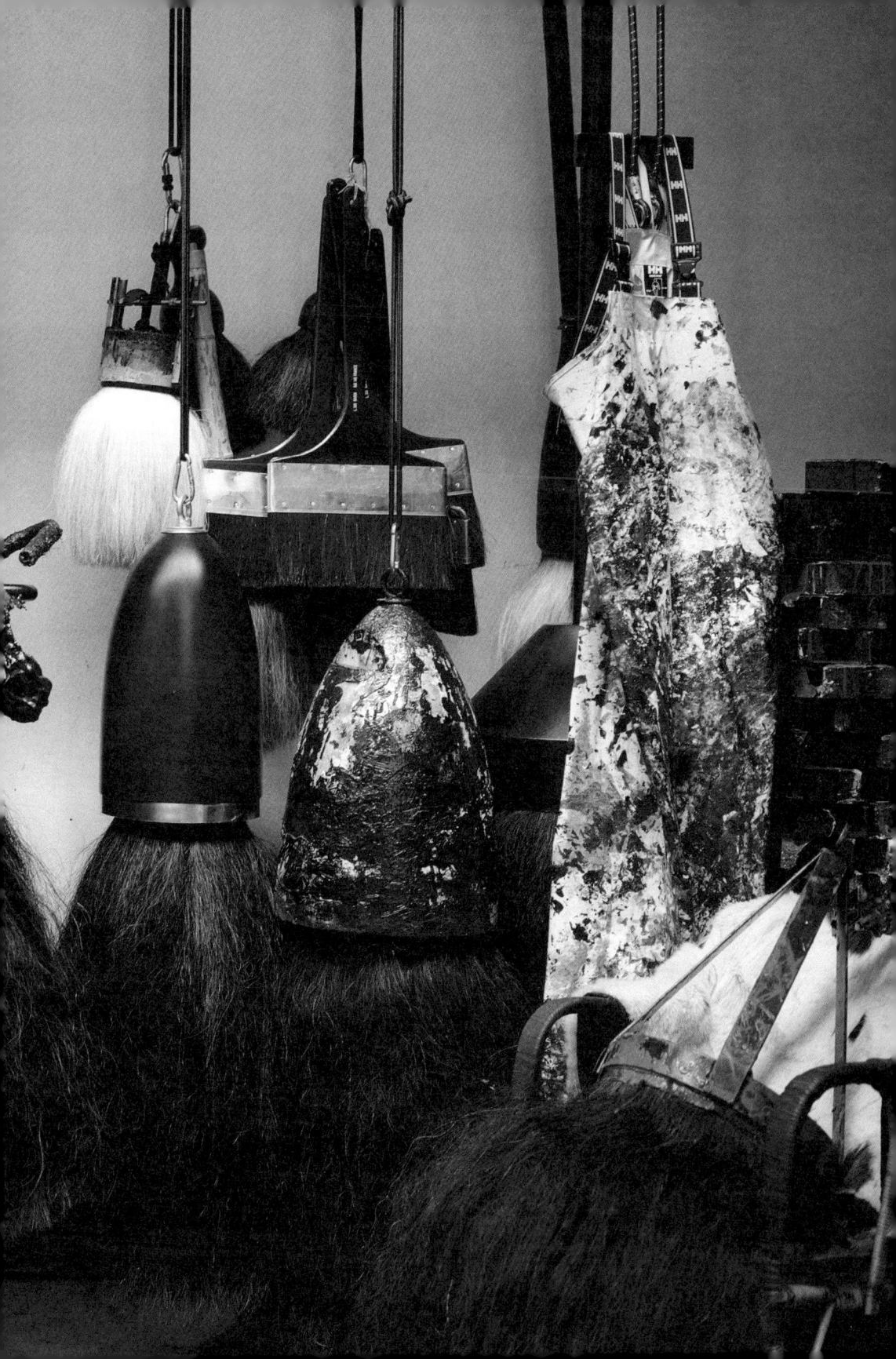

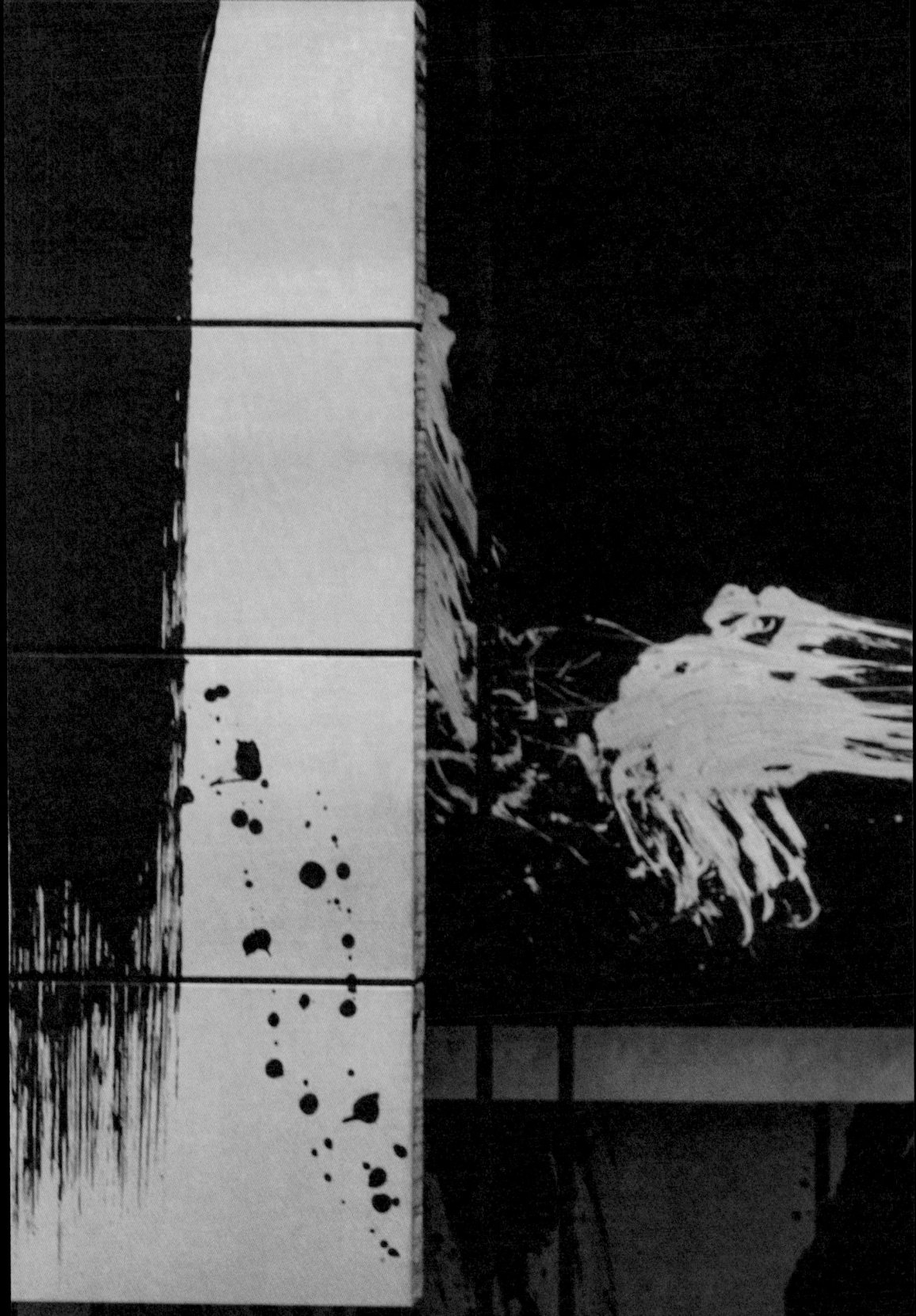

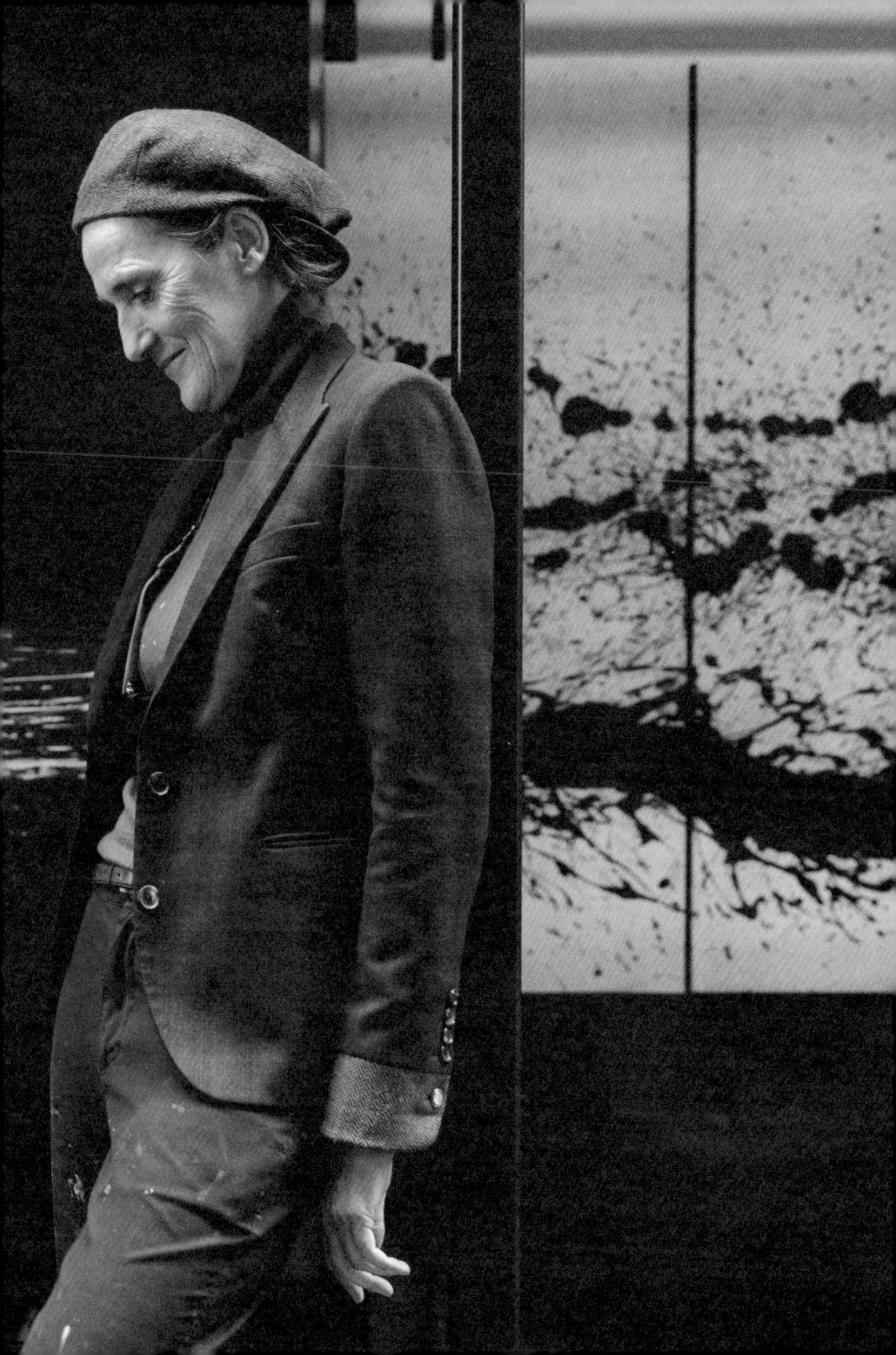

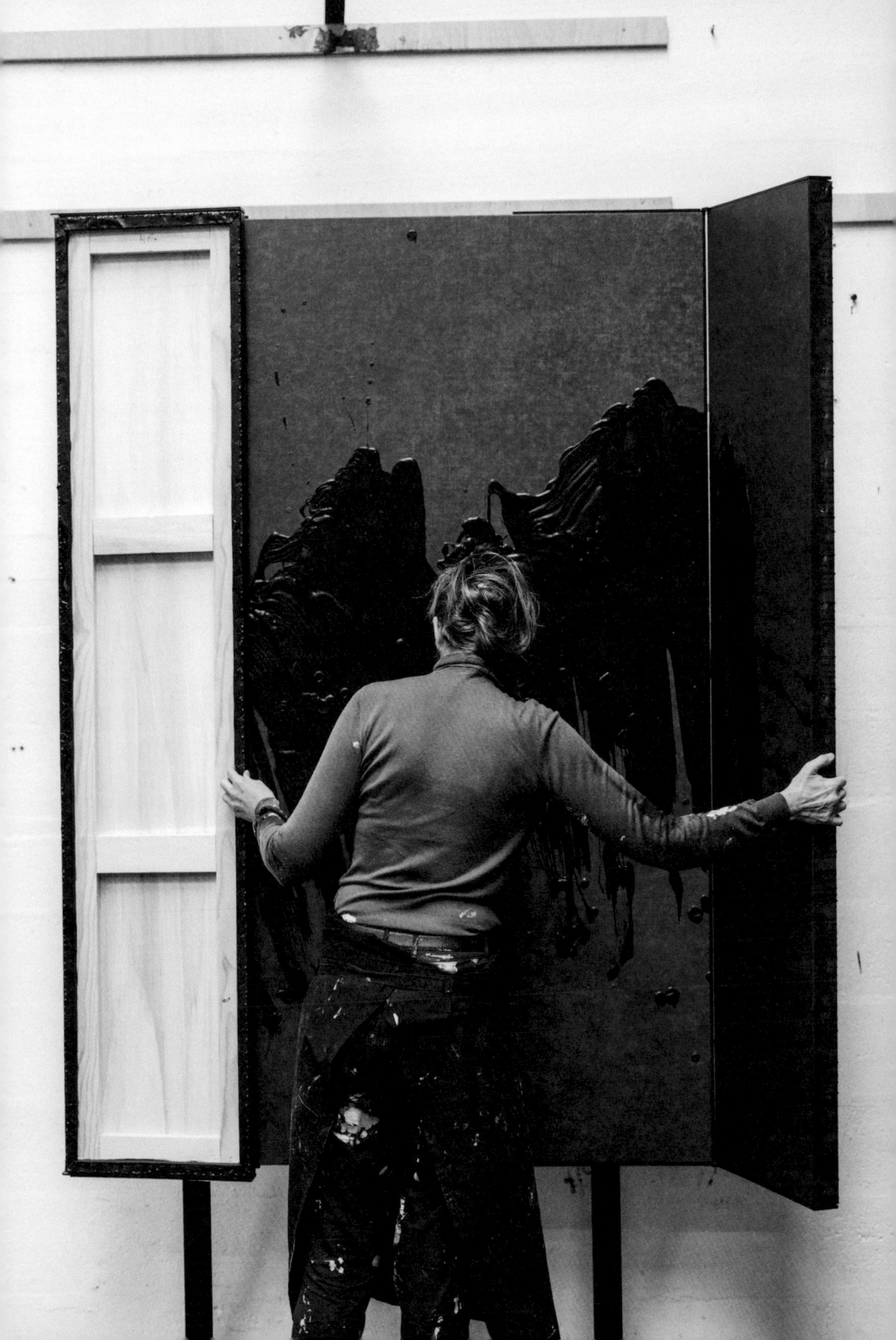

APPENDIX

CONCEPTS OF CHINESE AESTHETICS

For the English edition of *Passagère du Silence*, Fabienne Verdier has devised a supplement that brings together some fifty aesthetic notions she has studied over the years in China. They are listed alphabetically, but a random reading would no doubt be more appropriate to convey the richness and interconnectedness of many of these concepts. The entries are a selection of quotes from three fundamental reference works that Verdier has consulted time and again over the years and which she has annotated extensively.

These three books are:
- Pierre Ryckmans (PR), *Traduction et commentaire du traité de Shitao. Les propos sur la peinture du moine citrouille amère* (Brussels: Presse universitaire de France, 1970)
- Nicole Vandier-Nicolas (NVN), *Art et sagesse en Chine. Mi Fou (1051–1107)* [*Annales du Musée Guimet, Bibliothèque d'études*, vol. 70] (Paris: Presse universitaire de France, 1963)
- Yolaine Escande (YE), *Traités chinois de peinture et de calligraphie, traduits et commentés par Yolaine Escande* (Paris: Éditions Klincksieck, 2003)

At the end of each quotation are the initials of the sinologist who provided the definition and the page number of the corresponding book.

The first text mentioned is *Comments on Painting*, written in the seventeenth century by the Monk Bitter Pumpkin, who became famous under the name Shitao. One of the most celebrated Chinese painters and calligraphers, he condensed the reflections of a lifetime as a painter into book form. In the version edited and annotated by the Belgian sinologist Pierre Ryckmans, the book became a *vade mecum* for Verdier; indeed, Shitao, who is more than three hundred years older than Verdier, can be considered her first teacher. Verdier received the book as a gift shortly before her departure for China, and Shitao's unconventional and profound spirit, open to unorthodox paths and innovations, was a great help to her in overcoming the enormous challenges of her stay. At the same time, the text introduced her to the essence of traditional aesthetics, which demands the utmost vigilance and discipline from the student—a study of the past in order to "open up the present."

Verdier acquired the other two publications soon after her return from China. In Nicole Vandier-Nicolas's study on "Art and Wisdom in China," the author examines the work of the eccentric eleventh-century painter Mi Fu (French transcription: Mi Fou), who had a significant influence on the definition of "literati painting." Mi Fu is considered a seeker of truth, a master of spontaneity, and the pioneer of the aleatoric ink splotch. For this reason, in the recent past, connections have frequently been made with Jackson Pollock and the Abstract Expressionists, who are also important points of reference for Verdier. Vandier-Nicolas gives a detailed sense of how such concepts have been similarly applicable to modern and contemporary art, in particular the intellectual rigor that underlies the concept of spontaneity.

Finally, Yolaine Escande's seminal work makes more than thirty texts by Chinese painters and calligraphers since the sixth century available to the modern reader.

The basis of the teaching program Verdier experienced should be added here. It is summed up by the famous Chan (Zen) tale and painting series "Ten Scenes With an Ox" in which a cowherd loses his ox but manages to find it again and ride it home (becoming one with it), a metaphor for when knowledge is learned. Similarly, the studies culminate when the student has absorbed the most elusive subtleties of the training and becomes one with it. Only then, in the spirit of Shitao, is one free to face the challenges that arise.

—Corinna Thierolf
July 2024

Appearance – xing 形 – qu xing 取形
Capturing the formal appearance: *xing* designates formal appearance or "likeness" (*xing si* 形似). Initially seen as the goal of painting under the Han dynasty (206 BCE to 220 CE), in later eras the imperative of resemblance gradually gave way to the higher demands of expressing "spiritual rhythm" or "spiritual communion" with the essence of things, beyond external appearances. 筆取形，墨取意: (to use) the brush to take on the form, (to use) the ink to take on the meaning (or spirit, notion).
"Capturing the formal appearance and the inner impulse, painting from nature and conveying the spirit, revealing in totality or suggesting elliptically" (PR 26).

Bones, bone structure, skeleton – *gu* 骨
Skeleton, structure, physiognomy. Bones refer to a person's physical appearance as well as his or her general constitution. Applied to pictorial line drawing, it describes the structure of the line. The "bone manner in the use of the brush" (*gufa yongbi* 骨法用筆) is one of the six rules of painting (YE 375).

Breath – *qi* 氣
Breath, vital energy, energetic rhythm that binds strokes and ideograms together. Its etymology is vapor, exhalation, cloud-forming vapors. Under the Han (206 BCE to 220 CE), breath, especially in the form of clouds, was the object of close scrutiny. Everything that exists is formed of condensed *qi*. *Qi* can be positive or negative, good or bad. In pictorial theory, *qi* refers to the yang principle and implies a vigorous line or dynamic momentum in a composition (YE 380).

Qi yun sheng dong 氣韻生動, meaning "the resonance of breath gives life and movement," is the first of six rules of painting. The subject represented must emanate "vitality" and the execution must emanate "harmony" (YE p. 380).

Brushstroke – *bi hua* 筆劃 – *yi hua* 一畫
For the painter Shitao 石濤, the single brushstroke was the root and primary origin of calligraphy and painting (PR 127).
The brushstroke is not only the first stammering of pictorial language but also its final word: a single brushstroke is enough to reveal the hand of a master; a thousand ingenious brushstrokes could no more conceal a botched stroke than an orchestra could stifle a false note by a horn; touchstone or stumbling block, the brushstroke in Chinese painting synthesizes all the forms, metamorphoses, subtleties, and difficulties of this art (PR 15).
According to the painter Shitao, "The foundation of the Single Brushstroke lies in the absence of rules that generates the Rule, and the Rule thus obtained embraces the multiplicity of rules." 「立一畫之法者，蓋以無法生有法，以有法貫眾法也。」
If we are content to codify and describe phenomena, we remain slaves to these codifications; the essential thing is to grasp the why of phenomena; the rules of painting cannot be a simple inventory of classical procedures, a repertory of recited forms: they must start from a reflection on the very essence of the act of painting (PR 32).

Brush texture – *bi chu* 筆觸
In his technical research, the scholar-painter pursues the inexpressible quality of the

brushstroke. His aim is to eternalize the moment, and the brushstroke is moment, structure, and idea. Like the life of which it is the imprint, it suffers no repetition. Its mishaps, smudges, gaps, and omissions mimic the whims of nature. On a thin and firm support, watercolors and concentrated ink produce dots or draw lines that the brush does not correct but compensates. The heavy counters the light, darkness calls for clarity, short touches soften into longer strokes, voids, and solids that respond to each other. Contoured and shaped by colors, the figures breathe through their surrounding space (NVN 220).

Playing (fiddling) with the brush – *nong bi* 弄筆 The brush moves back and forth, reversing its direction; from the top to the bottom and back, from left to right and back, changing directions. The expression *nong bi* 弄筆 literally means "fiddling with the brush," a literati way of saying simply picking up the brush to write, or using the brush to perform calligraphy or painting. For the Song-dynasty calligrapher and painter Mi Fu 米芾 (1051–1107), fiddling with the brush was an art akin to illusionism. Brushes and ink must be handled with a disregard for balance, shattering planes to the point of splashing ink, like juggling with a ball. Place importance on naturalness, hold the brush lightly and paint spontaneously, with the hand and mind empty. The line must be lightning quick, completely natural, and spring from the idea (NVN 112).

Calligraphy – *shu fa* 書法

A discipline or method of writing, literally "writing rule" or "writing law," it refers to the Chinese art of writing, the noblest art practiced by literati officials in their spare time. Writing, poetry, painting, and music are among the essential arts (*yi* 藝) (YE 383). Calligraphy and painting are different names for the same practice. They are identical in origin, nature, principles, and techniques.

• He Liangjun 何良俊 (sixteenth-century painter): "Calligraphy and painting come from the same source." 「夫書畫本同出一源。」
• Zhu Tong 朱同 (painter of the second half of the fourteenth century): "Painting and calligraphy are the same discipline." 「畫之與書非二道也。」
• Zhao Xigu 趙希鵠 (thirteenth-century scholar): "Painting and calligraphy are in fact the same thing." 「書畫其實一事爾。」
• Jiang Qian 蔣乾 (painter from the second half of the sixteenth century): "The discipline of painting corresponds to that of calligraphy." 「粗知畫道與書通耳。」
• Yang Weizhen 楊維楨 (poet, musician, and painter, 1296–1370): "Scholars who are skilled in painting are necessarily skilled in calligraphy." 「士大夫工畫者必工書。」
Many painting treatises state that "the method of the brush is the same in calligraphy as in painting." 「書畫用筆同法。」
• Guo Xi and Guo Si 郭熙與郭思 (father and son, painters, critics, and theorists of the eleventh century), "Learning to paint does not differ from learning calligraphy." 「人之學畫，無異學書。」
• Hua Lin 華琳 (Qing-dynasty painter, 1791–1850), "Painting is an activity similar to that of calligraphy." 「作畫與作書相通。」
• Zhan Yanyuan 張彥遠 (Tang-dynasty

calligrapher and painter of the ninth century), "Painting and calligraphy have different names but share the same origin." 「書畫異名而同體也。」(PR 127).

Since painting is historically dependent on calligraphy, a thorough understanding of painting cannot be achieved without first studying calligraphy. This is true not only in terms of the aesthetic and critical appreciation of works—without calligraphic training, the connoisseur's criteria for judgment remain limited to the superficial interplay of forms and cannot penetrate the inner architecture of the brushstroke—but also on a theoretical level as pictorial treatises have borrowed a significant part of their terminology, their aesthetic and technical concepts, and their critical categories from calligraphic treatises. However, in the field of calligraphic theory, virtually nothing has yet been studied in the West (PR 129).

Historians of calligraphy believed that the will of the master was communicated to the disciple through an autograph work. The stronger and purer the calligrapher's genius, the more effective the energy diffused by his script. The timbre of the voice and the rhythm of the brush transmit a psychic vibration that certain spirits are able to capture. Beautiful script emanates a stimulating power, the benefits of which can be felt by the attentive copyist (NVV 13).

Feng liu 風流, literally "wind and flowing water," describes a spirit of total spontaneity, and presided over the birth of calligraphic art. The scholar Cai Yong 蔡邕 (132–192), creator of the flying white script (*fei bai shu* 飛白書), where bits of white appear in inky strokes due to the partial dryness of the brush, and skilled

in the Han-dynasty clerical script *ba fen* 八分, is credited with the following text: "Calligraphy has the spontaneity (*ziran* 自然) for origin. Once the spontaneity has been laid down, the yin and the yang become apparent. When the yin and yang are revealed, the design of the forms appears." 「夫書肇於自然，自然既立，陰陽生焉。陰陽既生，形勢出矣。」The spirit of *feng liu* 風流 implies willingness for spiritual escape, and is accompanied by a taste for elegance and keen, courageous cheerfulness (NVN 19).

Chaos – *hun dun* 渾沌 or 混沌

Original chaos is a Daoist concept and the primeval state of the universe in Daoist mythology. It is the first state of raw matter, still intact, undifferentiated, and unorganized. Chaos is the lack of differentiation between Full and Empty, Form and Formless, Having and Not-Having: it lies midway between these binaries, and is eliminated by openness, perception, distinction, and difference. According to Shitao, the brushstroke pierces, clears, and organizes the inert virtuality of the raw material of ink and the white void of the paper. By differentiating and ordering, it eliminates chaos (PR 63).

Coarse rawness – *sheng la* 生刺 rawness, skill – *sheng shou* 生熟

Sheng 生 means "raw, rough, unpolished"; *la* 刺 means "untamed, rough." This concept is frequently used in aesthetics; it is associated with *zhuo* 拙, "clumsy," as opposed to *shou* 熟, "mature, cooked" (and, by extension, "practiced, skillful, dexterous," and is in turn associated with *gong* 工, "elaborate," as in *gong bi* 工筆 "meticulously detailed brushwork"). Three successive levels are distinguished in an artist's development:

- In the beginning, one's craft is "raw, rough, primitive"— *sheng* 生;
- with practice, one becomes "mature, skillful"— *shou* 熟;
- when one has mastered the craft and can be free of the rigid schooling and summon the techniques at will, then one becomes capable of *sheng* 生—raw, primitive spontaneity.

We must therefore distinguish between untrained "rawness," which, tainted by impotence, remains inferior to "skill," and "rawness," the supreme quality, which can only be reached beyond "skill." It is to this second form of "rawness" that Shitao alludes in his treatise. As recorded by painter and theorist Tang Zhiqi 唐志契 (1579–1651), the Ming-dynasty painter Li Yanghuai 李仰懷 commented on making landscape paintings, "Too much skill leads to vulgarity; nor should there be too much rawness. Too much rawness is off-putting; but rawness rediscovered by dint of skill, that is marvelous." 「畫山水，不可太熟，熟則少文；不可太生，生則多戾；練熟還生，斯妙矣。」Another expression of the same phenomenon can be found, for example, in → Pablo Picasso's famous remark: "At sixteen, I was already drawing like Raphael (= skill); it took me fifty years to learn to draw like a child again (= rawness rediscovered through skill) (PR 96).

Composition – wei zhi 位置
Qing-dynasty painter and theorist Wang Yu 王昱 (1700–1750) wrote, "Regarding composition, don't follow the beaten paths of fashion, don't fall into hackneyed formulas;

let your bosom become pure and empty, no longer tainted by the slightest worldly dust; mountains and valleys will spring forth as the direct expression of your soul [...]" 「位置須不入時蹊，不落舊套。胸中空空洞洞，無一點塵埃。邱壑從靈性發出 ……」(PR 87).

Constant principle of internal order – li 理
"Principle, rule, sense; regulate; system, law; principle of intelligibility; internal principle of existing beings and things." The character's etymology is "vein in the jade"; it is the constant, structuring principle that governs the formation and becoming of all that exists (YE 378). This is the normative principle which, specified ad infinitum, gives each being and each thing its individuality, its reason for existence. In the world, all things are able to manifest their nature owing to their underlying principle. Wherever a thing exists, there must necessarily be a norm. Everything necessarily has its *li*, which is the principle of resplendence (*zhao* 照), i.e., of intelligibility (*lizhi* 理智) (NVN 187).
Li is a major issue in Chinese aesthetics and regards the relationship between the external form of things and the principle that animates them.
If the painter seeks to capture his subject through the harmony of the breath, he will also achieve its outward likeness. The artist aiming for outward resemblance neglects the total structure and his model's own movement will evade him. The idea underlying the unity of his object's parts will not appear to him and his work remains unintelligible. Nature models things from within: a landscape is no different from a face, whose true character is revealed in the brilliance of the eye. Every being, everything is just an idea of nature, and

it is these ideas that the artist must discover (NVN 188).

Contemplation, silent identification – *mo qi* 默契

The contemplative scholar experiences a state that the Chinese describe in two characters, *mo qi* 默契. The first character designates darkness, silence, and peace; the second evokes the precise fit of two beings like the wedge and the wheel merging into one. This expression denotes an ecstatic, intimate understanding of one another without having to use words. Divested of himself, the contemplative artist enters into communion with the principle of life (*shen* 神) and then finds himself in harmony with all beings and all things within the Whole (NVN 4).

Copy, copying – *mo* 摹 – *lin* 臨

Copying in China doesn't always mean reproducing the model line for line. It was important to distinguish between the slavish reproduction of a script and its free reproduction. The former, known as *mo* 摹 (copying, rubbing), required methodical precision. The second, known as *lin* 臨, was quite different: copying a work of art by getting close to it, in which case the copyist was no longer a craftsman, but an artist. The two methods served different purposes: the first, used by an expert hand, enabled the faithful memory of a unique masterpiece to be preserved, while the second was used by the artist to find his own inspiration in a painting or calligraphy that stimulated and guided him (NVN 110).

Creative spontaneity – *xing* 興

Improvisation; the instinctive predisposition that drives each being to act in accordance

with its own movement. To paint the landscape, don't apply your attention to particular details; instead, let yourself engage in an objectless meditation. Seated, forget in order to contemplate. To paint the sun, you must forget it as a phenomenon to retain only its idea, the visible and specified form of the total power of spontaneous realization. It would be a fatal error to claim to have achieved the particularized idea of the sun. Life is indivisible. If we try to treat it as an individual entity, we destroy it. The sun is a source of light and heat; reduced to its external appearance, it becomes inert. We must lose ourselves in the Whole to find each of the elements in total harmony. Return to the essence of the movement and intuitively discover the rhythm of each object. Only then does the artist's vision become active and in turn acquire the power to animate a movement in the viewer in sync with the artist's. This movement, recorded by memory, is set in motion when the magical double of the landscape is presented to view by the artist (NVN 54).

Creative spring, spontaneous dynamism – *tian ji* 天機

Creative spontaneity, in its dynamic aspect. Instinctive predisposition that impels each being to act in accordance with its own movement (NVN 184). → Spontaneity

Dao, Daoism – *dao* 道

Often translated as "the way," definitions of this term include "path, way; method, reason; truth; philosophical thought; skill, technique; to speak, to articulate; to lead, to guide." Etymologically, it is composed by the

element of the head (*shou* 首) and the radical that relates to walking (*chuo* 辶).
It designates the elusive movement of life, the universal principle inaccessible to rational knowledge or the discursive mind but manifested in the natural becoming of "the ten thousand existing beings" (*wanwu* 萬物). Dao is apprehended through an experience that "cannot be expressed or transmitted by words," as explained in the first sentence of *Tao Te Ching* (「道可道，非常道。名可名，非常名。」) (YE 374).

Detachment – carelessness, nonchalance, superior detachment, fantasy — *yi* 逸

Inner detachment must precede pictorial creation.
In painting, according to the painter Shitao, intention precedes execution and is the indispensable prerequisite to paint. Whereas the mind must be absolutely detached, idle, and unfettered, the idea must be firmly fixed and clearly determined: only then will the painter be able to take up his brush.
"In painting, the idea must first be fixed; if the brush begins to work before the idea has been fixed, it will have no inner guidance, there will be no coordination between hand and mind, and the work is condemned in advance,"
(「作畫須先立意，若先不能立意，而遽然下筆，則胸無主宰，手心相錯，斷無足取。」)
as Zheng Ji 鄭績 (active around the middle of the nineteenth century, physician, poet, and painter, author of the treatise *Menghuanju Huaxue Jianming* 夢幻居畫學簡明 *Summary of the Study of Paintings from Fantasia Residence*, 1866) wrote (PR 23–24).
Yi designates the nonchalance of the wise man who knows how to avoid the wearing effect of worries by happily managing his leisure time. *Yi* is the superior detachment that characterizes certain highly refined, very demanding minds, inclined to judge the vulgar with elegant disdain. It's also the fantasy that laughs at propriety and takes refuge "outside the cage" in the translucent universe of subtle essences. Zhang Zao 張藻 (or 張璪) was a renowned landscape artist during the Tang dynasty. He could wield two brushes at once, painting with one a branch filled with life, and with the other a rotting old trunk. He often worked with a bad and worn brush or painted on silk with his hand. When asked who had taught him his techniques, he would reply: "On the outside, I took my model from creation, and on the inside, I found the source of my own spirit." (「外師造化，中得心源。」) When he meditates "without attachment," the painter's mind illuminates the object and strips it of its envelope (NVN 69).

Emptiness – *xu* 虛

The painted part, less important than the empty space, tends to be no more than a support for the latter, a visual guide that directs the eye to the essential threshold of emptiness, where the mind takes over from the eye (PR 109). → Fullness
The inexperienced painter is unaware that it is pointless to set to work without spiritual preparation. The image is transposed onto the paper but is constructed in the mind. It cannot develop if it has not first come to life in the emptiness of thought. The idea is to the work of art what human thought is to creation: an inner principle of unity. The brush of a true artist reserves the center of his canvas

for the constructive impulse of the breath that distills forms in the void of space (NVN 226).

Flying white – *fei bai* 飛白

A style of calligraphic script in which slivers of white are left visible amid an inky brushstroke. "White" signifies the gaps that appear in a stroke where the bristles are drained of ink, as if the brush has run dry. "Flying" refers to the appearance of this type of script, which is generally large in size. The lightly inked line seems dry and light, airy, achieved with the brush swiftly going over the paper, as if flying (YE 374).

Form and Spirit — *xing* and *shen* 形神

From the very start, the relationship between form (*xing*) and spirit (*shen*) has been a subject of Chinese philosophy, which does not dissociate the two: "When form is complete, spirit comes into being" (「形具而神生」), asserted the philosopher Xunzi 荀子 (c. 316–237 BCE). Later, the Southern dynasties (420–589) philosopher Fan Zhen 范縝 (c. 450–515) specified: "The body is the matter of the mind; the mind is the function of the body" (「形者神之質，神者形之用。」). This concept had a profound influence on Chinese aesthetics. To be effective, form depends on something that is not form, namely energy from the spirit (*shen qi* 神氣) (YE 385). → Spirit

Free and relaxed – *song* 鬆

Casual, natural, relaxed. A quality on which painters placed great emphasis in the Qing dynasty. One author, Zhang Feng 張風 (?–1661), compares the painter's art to that of the chess player with his subterfuges, and concludes: "In painting, nothing is more wonderful than this detached nonchalance which, in a sparse composition, spreads by degrees the interplay of stains and washes, creating an effect of elegance and grace, and thus communicating a delightful feeling of elation. The initial application of the brush must be free and detached [. . .] without which the movement of life and spiritual dynamism cannot be expressed." The same idea is conveyed by the painter Wang Yuanqi 王原祁 (1642–1715) and by Zheng Ji 鄭績, physician and painter (active in the mid-nineteenth century). Shitao himself underlines this same quality in a colophon: "For the fingers, the rule is that they should be relaxed; this detached composure is the first condition to enable unlimited metamorphoses" (PR 92).

Fullness – *shi* 實

In China, the watchword of poetic criticism was the concept *shi* 實: solidity, density, the plenitude of material reality, the concrete weight that the words of the poem assimilate. In painting, on the other hand, the central concept of criticism was *xu* 虛, emptiness, i.e., the white areas left to the imagination (PR 109). → Emptiness

"In painting, it is important to grasp the subject with discernment, that is to say, in the tracing of forms; though the aim is to obtain an unqualified result, the whole art of execution lies in these fragmentary notations and interruptions. [. . .] The brushstroke is interrupted to better be invested with undertones; thus a mountain is represented by an empty outline, or a tree is amputated of its boughs: everywhere emptiness must be mingled with fullness." 「繪事要明取予，取者形象彷彿處以筆勾之。其致用遂在果

毅，而妙運則貴在玲瓏斷續。[...] 予者筆斷意含。如山之須廓，樹之去枝。凡有無之間是也。」Li Rihua 李日華 (1565–1635), government official, painter, calligrapher, and appraiser (PR 91–92).

Heart – *xin* 心

Shitao believes, "Painting emanates from the intellect." (「夫畫者，從於心者也。」) The character *xin* 心 literally means "heart," but in Chinese thought this term doesn't just have the affective definition as the physical organ; it designates above all spiritual and intellectual activity, as well as all of consciousness.

Unlike the craftsman, who is content to reproduce external formal appearances, the painter proper, i.e., the scholar, transcribes the content of his "heart." The primary issue of pictorial creation is therefore not technical or even aesthetic: it's ethical and philosophical. Painting is a difficult subject even before being practiced. The painter's first task is to develop within himself this inner source of the heart. The material execution of the painting is then no longer problematic but the natural and effortless consequence of this spiritual vision. As another author, Fu Zai 符載 (Tang-dynasty official and poet, 759–?), puts it: "Objects are not captured by sensory perception: they are enclosed in the dwelling of the soul, which is why the hand only responds to what the painter has apprehended in his heart" 「而物在靈府，不在耳目，故得於心，應於手。」(PR 19).

Idleness – *xian* 閒 or 閑

Within himself, the painter must maintain a heart that is idle (*xian* 閒 or 閑), silent, and tranquil (*jing* 靜), purified of emptiness (*kong* 空), possibly through the contemplation of nature or paintings, through study, through reading and poetry, or through music or wine to achieve a meditative state of purity and detachment. The painter must be calm and idle (*an xian* 安閒 or 安閑) when he takes up the brush. For the painter, calligrapher, and critic Li Rihua 李日華 (1565–1635): "It's no small matter to impregnate paper with a single drop of ink: the heart must become immense and empty without containing a single object."

For landscape painter Wang Yu 王昱 (1700–1751), "The heart must be absolutely empty, without the shadow of a speck of dust, and the landscape will emerge from the innermost depths of the soul [...]. Before painting, the painter must calm his heart and keep his thoughts distant [...]" 「胸中空空洞洞，無一點塵埃。邱壑從靈性發出 ……士人作畫第一要平等心，弗因識者而加意揣摩……。」(PR 123). → Composition

Imagination – *xiang xiang* 想像

In the Chinese tradition, the painter's imagination is sparked by a schema that retains the living lines, the arteries of the breath, and the balanced curve of the vital movement of nature. What sustains the world and gives each object its own reality is the set of relationships that each element maintains with all the others under the action of the movement. Thought records its relationships, then closes in on itself and looks beyond the relative, seeing the movement itself. Shaken in its depths, it goes to work and recreates the contemplated object in an idealized, concentrated, unified form. The creative operation is complete when the image has blossomed on the surface of consciousness. Seen by the mind, it is as though it had been born within it (NVN 192–93).

Intention – *Yi* 意

Yi is the intention that precedes execution; as the classical maxim goes, "the idea must precede the brush" (「意在筆先」 attributed to Wang Wei 王維 , 699–759). Intention is the indispensable prerequisite for painting. Whereas the mind must be absolutely detached, idle, and unfettered, the idea must be firmly fixed and clearly determined: only then will the painter be able to take up his brush. "In painting, the idea must first be fixed; if the brush begins to work before the idea has been fixed, it will have no inner guidance, there will be no coordination between hand and mind, and the work is condemned in advance." Zheng Ji 鄭績 (active around the middle of the nineteenth century, physician, poet, and painter, author of the treatise *Menghuanju Huaxue Jianming* 《夢幻居畫學簡明》, 1866) (PR 23–24).

Interruption or ellipsis

Don't represent the whole subject but isolate one of its significant elements (PR, Appendix). By schematizing the object, thought gives life to what it represents. By writing in cursive style, the painter or calligrapher imbues his ideograms with powerful schemas and communicates the cyclical movement of life (NVN 3).

The pictorial ideal is represented by the ellipsis, a fragmentary view: the object is deliberately removed from its context to better strip away its "vulgar" materiality, the mountain is glimpsed only between two banks of mist, the flower or fruit has been torn from its branch

and thrown into the emptiness of the white page where, removed from all trivial detail, it becomes an abstract sign (PR 110).

And shortly afterwards, at the beginning of the Qing dynasty, calligrapher and painter Shen Hao 沈顥 (1586–1661) continued in the same vein: "It is not necessary to show the foot of mountains or the root of trees: the viewer must be allowed to ascertain all that the brush leaves to guess [. . .]. When the ancients painted plum trees or bamboos, they only showed a branch protruding from behind a wall and, with this original approach, totally captured its character; if they had painted the tree with all its branches, they would have fallen into insipid banality" (PR 91).

Intuition – *Shen hui* 神會, universal consonance

The supreme faculty that qualifies a man for the service of art. The gift of discovery and invention that cultivates the mind. Zhang Yanyuan 張彥遠 (810–880), author of the monumental history of art (*Li dai ming hua ji* 《歷代名畫記》, 847), was already talking about the role of intuition (*shen hui* 神會) in artistic creation, an intellectual sympathy that informs the mind of the inexpressible aspects of an object. Sensitive to the rhythm that ancient painters infused in their work, he knew that rhythm is breath, idea. He said that painting was only truly animated by the breath of the idea. "The idea dwells (in the mind) before the brush (comes into play), and when the painting is finished, it remains present" (NVN 67).

When detached from everything, the artist's soul becomes depersonalized and dissolves into phenomena. It becomes an aptitude for spontaneous realization, through which the universe is seen and developed. This is the union of *shen hui*, silent identification and absolute vitalization. Having achieved this high degree of abstraction, the artist can use the tip of his brush to create small, impermeable, living worlds, inviolable retreats where he expresses himself in the universal. All that's required is for him to unroll the fragile roll of silk or paper, in the company of a chosen friend, to escape from everyday life, to wander along paths that wind through damp woods, to pass through the narrow gate that leads to the ever-near afar (NVN 246). The painting of scholars is a religious game, a mystery of grace where all is consideration and freedom, outpouring, superabundance, and deliverance. Suddenly aware of his unlimited autonomy, the artist who devotes himself to it paints in the spontaneous manner that the bird sings, the wind blows, and living water gushes forth. His thought escapes the control of his will, insofar as the latter is an effort, and not the irresistible impulse of spiritual life. His brush is no longer directed by speech, but by intellectual intuition, absolutely free awareness (NVN 180).

Landscape – *shan shui* 山水

Mountain and water, an expression that appeared in the third century BCE to designate the Chinese literary and pictorial landscape. The first treatises on *shan shui* appeared in the fourth century. By the tenth century, *shan shui* had become the main genre of Chinese painting, embodying the → microcosm within the macrocosm (YE 381). Shitao's ideal of a landscape: "The landscape expresses the form and momentum of heaven and earth. Within the landscape, wind and rain, darkness and clarity constitute the atmospheric mood; scattering or grouping, depth and distance constitute schematic organization; verticals and horizontals, hollows and reliefs constitute rhythm; shadow and light, heaviness and thinness constitute spiritual focus; mists and clouds, in their gathering and dispersal, constitute connection and belonging; the folds and rises that form the valleys and ridges constitute the alternation of action and retreat." 石濤《畫語錄》：「山川，天地之形勢也。風雨晦明，山川之氣象也；疏密深遠，山川之約徑也；縱橫吞吐，山川之節奏也；陰陽濃淡，山川之凝神也；水雲聚散，山川之聯屬也；蹲跳向背，山川之行藏也。」(PR 67–68).

Light, alert – *qing* 輕

This term can be positive or negative. When it describes a line drawn too quickly, lacking internal tension, a little transparent and inconsistent, it indicates a defect. Conversely, it can be positive with regard to the lightness of a brushstroke and the dexterity this emanates (YE 381).

If the artist brings alert thought (*qing* 輕) to his work, he will spontaneously transmit the spirit of his model. In this way, his painting will have the power to call to life everything it represents (NVN 26).

According to Shitao, when the painter directs the breath, he not only becomes regenerated physically but also strengthened spiritually. He nourishes his essence and spirit, and by feeding the vital principle within himself, he keeps his creative faculties awake. Alert and keen, they go to work, creating a work that is pure energy (NVN 29).

Microcosm / Macrocosm – *yin yun* 絪縕 or 氤氳

According to Shitao, who associates the brush with the mountain and ink with water (he uses the terms "brush mountain" 筆山 and "ink sea" 墨海), the union of macrocosm (i.e., the great universe) and microcosm (i.e., the small universe) generates pictorial phenomenon, just as the union of *yin* and *yang* produced the multitude of creatures. Painting is not a description of the spectacle of Creation: it is itself a Creation in the literal sense of the word, a microcosm whose essence and mechanism are identical and parallel to those of the macrocosm; painting is no less concrete and real than the world: it is the world's sister, begotten in accordance with the same laws (PR 63).

Momentum, power – *shi* 勢

Etymologically: power conferred by possession of land. It can mean "position; impact; dynamism, momentum; shape and form; condition, status; opportunity." In calligraphy and painting, this term covers both the concrete line and its visual result, the impression of momentum or dynamism suggested in the viewer's mind by the line and therefore by the handling of the brush and the strength of the line. It is opposed to the term *xing* 形, the appearance, outward form. *Shi* 勢 is dynamic, *xing* 形 static: *xing* 形 refers to the form of the stroke, while *shi* 勢 designates its effect (YE 382).

Movement of life – *sheng dong* 生動, breath harmony – *qi yun* 氣韻

Jing Hao 荊浩, a reclusive painter living from late Tang dynasty to the early Five Dynasties period, tells the following story in his painting treatise *Bifaji*《筆法記》: a young painter meets an old man in the mountains who initiates him into the mystery of painting. Inexperienced, the young artist believes that it's enough to convey the exterior likeness to find the truth of the model (曰:「畫者，華也。但貴似得真，豈此撓矣。」). The old man replied, "The likeness seizes the appearance (*xing* 形) but leaves behind the animating breath (*qi* 氣). Truth (*zhen* 真) pulls everything together, breath (*qi* 氣) and matter (*zhi* 質)" 「叟曰：『似者，得其形，遺其氣。真者，氣質俱盛。』」. Breath is understood here as the movement that animates inertia and wrests beings and things from chaos (NVN 189).

Nature – *tian ran* 天然 (spontaneous, natural)

The great literati of the eleventh century seem to have attached eminent value to landscape painting, to that of trees and grasses, mountains and stones, clouds and water. They saw nature constantly changing before their eyes and hence understood better that the painter's mission is not to set down the fleeting appearance of objects but to capture the organizing principle that makes them what they are (NVN 186).

According to Shitao:

- The state of nature contrasts with the state of civilization.
- Travel and visits to mountains are part of a painter's training.
- Nature is the painter's only master.
- Only the direct contemplation of nature enables painting to achieve higher categories.
- Nature is the absolute limit and criterion of all painting (PR, Appendix).

According to the eleventh-century painter Mi Fu 米芾 (c. 1051–1107), the artist must not copy nature but create as nature creates. Nature's dynamism is spontaneous, and so is that of art (NVN 63).

Natural arrangements, natural harmonies – *tian qu* 天趣

According to the aesthete and collector Zhao Xigu 趙希鵠 (1180–1240), in his book *Dong Tian Qing Lu* 《洞天清錄》, written around 1230, the painter Mi Fu, by imitating each day what his eyes saw, grasped the mystery of natural harmonies or *tian qiu*. He owed his virtuosity to calligraphers, but he owed the vigor, lightness, and originality of his style to nature and to his temperament (NVN 118).

Poetry and painting – *shi yu hua* 詩與畫

In China, the close union between painting and poetry is a fundamental principle. Painting and poetry do not seek to complement one another, but to exchange and invert their respective functions and conditions. Poetry is, by nature, a more abstract and symbolic art form, since it can only render things present through the intellectual medium of words; painting, on the other hand, is more concrete, enabling us to grasp the world more directly and sensitively through the sensual medium of the eye. Contrary to their nature, poetry strives to put before the eye a picture of things that is as concrete and real as possible, while painting aims to free itself from any function of representation or material figuration, and becoming as evasive and abstract as possible, a poetic allusion speaking to the spirit far more than a concrete object submitted to the gaze. Thus, the keyword in poetic criticism is the concept *shi* 實: the fullness, density, and plenitude of material reality, the concrete weight of which the words of the poem manage to assimilate. In painting the central concept of criticism is *xu* 虛, emptiness, i.e., those white areas left to the imagination. The painted part, less important than the empty spaces, tends to be no more than a support for the latter, an aid that guides the eye and brings it to that essential threshold of emptiness, where the mind takes over from the eye. Poetry uses a rich array of colorful adjectives, both abundant and precise, while painting, from the end of the Tang period onward, sometimes rid itself of color and found its highest form of expression in the monochrome ink wash (PR 109).

Quintessence, essence – *hua qing* 畫情

The landscape painters of the Song knew that the effect of painting is not to represent things as the eye sees them, but as they are to the soul, totally internalized. For a true artist, a true image is will, a vital force. It appears and immediately manifests its dynamic, organizing power (NVN 240).

In art, the spirit is communicated and transmitted. How can a calligrapher's, a painter's, or a poet's mind reach out and unite with all that solicits it if it has not first grasped its own essence? [. . .] Creative work consists in evoking the spirit hidden in the body of things, and thus attracting into the universal materiality all that lives, sparks, and sings (NVN 26).

The eye records and compares sensations, transmitting a synthetic perception to the mind (*xin* 心). When the memory does not carry out an initial purification, thought does not react to the excitation received and the mind is not even reached.

In China, art is not an imitation of reality, but the creation of a world consubstantial with the mind. Nor is it pure subjectivity, since the assent of the eye is first required. To possess the indefinable quality that makes it a "mental thing (*xin shi* 心事 or *qing shi* 情事)," the work of art must correspond to an inner necessity and arise from the depths of the mind (NVN 33).

Receptivity, perception, reception – *shou* 受, and knowledge – *shi* 識

According to the painter Shitao, it is a question of *venerating receptivity*. As far as receptivity and knowledge are concerned, it is receptivity that precedes, and knowledge that follows; receptivity that would be posterior to knowledge would not be true receptivity (PR 43).

These are originally two concepts from Buddhist philosophy. Shou refers to the way in which the mind comes into contact with and perceives the external universe. Shi is another word for the mind as a capacity to understand and distinguish. Knowledge, *shi* 試, is the intellection and distinctions made by the mind about the external world. Chan Buddhism is known to have had a decisive influence on Shi Tao's intellectual training. Chan thought, moreover, with its extraordinary insistence on the objectivity of reality, has, since the Song period, encouraged an attitude of humble, attentive contemplation of the world, down to the most trivial, minute, and concrete of its manifestations, an attitude that was particularly fruitful for painting (PR 45). Before painting, the painter's discipline is to be a seer (PR 45).

Spirit – *shen* 神

Spirit, spiritual power, force that animates the sensible, vital principle, its etymology unites the radicalness of sacrifice and an element signifying spiritual power. *Shen* is an aesthetic category just below that of the natural (YE 382). → Form

According to Shitao:
- Painting is a spiritual operation, freed from the contingencies of materials and instruments.
- Painting emanates from the intellect.
- Conscious intention must precede the brush.
- The intention of the work must precede the brushwork (PR 9).

Spiritual rhythm – *qi yun* 氣韻

The brushstroke is considered the privileged channel through which "spiritual rhythm" (*qi yun* 氣韻) is expressed—an expression that constitutes the absolute limit toward which all painting tends. For the painter Shitao, this notion goes far beyond the realm of technique: the brushstroke is seen as the only intermediary capable of transmitting the vision of the spirit in the universe of forms (PR 16).

The supreme value of painting lies in its ability to transmit spiritual influx or spiritual rhythm. This ability does not depend on technical or plastic execution, but on the heart that precedes and guides it. "Spiritual influx is produced by the brush when its movements follow the heart." "The spiritual rhythm of painting originates in the free flow of the heart" (Guo Ruoxu 郭若虛, author of the most important work on the history of art from the Northern Song period, *Tuhua Jianwenzhi* 《圖畫見文誌》, 1074) (PR 20).

Spontaneity – *ziran* 自然

Of its own, by itself, and thus natural, nature, not in the sense of what is in itself, but of what happens without cause or reason, *ziran* is an aspect of the Dao, by which is meant being such "by itself." *Ziran* is the superior artistic (technical) and aesthetic (plastic) criterion of pictorial and calligraphic creation, which applies to both artists and works of art (YE 390). Painting, like calligraphy, "originates in the spontaneous." When a landscape is constructed in the intimacy of the brain, where it is nourished by the breath of life, it possesses all the qualities that scholars expect of painting. It is simple and unpretentious (*ping dan* 平淡); it is true, like nature in its prime purity (*tian zhen* 天真); it is alive like the spirit that directs the brush. According to Dong You 董逌 (twelfth-century art critic and author), "Painting owes its excellence to the dynamism of thought that never lets the truth of things slip away" (NVN 192).

When the painter or calligrapher works spontaneously, he naturally transmits the movement of life to his line and triggers creative mutations with his brush. In the universe, beings and things only appear in order to disappear, carried along by the flow of becoming. According to ancient texts, "Mutation is the first graspable manifestation of vital energy. The painter must let this power work through him. He then becomes capable of evoking life in all its aspects, that of beings that sit and get up, move and fly, come and go, lie down and stand up [. . .] that of insects that eat the leaves of trees, that of water and fire, clouds and mists, sun and moon" (NVN 20). → Creative Spontaneity

Strength – *li* 力

Fundamental quality of the brushstroke (YE 378). All the force of the stroke must be concentrated in the tip of the brush; the stroke is removed without smudges or lateral pentimenti. Good painters draw with the incisiveness of an awl on sand, like the imprint of a seal on paper (PR 119). → Brush/Brushstroke

According to Shitao, the force that expresses itself through strong means is not true force, unlike the force that succeeds in manifesting itself through meager and dull means; the density that expresses itself through a thickness of matter is only a false density, unlike the density that succeeds in imposing itself by means of light, sparse material (PR 122).

Supreme simplicity – *tai pu* 太樸

Daoist expression whose original meaning is that of a block of rough, uncut wood; absolute simplicity, i.e., pure virtuality, containing all possibilities, without having yet mutilated itself to become the limited, specialized expression of one of them (PR 12). Simplicity is the basis for embracing the universal. In Daoist thought, it is precisely the simple, the easy, the concrete, the infinitely small, and the infinitely humble that constitute the seat and source of the Wise Man's omnipotence, universal mastery of phenomena, and intellection of the most complex and abstract. This is the Taoist paradox, which sees in the most immediate superficiality the true gateway to the deepest mysteries; the key to all difficulties lies in the humble facility that powerful minds disdain. "The wise man never undertakes great things, which enables him to achieve his goals; he unravels difficulty by attacking it on its easy side, he tackles great undertakings starting with their smallest elements" (PR 25).

Textured strokes – *cun* 皴

The effect given by rubbing with a pointed brush held at an angle is called *cun*, an overpainting added with a dry brush after (the outlines) to give volumes a fragmentary appearance. Once the outlines have defined the contours of a given object (stone, mountain, tree trunk, etc.), *cun* is added inside the outlines, or built on them, to depict the relief, texture, grain, luminosity, surface irregularities, and volume of the object. In other words, in Chinese painting, *cun* combines the various functions that, in the West, are assigned to the line, color, shading, and perspective, since they describe the form, matter, lighting, and mass of things at the same time (PR 78).

Transcribing the idea – *xie yi* 寫意; poetic abstraction in painting

Xie 寫 means to write, and by extension can mean to create, to capture, or to draw from what is there. Chinese has two opposing expressions: *xie xing* 寫形 that reproduces the external form of the object; *xie yi* 寫意 that reproduces the idea behind the object. *Xie xing*

寫形 stops at the simulacrum, while *xie yi* 寫意 brings out the resemblance of objects to their models (*exempla*). *Xin* 形 is differentiated from *yi* 意 in the same way that, in the thought of the West's early medieval period, the sensible world, *mondus sensilis*, is opposed to the intelligible world, that of the models (*exempla*) (See Étienne Gilson, *La Philosophie au Moyen-Age*) (NVN 195).

A painter can only enter into sympathy with beings and things if he brings to his art a healthy, vigorous body, a serene heart, and a light, lively mind. If he is depressed and melancholic, if trivial worries hinder the momentum of his imagination and the supple movement of his thought, he will not respond to nature's subtle promptings and, in his troubled soul, no reflection will arise (NVN 195).

Travel / Journeys

According to Zhao Xigu 趙希鵠 (1180–1240), a scholar and aesthete, in his guide for aesthetes and collectors: "A painter's normal training must not only include a thorough literary culture and knowledge of the works of art of Antiquity, it is also necessary that the artist travel around a good half of the Universe, whether by carriage or on horseback, and only then will he be in a position to take up his brush" (PR 72–73). Since then, travel and journeys have always been part of the painter's apprenticeship.

Variation, transformation, mutation – *bian* 變

Variation, varying, change. Variation is the quality of being able to never repeat the same line twice, and therefore not to allow oneself to be carried away by automatisms acquired during training. "Variation" denotes the ability to create something new, an essential criterion in calligraphy and painting (YE 372). Mutation is the universal law, everything changes, and at every moment we change with the All. The wise man must therefore abandon himself to the rhythmic movement that reigns over the universe, and follow the impulse of his nature. If he lives like this, he will find not only joy, but life (NVN 4).

Vertical tip (of the brush) – *zheng feng* 正鋒

Together with the "hidden tip (*cang feng* 藏鋒)," one of two basic calligraphic and pictorial techniques. *Zheng feng* is when the brush is held constantly perpendicular to the paper, with the tip in line with the axis, and the tip alone makes a mark, so as to concentrate maximum force in each stroke. Painting in ancient times made almost exclusive use of this difficult, demanding, and rather austere technique, but one of incomparable power (PR 119).

Working freehand or *xuan wan* 懸腕, the hand and wrist must hover over the paper without leaning on the desk for support; the movements of the brush no longer depend on the fingers, but on the wrist: hand, fingers, and brush become a single entity; the fingers hold onto the brush just tight enough so that the brush becomes the natural extension of the whole arm; the force that moves the brush starts from the shoulder and is transmitted from one point to the paper, giving the slightest stroke an incomparable concentration of energy. This technique is obviously much more difficult:

as the hand is suspended in air, its slightest movements must be entirely controlled and sustained by the muscular strength of the whole arm. For the Chinese painter, the difference in line quality—meager and constricted when the hand is supported and the brush is maneuvered by the fingers, free and powerful when the grip of the fingers is rigid and the movements are transmitted by the motion of the wrist held above the paper by the strength of the arm—is not a mere technical phenomenon: it's a question of imparting the influx of *qi* 氣 into the painting, a breath that it would be futile to try and define in spiritual or physical terms since the notions of matter and spirit are opposed only in the arbitrariness of Western analytical classifications. Painting freehand, the painter has no other contact with the surface to be painted than the tip of his brush, where the totality of his energy is concentrated—the creation-generating fluid flowing from the artist's heart to the tip of the brush, without intermediation or divergence. If the wrist comes to rest on the table, this flow, on the contrary, loses momentum and, revived as much as possible by the agility of the fingers alone, is distributed no more than thinly (PR 24).

For Shitao, the painter must work with freehand ease: the brushstroke will consequently be capable of abrupt mutations. If the brush is incisive in its opening and finishing movements, the form will be without clumsiness or confusion. The firmness of the wrist allows the brush to settle and penetrate deeply; the lightness of the wrist makes the brush fly and dance with cheerful detachment; the rigorously straight wrist makes the brush work from the tip; it bends, and the brush works at an angle; the wrist accelerates its stroke and the brushwork gains in strength; the slowness of the wrist gives rise to delightful curves; the variations of the wrist enable effects of unconstrained naturalness; its alterations generate unexpected and bizarre effects; its eccentricities work miracles, and when the wrist is animated by the spirit, rivers and mountains deliver up their soul (PR 56).

Weak, light, pale, dull – *dan* 淡

This concept plays an important role in aesthetics and is typical of China's conception of beauty. *Dan* literally means "weak" (as opposed to "thick, heavy, dark," *nong* 濃) or "light," "bland," "pale," "dull," "faded," referring to a color (as opposed to a bright or vivid color). In painting, it refers to ink with a high content of water. This diluted, fluid ink (as opposed to thick *nong* ink) has all the aesthetic characteristics suggested by the above terms: unlike thick ink, which allows the creation of luminous effects of external force, diluted ink results in weak, light, faded appearances. The latter is much more difficult to use than thick ink; thick ink enables spectacular effects, but its potency is derived more from the material itself than from the painter's art, and its usage is therefore an easy solution. The use of pale ink, in contrast, which is a thankless process in principle, offers no intrinsic beauty and thus all depends on the painter's art. The force that expresses itself through strong means is not true force, unlike the force that manifests itself through meager and dull means; the density that expresses itself through a thickness of matter is only a false density, unlike the density that imposes itself

by means of light, sparse material (PR 121). The concept *dan* 淡 refers to all that is rare and exquisite, but—when compared with our Western understanding—it has a fundamental difference, as for the Chinese mind the rare and exquisite are associated with a stark sobriety that is the very opposite of "precious." The taste of the "insipid" is almost inexpressible. The same applies to *yi* 逸, superior detachment, elegant nonchalance, whimsical and sovereign naturalness, noble idleness. The two terms *dan* 淡 and *yi* 逸 are closely related. For some authors, including Dai Xi 戴熙 (1801–1860), the two terms constitute one of the "four essential beauties" of painting, the other three being "idle nonchalance" or *xian* 閒, "motionless silence" or *jing* 靜, and "far distance" or *yuan* 遠. For another author, Yun Xiang 惲向 (1586–1655), painting becomes capable of exhausting the reality of all phenomena if it succeeds in making itself "totally pale," "totally flat," "totally devoid of intention" (PR 122).

Yin and *Yang* 陰陽

Yin and *yang* symbolize the traditional conception of the world in constant mutation through the intermediary of two opposing and alternating principles: *yang*, the masculine principle, embodies the sun, sky, mountains, hardness, etc., and corresponds in graphic arts to the white of the support; *yin*, the feminine principle, embodies the moon, earth, water, shadow, suppleness, etc., and corresponds to the black of the ink (YE 388).

INDEX AND GLOSSARY

The page numbers in italics refer to the key entries in *Concepts of Chinese Aesthetics*.

Manual for calligraphy from the seventeenth to eighteenth century. "Mustard seed" stands for "growing great." See for example *The Mustard Seed Garden Manual of Painting* (Princeton, NJ: Princeton University Press, 1956).

Zhuangzi → Zhuangzi 54, 79, 81, 124

Breath 75, 80, 263, 267, 285, 296, 298, *326*

Brush: Ink brushes are made of soft or hard hairs with different sizes, from goats, weasels, pigs (hog bristles), to horses. They can also be made from feathers of an eagle. Also the handle, made of buffalo horn, wood, or bamboo, with different sizes and forms, is important for the quality of the brush strokes. 9, 27, 46, 52, 53, 55, 59, 71, 73, 74, 76, 78, 79, 83, 88, 98, 140, 158, 173–75, 202, 265, 266, 271, 280–82, 296–98, 302, 314

Brushstroke 11, 17, 46, 57, 63, 69, 74–78, 83, 85, 87–92, 171, 181, 268, 283, 286, 295–97, *326*

Brush texture *326*

   Playing (fiddling) with the brush *327*

Buddha Amitabha: A Buddha, known for his longevity, discernment, pure perception, and the purification of aggregates with deep awareness of the emptiness of all phenomena. 160

Buddhism: Buddhism was founded in India by the wandering ascetic and religious teacher Siddhartha Gautama (563–483 BCE). About two centuries after his death, he came to be known by the title Buddha. One of his names was → Shakyamuni.
Buddhism was first introduced to China during the Han dynasty. Chinese or Han Buddhism is a form of Mahayana-Buddhism ("Great Vehicle") that draws on numerous Chinese traditions. 54, 147, 152, 156, 157, 160, 162, 163, 180, 283, 284, 296

Bund 172 → Shanghai

Buyi 129, 210, 240, 293 → Ethnic groups

Calligraphy 13, 14, 17, 29, 46, 54, 59, 62, 63, 65–69, 71, 73, 74, 76–79, 81, 82, 86, 87, 113–16, 128, 147, 168–79, 180–84, 202, 240, 248, 254, 264, 268–70, 277, 283, 284, 290, 291, 294, 295, 324, 325, *327*

Camphor wood: Used for storage for its insect-repellant properties. 173, 262, 267

Carmen: Opera written in 1875 by Georges Bizet (1838–1875). 61

Carving 30, 33, 35, 71–73, 78, 80, 120, 122, 128, 129, 136, 154, 161, 172, 173, 184, 240, 325 → Lacquer

Ceramic 173, 266

Chan → Zen 128, 147, 180, 325

Chaos 121, 159, 160, 296, *328*

Chaozhou-style tea 170

Chengdu: Capital of Sichuan province 108, 120, 122, 123, 132, 139, 141, 255, 260

Chess 33, 44, 45, 87, 88

Chongqing: Municipality with thirty-two million inhabitants at the confluence of Yangtze and Jialing rivers, 1,700 kilometers southwest of Beijing.
The **Sichuan Fine Arts Institute** was established in 1940. In the 1950s and 1960s the Institute's focus was handcraft arts; in the 1970s it was sculpture; in the 1980s it was oil painting. 18, 22–35, 44, 50, 59, 62, 98, 112, 120, 134, 165, 172, 181, 248, 257, 258, 291

Christianity 53, 70, 148

Circle 127, 128, 160, 286, 298 → Mandala

Civilization 7, 53, 70, 125, 279

Classic of Mountains and Seas 150→ Books

Classic of the White Madam → Books

Classical Era 73 → Dynasties, Han

Clouds 75

Coarse rawness *328*

Color/monochrome 9, 62, 81, 162, 282, 283, 292, 297, 337

Comments on Painting 18, 73 → Shitao

Communism 45, 55, 56, 130, 169, 261 → History

Composition 9, 27, 62, 79, 87, 88, 89, 90, 92, 158, 171, 180, 187, 269, *329*

Confucianism: A system of thought and behavior, following the teachings of → Confucius (c. 551–479 BCE), philosopher of the Spring and Autumn period (770–481 BCE). Confucianism is omnipresent throughout Chinese history as a formative mindset. It is associated with a rigorous ethos, characterized by rituals, kindness, and respect, while Daoist philosophy leads to more open and poetic associations. 54, 141, 144, 152, 171, 172, 174, 296

Constant principle of internal order *329*

Contemplation, silent identification 15, 48, 68, 83, 181, 187, 262, 265, 266, 267, 286, *330*

Copy, copying 11, 13, 60, 61, 64, 66, 68, 72, 74, 78, 85, 87, 175, 177, 178, 179, 184, 240, 294, 295, *330*

Craftsmen-painters 162, 163

Creative spontaneity *330*

Creative spring, spontaneous dynamism *330*

Cremation 96, 97, 137, 138

Crickets 122, 165–68

Cultural Revolution: Sociopolitical movement, launched by → Mao Zedong in May 1966, lasting until his death in 1976. At the beginning it marked the

effective return of Mao to the center of power in China after his political sidelining, in the aftermath of the → Great Leap Forward (1958–1962) and the Great Chinese → Famine (1959–1961). Its stated goal was to preserve Chinese communism by purging remnants of capitalist and traditional elements from the society. One of the instruments of power was → self-criticism. The Gang of Four rose to power in 1971 and had significant influence over the Cultural Revolution. The Cultural Revolution continued until Mao's death in 1976, soon followed by the arrest of the Gang of Four. → History → Jiang Qing
During the Cultural Revolution, tens of millions of people were persecuted, with an estimated death toll ranging to sixty-five million. 7, 29, 30, 33, 47, 49, 51, 53, 64, 69, 70, 71, 98, 101, 130, 134, 141, 143, 151, 169, 179, 181, 185, 187, 256, 265, 272, 278, 279, 291–93
Currency: 100 USD = 232.70 *yuan* or *renminbi* in 1984. Today (2024) the rate is about 700. Fabienne Verdier got 120 *yuan*/month, the other students 60 *yuan*/month (about $25 or 18£).
1 *yuan* = 10 *jiao* (or *mao*) = 100 *fen* 分. 35

Dao, Daoism 296, *330*
Detachment – carelessness, nonchalance, superior detachment, fantasy 64, 88, 159, 161, 171, 188, 258, 269, 285, *331*
Didone 13 → Styles/Western styles
Diplomat 20, 22, 103, 260, 261, 263, 268, 269, 274
Discourse on art and literature 30 → Mao Zedong
Divining rod 158
Dollar 102, 178, 270 → Currency
Double Five 95
Dream stone: Marble slabs mined, cut, and polished to reveal extraordinary patterns resembling landscapes of traditional Chinese painting, celestial landscapes, or abstract depictions of natural phenomena. 145, 169, 180, 187, 275, 280
Drying oil 48→ Lacquer
Du Fu Cottage 121 → Chengdu
Dunhuang Caves: The Caves of the Thousand Buddhas are a system of five hundred temples twenty-five kilometers southeast of Dunhuang, a town in the northwest of Gansu province. 265
Dynamism → Creative spontaneity
Dynasties 48, 121, 135, 162, 166, 220, 266 → History
BC = Before Christ (BCE = Before Common Era), AD = Anno Domini (CE = Common Era) 73, 110, 121, 170, 187

1600–1046 BC	Shang: Ruling in the Yellow River valley		
1000–750 BC	Western Zhou: Capital Zongzhou		
771–256 BC	Eastern Zhou: Capital Chengzhou	770–476 BC	Spring and Autumn Era
		475–221 BC	Warring States Period
202 BC–220 AD	Han: Beginning of classical era	202 BC-220 AD	Western Han
		25–220	Eastern Han
220–589	Six Dynasties Period	220-280	Three Kingdoms Period
		386-535	Northern Wei
		386-589	Northern and Southern Dynasties
618–907	Tang: Historians generally regard the Tang as a high point in Chinese civilization, and a golden age of cosmopolitan culture		
960–1127	Northern Song		
1127–1279	Southern Song		
1271–1368	Yuan or Mongolian: Mongol-led imperial dynasty of China and a successor state to the Mongol Empire after its division		
1368–1644	Ming: Last imperial dynasty of China ruled by the Han people, the major ethnic group in China		
1644–1912	Quing: Last dynasty, until 1912, when it was overthrown during the Xinhai Revolution	1850–1864	Taiping Rebellion

Eight Immortals: Group of legendary immortals in Chinese mythology. 109

Emei: Mountain in Sichuan province, 150 kilometers southwest of → Chengdu. At 3,099 meters above sea level it is the highest of the "Four Sacred Buddhist Mountains" of China. There are many temples, including the **Temple of Ten Thousand Years** (Wannian Temple) at the foot of the Camel Mountain Range, one of the six earliest Buddhist temples on Mount Emei. 141, 162

Emptiness 81, 86, 88, 127, 153, 156, 160, 170, 282, 286, 296, *331*

Engraving 48, 140, 173, 267 → Seal

Essence 78, 282, 286 → Quintessence

Ethnic groups 31, 57, 129, 132, 135, 140, 292, 293

> **Han:** The world's largest ethnic group with 17.5% of the global population and 1.3 billion members in China in 2020, i.e., 91% of the Chinese population. Besides the Han there are fifty-five recognized ethnic (minority) groups in China. 31, 121, 134, 184, 275

> **Buyi:** 3.6 million members. They live among related ethnic groups primarily in the Guizhou province. 129, 210, 240, 293

> **Miao:** 11 million members, neighbors of Buyi, living in the mountains of southern China. They are known for making and donning silver accessories. There have been massacres by → Kuomintang and plundering by the → Red Guards. 57, 129–30, 132, 202, 210, 243, 293

> **Naxi:** 323,000 members, living in the northwestern part of Yunnan province. 57, 293

> **Shakya:** Ethnic group living in the time of → Shakyamuni in the Terai, an Indian area south of the foothills of the Himalayas.

> **Yao:** 3 million members, living in the mountainous southwest and south of China. 57, 293

> **Yi:** 9.8 million members, living primarily in rural areas of Sichuan, Yunnan, Guizhou, and Guangxi provinces. 63, 131–40, 202, 210, 220, 293

Evil spirits 32, 134, 174 → Zhong Kui

Excursions 97, 119, 123, 141, 152 → Travel

Exhibitions 13, 30, 57, 178, 25–57, 254, 255, 256, 263, 270, 271, 280, 294, 302

Expressionism 15, 52

Fabrics 121, 127, 129, 138, 170, 171, 183, 271

Famine 130, 133 → Cultural Revolution/Great Chinese Famine

Fantasy 150 → Detachment

Father 8–10, 14, 37, 111, 112, 117, 123, 273 → François Verdier

Festivals 94–96, 99, 102–5, 134, 140, 157, 210, 220, 263

Films 36, 39, 50, 51, 89, 98, 99, 105, 113 133, 278, 297, 298, 314

> *From the Masses to the Masses: As Artist in Mao's China* (2016) Film by Dodge Billingsley

> *How Yukong Moved the Mountains* (**Comment Yukong déplaça les montagnes**) (1976)

> *In the Mood for Love* (2000) Film by Wong Kar-Wai

> *The Mystery of Picasso* (**Le Mystère Picasso**) (1956) Film by Henri-Georges Clouzot

> *Evening Rain* (**Bashan Yeyu**) (1980) Film by Wu Yonggang and Wu Yigong

> *Still Life* (2006) Film by Jia Zhangke (b. 1970)

> *A Tale of the Wind* (**Une Histoire de vent**) (1988) Film by → Joris Ivens and → Marceline Loridan

> *The Chinese Ghostbuster* (1994) Film by Wu Ma (1942–2014)

Flemish painting, Flemish primitives: Painting in the Flemish part of the Netherlands in the fifteenth and sixteenth century. See Fabienne Verdier, *L'Esprit de la peinture: Hommage aux maîtres flamands* (Paris: Albin Michel, 2013). 15, 48, 282

Flying white *332*

Folk 16, 29–31, 45, 57, 63, 95, 98, 129, 141, 152, 161, 270, 272, 293

Folk art 29, 30, 63, 161, 271, 272, 293

Folk legends 29, 31

Folk traditions 16, 98, 129

Forbidden City 262, 268 → Beijing

Forest of Steles 78 → Xi'an

Form and Spirit *332*

Foundation 74, 296

Four Olds: Old ideas, old cultures, old habits, and old customs. The elements of Chinese culture prior to the Chinese Communist Revolution that the Red Guards set out to destroy at the beginning of the Cultural Revolution. 292

Four-handed sessions, exercises 86, 88, 90, 91, 277

Free and relaxed *332*

Fullness 77, 128, 282, *332*

Ganyan: Hepatitis 94, 102, 108, 126, 248, 257

Garden and Palace of Tranquil Longevity 262 → Beijing/Forbidden City

Go: Abstract strategy board game invented in China

more than 2,500 years ago, believed to be the oldest board game continuously played to the present day. 100

Grass (cursive) script 269 → Styles

Gravity 75, 298

Great Fire Festival 134, 140 → Festivals

Great Formulary of State Pharmacies 110 → Books

Great Helmsman: Chinese honorific title. It most commonly refers to → Mao Zedong. 56, 181, 256

Great Leap Forward 179 → History

Grinding 29, 65, 74, 173 → Ink

Guizhou 128, 202, 210, 240 → Provinces

Hall of Original Chaos 121 → Chengdu

Han 31, 121, 134, 184, 275 → Ethnic groups

Hangzhou 22, 144, 181, 182, 185, 186, 248, 260 Capital of Zhejiang province. The **China Academy of Art** is a provincial public college of fine arts, founded in 1928.

Harmony 9, 72, 77, 79, 83–85, 153, 160, 180, 187, 270, 296 → Movement of life → Breath → Natural arrangements

Heart 69, 75, 80, 81, 83, 84, 89, 90, 91, 153, 154, 155, 160, 161, 180, 276, 285, *333*

Heaven 32, 75, 119, 120, 123, 136, 146, 150, 153, 155, 159, 160, 166, 276, 281, 296, 298

Herd-Boy 171→ Du Mu 杜牧

Hermit 154, 155, 280, 286

History

BC = Before Christ (BCE = before common era)

c. 8000–1600 BCE: Neolithic cultures

1600 BCE–1912 CE: → Dynasties

  Republic:

  1911/12: **Xinhai-Revolution** (Xinhai = name of the year January 30, 1911–February 17, 1912)

  1912–1949: **Republic of China (ROC)**

  1927–1949: **Civil War** with **Long March** (1934/35, retreat by the Red Army from advancing Nationalist forces)

  1937–1945: Second **Sino-Japanese War** (with Nanking massacre in 1937, a mass murder of Chinese civilians by the Japanese Army)

  From October 1, 1949: **People's Republic of China (PRC)**

  1958–1962: → Great Leap Forward (important economic and social campaign to reconstruct the country from an agrarian economy into an industrialized society)

  1959–1961: → Great Chinese Famine (with fifteen to fifty-five million deaths)

  1966–1976: → Cultural Revolution

Parties:

Kuomintang (KMT): Major political party in the ROC, sole ruling party until 1949, when the party retreated from the mainland to Taiwan.

Chinese Communist Party (CCP): The party was founded in 1920 with the help of the USSR and the Communist International. Up to 1927 the CCP aligned itself with the KMT as the organized left wing of the larger nationalist movement. When the right wing of the KMT, led by Chiang Kai-shek, turned on the CCP and massacred tens of thousands of the party's members, the two parties split and began a prolonged civil war.

Communist Party of China (CPC): After the KMT's retreat to Taiwan in 1949, the CCP established the People's Republic of China. General Secretary: since 2012 Xi Jinping.

Armies:

Red Army: The Red Army was the military wing of the CCP from 1928 to 1937.

People's Liberation Army (PLA): After the Japanese surrender in 1945, the CCP continued to use the National Revolutionary Army unit structures. In 1947 it was renamed PLA.

Red Guards: The Red Guards were a mass, student-led, paramilitary social movement mobilized by Chairman → Mao Zedong in 1966 until their abolishment in 1968. The Red Guards attacked the "Four Olds" of Chinese society (old ideas, old culture, old customs, and old habits).

Hong Kong 111, 258, 269, 276, 280, 290

Horizontal/vertical 13, 27, 74, 77, 271, 283, 296–98

Hua 46, 75, 123 → Brushstroke

Huangping: Village in Guizhou province. 202, 210

Huoguo: Hotpot, Chinese dish like fondue. 115

Hyperrealism: Painting technique in which the depiction of realities, akin to photography, is exaggerated. 102

I Ching (Book of Changes) 54 → Books

Idleness 88, *333*

Identification → Contemplation

Ideology 28, 29, 30, 33, 34, 38, 40, 45, 52, 55, 57

Imagination 56, 82, 87, 89, 92, 128, *334*

Imperial Garden 262 → Beijing/Forbidden City

Imperial Palace 31→ Beijing/Forbidden City

In the Mood for Love 113 → Films

Initiation 18, 86, 99, 154

Ink: Ink sticks or **cakes** are made mainly of soot and animal glue. An **ink stone** is a stone mortar for **grinding** and containment of ink. It is also manufactured from clay, bronze, iron, or porcelain. The finish of the stone can be delicately carved or rough, its appearance humorous or ferocious. To make ink, the ink stick is ground against an ink stone with a small quantity of water to produce ink, which is then applied with the **ink brush**. For calligraphers and painters, a good ink stone is as important as the quality of the ink, and indeed affects the texture of the ink ground upon it. 27, 29, 30, 33, 52, 55, 65, 68, 74, 77, 78, 81, 86, 88, 146, 158, 160, 173, 174, 176, 282, 292, 296, 297, 325

Ink brush 173→ Brush/Brush and ink
Ink cake, stick, stone 27 → Ink
Intention 268, *334*
Interruption or ellipsis *334*
Intuition 9, 69, 79, 84, 89, 152, 160, 284, 291, *334*
Isolation 9, 40, 124
Italian primitives 15, 281

Jesuits 138, 148
Jiu Long Po 39, 240 → Teahouse

Kabuki: Traditional Japanese theater. 61
Kaishu (regular script) 169 → Styles
Karachi 19, 20
Kathakali: Traditional form of classical Indian dance and one of the most complex forms of Indian theater. 61
Kite 268
Kuang Cao (wild cursive) 269 → Styles
Kuomintang (the Nationalist Party) 120, 130 → History/ Parties
Kwok On Museum: The **Collection of Musée Kwok On**, founded 1972 in Paris by → Jacques Pimpaneau, is now the Museu do Oriente in Lisbon. 16, 17

Lacquer 47, 48
    Drying oil 48
Lake of Ten Buddhist Monasteries 275 → Beijing
Lake Tai 262 → Yangtze
Landscape *335*
Landscape painting 57, 62, 81, 82, 86–90, 92, 123, 147, 150, 158, 161, 163, 174, 180, 181, 182, 187, 265, 271
Les singes orient leurs chagrins 17, 27 → Books
Lhasa 124
Li 148 → Constant principle of internal order

Liangshan: Autonomous prefecture occupying much of the southern part of Sichuan province. 220, 248
Light, alert *335*
Literati 19, 70, 173, 291, 292, 296, 324
Little Red Book 144→ Mao Zedong
Long March 56 → History
Lyrical abstraction 11, 15

Mad old man: Well-known fable from Chinese mythology about a man called Yugong. 83 → Films/*How Yukong* → Mao Zedong
Mahjong (*mah-jongg*) 44, 65
Maîtres Flamands → Flemish painting
Mandala: Geometric configuration of symbols, which often takes the form of a square with four gates (one on each side) and a circle (in its center). It is an archetype of the universe in Buddhism, Hinduism, Jainism, and Shintoism. Mandalas may be employed for focusing attention of practitioners and adepts, as a spiritual guidance tool, and as an aid to meditation. 127
Marouflage: Marouflage (from French *maroufle* = strong glue) is a technique that consists of gluing a work of art to a support and fixing the pigments. 61–63, 243, 244
Marxism 42
Medicine 107, 109, 110, 120, 133
Meishan: City with three million inhabitants, located in Sichuan province. 141
Men of letters 124, 141, 149, 162, 187, 267, 278
Miao 57, 128–130, 132, 198, 208, 243, 293 → Ethnic groups
Microcosm *336*
Ming 162, 166, 173, 218, 262, 267 → Dynasties
Minorities 31, 52, 57, 58, 104, 127, 131, 292, 293 → Ethnic groups
Momentum *336*
Monasteries 32, 121, 125–28, 137, 144, 150, 151, 156, 157, 275 → Beijing → Shigatse
Mongolian 48, 57 → Dynasties
Mother 8, 282 → Marie-France Guibert
Mountain of Purity: Daoist temple complex on Mount Lao or Laoshan near the eastern coast of China (Shandong province). The Temple of Supreme Purity is located near the coast on the southeastern foot of Mount Lao. 122
Movement of life *336*
Mustard Seed Garden Manual of Painting 87 → Books

Nanking (Nanjing) 105, 113, 115
Natural History Museum 16 → Toulouse
Nature 8–10, 12–15, 52, 57, 58, 74–76, 81, 83, 85, 92, 123, 147, 149, 153, 167, 172, 176, 181, 187, 263, 267, 284, 286, 291, 292, 298, *336*
Natural arrangements, natural harmonies *337*
Naxi 57, 293 → Ethnic groups
New Year 29, 30, 94, 119 → Festival
Night Rain in the Bashan Mountains 50 → Films

Old concessions district 169, 172 → Shanghai
Old masters 42, 60, 83, 91, 154, 179, 180, 181, 259, 270, 273, 277, 281, 286
Opera 17, 50, 61, 77, 97, 98, 121
OuLiPo: "Ouvroir de Littérature Potentielle" ("Workshop of Potential Literature"), a group co-founded in 1960 by the French writer → Raymond Queneau. 158
Overpopulation 96, 97, 120

Painter 7–10, 13, 15, 19, 24, 29, 31, 42, 46, 48, 55, 57–60, 77, 81, 84, 85, 87, 89, 91, 92, 102, 105, 117, 118, 122–23, 127, 134, 147, 149, 153, 154, 158, 160, 163, 168, 169, 173–75, 179, 180–84, 261, 262, 264, 267, 271–75, 277, 280, 282–84, 286, 295, 324, 325
Painting 7, 9, 11, 17, 18, 27–29, 41, 43, 44, 46, 48, 52–60, 62, 63, 70, 72–74, 76, 81–92, 101, 109, 122, 123, 131–34, 144–48, 150, 154, 155, 158, 159–63, 169, 170, 173, 174, 176, 179, 181, 183–86, 188, 258, 265, 271, 273, 274, 277, 280–83, 285–87, 290–94, 296–99 → Poetry and painting
Painter-scholars 162
Palette knife: Blunt tool with a flexible blade, used for mixing or applying paint to the canvas, mixing paint colors, and adding texture to the painted surface. 27, 55
Paper: Paper from hemp was invented in China. The first documents are from the Eastern Han dynasty (25–220). A pivotal moment in the history of paper is when → Cai Lun (63–121) added pulp via tree bark, hemp, and bamboo ends, which resulted in the large-scale manufacture and worldwide spread of paper. 12, 27, 29, 30, 33, 52, 62, 66, 67, 73, 75, 77, 81, 86, 88–90, 121, 158, 159, 161, 170, 173–77, 181, 270–72, 277, 278, 292, 293, 296, 297
   Mulberry paper: Asian craftsmen showed remarkable creativity in producing different types of paper using mulberry fibers, which are smooth, resistant to pests, very white, and strong. They absorb and react well to the inflexions of the brush.

Mulberry paper is used also to cover windows and sliding doors.
   Xuan paper: A paper renowned for being soft and fine textured, suitable for conveying the artistic expression of both calligraphy and painting. It is often a mixture of blue sandalwood, hemp, and mulberry fiber. The name comes from the city of Xuancheng (Anhui province). 173
Paper cutouts: Paper cutting is a treasured traditional Chinese art dating back to when paper was developed. It became popular as a way of decorating doors and windows. 29, 271, 272
Party 24–27, 29, 31, 34, 39, 40, 42, 47, 52, 58, 67, 70, 93, 102–4, 107, 109, 110, 114, 116, 130, 138–40, 143, 161, 184–87, 255–57, 262, 270, 292 → History/Parties
Pelléas et Mélisande: Opera by Claude Debussy (1902). 275
People's Republic of China → History
Pigeons: Pigeon whistles are tied on the tails of pigeons so that when they fly the air that flows through the whistle creates a harmonic sound. 31, 268 → Crickets
Poetry and painting *337*
Politics 15, 24, 28, 30, 41, 56, 60, 105, 130, 143, 144, 161, 181, 182, 184, 185, 273, 274, 292, 296
Porcelain 44, 56, 167, 173, 267 → Ceramic
Portfolio: Folder with drafts, paper, and cards, always accompanying the painter. 11, 16, 29, 52, 58, 119, 134, 139
Power 60, 71, 83, 88, 135, 152, 266, 286, 296, 298 → Momentum
Prayer flag: Colorful rectangular cloth, often found along trails and peaks high in the Himalayas. Prayer flags are used to bless the surrounding countryside. They often include → woodblock printed texts and images. 124, 156
Principle 9, 75–79, 146–48, 159, 184, 263, 286 → Constant principle of internal order
Prison 106, 142, 143
Provinces 15, 18, 21, 22, 28, 31, 48, 50, 71, 95, 101, 104, 115, 120, 128, 139, 173, 175, 184, 260, 272
Puding: Village in Guizhou province. 240

Quintessence, essence 7, 78, 82, 145, 282, 286, 324, *337*

Rawness 174 → Coarse rawness
Receptivity, perception, reception *338*
Red Guards 50, 130, 133, 141 → History/Army
Regular script 169, 171, 172, 177, 183 → Styles

Relaxed → Free and relaxed

Republic 10 → History

Ripolin: Trademark for paint. 101

Romantic realism: Part of → socialist realism, elevated the common worker, whether factory or agricultural, by presenting his life, work, and recreation as admirable. Its purpose was to show how much the standard of living had improved thanks to the revolution. 55

Room of the Tranquil Heart 276 → Beijing

Rubbing: Ancient way to retrieve patterns, calligraphy, or characters engraved on bronze ware, etc., with rubbings using rice paper, ink, and a cloth ball. 64, 68, 69, 74, 77, 78, 161, 172, 175, 177–80

Scholars 16, 21, 30, 45, 52, 92, 122, 144, 150, 165, 166, 175, 269

Scripts 13, 78, 169, 171, 172, 174, 177, 183, 284 → Styles

Sculpture 27, 32, 40, 47, 123, 161, 174, 272

Seal 71–73, 78, 162, 184, 240, 264, 278, 283

Self-criticism, self-censorship 45, 57, 140, 264, 293 → Cultural Revolution

Shaanxi 271, 272 → Provinces

Shamanism 130, 132, 133, 136, 137, 138, 158

Shandong → Provinces

Shang 73 → Dynasties

Shanghai 105, 164, 165, 167–70, 172, 173, 175, 177, 184, 185, 248, 254, 260, 294

Shigatse (or Xigazê): Second largest city of Tibet, 250 kilometers west of Lhasa, with splendid natural landscapes like Mt. Everest, and about nineteen monasteries in total. 125, 126

    Tashi Lhunpo Monastery: Culturally important monastery, founded in 1447 by the first *Dalai Lama*. It is the traditional monastic seat of the *Panchen Lama* (an emanation of → Buddha Amitabha). The frescos inside depicted → Sakyamuni, the arhats and → Bodhisattvas.

    Shalu Monastery: Twenty-two kilometers south of Shigatse. It was the first of the major monasteries to be built by noble families during Tibet's great revival of Buddhism.

Sichuan 18, 20, 21, 24–26, 28, 35, 50, 60, 65, 98, 120, 124, 154, 164, 165, 169, 220, 248, 260–62, 273, 277, 291 → Provinces

Silk: The production of silk originated in Neolithic China. China maintained a virtual monopoly over silk production for another thousand years. 24, 48, 127, 170, 171, 282

Simplicity 89, 155, 267, 281, 285 → Supreme simplicity

Singapore 44

Sino-Japanese War 105 → History

Skeleton 12 → Bones

Socialist realism: Official cultural doctrine of USSR, which mandated an idealized representation of life under socialism in literature and the visual arts. The present and the future were constantly idealized. Socialist realism had a sense of forced optimism. Tragedy and negativity were not permitted, unless they were shown in a different time or place. The term was approved in meetings that included politicians of the highest level such as Joseph Stalin and Maxim Gorky in 1932/33. In the 1950s the ideas of socialist realism were adapted by communist countries like GDR and China. 24, 28, 30, 57, 161, 292

Solitude 9, 10, 40, 89, 109, 112, 113, 127, 164, 285

Song 128, 170, 181, 266, 267 → Dynasties

Spirit *338*

Spiritual rhythm *338*

Spontaneity *339*

Spring and Autumn 73 → Dynasties

Stardust: A sort of cosmic dust, composed of particles in space. Used metaphorically also for a technique of painting suggesting the cosmos. 145, 266 → Hubert Reeves

Steatite: Ceramic on the base of magnesium silicate. Steatite stones are used for carving. 72

Stele 55, 69, 71, 78 → Xi'an/Forest of Steles

Still life: Work of art depicting mostly inanimate subject matter. 9, 11, 52, 267

Strength *339*

Strokes 13, 14, 28, 29, 38, 46, 59, 71, 74–76, 77, 78, 83, 87, 159, 161, 171, 174, 175, 265, 269, 271, 280, 281, 292, 295

Styles 7, 13, 14, 24, 27, 29, 31, 46, 56, 58, 60, 61, 63, 64, 73, 78, 114, 127, 128, 141, 161, 162, 163, 169, 170, 172, 173, 175, 184, 268, 269, 283, 292, 295

    Western styles: Types of scripture used in Europe, for example with rustic capitals, Roman square capitals, or Latin primitive uncial, Roman cursive, Merovingian, Visigothic, bastarda, and didone (named after the French printer firm Didot).

    Kaishu: Calligraphy style which served as the basis for printed characters. Newest of the Chinese script styles, also called regular script.

    Kuang Cao: Wild cursive style, particularly aestheticized, used in calligraphy and difficult to decipher. It is a style of → Grass (Cursive) Script.

Zen (in Japanese) / Chan (in Chinese): A school of Mahayana Buddhism that originated during the Tang Dynasty. Zen/chan emphasizes meditation practice, direct insight into one's own true nature, and the personal expression of this insight in daily life for the benefit of others. 128, 147, 180

Zhejiang 175 → Provinces

Zongzi: Traditional Chinese rice dish with different fillings and wrapped in bamboo leaves. 95

PERSONS

Alighieri, Dante: (1265–1321) Italian poet and writer. The quotation is from his *Divina Commedia* (1307–1320), Paradiso, Canto 1, 112–114: "[. . .] onde si muovono a diversi porti / per lo gran mar de l'essere, e ciascuna / con istinto a lei dato che la porti." Following the advice of → Huang Laoshi, here is a different translation (H. W. Longfellow): "Hence they move onward unto ports diverse / O'er the great sea of being; and each one / With instinct given it which bears it on." 99

Arin, Bernard: (1938–2019) Ex-director of Scriptorium de Toulouse, calligrapher, teacher, and typographer. 13, 14

Bach, Johann Sebastian: (1685–1750) German composer and musician of the late Baroque period. 284

Bachelard, Gaston: (1884–1962) French philosopher. 99, 285

Bada Shanren (or Zhu Da): (1625–1705) Chinese painter, calligrapher, and poet. 73, 147, 149, 181

Baizeau, Ghislain: (1963–) Husband of Fabienne Verdier, their son is → Baizeau, Martin. 218, 274, 275, 276, 277, 278, 280, 298

Baizeau, Martin: (1994–) Son of Ghislain Baizeau and Fabienne Verdier. Filmmaker of *Le chant des étoiles* (2022), *Sur les terres de Cézanne* (2019), and *L'Atelier nomade* (2018). 280

Baudelaire, Charles: (1821–1867) French poet, essayist, art critic, and translator. The quotation is from *Salon de 1846* (Oxford: Clarendon Press, 1975). 82

Beethoven, Ludwig van: (1770–1827) German composer. 11, 28, 262

Bing Xin: (1900–1999) One of the most prolific Chinese women writers in the twentieth century. 82

Blake, William: (1757–1827) English poet, painter, and printmaker. The quotation is from the poem "Auguries of Innocence" (1803), see for example *Poets of the English Language* (New York: Viking Press, 1950). 99, 146

Bodhidharma: (c. 470–573) Semi-legendary Buddhist monk, traditionally credited as the transmitter of Chan Buddhism to China. He is regarded as the twenty-eighth Indian and first Chinese Patriarch. 66

Boissard, Fernand: (1813–1866) French painter. 55

Boudin, Eugène: (1824–1898) French landscape painter. 271

Braque, Georges: (1882–1963) French painter. 11, 60

Brook, Peter: (1925–2022) British film and theater director. 61

Buren, Daniel: (1938–) French conceptual artist, painter, and sculptor. 101

Cai Guo-Qiang: (1957–) Chinese artist. 101

Cai Lun: (63–121) Chinese eunuch court official of the Eastern Han dynasty. He is traditionally regarded as the inventor of paper. 30 → Paper.

Cézanne, Paul: (1839–1906) French painter. 58, 163, 271, 294

Chagall, Marc: (1887–1985) Russian-French artist. 58

Champollion, Jean-François: (1790–1832) French philologist and orientalist, decipherer of Egyptian hieroglyphs. 271

Chapuis, Nicolas: (1957–) French diplomat, translator, and essayist. 263

Chassériau, Théodore: (1819–1856) French painter of romantic classicism. 37

Cheng, François: (1929–) Chinese author and calligrapher, living in France. 7, 14

Cheng Jun: Master of seal engraving. 71, 234–36

Cixi: (1835–1908) Dowager Empress of Emperor Xianfeng, noblewoman who effectively controlled the Chinese government in the late Qing dynasty for almost fifty years (1861–1908). 34

Clastres, Hélène: (1936–2023) Ethnologist, specializing in religious and political anthropology. 259

Confucius Kongzi: (c. 551–479 BCE) Founder of → Confucianism, philosopher, historian, and educator. Considered the Greatest Saint in Chinese culture since the Han dynasty when Confucian text was promoted as supreme knowledge by the emperors. See for example

The Analects (Hong Kong: Chinese University Press, 1983). 144, 152

Conrad, Joseph: (1857–1924) Polish-British novelist and story writer. 61

Corot, Camille: (1796–1875) French painter. 271

Courbet, Gustave: (1819–1877) French painter who led the Realism movement. Works mentioned are *Les Casseurs de pierres* (*Stone Breakers*, 1849, destroyed in Dresden 1945), *L'Atelier du peintre* (*The Artist's Studio*, 1855, Musée d'Orsay, Paris), and *Les Trellis* (*The Trellis*, 1862, Toledo Museum of Art, Ohio). 52, 56, 60

Cozens, Alexander: (1717–1786) British landscape painter in watercolors, born in Saint Petersburg. 158 → Hugo, Victor

Cui Jian: (1961–) Chinese rock musician. 278

Dante → Alighieri, Dante

Daubigny, Charles-François: (1817–1878) French painter, Barbizon School. 60

Daumier, Honoré: (1808–1879) French painter. The picture mentioned is *Don Quixote and Sancho Panza* (1868, Neue Pinakothek, Munich). 52

De La Tour, Georges: (1593–1652) French Baroque painter. 44

Delacroix, Eugène: (1798–1863) French painter. 53, 55

Delon, Alain: (1935–2024) French actor, singer, and filmmaker. 36

Deneuve, Catherine: (1943–) French actress, producer, and model. 36, 98

Derain, André: (1880–1954) French artist, painter, sculptor. 58

Du Fu: (712–770) Chinese poet and politician during the Tang dynasty. 121

Du Mu: (803–852) Chinese calligrapher, poet, and politician who lived during the late Tang dynasty. For the quotation from "Autumn Evening" see Red Pine, *Poems of the Masters* (Port Townsend: Copper Canyon Press, 2003). The poem is about the "Cowherd and the Weaver Girl," the story of two star-crossed lovers who can only meet once a year, represented by the stars *Altair* (Herd-Boy) and *Vega* (Weaver Girl). 177

Duchamp, Marcel: (1887–1968) French painter, sculptor, chess player, and writer. 101

Dürer, Albrecht: (1471–1528) German painter, printmaker and theorist. The picture mentioned is *Das große Rasenstück* (*The Great Piece of Turf*, 1503, Albertina, Vienna). 149

Einstein, Albert: (1879–1955) German theoretical physicist who stated that the void is not filled with ether in the form of a substance. But it is *not* empty: it is filled with *fields* like the gravity field and the electromagnetic field. 282

Escande, Yolaine: French historian and sinologist. 324, 325

Fan Kuan: (c. 960–1030) Chinese landscape painter of the Song dynasty. 282

Feng Jianwu: (1910–1989) Founder of the Oriental Fine Arts College in Chengdu in 1932, where he was the principal of the Chinese Painting Department. After 1956, he taught at the Sichuan Fine Arts Institute. 64

Flaubert, Gustave: (1821–1880) French novelist. For the quotation see Jean-Yves Leloup, *Il n'y a qu'un seul dieu, lequel?* (Paris: Philippe Rey, 2018). 153

Friedrich, Caspar David: (1774–1840) German painter. The quotation is attributed to him. More about nature can be found in H. Börsch-Supan, *Caspar David Friedrich* (Munich: Prestel, 1976), with excerpts from his letters. 89

Gauguin, Paul: (1848–1903) French painter, sculptor, printmaker, ceramist, and writer. 58

Ge Hong: (283–343) Eclectic philosopher who dedicated his life to searching for physical immortality, which he thought was attainable through alchemy. 155

Géricault, Théodore: (1791–1824) French painter and lithographer, one of the pioneers of the Romantic movement. 55

Ghislain → Baizeau 220, 274–78, 280, 298

Giacometti, Alberto: (1901–1966) Swiss sculptor and painter. The quotation is from "Color and I," Zurich, a 1934 radio broadcast. 12, 161

Giotto di Bondone: (1267–1337) Italian painter and architect. 281

Goethe, Johann Wolfgang von: (1749–1832) German polymath (poet, playwright, novelist, scientist, statesman, theatre director and critic). The quotation is from his poem "Vermächtnis" (*A Legacy*, 1829): "Dann ist Vergangenheit beständig, Das Künftige voraus lebendig, Der Augenblick ist Ewigkeit." 145

Gong Li: (1965–) Chinese actress. 272

Goya, Francisco de: (1746–1828) Spanish artist of the late eighteenth and early nineteenth centuries. 56

Gu Kunbo: (1905–1970) Chinese painter, famous for his landscapes. 178, 179

Guanyin: → Bodhisattva associated with compassion

often referred to as the "most widely beloved Buddhist divinity." 32

Guibert, Marie-France: (1941–) Mother of Fabienne Verdier. 8

Guo Xi: (c. 1020–1090) Chinese landscape painter from Henan Province. 282

Gutenberg, Johannes: (c. 1400–1468) German craftsman. He invented the movable-type printing press in 1450. 30

Hanshan: (eighth or ninth century) Chinese Buddhist and Daoist poet associated with a collection of poems from the Tang Dynasty. Of the six hundred poems he is thought to have written at some point before his death, more than three hundred were collected and have survived. His name means "cold mountain." 155 → Books/Cold Mountain

He Duoling: (1948–) Chinese painter, lives and works in Chengdu. 59

Heraclitus: (c. 520–460 BCE) Greek pre-Socratic philosopher. For his texts see for example *The Fragments of Heracleitus* (Bray: Guild Press, 1976). "The soul is a spark of stellar essence" is attributed to Heraclitus and was often cited by the psychologist C. G. Jung. It probably refers to fragment 118: "A dry gleam of light is the wisest and best soul." "All things are one and from one" refers to fragment 10: "The one is made up of all things, and all things issue from the one." "Nature loves to hide" is fragment 123. Another translation (D. W. Myatt): "Physis naturally seeks to remain something of a mystery." 14, 74, 145

Hokusai, Katsushika: (1760–1849) Japanese painter and printmaker. 14

Horvat, Frank: (1928–2020) Italian photographer who lived and worked in France. 98

Houmei: Friend of Fabienne Verdier. 43, 47, 52

Huang Laoshi: (1922–2007) Mentor, teacher, and friend of Fabienne Verdier. She calls him *Laoshi* 老師, which means teacher, a colloquial title that shows respect, even for those whose profession is not in education. 64, 66, 68–71, 73–76, 78, 81, 84, 85, 86, 89, 90, 92, 99, 108, 110, 114, 121–24, 128, 136, 141, 143–46, 149, 150, 151, 152, 154, 155, 157–59, 162, 164, 171, 240, 258, 264–66, 269, 273, 274, 277, 282, 294

Huang Yong Ping: (1954–2019) Chinese-French artist, founder of the avant-garde Xiamen Dada group. 57, 101

Huang Yuan → Huang Laoshi

Hugo, Victor: (1802–1885) French Romantic writer and politician. The quotation is from the poem "Ce que

dit la bouche d'ombre" ("What the Mouth of Darkness Says," 1856). See Bettina Knapp, "Victor Hugo: What the Mouth of Darkness Says," *L'Esprit créateur* 16 (1976): 178–97. Klecksography is the art of making images from inkblots, which was pioneered by Hugo (see his *Inkblot Art*) and Justinus Kerner (1786–1862, German poet and physician). Since the 1890s, psychologists have used it as a tool for studying the subconscious, most famously Hermann Rorschach (1884–1922, Swiss psychiatrist) in his inkblot tests. 149, 158 → Cozens

Ingres, Jean-Auguste-Dominique: (1780–1867) French neoclassical painter. 37

Ivens, Joris: (1898–1989) Dutch documentary filmmaker. 98

Jankélévitch, Vladimir: (1903–1985) French philosopher and musicologist. 92

Jean-Louis → Jean-Louis Verdier 259

Jiang Qing: (1914–1991) Chinese communist revolutionary, actress, and major political figure during the → Cultural Revolution. She formed the radical political alliance known as the Gang of Four, fighting against the Four Olds (ideas, culture, customs, habits). 182

Jin Zhilin: (1928–2018) Chinese modern and contemporary artist, accomplished also in the fields of archaeology, folklore, and folk art. 270, 271 → Films/ *From the Masses to the Masses*

Jolas, Tina: (1929–1999) Ethnologist and translator, friend of Fabienne Verdier. 259

Kandinsky, Wassily: (1866–1946) Russian painter and art theorist. The text mentioned is from *Über das Geistige in der Kunst, insbesondere in der Malerei* (1946), see *On the Spiritual in Art* (New York: Solomon R. Guggenheim Foundation, 1946). 15

Keats, John: (1795–1821) English Romantic poet, along with Lord Byron and Percy Bysshe Shelley. The quotation is the title of the first book (of four) of *Endymion: A Poetic Romance* (London: Taylor and Hessey, 1818). 14

Khrushchev, Nikita: (1894–1971) First Secretary of the Communist Party of the USSR, 1953–1964. 55

Klee, Paul: (1879–1940) Swiss-born German artist. 63

Klimt, Gustav: (1862–1918) Austrian painter. 31

Kline, Franz: (1910–1962) American abstract painter. 291

Kwok On: Chinese (Hong Kong) banker, theater enthusiast, and collector of musical instruments, Asian folk art puppets, and dolls. 16, 17

Nerval, Gérard de: (1808–1855) French writer, poet, and translator. The quotation is from *Aurélia ou le rêve de la vie* (1855), see *Aurélia and letters to Aurélia* (Guildford, Surrey: Grosvenor House, 2013). 149

Newman, Barnett: (1905–1970) Influential abstract American artist. 60

Pei, Ieoh Ming or I.M. Pei: (1917–2019) Chinese-American architect. 278

Pepin the Short: (c. 714–768) King of the Franks, first Carolingian to become king. 14

Pessoa, Fernando: (1888–1935) Portuguese poet. In his *Livro do Desassossego* (Book of Disquiet, 1913–1934, first published in 1982) the hero, Bernardo Soares, assistant bookkeeper, is and is not-being. He lives, to live his not-living. 85

Petrarch (Petrarca), Francesco: (1304–1374) Italian poet who wrote about his ascent of Mont Ventoux (in Provence, 1909 meters above sea level) in 1336 in a well-known letter to Dionigi di Borgo San Sepolcro. Petrarch claimed to be the first person since antiquity to have climbed a mountain for the view. See Petrarch's *Letters on Familiar Matters (Rerum familiarium libri)* (New York: Italic Press, 2005). 150

Picasso, Pablo: (1881–1973) Spanish artist. The work mentioned is *Les Demoiselles d'Avignon* (1907, Museum of Modern Art, New York). For the film mentioned see → Films/*Le Mystère Picasso*. 56, 58, 60, 89, 294

Pimpaneau, Jacques: (1934–2021) French scholar of Chinese. 16, 18 → Kwok On Museum

Pisanello, Antonio: (1395–1455) Painter of the early Italian Renaissance and Quattrocento. 15

Pollock, Jackson: (1912–1956) American painter, major figure in the Abstract Expressionist movement. 27, 60, 325 → Vertical tip

Pu Songling: (1640–1715) Chinese writer during the Qing dynasty. 166

Qi Baishi: (1864–1957) Chinese painter. 57

Qi Gong: (1912–2005) Chinese calligrapher, artist, painter. 254, 277

Qu Yuan: (c. 340–278 BCE) Chinese poet and aristocrat during the Warring States period. 95

Queneau, Raymond: (1903–1976) French novelist, poet, critic, editor, and co-founder and president of → OuLiPo. Famous for *Zazie dans le métro* (1959, also a film by Louis Malle). 158

Racine, Jean: (1639–1699) French dramatist. 70

Raysse, Martial: (1936–) French artist and actor, co-founder of the Nouveau Réalism group. 60

Reeves, Hubert: (1932–2023) Canadian astrophysicist and popularizer of science. In his book *The Universe Explained to My Grandchildren* (London: Salammbo Press, 2012) he explains: "We are made from → stardust! [. . .] After the death of a star, its atoms break free and wander into space. And one day they enter the life cycle of living beings." 145

Rembrandt van Rijn: (1606–1669). Dutch artist. 56, 294

Rodin, Auguste: (1840–1917) French sculptor. Fabienne Verdier promoted an exhibition of Rodin in China in 1992. 263

Rothko, Mark: (1903–1970) American abstract painter. 60, 282

Rubens, Peter Paul: (1577–1640). Dutch artist and diplomat. 70

Ryckmans, Pierre: (1935–2014) Belgian-Australian writer, essayist, literary critic, translator, art historian, and sinologist. 324

Sablon, Jean Leclerc du: (1942–2012) Journalist, author. See his book *L'Empire de la poudre aux yeux. Carnets de Chine 1970–2000* (Paris: Flammarion, 2002). 270

Sakyamuni: Name of → Siddhartha Gautama, the founder of Buddhism. Sakyamuni means "Sage of the Shakya." 125 → Ethnic groups

Seneca, Lucius Annaeus: (c. 4 BCE–65 CE) Stoic philosopher, statesman, and dramatist. The quotation refers to *De Tranquillitate Animi* (On the tranquility of the mind, c. 60). See *Dialogues and Letters* (London: Penguin, 1997). 14, 284

Sha Menghai: (1900–1992) Master of calligraphy and seal carving, theoretician of traditional Chinese art. 182

Shakespeare, William: (1564–1616). English playwright, poet and actor. 61

Shen Dali: (1938–) Chinese writer and politician. See his book *Femmes poètes dans la Chine d'aujourd'hui* (Beijing: Chinese Literature Editions, 1991). 278

Shitao: (1642–1707) Chinese painter and calligrapher, later Buddhist monk and Daoist. In his *Comments on Painting from Monk Bitter Pumpkin* he repeatedly stressed the use of the "single brushstroke" or the "primordial line" as the root of all his painting. See Earle Coleman, *Philosophy of Painting by Shih-T'ao* (The Hague: De Gruyter Mouton, 1978); and Shitao, *Comments on Painting from Monk Bitter Pumpkin*. 18, 21, 38, 53, 73, 99, 182, 265, 324, 325

Sinatra, Frank: (1915–1998) American singer and actor. 94

Sisley, Alfred: (1839–1899) Impressionist landscape painter. The work mentioned is *The Gamekeeper in Fontainebleau Forest*. 271

Su Shi (or Su Dongpo): (1037–1101) Chinese poet, essayist, statesman, calligrapher, and painter, living during the Song dynasty. 141–44, 162

Soutine, Chaim: (1893–1943) French painter of Belarusian-Jewish origin. 56

Tang Yun: (1910–1993) Chinese painter known for his flower-and-bird paintings, landscapes, and portraits. 179

Tao Yuanming (or Tao Qian): (c. 365–427) Chinese poet and politician during the Six Dynasties period. The quoted poem is "Returning to the Farm to Dwell." See *The Complete Works of Tao Yuanming* (Hong Kong: Joint, 1992). 142, 158

Tàpies, Antoni: (1923–2012) Spanish painter, sculptor, and art theorist. 60

Valéry, Paul: (1871–1945) French poet, essayist, and philosopher. The quotation is from "La Fileuse" (The Spinner, 1891): "Un arbuste et l'air pur font une source vive." See *Selected Writings* (New York: New Directions, 1950). 144

Vandier-Nicolas, Nicole: (1906–1987) French sinologist and philosopher. 295, 324, 325

Van Gogh, Vincent: (1853–1890) Dutch Post-Impressionist painter. 58, 117, 291, 294

Verdier, François: (1939–) Father of Fabienne Verdier, artistic director at several communication firms. 8–10, 14, 37, 111, 112, 117, 123, 273

Verdier, Jean-Louis: (1935–1989) Mathematician, uncle of Fabienne Verdier. 259

Verdier, Yvonne: (1941–1989) Ethnologist, anthropologist, aunt of Fabienne Verdier. 16, 112, 259

Verlaine, Paul: (1844–1896) French poet. 265

Vermeer, Jan: (1632–1675) Dutch Baroque painter. 70

Villepoix, Gilles de: Friend of Fabienne Verdier, cultural attaché at the French embassy in Beijing. 274

Wang Xizhi: (c. 303–361) Chinese politician and writer of Jin dynasty, known for his mastery of calligraphy. 184

Wang Yishi: (1939–) Chinese painter, one of the founders of the School of Fine Arts in Chongqing. 30

Warhol, Andy: (1928–1987) American visual artist, film director, and producer. 60

Wen Yiduo: (1899–1946) Chinese poet and scholar. 72

Weyden, Rogier van der: (c. 1399–1464) Dutch painter. 283

Whitman, Walt: (1819–1892) American poet, essayist, and journalist. 99

Wu Daozi: (c. 680–759) Influential Chinese painter of the Tang dynasty. 144

Wu Zuoren: (1908–1997) Chinese painter and educator who studied under → Xu Beihong. 57, 254, 275

Xia Gui: Chinese landscape painter of the Song dynasty. 265

Xie Zhiliu: (1910–1997) Traditional painter, calligrapher, and art connoisseur. 182

Xu Beihong: (1895–1953) Chinese painter and educator. 24, 56, 57, 271

Xuanzong, Emperor (685–762) Emperor of the Tang dynasty. 33

Xue Tao: (c. 768–831) Chinese poet and courtesan. She was one of the most famous women poets of Tang poetry. 121 → Chengdu

Ye Yongqing: (1958–) Chinese painter, teaching at Sichuan Academy of Fine Arts, Chongqing. 59, 248

Yourcenar, Marguerite: (1903–1987) Belgian-born French novelist and essayist. 90

Yo-Yo Ma: (1955–) Chinese-American cellist. 7

Zao Wou-Ki: (1920–2013) Chinese-French painter. 7

Zhang Daqian: (1899–1983) Chinese artist of the twentieth century. 179

Zhang Xiaogang: (1958–) Chinese painter. 59

Zheng Zhenduo: (1898–1958) Chinese journalist, writer, historian, archaeologist, and scholar. 30

Zhong Kui: Taoist deity in Chinese mythology. 31, 32, 37

Zhou Chunya: (1955–) Chinese painter. 59

Zhu Qizhan: (1892–1996) Chinese artist. 169

Zhu Xiao-Mei: (1949–) Chinese-French classical pianist and teacher. 270

Zhuangzi: (c. 365–290 BC) Born Zhuang Zhou, known with respect as Zhuangzi, Chinese philosopher who lived during the Warring States period. He is credited with writing the work also known as *Zhuangzi*. It is one of the two foundational texts of Daoism, alongside the → *Tao Te Ching*. 54, 79, 81, 124

Zhuge Liang: (181–234) Chinese statesman, strategist, and engineer. 121

Zola, Émile: (1840–1902) French novelist, journalist, playwrighter. 72

Corinna Thierolf is an art historian and founding curator of the Pinakothek der Moderne in Munich, Germany, where she served as chief curator for more than twenty-five years. At the Pinakothek, she significantly expanded the museum's collection of postwar art, curated numerous exhibitions, and published books and essays on artists such as Georg Baselitz, Joseph Beuys, John Cage, Dan Flavin, Anselm Kiefer, Donald Judd, Walter De Maria, Arnulf Rainer, and Andy Warhol, among others. Her exhibition series "Königsklasse" (2013 to 2020) showcased contemporary works in the historic Herrenchiemsee Palace. Since 2020, she has worked as a freelance curator, writer, and consultant for various museums.

Young Kim is a writer based between New York and Paris who works in art, fashion, film, music, and literature while managing the estate of Malcolm McLaren, her late boyfriend and creative/business partner. She is the author of the controversial but highly acclaimed memoir *A Year On Earth With Mr. Hell* and has published pieces in *Vogue US*, *Holiday*, *Drugstore Culture*, *GQ UK*, *Liber*, *A Rabbit's Foot*, *The Evening Standard*, and *Gagosian Quarterly*. *Passenger of Silence* is her first translation.

ACKNOWLEDGMENTS

The publisher wishes to thank Albin Michel and the Waddington Custot Gallery for making this editorial project possible. Special thanks to Solène Chabanais, Stéphane, and Laurence Custot.

We would also like to thank Stéphanie Cooper-Slokyj and Young Kim for the English translation of the manuscript; Louise Malcolm, Kelly Ma, Miranda Chance, Timothy Stroud for their assistance with the glossary of Chinese aesthetics concepts, and Carl Freytag for the Glossary and Index; Charles Gute for editing and proofreading all the texts.

Special thanks to Emmanuel Constant for his research and development of the iconographic sections, and to photographers Martin Baizeau, Ned Burgess, Philippe Chancel, Thierry Cron, Dolorès Marat, Benjamin McMahon, and Laura Stevens for the images reproduced in the color pages of this book.

We would like to thank Corinna Thierolf for writing the Afterword and for her support and dedication throughout the project.

A special thank to Ghislain Baizeau for coordinating the various stages of this project.

Finally, sincere thanks go to Fabienne Verdier for entrusting us with the first publication of her work in English.

PHOTO CREDITS

Ned Burgess: 312–313
Philippe Chancel: 303, 307
Thierry Cron: 316–317
Martin Baizeau and Ned Burgess: 301–302
Benjamin McMahon, 315, 322
Dolorès Marat: 311
Laura Stevens: 304–305, 320–321
Laure Vasconi: 288, 318–319
Fabienne Verdier Archive: 308–309

Front cover: Fabienne Verdier Archive
Back cover: Benjamin McMahon

The reproductions of black-and-white images on pages 189–253 are taken from archival photographic prints that Fabienne Verdier brought back from her travels in China's forbidden territories, many of which were offered by the students who accompanied her. Some of them were taken by the Sichuan Academy of Fine Arts photographer Zhang Tianming. We would like to thank him for entrusting the author with these memories before she left China.
The portraits of the last great masters of Chinese painting and calligraphy are extremely rare photographic documents kept as part of the author's collection of various Chinese artworks and ephemera.

5 CONTINENTS EDITIONS

Editor-in-Chief: Aldo Carioli
Art Director and Layout: Stefano Montagnana
Editing: Charles Gute
Translation from German (*Transposing and Inventing*): Gérard Goodrow

Index and Glossary: Corinna Thierolf,
Carl Freytag, Kelly Ma

Pre-press: Maurizio Brivio, Milan, Italy

ISBN 979-12-5460-063-4

Printed and bound in Italy in October 2024
by Tecnostampa – Pigini Group
Printing Division Loreto – Trevi
for 5 Continents Editions

5 Continents Editions s.r.l.
Piazza Caiazzo 1, 20124 – Milan, Italy
info@fivecontinentseditions.com
www.fivecontinentseditions.com